Fear and Learning

Fear and Learning

Essays on the Pedagogy of Horror

Edited by Aalya Ahmad *and* Sean Moreland

Foreword by Glen Hirshberg

McFarland & Company, Inc., Publishers
Jefferson, North Carolina, and London

LIBRARY OF CONGRESS CATALOGUING-IN-PUBLICATION DATA

Fear and learning : essays on the pedagogy of horror /
  edited by Aalya Ahmad and Sean Moreland ; foreword by
  Glen Hirshberg.
      p.   cm.
    Includes bibliographical references and index.

  ISBN 978-0-7864-6820-1
  softcover : acid free paper ∞

   1. Horror films — Study and teaching.   2. Horror
films — History and criticism.   3. Horror tales,
American — Study and teaching.   4. Horror tales,
English — Study and teaching.   I. Ahmad, Aalya,
1971– editor of compilation.   II. Moreland, Sean,
1975– editor of compilation.
PN1995.9.H6F395 2013
791.43´6164 — dc23   2012047507

BRITISH LIBRARY CATALOGUING DATA ARE AVAILABLE

© 2013 Aalya Ahmad and Sean Moreland. All rights reserved

*No part of this book may be reproduced or transmitted in any form
or by any means, electronic or mechanical, including photocopying
or recording, or by any information storage and retrieval system,
without permission in writing from the publisher.*

Front cover images © 2013 Shutterstock

Manufactured in the United States of America

McFarland & Company, Inc., Publishers
  Box 611, Jefferson, North Carolina 28640
    www.mcfarlandpub.com

To Robin Wood,
who has taught us so much

Acknowledgments

Our partners Dietrich Sider and Madeleine Mony were gracious and helpful throughout the progress of this project and we are very, very grateful to them both for their assistance with manuscript preparation, child care and giving us space to work. We would also like to thank all our wonderful contributors who bore with us patiently and adopted many of our editorial suggestions and whose work and critical insights have made this one hell of a ride.

—AA & SM

Table of Contents

Acknowledgments — vi
Foreword by Glen Hirshberg — 1
Introduction: Horror in the Classroom
    AALYA AHMAD and SEAN MORELAND — 5

Postmodernism with Sam Raimi (or, How I Learned to Stop Worrying About Theory and Love *Evil Dead*)
    JEFFREY ANDREW WEINSTOCK — 19

Towards a Monster Pedagogy: Reclaiming the Classroom for the Other
    JOHN EDGAR BROWNING — 40

When the Women Think: Teaching Horror in Women's and Gender Studies
    AALYA AHMAD — 56

Acts of Re-Possession: Bollywood's Re-Inventions of the Occult Possession Film
    SEAN MORELAND and SUMMER PERVEZ — 75

Beyond the Lure: Teaching Horror, Teaching Theory
    BRIAN JOHNSON — 95

A Raven's Eye View: Teaching Scopophilia with Dario Argento
    K. A. LAITY — 124

The Hulking Hyde: How the Incredible Hulk Reinvented the Modern Jekyll and Hyde Monster
    LANCE EATON — 138

Critical Thinking on the Dark Side
    LISA MARIE MILLER — 156

"Inside...*Doesn't Matter*": Responding to *American Psycho* and Its Dantean Agenda
    MILES TITTLE — 179

In the Dark of Your Own Psyche: Jungian Theory and Horror
    J. A. WHITE   200

Skins and Bones: The Horror of the Real
    JOHN EDWARD MARTIN   224

The Pedagogical Value of Mary Shelley's *Frankenstein* in Teaching Adaptation Studies
    BEN KOOYMAN   245

About the Contributors   265
Index   269

Foreword
by Glen Hirshberg

I couldn't have been less surprised.

The very first question I was asked, in my first face-to-face interview for a professor of fiction writing position at Cal State San Bernardino, was, "Why horror?"

I'd prepared thoroughly for that moment, had developed what seemed to me an imposing, ivy-clad tower of a response. My bricks would be horror's rich, cross-cultural history — as old as storytelling itself— and my mortar would be the profound and lasting psychological, psychosexual, gender- and class-specific power of its imagery, its ability, as Robert Aickman pointed out, to plumb Freud's "submerged nine-tenths," meaning the ninety percent of our brains we never consciously use.

In the heat of the moment, though, what spilled out of me was a grin, and the words, "Why on earth not?"

The truth is that at least until 1965 or so, virtually every major American author dabbled — and in more than a few cases, did their most significant work — with supernatural elements. In considering everyone from Charles Brockden Brown to Washington Irving to Nathaniel Hawthorne to Charles Waddell Chesnutt to Herman Melville to Edgar Allan Poe to Henry James to Willa Cather to Edith Wharton to Shirley Jackson to Toni Morrison, one could even make the case that there have been more truly great American short stories written *with* ghosts than without them.

Ghost and horror stories appear, in one form or another, in virtually every human civilization. Even the most overly familiar, seemingly tired tropes of the genre (vampires, say, or boy magicians, or the walking dead), have enduring and significant power, and have proven remarkably malleable. We may (or may not) be living in a more secular age, but the impact of horror imagery turns out to have little to do with belief.

In the end, the root of the horror story is wonder. These tales concern themselves with our mutual and collective quest to understand where feelings come from, why we dream what we dream, how hope gets born, why we always feel so vulnerable and so hungry for more, and why there's no cure for the vulnerability or the hunger, and why we really don't want there to be. What horror is really about — what it has always been about — is the fundamental human quest to understand the elements of human experience we can never touch or name or know. And that is why books like *Fear and Learning*, which contribute so much to the growing but still-nascent field of serious horror scholarship, matter.

Academia remains particularly, perhaps inherently difficult terrain for this kind of work, because academia, at least as it has evolved in the West, is peculiarly resistant to wonder. That may be a cliché, but I have found it a true one. In the overture to his collection *Air Guitar*, critic Dave Hickey describes his own frustrations as an academic, and he does so in imagery redolent of the ghost story: "(w)ithin the cloister, we moved among one another, and among all the treasures of human invention, like spiteful monks sworn to silence ... while all the joys that bind the world together kept us sullenly apart."

What Hickey is specifically decrying is the lack of joyful conversation, of shared awe at what human beings create. But the passage also suggests an even more fundamental conflict between current academic Western biases and lasting art: in devaluing everything but the rational, the so-called "real," we are missing the fundamental truth that what we wish for and what we dream make up significantly more of who we are and what we know than what we consciously or directly experience.

The first time I taught my graduate seminar in the literature of the ghost story, I suggested to my students that to honor these stories' intentions and illuminate their treasures, they might have to check their critical-theory skills at the door for a while. What I meant was not that that the students should shut off their brains, but that they would also need their Freudian nine-tenths, their Jungian hive-mind, their childhood nightmares, their (generally) quieter, more nagging grown-up fears and hopes and anguishes. They'd need themselves, in other words.

What happened over those next 10 weeks surpassed my expectations. For a while, the students talked about what a "relief" it was just to read, to remember why they'd loved reading in the first place. Then they started to talk about what they loved, and argue about what they thought they were reading. And then they began to dazzle me, and each other, and themselves. At the end of the quarter, I got stunning papers on contrasting notions of female sexuality in Japanese versus American ghosts, an examination of the secret anguish in Roald Dahl's stories that I found more perceptive and anguished than Dahl's stories themselves, and a dozen other fully fledged works of critical exploration remarkable equally for their insight and their heart.

That course confirmed my passionate belief that the underexamined literature and film and art of the supernatural can inspire and support criticism of the highest order. Indeed, this literature and film and art demand it.

The existence of *Fear and Learning* strikes me as both encouraging and necessary. In offering thoughtful and contemporary perspectives on gender roles in the field, on "monster pedagogy," on the ways horror film and literature inform, transform, and sometimes upend critical theory, on what Bollywood's "re-possession" and "re-invention" of the possession film tells us about contemporary notions of gender and class at precisely the point where west and east collide, *Fear and Learning* presents serious scholars engaging serious (and, sometimes, seriously goofy) literature and film with their critical minds intact, and with the rest of themselves switched on and wide open. That's the only way we will ever begin to come to grips with an art form permanently and resolutely rooted in wonder, which has always been the spark for all human creativity, and which so little contemporary scholarship *or* art even aspires to, let alone achieves.

Glen Hirshberg won the 2008 Shirley Jackson Award for his novella The Janus Tree. *His two story collections,* American Morons *and* The Two Sams *(Publishers Weekly best book, 2003), were International Horror Guild and Locus best of the year award winners. He teaches writing at California State University, San Bernardino.*

Introduction: Horror in the Classroom

AALYA AHMAD *and*
SEAN MORELAND

As studies of horror have increasingly gained scholarly acceptance, more horror texts are finding their way onto curricula in a number of disciplines. These fictions have always invited a powerful response from their readers and audiences, reactions that have generated numerous interpretations and attempts to explain horror's popularity despite, and possibly even because of, horror's supposedly lowly status, a status that used to be uncritically accepted and accorded also to horror's readers and audiences. Since the late 1980s, the assumption that literary and cinematic horror texts are low cultural forms unworthy of serious critical attention has been successfully challenged on a number of fronts. The essays in this book are therefore no longer constrained by the requirement to bring horror into the realm of scholarly concern. Instead, they explore what *the study* of horror makes possible, conveying fresh insights into both the genre and its audiences. *Fear and Learning* incorporates diverse thematic, stylistic and methodological perspectives on the pedagogy of horror, presenting practical studies of horror fictions that reveal important intersections between the academy, culture and society. This book is not only for teachers. It is for everybody who is interested in what we can learn from horror.

While many provocative studies of horror as a genre have appeared from the 1990s onward, much less has been said about the theory and practice of teaching horror texts. Such practices vary across disciplines — for example, certain horror films and even whole courses on horror are a staple of film and cultural studies undergraduate classes, while in English literature, the emphasis often remains squarely upon the Gothic, rather than horror, as an appropriate field of study. In other disciplines, horror nomenclature and concepts may appear as metaphors — "zombies," for example, appear in philosophy and more recently, economics — or interesting case studies on the reception of a particular text; for example, the "video nasties" debates. Here you will find a diversity of approaches to the pedagogy of horror that could be said to address the following questions. What considerations exist for teaching horror to students? Are there patterns of reception and response that are particularly important for developing pedagogies of horror? How do certain cultured, classed and gendered contexts change our perspectives on horror texts?

The scant existing scholarship on the pedagogy of horror has tended to mirror the English literary bias of subordinating contemporary horror texts to the critical rubric of the Gothic. Two books in particular bear specific mention: *Approaches to Teaching: Gothic Fiction—The British and American Traditions*, edited by Diane Long Hoeveler and Tamar Heller (2003) and *Teaching the Gothic*, edited by Andrew Smith and Anna Powell (2006). These collections gather a variety of scholarly approaches to teaching Gothic fiction and include essays that refer to works of contemporary horror as extensions of the Gothic paradigm. While many critical insights are gained through the emphasis on this continuity, the collapse of horror into the Gothic frequently skews the academic reception of horror texts by emphasizing primarily those modern fictions which are the most obviously indebted to Gothic precursors and excluding or distorting in a Procrustean fashion, texts that are less well suited to this model. The assimilation of modern horror into the Gothic obscures some of the more original and challenging qualities of contemporary texts in favor of emphasizing their membership in a literary tradition. This emphasis has caused gaps in the critical and scholarly treatment of horror that the present collection will help to address.

Fear and Learning complements a growing corpus of conceptual studies of horror, including well-known books by James Twitchell (1987), Noël Carroll (1990), Carol Clover (1992), Harry Benshoff (1997), Isabel Cristina Pinedo (1997), Cynthia Freeland (2000), and Matt Hills (2005). Collections of essays mainly devoted to horror cinema have also established the field, including *The American Nightmare* (Wood et al., 1979), *The Dread of Difference* (Grant, 1996), *The Horror Reader* (Gelder, 2000), *The Horror Film Reader* (Jancovich, 2002) and *Fear Without Frontiers* (Schneider, 2003). While these studies have contributed much to the academic recognition of the importance and complexity of the horror field, each has also tended to subordinate horror texts to particular conceptual or methodological schemes such as psychoanalysis, implicitly suggesting that horror fictions are important *only* insofar as they reveal the truth, or the use, of a particular theoretical system. The essays in this volume variously challenge this restrictive emphasis.

Matt Hills calls the practice of using horror to illustrate a particular pet theory "horror-as-schooling." This "theory-first, pleasure-second" tendency,

Hills argues, has been a recurring problem for academics who study and teach horror:

> All such theories (including sociologies and cognitive philosophies of horror) appear to proceed from the basic notion that horror's pleasures stand in need of explanation, whether this is done by relating horror texts to the "real" cultural anxieties of a time period, or to transhistorical notions of "the unconscious." I am suggesting here that theoretical approaches to horror have explained (away) the genre's pleasures by invoking their own disciplinary and theoretical norms.[1]

As Hills notes, "horror-as-schooling" tends to radically oversimplify crucial aspects of the texts, where "theoretical answers seem to be determined in advance of critics' encounters with horror texts, while at best scholarly theories continue to be accorded discursive primacy."[2] Hills argues that taking pleasure in the text's affects[3] is far too redolent of fandom for the established hierarchies of knowledge that distinguish academic work. Such hierarchies also have an unfortunate tendency to suppress textual specificities in subordinating horror fictions to theoretical frameworks. This habit of avoidance then obscures the formal qualities of the text itself, restrictively pre-determining the text's appearance in the classroom as well as the range of responses and treatments of that text available to students and instructor.

Our collection is an attempt to remedy this situation by critically examining the practice as well as the theory of "horror-as-schooling." We contend that far too many scholars hasten towards theoretical formulations, offering only a passing nod to a text or two before proclaiming that horror is really "about" Kristevan abjection (Creed), "about" gender normativity (Twitchell), "about" Deleuzian schizoanalysis (Powell), or some other enticing theoretical blank. Such tidy "accounts" of horror, clever, compelling and insightful as they are, might be one reason many horror fans and writers scorn academic work, instead preferring to produce their own analyses, reviews, publications, conferences and anthologies.[4] Notably, few scholars in the academy refer to any of this copious work, beyond a few references to Lovecraft's "Supernatural Horror in Literature" (1927), Stephen King's *Danse Macabre* (1981) and one allusion to Les Daniels's *Living in Fear* (1975).[5] Few so far have paused to consider the pedagogical implications of bringing horror texts into the classroom. Effectively teaching horror forces us to stop and pay attention to the texts themselves, as well as to extant considerations of them, whether these are produced by scholars, reviewers, critics, or informed fans. While the contributors to this volume certainly recognize the value of horror as a tool to teach theory, by foregrounding the pedagogical aspect of such a practice, they also acknowledge the many other possibilities of the texts they discuss.

For Matt Hills (2005), a "generic" characteristic of horror fiction is precisely its ability to penetrate "the hallowed, jargon-heavy world of 'Theory,'"[6] challenging theoretical formulations, while simultaneously informing these theories in a process of reciprocal destabilization. Both Jeffrey Andrew Weinstock and Brian Johnson's contributions to this project recognize and address horror's permeable discursivity. Rather than merely mapping a particular theoretical paradigm over the texts in the way that Hills critiques, they consider some of the ways in which these films can embody and exemplify theories of postmodern intertextuality in both an intuitive and accessible manner.

Our book is also informed by the desire to address the schismatic division between horror as a non-subject (in the case of literary fiction) and horror as fetishistic stand-in for some other subject (in the case of cinematic fiction). Such an inclusive approach recognizes the degree to which those working in the field of horror (whether as fictionists, filmmakers, scholars, fans, reviewers, etc.) often influence one another across media boundaries. Those involved in producing and consuming horror knowingly and lovingly partake of a multiplicity of texts, intertexts and adaptations in keeping with their "intertextual subcultural capital."[7] Such intertextuality, which is also invoked in Philip Brophy's useful concept of "Horrality — horror, textuality, morality, hilarity"[8] tends to resist easy or absolute compartmentalization of any sort. The effect that intertextuality has on the production of horror as both an affect and an attribute of the text is as vital a topic for horror fans as it is for those who teach horror,[9] and it is aptly emphasized by Stephen Jay Schneider's call for a "historical poetics" of horror.[10] Schneider employs Henry Jenkins' description of historical poetics as going against the grain of much film criticism, which excavates either "the world-view of a particular film-maker" or "dominant ideological assumptions in the culture at large":

> Historical poetics forestalls this search for meanings in order to ask other questions about how film narratives are organized, how films structure our visual and auditory experience, how films draw upon the previous knowledge and expectations of spectators.

Schneider further comments that "what is needed is an in-depth understanding of those principles, techniques, and devices that have proven most capable of eliciting horror responses in audiences."[11] In the classroom where horror texts come alive, in a sense, through being read, watched and discussed, we are brought closer to an understanding of such "principles, techniques and devices" rather than being able to comfortably assume a one-size-fits-all horror experience.

Stanley Fish's reader-response theory raises some interesting questions about the experience of teaching horror fiction. Fish confesses that "in general I am drawn to works which do not allow the reader the security of his normal patterns of thought and belief," suggesting instead that readers might "erect a standard of value on the basis of this preference—*a scale on which the most unsettling of literary experiences would be the best*" [our emphasis].[12] Reader-response solves horror's dilemma of "high" versus "low" literary status by pronouncing literature itself as merely "a conventional category ... a function of a communal decision as to what will count as literature."[13] This approach frees criticism from the deterministic task of having to impose "a correct way of reading," allowing it to determine, instead, "from which of a number of possible perspectives reading will proceed,"[14] rather than having to try on ill-fitting subjectivities. Such an approach is complemented in film studies by Carol Clover's idea of cross-gender identification[15] and Judith Mayne's emphasis on the active participation of the audience.[16]

Fish urges us to consider meaning as a function of "what does this sentence do?" Rather than seeing it as "an object, a thing-in-itself," we are asked to look at the sentence or the film as "an *event*, something that *happens* to, and with the participation of, the reader.[17] Reader-response can thus be employed to bridge a distance from film theory to literary theory, another reason it is useful for a historical poetic approach to horror studies. The emphasis upon "temporal flow" and "meaning as an event" is also peculiarly suited to horror, which presents its affect as a frightening or shocking "event" that precedes deeper analysis. A "new look at the question" of what a text does, Fish writes, "may result also in a more accurate account of works whose formal features are so prominent that the critic proceeds directly from them to a statement of meaning without bothering to ask whether their high visibility has any direct relationship to their operation in the reader's experience."[18] Again, it is undeniable that horror's "formal features" are perhaps the most prominently visible of all. In keeping with Fish's theory, these features have been least dwelt upon by horror's critics.

Responses to horror include not only the immediate and recognizable response of startling, characterized by a fight-or-flee response to the jumps and shocks of cinematic horror techniques, but responses that call into question the borders between mind and body, how we "know" our fears. These responses have occasionally been raised, albeit in film studies rather than literature: for example, Anna Powell has viewed affective responses to horror films through Deleuzian concepts of body and faciality.[19] Martin Barker has also drawn attention to the ways in which cinematic narratives offer a variety of memorable textual experiences, including "resonant" moments that linger in the viewer's mind as well as "punctuation" moments that hammer a particular sight, spectacle or scene home.[20] Dennis Giles has discussed what he calls, following Lyotard, *figures* in film, techniques that create an "anticipatory vision" and thus cause the audience or viewer to experience fear although nothing fearful is visible.[21] In the classroom, such insights may also be adapted to literary horror texts, providing a fuller sense of how "horror" as an affective response may be elicited and sustained. Interest in the affects[22] associated with horror texts and the historical poetics that enable them is everywhere evident in this collection.

The definition of horror is far from a simple matter. As Jack Sullivan puts it, "horror is unusual in that it is both a genre and a subject, one treated in all the arts." How, then, might one distinguish it? Sullivan's prompt response is: "Fear, in fact, in its many forms and intensities."[23] Horror writers such as H. P. Lovecraft and Stephen King have voiced a common definition of horror as fundamentally *affective*, as fear-inspiring, as out "to get you,"[24] as inducing a *response*, rather than a scholastic enumeration of elements that may or may not distinguish a horror text. As Yvonne Leffler, Hills and Schneider have noted, the affective function of horror has long been under-theorized, with the notable exception of Noël Carroll's influential theory of "art-horror," which builds the experience of fear into his conception of the genre.

The construction of definitional categories more often than not fulfills the agenda of privileging one form of horror over another, such as "terror" over "horror" in Radcliffe's classic distinction,[25] the ghost story over the slasher narrative, the slasher narrative over "torture porn,"[26] or the "Golden Age" over the contemporary horror film. In this process, certain textual strategies are subordinated or ignored in favor of others which serve to support the particular theory of "terror," "dread," or "horror" which is being advanced. Stephen King asserts that the horror story is "a dance — a moving rhythmic search. And ... it's looking for what I would call phobic pressure points."[27] King argues that horror can best be understood as the more-or-less successfully crafted work that will touch those pressure points:

> The closest I want to come to definition or rationalization is to suggest that the genre exists on three more or less separate levels [....] The finest emotion is terror [....] It's what the mind sees that makes these stories such quintessential tales of terror [....] The horror comics of the fifties still sum up for me the epitome of horror, that emotion of fear that underlies terror, an emotion which is slightly less fine, because it is not entirely of the mind. Horror also invites a physical reaction by showing us something which is physically wrong [....] But there is a third level — that of revulsion.[28]

King calls this sub-level "the gross-out" and defines it as a last resort for the writer of horrific fiction: "If I find I cannot horrify, I'll go for the gross-out. I'm not proud."[29] The gross-out is what many point to when they either attempt to refute the claim that horror is a legitimate art form or allege that horror, along with pornography, has a degrading, "nasty" effect. The moral panic over the "video nasties" in the 1980s illustrates how the transgressive excesses of horror become attributed to those who partake of its pleasures.[30]

Challenges along these lines frequently arise for teachers of horror, who must engage not only with the resistance of their students, but also the predispositions of their peers towards subject matter that has not been well-established. While, as we already maintained, it is no longer necessary to exonerate horror as a worthwhile subject of study, it does seem to be necessary to consider such allegations and hierarchizations. For example, Lisa Marie Miller writes in this volume about the barriers she faced in trying to introduce a critical thinking class on the subject of the paranormal, while Miles Tittle describes his students grappling with their revulsion towards the violent excesses of *American Psycho* (1991). Often, this tendency to dwell on horror's ill effects— whether to refute or to uphold them — arises from within the psychoanalytic intellectual traditions that have historically had the most to say about horror literature and film. As Andrew Tudor has pointed out, many psychoanalytic approaches are, unfortunately, occasioned by the "widespread belief that horror fans are a peculiar bunch who share a perverse predilection. A taste for horror is a taste for something seemingly abnormal and is therefore deemed to require special explanation."[31] Both drawing on and moving beyond the psychoanalytic film theories of Christian Metz and Laura Mulvey, K. A. Laity's contribution to this collection explores the way that Dario Argento's *giallo* and horror cinema presents an embodiment of the perceptual and psychological structures of scopophilia, and provides students with a vital instrument to critically engage with these theories that does not stigmatize their experiences of and responses to the film. Similarly, J. A. White provides a strong argument for the pedagogical possibilities of Jungian theory applied to horror texts.

In *The Pleasures of Horror*, Hills argues persuasively that "the pathologization of horror's pleasures as a 'problem'— and hence also the genre's fans — never seems far from the surface of literalist readings."[32] While we take Hills' point that the need for answers to horror's "problem" is somewhat suspect because this tends to validate the insinuation that horror is a sort of "mimetic infection" or "pollution,"[33] it is not appropriate to simply dismiss the "problem" of horror's pleasures as always fortifying a "literalist" reading. In fact, many horror texts compel and foreground the sort of pathological problematization that Hills denounces. While Hills insists that we should not ask any audience to "account for its pleasures,"[34] we suggest that horror texts often more or less playfully and consciously invite such accountings and pressurized readings as part of both their pleasure and their cultural work, which again makes them particularly fascinating to teach. Engaging in such pedagogy invokes what Mark Jancovich calls the "cultural politics of shocking images,"[35] signifying a particular kind of subjectivity characterized not only by a gleeful response to surreal, graphic and taboo images, but by an ongoing concern with the analysis of horror's effects on readers, audiences and their societies.

Horror fictions including Lewis's *The Monk* (1796) King's *The Dark Half* (1989), Cronenberg's *Videodrome* (1984) and Haneke's *Funny Games* (1997/ 2008) have variously but deliberately invited their readers/audiences to critically examine the affects of horrific entertainment, as well as the historical tendency to characterize horror's "ill effects," portraying its fans as deviant, suspect or marginal, and dangerously prone to acting out the violence and excess which their preferred fictions portray. Going back to the popularity of the "penny dreadfuls," G. K. Chesterton wrote at the turn of the twentieth century: "It is the custom, particularly among magistrates, to attribute half the crimes of the Metropolis to cheap novelettes."[36] Similarly, Robert Bloch, defending H. P. Lovecraft's work, which was kept in print due to the tenacity of a handful of fans despite being labeled "sick," writes "If safeguarding our mental health requires us to avoid the work of those whose life-styles depart from the accepted norm, then our bookshelves would soon be stripped bare."[37] Barker and Petley have also drawn attention to the class inequities and oppressions masked by the high moral indignation whipped up against horror texts that are said to instigate crimes.[38]

As others have noted,[39] allusions to horror's "sick-making" pleasures raise the specter of Pierre Bourdieu's theory of cultural capital, where the taste or distaste for horror more properly "classifies the classifier."[40] For Bourdieu, "tastes are perhaps first and foremost distastes, disgust provoked by horror or visceral intolerance ("sick-making") of the tastes of others.[41] Horror's "guilt by association" seems to haunt those interested in the field, who often describe their engagement with horror as an inherently agonistic struggle to define the relationship between their enjoyment of and interest in the texts, and their perceptions that they are viewing or reading material that may not be compatible with the progressive concerns they voice. These concerns, as Aalya Ahmad discusses elsewhere in this collection, are often especially acute for feminist critics such as Linda Williams. However, Ahmad describes how critically reflecting on horror in the context of the classroom engenders subversive feminist performances that resist the strictures of "the male gaze." Also in this collection, drawing on the work of philosophers of monstrosity such as Donna Haraway and Judith Halberstam, John Edgar Browning's contribution considers the tremendous pedagogical value that horror monsters have for recognizing and articulating complex issues of alterity.

While books on horror proliferate, horror's presence in the academy continues to create confusion and uncertainty. The shocking imagery and graphic excesses of many horror fictions, moreover, engender discomfort, which further challenges the established protocols of how "good" and "bad" cultural objects may be handled. For Steffen Hantke, horror's powerful sensory and affective impact resists attempts to canonize its texts and thus confounds academic attempts at mediation between the text and the reader.[42] The "imagined subjectivity," as Hills puts it, of the scholar as antithetical to the fan simply does not permit such room to be made. The opposition between fandom and scholarship has in fact been viewed as somewhat artificial and reflective of a "torn social dynamic" between fans and scholars.[43] Both communities have constructed mutually marginalizing boundaries around particular ways of knowing about horror. This false dichotomy can be challenged in the classroom in which horror texts are taught and studied. Hills observes that "Scholars who are also fans are, perhaps, particularly sensitive to the ways in which academia silences or devalues their objects of fandom, as well as being especially alert to the minutiae of cultural distinctions that pervade both academic and fan cultures."[44]

Another fascinating possibility for pedagogical intervention in the horror field is raised by a question that King claims to be frequently asked: "Why do you want to make up horrible things when there is so much real horror in the world?"[45] When our headlines are full of the material that Jonathan Lake Crane calls "the terror of everyday life,"[46] what distinctions and connections are made between fictional horror and real-life horror, or what Carroll calls "art-horror" and "natural horror"?[47] When these boundaries are increasingly blurred, what does fictional horror become and what cultural work does it do? Hills mentions Stephen King's designation of "real horror" as "the six-o-clock news" on television,[48] asking us to consider that many horror texts blur the boundaries between "real" (factual) and "unreal" (fictive) events and that "fictional horror's tropes, devices and discursively assumed affects play a material and cultural role beyond their usually perceived parameters."[49]

For Hills, the news operates as a horror "para-site" in that news stories, such as those covering the events of September 11, 2001, can assume the "aesthetic structures of fictional horror." In addition to Hills's "true horror," we might also recall Cathy Caruth's theory of "trauma" in *Unclaimed Experience: Trauma, Narrative and History*. Trauma as a concept bears some relation to horror in that it affords insight into "the story of a wound that cries out, that addresses us in the attempt to tell us of a reality or truth that is not otherwise available.[50] By linking trauma to "what is known, but also to what remains unknown in our very actions and our language," Caruth opens up the possibility of studying horror as not only a "para-site," but as a language of the traumatized representation of horrific reality. Part of the cultural work of horror, then, is to brutally and repetitively expose trauma's wound, insisting upon nightmarish realities in the face of all attempts to suppress them. John Edward Martin's essay describes how his students have interpreted certain horror texts in terms of their own brushes with the horrific event of Hurricane Katrina.

What Valdine Clemens terms the "return of the repressed"[51] not only describes horror's relationship to horrific realities, but may also account for the particular *serial* quality of horror, its ability to produce sequels, spin-offs and copies in an endless chain of reanimation. Seriality has also become a vehicle of parody as familiarity with certain horrific conventions reaches the point of contempt. Lately, the question has become more complicated, with the appearance of numerous remakes of horror films.[52] For example, there has been a re-emergence in the twenty-first century of the "monster redneck family" once hailed by critic Robin Wood as a radical vision from the American Seventies, in a series of remakes of cult films such as *The Texas Chainsaw Massacre*, as well as in the lovingly intertextual tributes by fan and horror musician Rob Zombie to those films, *House of 1000 Corpses* (2003) and *The Devil's Rejects* (2005). The recent spate of horror film remakes from Hollywood has revived interest in the horror film genre at the same time as it has prompted denunciations of an "exhausted" and over-saturated field.

The wistful elitism (not to mention ethnocentrism) inherent in the notion of literary exhaustion also characterizes what Linda Hutcheon calls "fidelity criticism" which measures how well or how poorly the remake or adaptation "lives up" to its "original" according to traditional standards.[53] A "fidelity criticism" that focuses upon the verisimilitude of an adaptation in relation to its original conceals the power of intertextuality as a process of audience reception (and the mark of the reader-responsive text) as Hutcheon's example of the *Hellboy* DC comic series, the Guillermo del Toro film adaptation and the 2004 Yvonne Navarro novelization shows. Ben Kooyman's essay in this collection examines various inter-media adaptations of Shelley's *Frankenstein* in terms of the insights provided by the adaptation theories of Hutcheon and others, emphasizing the way the horrific elements of these adapted texts can help students examine their adherence to particular versions of these texts. Lance Eaton's detailed analysis in the present work of the role that the Incredible Hulk has played in interpreting Hyde to contemporary audiences and students of culture also takes us beyond fidelity criticism.

It is clear that simply continuing to elaborate the generic status of horror fiction is far too reductive, given what Cynthia Freeland has called the "slippery" nature of horror's boundaries and contemporary artistic productions' tendency to play with generic elements.[54] The vexed question of genre should not determine the study of horror fiction. This is not to say that generic conventions are not important, only that they are not the only means of analyzing our responses to horror fictions. Examining the pedagogy of horror, then, takes on renewed importance as interest in horror fiction has become pervasive, not only in a wide variety of popular cultural forms, but also in film, literary and cultural studies. Not only has this interest escalated in the academy, the awareness of a newer and more international cycle of horror production is also evident, as well as a multi-cultural preoccupation with figures such as the vampire and the zombie. Here, Sean Moreland and Summer Pervez focus specifically on the tropic transformation of the occult possession narrative performed by a number of Bollywood films, which invite both a re-consideration of this subgenre of supernatural horror, and a meditation on some of the key differences that distinguish South Asian from Anglo-American cinematic practice.

The study of horror is becoming a rich and fruitful field for educators across a broad range of disciplines. Indeed, horror has unmistakably gained a foothold in the academy, and these essays show us what can be and is being done there by providing both practical experience and critical reflection on what it means to teach and learn from horror texts.

Notes

1. Matt Hills, *The Pleasures of Horror* (London: Continuum, 2005), 2.
2. Hills, *Pleasures*, 2.
3. We deliberately use "affects" here instead of "effects" to describe the horror responses evoked by the text in order to avoid confusion with the debate about horror's "ill effects" on society. See for example Martin Barker and Julian Petley, eds. *Ill Effects: The Media/Violence Debate* (New York: Routledge, 2001).
4. See Mark Kermode, "I Was a Teenage Horror Fan: Or How I Learned to Stop Worrying and Love Linda Blair," *Ill Effects: The Media/Violence Debate*, and Hills, *Pleasures*, for a discussion of how extensive fan culture's horror connoisseurship and knowledge production can be.
5. Few references exist to this non-fiction survey of horror by a well-known horror writer, with the exception of Yvonne Leffler, *Horror as Pleasure: The Aesthetics of Horror Fiction* (Stockholm: Almqvist and Wiksell, 2000).
6. Hills, *Pleasures*, 145.
7. See Hills, *Pleasures*, 188, and Kermode, "Horror Fan," 12.
8. Philip Brophy, "Horrality," *The Horror Reader*, ed. Ken Gelder (London: Routledge, 2000).
9. The term "intertextuality" has been broadly expanded since Julia Kristeva, interpreting Bakhtin, launched the concept in 1967. Here we take it in its original sense as indicating the connections between texts, discourses and traditions as "a mosaic of quotations." See Julia Kristeva, *Desire in Language* (New York: Columbia University Press, 1980), 66–69.
10. Steven Jay Schneider, "Toward an Aesthetics of Cinematic Horror," *The Horror Film*, ed. Stephen Prince (New Brunswick, NJ: Rutgers, 2004).
11. Schneider, "Aesthetics," 134.
12. Stanley Fish, *Is There a Text in This Class? The Authority of Interpretive Communities* (Boston: Harvard University Press, 1980), 51.
13. Fish, *Is There a Text*, 10.
14. Fish, *Is There a Text* , 16.
15. Carol Clover, *Men, Women and Chainsaws* (Princeton, NJ: Princeton University Press, 1992).
16. Judith Mayne, "Paradoxes of Spectatorship," *Viewing Positions: Ways of Seeing Film*, ed. Linda Williams (New Brunswick, NJ: Rutgers, 1995).
17. Fish, *Is There a Text*, 25.
18. Fish, *Is There a Text*, 41.
19. Anna Powell, *Deleuze and Horror Film* (Edinburgh: Edinburgh University Press, 2005).
20. Martin Barker, "The Newson Report: A Case Study in 'Common Sense,'" *Ill Effects*, 27–46.

21. Dennis Giles, "Conditions of Pleasure in Horror Cinema," *Planks of Reason*, ed. Barry Keith Grant (Metuchen, NJ: Scarecrow, 1984).

22. In thinking about affective responses to horror texts, we want to include not only Noël Carroll's "art-horror" but also Lovecraft's celebrated "cosmic fear" as well as the creeping dread caused by a fiction, which often lingers long after the text has been read, and perhaps the intransient emotional disposition of angst so important to existentialist thought, with which films including Russell's *The Devils* (1971), Zulawski's *Possession* (1981) and von Trier's *Antichrist* (2009) appear to be engaged. See, for example, Noël Carroll, *The Philosophy of Horror or, Paradoxes of the Heart* (New York: Routledge, 1990) and H. P. Lovecraft, "Supernatural Horror in Literature," *Dagon and Other Macabre Tales* (Sauk City, WA: Arkham House, 1965), 367.

23. Jack Sullivan, *The Penguin Encyclopaedia of Horror and the Supernatural* (New York: Viking, 1986), vii.

24. Carroll, *Philosophy*, 35.

25. Anne Radcliffe, "On the Supernatural in Poetry," *Gothic Documents*, ed. Emma Clery and David Miles (Manchester: Manchester University Press, 2000).

26. "Torture porn" was a term originally coined by *New York Magazine* film critic and self-confessed "horror maven" David Edelstein in 2006 to describe *Hostel, Wolf Creek, The Devil's Rejects* (all 2005) and other recent films in which "explicit scenes of torture and mutilation" occur (n. pag.). Tellingly, Edelstein implies that torture porn is a foreign import: these scenes "were once confined to the old 42nd Street, the Deuce, in gutbucket Italian cannibal pictures like [*Cannibal Ferox*] *Make Them Die Slowly* [1981], whereas now they have terrific production values and a place of honor in your local multiplex." David Edelstein, "Now Playing at Your Local Multiplex: Torture Porn," *New York Magazine*, January 28, 2006, http://nymag.com/movies/features/15622/.

27. Stephen King, *Danse Macabre* (New York: Berkley, 1981), 176.

28. King, *Danse Macabre*, 18.

29. King, *Danse Macabre*, 35–36.

30. The term "video nasties" refers specifically to a list of seventy-four films which were banned in the United Kingdom under the *Video Recordings Act*, which was introduced as a private member's bill in the British Parliament in 1982 and became law in 1984.

31. Andrew Tudor, *Monsters and Mad Scientists: A Cultural History of the Horror Film* (Oxford: Blackwell, 1997), 446.

32. Hills, *Pleasures*, 4.

33. Hills, *Pleasures*, 3.

34. Hills, *Pleasures*, 5.

35. Jancovich notes somewhat ruefully that horror films (and those who study them) have become less "disreputable" and implicitly less interesting and subversive, ignoring the struggles against censorship and regulation of horror that characterized a more "underground" era of horror scholarship. This lament echoes Hills's dismissal of the "now rather conventional" scholar-fan and is equally oblivious to the world outside the charmed circle of British cultural studies. By wearily implying that they have "done it all," both Hills and Jancovich are rather prematurely cordoning off the field of horror fiction from other critical interventions and re-examinations. See Hills, *Pleasures*, and Jancovich, "Introduction," *Horror: The Film Reader*, ed. Mark Jancovich (London: Routledge, 2002).

36. G. K. Chesterton, "A Defence of Penny Dreadfuls," *The Defendant*, http://www.fullbooks.com/The-Defendant.html

37. Robert Bloch, *Best of Lovecraft* (New York: Ballantine, 1982), viii.

38. Petley, "The Newson Report," *Ill Effects*.

39. Ken Gelder, "Introduction," *The Horror Reader*; Matt Hills, *Fan Cultures* (New York: Routledge, 2002); K.A. Laity, "From SBIGs to Mildred's Inverse Law of Trailers: Skewing the Narrative of Horror Fan Consumption," *Horror Film: Creating and Marketing Fear*, ed. Steffen Hantke (Jackson: University Press of Mississippi, 2004).

40. Pierre Bourdieu, *Distinction: A Social Critique of the Judgement of Taste* (New York: Routledge, 1984), 6.

41. Bourdieu, *Distinction*, 56. Gelder, Kermode, Laity, Jancovich, Hills and others have also taken up Bourdieu's theory of cultural distinctions to discuss horror production and the cultural capital wielded by horror fans, and to weigh the pleasures of horror connoisseurship,

reading and viewing against the broader expression of distaste for horror in mainstream reception, which is often evinced as distaste for its fans. Before Bourdieu, the Frankfurt School defined a "culture industry" where the differentiation between "A and B films" serves as a mechanism for "classifying, organizing, and labelling consumers." See M. Horkheimer and T. Adorno, *The Culture Industry: Enlightenment as Mass Deception* (London: Continuum, 1976). In light of Bourdieu's work, with its figurative feet firmly placed on the B side, horror defines *us*, not the other way around.

42. Steffen Hantke, "Shudder as We Think: Reflections on Horror and/or Criticism," *Paradoxa* 17 (December 2002), http://paradoxa.com/excerpts/17intro.htm; Hills, *Fan Cultures*, 2.

43. Matt Hills, *Fan Cultures* (New York: Routledge, 2002), 2.

44. Matt Hills, "Para-Paracinema: The Friday the 13th Film Series as Other to Trash and Legitimate Film Cultures," *Sleaze Artists: Cinema at the Margins of Taste, Style, and Politics*, ed. Jeffrey Sconce (Durham, NC: Duke University Press, 2007), 236.

45. King, *Danse Macabre*, 26.

46. Jonathan Lake Crane, *Terror and Everyday Life* (SAGE: Thousand Oaks, CA, 1994).

47. Carroll, *Philosophy*, 12.

48. King, *Danse Macabre*, 212.

49. Hills, *Pleasures*, 130.

50. Cathy Caruth, *Unclaimed Experience: Trauma, Narrative and History* (Baltimore: Johns Hopkins University Press, 1996), 4.

51. Valdine Clemens, *The Return of the Repressed: Gothic Horror from* The Castle of Otranto *to* Alien (New York: State University of New York, 1999).

52. The outpour of horror film remakes from Hollywood shows no signs of abating at the time of this writing and now includes 1980s films such as *A Nightmare on Elm Street* (1984, 2010) as well as earlier Universal classics such as *The Wolf Man* (1941, 2010). Some of the remakes that have been pouring out of studios in the last five years are: *The Texas Chainsaw Massacre* (1973, 2004); *The Hills Have Eyes* (1977, 2006); *Dawn of the Dead* (1978, 2004); *Black Christmas* (1974, 2006); *The Amityville Horror* (1979, 2005); *It's Alive* (1974, 2008); *The Last House on the Left* (1972, 2009); *The Wicker Man* (1973, 2006); *When a Stranger Calls* (1979, 2006); *The Fog* (1980, 2005); *Poltergeist* (1982, 2011); *Halloween* (1978, 2007); *Friday the Thirteenth* (1980, 2009); and *The Stepfather* (1987, 2009).

53. Linda Hutcheon, *A Theory of Adaptation* (New York: Routledge, 2006), 8.

54. Cynthia A. Freeland, *The Naked and the Undead: Evil and the Appeal of Horror* (Boulder, CO: Westview, 2000), 10.

Postmodernism with Sam Raimi (or, How I Learned to Stop Worrying About Theory and Love *Evil Dead*)

JEFFREY ANDREW WEINSTOCK

Projecting the Exploding Projector

A little more than an hour into Sam Raimi's cult classic, *The Evil Dead* (1981), Ashley "Ash" Williams (Bruce Campbell), now the only surviving member of the initial group of five to visit the secluded cabin in the Tennessee woods, returns to the cabin's cellar seeking shotgun shells. As he does so, an old phonograph winds itself and begins to play a scratchy vaudevillian tune and a film projector switches itself on, capturing Ash in a bright rectangle of white light. While the blinded Ash struggles to regain his composure, the omnipresent blood that has been seeping from electrical sockets, pouring from broken pipes, streaming through cracks in the walls, and even filling the overhead incandescent light bulb begins to trickle onto the projector lens, casting an image of dripping blood across and behind Ash. Then, as the lens is slowly covered with "real" blood, the wet projector emits sparks and explodes.

This sequence in which Raimi's fictive protagonist flickers between being a spectator trapped by projected light and a character trapped within a film while a film projector doused in blood catches fire arguably encapsulates the *Evil Dead* films' postmodern ethos in general as it self-referentially foregrounds the absorptive character of conventional film and then pushes generic conventions past the breaking point. The moment at which Ash becomes a spectator covered in projected blood is a moment at which the film foregrounds itself as "metafiction"—a film about film; the moment at which the room becomes so filled with blood that the projector explodes, the film becomes parody—a horror film so excessive, so "over the top," that it uses the conventions of horror to poke fun at horror. What this scene thereby makes explicit is what has been implicit since the very beginning of the film when the iconic *Evil Dead* "attacking camera" rushes for the first time through the woods and almost collides with the car carrying Ash, Linda (Betsy Baker), Cheryl (Ellen Sandweiss), Scott (Richard Demanicor appearing as Hal Delrich), and Shelly (Theresa Tilly appearing as Sarah York) to the cabin: *Evil Dead* is a film that refuses to play by the rules. In its gleeful transgression of Hollywood cinematic and generic conventions, it is characteristically postmodern — a sensibility that its two "sequels," *Evil Dead II* (1987) and *Army of Darkness* (1992), not only share but accentuate through even campier special effects leading to heightened self-reflexivity, more pronounced intertextuality, conscious toying with continuity, and ultimately a persistent interrogation of subjectivity that fragments the notion of a stable, coherent self into multiple cyborg selves.[1]

There are of course any number of ways one can introduce postmodernism into the classroom. One can, for example, turn to the now-canonical but nevertheless daunting theoretical texts including Jean-François Lyotard's *The Postmodern Condition* (1979) to learn about distrust of "metanarratives," Fredric Jameson's *Postmodernism, or, The Logic of Late Capitalism* (1991) for a consideration of pastiche and the crisis in historicity, Donna Haraway's "Cyborg Manifesto" (1985) for meditations on the ways in which the human experience of the world is invariably mediated by various technologies. Or, as this chapter will assert, one can just watch Sam Raimi's *Evil Dead* films. The objective of this chapter is to present a pedagogical framework for considering postmodernism through a quick survey of the postmodern elements of the *Evil Dead* movies, with an emphasis on the ideas of metafiction, suture, and camp. The idea here is that these Raimi films — which I will assert are exemplary postmodern texts — offer ready illustrations of many of the characteristics associated with postmodernism. Instructors and students are then invited to elaborate further on the propositions presented here and to extend the conversation to other aspects of the *Evil Dead* films and beyond. In this way, the films can be utilized — in all their glorious, disgusting absurdity — as tools for teaching us not just about modern cinema, but about our contemporary moment.

Your Sutures Are Showing: Opening the Wound

Now let's move upstairs from the cellar and outside the cabin as we turn to another short sequence of shots that again has the effect of highlighting, rather than obscuring, the role of the camera in mediating the images before us — this time from *Evil Dead II* (*EDII*), Raimi's part re-make, part sequel to

The Evil Dead (*EDI*). Ash (again played by Bruce Campbell) — having already decapitated his possessed girlfriend Linda (played this time by Denise Bixler) and having himself been briefly possessed — wakes up with a start on his back in the woods, feet dangling in a muddy puddle of water. As his eyes open, the camera detaches itself from a close-up on Ash's face and shoots rapidly upward with a dizzying spiral motion until it seemingly comes to rest in the trees, some thirty feet or so above Ash who, shown from above, struggles to sit up. In the next shot, the camera is again eye-level with and focused on the now-standing Ash. As Ash slowly turns his head to his right, the camera pans with him and then begins a continuous 360° shot that moves past Ash's face and revolves to take in the woods behind him and to his right, the cabin and 1973 Oldsmobile that he faces, and the cross he has erected marking Linda's burial spot to his left. The camera then completes its circle by returning to a close-up on Ash's dazed face, now looking to his left. Following these two dizzying shots are then two much more traditional sequences. In the first, Ash cocks his head upward and the camera cuts to a shot of the presumably setting sun and then back to Ash, whose attention has been captured by some spooky sounds. In the second, the camera starts on Ash's face, cuts to the cabin over which a sort of creepy face is superimposed as a distorted voice intones "join us," and then returns its gaze to the disconcerted Ash who has decided it is time to get the hell out of Dodge (an escape attempt that predictably fails).

This series of shots is again exemplary of the push and pull of the *Evil Dead* films as they both work within and transgress established conventions of cinema and genre and direct us toward a consideration of the films as postmodern texts that persistently and metatextually foreground their own status as cultural artifacts. The sequences of Ash looking at the sun and looking at the cabin are good examples of a process discussed by film theorists as "suture."[2] In medical discourse, a suture stitches together a wound. In film theory, suture refers to the ways in which the viewer is "stitched into" the world of the film; the "wound" here that is covered over is the viewer's awareness that this world is fictive and that someone else is controlling what one can and cannot see. One common technique for achieving this forgetting of the spectator's disempowered position in classic Hollywood film is through character identification. In the sequences of Ash looking at the sun and the cabin, this is effected by introducing a familiar pattern of three quick shots: we see Ash looking, we see what he sees, and we see Ash responding. The effect that these shot/reverse shot sequences create is of seeing the world through Ash's eyes. The viewer becomes "sutured" to Ash and, in the process, is manipulated into forgetting the mediating gaze of the camera.

Successful suturing — for which traditional Hollywood film strives and for which students could be invited to look in other places — results in what can be referred to as cinematic false consciousness. Absorbed into the world of the film, the viewer forgets that the imaginary reality of the film has been constructed by absent forces (what Daniel Dayan, following Jean-Pierre Oudart's Lacanian-influenced film theorizing, refers to as "the absent one"[3]) and overlooks the "seams" at which the fabric of the film has been stitched together. This cinematic sleight of hand by which the role of outside controlling forces is obscured secures the ideological effect of the film as the viewer is interpolated into the cinematic world.[4] In other words, if the suturing is successful, the film has essentially "tricked" the spectator into forgetting the ways in which he or she is being manipulated.

Part of the postmodernism of the *Evil Dead* films however — and what students productively can be prompted to consider — is that, even as they make use of the conventions of traditional Hollywood cinema such as suture, they also persistently parody them. By juxtaposing these conventions with non-traditional techniques, their artifice is foregrounded, resulting in ideological demystification — that is, the films prevent the viewer from being wholly absorbed into the cinematic world by continually calling attention to their status as films. This is where the two circling camera shots come in. The first shot in which the camera swirls rapidly upwards into the trees is what one could refer to as a ridiculous shot. It positions the camera where no person could possibly be and shocks the viewer out of his absorption by foregrounding the mediating role of the camera. In fact, as Ash wakes up, the cinematic gaze distances the viewer from him rather than allowing for identification. The second shot that begins with a close-up on Ash's face and then rotates 360° around until it ends up back on Ash's face again can be described as an impossible shot. Rather than suturing the viewer's consciousness to Ash's as the conventional shot/reverse shot sequence would do, the slow rotation, including what Ash could not possibly see, again alienates the viewer from Ash and in fact positions the viewer as an invisible presence *in front* of him.

Part of the postmodernism of the *Evil Dead* films is this insistent self-reflexivity, this calling attention to rather than obscuring the constructed character of the cinematic text. As Brenda K. Marshall observes, "the postmodern moment is an awareness of being-within, first, a language, and second, a particular historical, social, cultural framework."[5] Postmodern works thus characteristically highlight their own textuality, their own status as constructed artifacts told from particular perspectives — and, in so doing, they foreground the constructed, perspective status of larger narratives such as history and identity. The two spinning shots, rather than obscuring the role of the camera in mediating the images presented to the spectator, instead consciously call attention to it and the effect is particularly uncanny because the perspectives represented — from above and from an unseen presence in front of Ash — literally belong to no one. To these two spinning camera shots, students can certainly add any number of other intrusive and expressionistic shots and effects that call attention to rather than obscure the mediating gaze of the camera. Indeed, part of what distinguishes the *Evil Dead* films in general (especially *EDI* and *EDII*) is the camera's mischievous refusal to conform to conventional cinematic expectations concerning position and movement. Raimi's camera instead is constantly shifting, tilting, spinning, and flying. This is particularly obtrusive late in *EDI*, for example, when Ash is first viewed from below, through cracks in the floorboards; then he is viewed at a 45° angle; then, in an especially disorienting shot, he is viewed *upside down* from behind by a camera that then flies over his head and rights itself like a trapeze artist in front of Ash.

All of these unusual and unexpected shots and angles function in a dual capacity: they are first and foremost expressionistic, establishing as they do Ash's interior state. Ash's ontological grounding (his sense of the world and how it works) has been wholly unsettled by the dramatic paranormal events in which he has been involved. His grip on sanity is tenuous and this sense of being off-balance and, indeed, of being turned on one's head is conveyed by the drunken camera and trick shots. Beyond establishing and exteriorizing Ash's subjective experience, however, the crazy camera is doubly disorienting in that it rips apart the sutures and opens the wound, so to speak, as it reminds the viewer that he or she is watching a film. The characteristic rhythm of the *Evil Dead* films is thus one in which the spectator is repeatedly invited into the cinematic world and then barred by the camera, provided with a subject with whom to identify and then alienated. Sutures are sewn and then repeatedly ripped open until the films are revealed for what they are: Frankenstein's monsters constructed, as we shall see below, from the scraps of cinematic history and roughly sewn together by a mad scientist. Students familiar with the films likely will have little difficulty pointing to other moments when the camera becomes especially intrusive, and this awareness can be used to prompt a consideration of the ways in which the technological mediation of the camera is either obscured or foregrounded and how this (in)visibility of the camera manipulates the viewer's cinematic experience.

Camping Out and PoMo Parody

The self-reflexivity of the *Evil Dead* films (and hence their postmodern aesthetic) is also inevitably emphasized by their campy special effects. Camp, as famously developed by Susan Sontag in her 1964 essay "Notes on 'Camp,'" can be described as a sensibility that derives pleasure from artifice and exaggeration. It is a postmodern aesthetic that celebrates the deliberately artificial, vulgar, banal, or affectedly humorous. Camp in short is bad taste elevated to the status of art. The *Evil Dead* films, of course, are Grand Guignol that, through ridiculously exaggerated special effects and buckets of blood, ichor and goo, intentionally transgress genre by pushing horror into comedy. As with the unorthodox camera shots, over-the-top intentionally excessive special effects are evident at every turn. One could include here the rapid stop-motion disintegration of corpses in *EDI* and *II* and the sequence in *EDII* when, after having severed his own possessed hand with a chainsaw, Ash is flipped off by the animate detached hand before it disappears into a mouse hole. Ash fires several shots into the wall and is doused with blood as from a fire hose for his troubles. Equally unforgettable is the later scene in *EDII* when the trapdoor to the cellar is forced down on the head of the reanimated Henrietta Knowby (Lou Hancock) and her eyeball pops from its socket and flies through the air right into the mouth of Bobby Joe (Kassie Wesley). Fans of the *Evil Dead* films will of course have their own favorite gross-out moments of over-the-top gore and mayhem and students, especially if asked to watch for these moments in advance, likely will be quick to identify the moments that stand out for them as being simply ridiculous — the point here is that these scenes are so exaggeratedly grotesque and absurd that the viewer with the requisite camp sensibility, far from being horrified, enjoys them for their comedic effect (Ndalianis refers to such scenes as "morbidly hysterical").[6]

The overall effect of the campiness of *EDI* and *II* is to transform the films into what Linda Hutcheon refers to as "postmodern parody." Camp, according to Sontag, "sees everything in quotation marks. It's not a lamp, but a 'lamp'; not a woman, but a 'woman.' To perceive Camp in objects and persons is to understand Being-as-Playing-a-Role. It is the farthest extension, in sensibility, of the metaphor of life as theater." Hutcheon interestingly says almost precisely the same thing about postmodern parody when she writes that, "It is rather like saying something whilst at the same time putting inverted commas around what is being said. The effect is to highlight, or 'highlight,' and to subvert, or 'subvert,' and the mode is therefore a 'knowing' and an ironic — or even 'ironic'— one."[7] Brian McHale has yet another way of saying the same thing when he discusses the characteristic postmodern gesture of putting something *sous rature* or "under erasure." Taken from the post-structuralist theorizing of French philosopher Jacques Derrida, to put something under erasure is to cross it out: "Physically canceled, yet still legible beneath the cancellation, these signs *sous rature* continue to function in the discourse even while they are excluded from it."[8] Like putting something in quotation marks, to put it under erasure is to use a concept even while calling it into question.

With this in mind, all three *Evil Dead* films, the instructor might propose, are not horror, but "horror" or perhaps even ~~horror~~. They are horrific in places and clearly deploy the conventions of the horror film genre, but because they are so campy, so out-and-out silly, they refuse to sustain the affect — the emotional response — typically elicited by horror films. So although they look a lot like horror films, they are more properly "metahorror films," horror films that incorporate and exaggerate the conventions of horror in order to subvert them — which is essentially the process defined by Hutcheon as postmodern parody. The parodic thrust of the films is most evident, as mentioned above, in the incorporation of over-the-top patently ridiculous special effects — effects that become more pronounced as the series progresses until *Army of Darkness* confronts the viewer with platoons of claymation stop motion skeleton warriors and the absurd elongation of Ash's face after he is almost sucked into a decoy *Necronomicon* (again foregrounding the absorptive quality of narrative even as the campy special effects obstruct such absorption in the films!).

Hail to the King of the Hills with Eyes: Intertextuality

Students watching *EDI* with a close eye will note a promotional poster in the basement of the cabin for the 1977 Wes Craven horror film, *The Hills Have Eyes* (about a suburban American family stalked by a clan of psychotic mutant cannibals who live in the Nevada desert [remade in 2006 by Alexandre Aja]). According to Ndalianis, Raimi in fact spoke to the role of allusion within the horror film in a 1983 interview: "Discussing Wes Craven's allusion to *Jaws* (via a poster) in *The Hills Have Eyes* (1977), Raimi stated that in Craven's film, the poster was there to make the point that *Jaws* was 'pop' horror whereas *The Hills Have Eyes* was 'real' horror."[9] Ndalianis then asserts that "The subsequent appearance of a *The Hills Have Eyes* poster in the basement of *The Evil Dead* undercuts its predecessor by suggesting that, by 1983, it was Craven's film that produced 'pop' horror and Raimi's that presented 'real' horror."[10]

While Ndalianis astutely observes the chain of intertextual references at play here — Raimi's referencing Craven's referencing of Spielberg's blockbuster 1975 adaptation of Peter Benchley's 1974 novel — far from asserting or establishing any kind of generic purity or authenticity, it seems to me that the *Evil Dead* films' increasingly obvious incorporation of allusion, quotation, and intertextual punning — culminating with *Army of Darkness* as generic pastiche — instead precisely calls into question (or puts under erasure) the notion of "real horror." Returning to the idea of postmodern parody, Hutcheon asserts that, "through a double process of installing and ironizing, parody signals how present representations come from past ones and what ideological consequences derive from both continuity and difference."[11] The anachronistic *The Hills Have Eyes* poster in the basement of the secluded cabin in *EDI*—like the exploding movie camera later in the film—effectively highlights the artifice of the film one is watching by playfully reminding the viewer that one is watching a "horror" film and inviting a comparison between Raimi's film about a terrorized group in the woods and Craven's about a terrorized group in the desert. The film "installs" conventions of the horror genre, but then ironizes them through the gesture of situating them in a horror genealogy of sorts. Again to refer to Derrida, the "meaning" of *The Evil Dead* films then becomes a function of *différence*—their difference from other horror films and their place within a chain of signifiers. *The Evil Dead*, which is different from *The Hills Have Eyes*, which itself was different from *Jaws*, nevertheless is related to all three and retroactively alters the meaning of each link in the chain. What was real becomes pop (or, put differently, what was avant-garde becomes mass culture)—until one reaches the point where there no longer seems to be any difference.

While *EDI* and *EDII*, characteristic of postmodern texts, are full of intertextual allusions and citations—among them the references to early twentieth-century American author H. P. Lovecraft's book of forbidden spells and lore, the *Necronomicon*; the bad pun on Hemingway's *A Farewell to Arms* (a groaner then exacerbated by crediting the book to author Stubby Kaye) when Ash severs his own hand and the ensuing allusion to the animate hand Thing from *The Munsters*; arguably to Carl Theodor Dreyer's surreal 1932 *Vampyr* when the ghost of the father (played by John Peakes) of Annie Knowby (Sarah Berry) appears in *EDII*, to *Poltergeist* (Tobe Hooper, 1982) when the tree attacks at the end of *EDII*, to Kubrick's *The Shining* (1980) and Craven's *Nightmare on Elm Street* (1984) when torrents of blood pour from walls and douse Ash, etc.—*Army of Darkness* is even broader in its scope and must be considered as a kind of transgeneric pastiche as it incorporates, juxtaposes, and parodies not only elements of the horror film, but of the sword-and-sorcery fantasy epic, the science fiction film, the Western, and the action film as well. Another way to put this is that whereas *EDI* and *EDII* can be described as horror films under erasure or "horror films," *AOD* in good postmodern form scuttles the notion of genre almost entirely as, in keeping with Hutcheon's discussion of the postmodernism of Terry Gilliam's *Brazil* (1985), it juxtaposes "heterogeneous filmic genres."[12]

AOD is at bottom a patchwork quilt—or Frankenstein's monster—of appropriations from and allusions and references to other cinematic, literary, and popular culture genres, works, and figures (here again, students can be prompted to look for these intertextual moments). Some of these allusions are related to cinematic techniques—for example, the recurring intrusive fast zoom during the fashioning of Ash's prosthetic hand is a clichéd convention of the Kung Fu film. Others are conveyed through image, dialogue, and action. Among the more obvious ones are the repeated appropriations from and allusions to the Three Stooges through stylized comedic violence and insult, the allusion to Jonathan Swift's *Gulliver's Travels* (1726) when Ash is bound by a gaggle of Lilliputian mini–Ashes, and the homage to stop-motion film pioneer Ray Harryhausen — especially *Sinbad the Sailor* (1949) — conveyed through the incorporation of claymation skeleton warriors. Further, the hand that reaches up through the murky water when Ash is thrown into the pit early in the film is a visual reference to fantasy epic *Excalibur* (1981), the windmill into which Ash ventures is taken from the end of James Whale's classic *Frankenstein* (1931), and the incantation Ash must use to claim the *Necronomicon*, "Clatto Verata Nicto," is an obvious reference to "Klaatu, Barada, Nikto," the words used to command the robot Gort in *The Day the Earth Stood Still* (1951). More broadly, from Ash's prosthetic hand to the collapsing walls of the pit, the first three films released in the *Star Wars* series (*Star Wars* 1977, *The Empire Strikes Back* 1980, *Return of the Jedi* 1983) seem to be persistent points of reference, while Ash as supremely confident rifle-bearing bad-ass with his stylized assertive delivery of lines (Steve Biodrowski refers to him in an online 2008 review as a "self-centered, loud-mouthed jerk who happens to be good at fighting monsters") seems to borrow in equal measure from tough guy roles played by James Cagney and Clint Eastwood (with a dash of Elvis, foreshadowing Campbell's role in 2002's quirky *Bubba Ho-Tep*, tossed in for good measure).

The point is here that, as one watches *AOD*, one is not watching one film, but many. The film — indeed all the *Evil Dead* films — constructs what McHale would refer to as "intertextual spaces"[13] (or, as I will discuss below, Foucaultian "heterotopias) that are characteristically postmodern in their mixing, parodying, and ultimate destabilization of genre. The internal "spaces" of these films are thus in a dizzying way constituted by their outsides as the films are "postmodernist contradictory texts" that, in keeping with Hutcheon's discussion of such texts generally, are "specifically parodic in their intertextual relation to the traditions and conventions of the genres involved."[14] This observation could then be developed into classroom considerations of genre, as well as the relationship between intertextuality and originality. How does one "classify" a film such as *AOD*? And is the originality of the film in some way diminished by virtue of its reliance upon the cinematic tradition?

Heterotopic Juxtaposition

I now wish to spiral back around to my earlier discussion of the ridiculous and impossible camera shots in *EDII* — the circling shots taken from above

Ash and from in front of him that I described as belonging to no one. The *Evil Dead* films, I should point out, do in fact offer one possible explanation for the camera's uncanny gaze that students are likely to suggest: the supernatural. That is, although no *person* is gazing down at Ash from the trees or standing invisibly in front of him, the viewer could be seeing from the perspective of the demonic force tormenting him. While there are some problems with this explanation in the cases of the two spinning shots — the camera's quick retreat in the first seems uncharacteristic of the aggressive demonic force within the *Evil Dead* films, while the camera's cautious pan in the second clearly reflects Ash's anxious gaze even if it does not embody it — the first two *Evil Dead* films in general do correlate disembodied gazes with supernatural forces and this is most especially the case for what I refer to as the films' iconic *attacking* shots.

Tracking shots in which the camera follows along a path parallel to that of a person being filmed are a familiar convention of the horror genre, as are voyeuristic shots in which a protagonist is viewed by an unobserved malevolent force. Such shots — sometimes referred to as "killer cam" shots — establish the vulnerability of the protagonist as an antagonist surreptitiously observes or in some cases chases her (in the gendered dynamic of the horror genre, it is conventionally a woman who is tormented[15]) and these shots are often filmed using an unsteady camera to connote that they are first-person perspectival shots as seen by the killer or monster — what cultural critic Mark Edmundson refers to as the "I-camera technique."[16] The first two *Evil Dead* films appropriate and exaggerate these techniques through the recurring device of the rapidly moving unsteady camera that aggressively "flies" through the woods toward the main characters and the cabin. This camera movement — which may be a sort of intertextual allusion to the drunkenly lilting, flying camera that tracks the Torrance family car across the beautiful and forbidding landscape at the start of a film that came out one year prior to *EDI*, Stanley Kubrick's *The Shining* (1980) — in fact opens *EDI* and is quickly established as belonging to an evil supernatural force as it almost seems to collide with the car carrying Ash, Linda, Cheryl, Shelly, and Scott.

This type of shot, featuring what Ndalianis refers to as a "hyperkinetic camera,"[17] perhaps the most insistent feature of the first two films, is then repeated multiple times throughout both *EDI* and *II* with the camera increasingly becoming more aggressive. At the end of *EDI*, as the battered and beleaguered Ash emerges from the cabin, the camera — seemingly getting a running start from behind the cabin — flies out of the woods swaying dangerously as it goes, slams through the cabin, breaks through the front door, and charges right into Ash's open and screaming mouth. *EDII*'s truncated (and altered) recapitulation of the events of *EDI* culminates with this shot — and then continues with Ash actually being sent flying and spinning wildly through the air with impossible velocity. He has seemingly been knocked into the woods by the camera!

The hyperkinetic camera creates two important postmodern effects. First, as with the spinning camera shots referenced above, this unusual technique — one that violates the standard conventions of Hollywood filmmaking — self-reflexively foregrounds the cinematic qualities of the film and again calls attention to, and to a certain extent implicitly critiques, the expectations and conventions of "traditional" cinema. Beyond this, the conflation of camera with supernatural forces participates in what we could refer to as the postmodern process of "unworlding" — of calling into question explanatory metanarratives that offer coherence to one's experience of existence.

In *Postmodernist Fiction*, McHale's first "thesis" about postmodernist fiction is that its "dominant" — its organizing questions and premises — are "*ontological*" in nature.[18] By this, he means that postmodernist fiction "deploys strategies which engage and foreground questions" about "modes of being." Among these questions are "Which world is this? What is to be done in it? Which of my selves is to do it?" Additional questions include "What is a world? What kinds of world are there, how are they constituted, and how do they differ? What happens when different kinds of world are placed in confrontation, or when boundaries between worlds are violated?"[19] Given this cluster of questions, it isn't hard to see why McHale privileges science fiction as the "ontological [and thus postmodern] genre *par excellence*"[20] — but McHale does extend this analysis to supernatural horror when he observes the "*dual ontology*" of such texts: "on one side our world of the normal and everyday, on the other side the next-door world of the paranormal or supernatural, and running between them the contested boundary separating the two worlds."[21] Supernatural horror thus inevitably engages these questions of ontology as characters and viewers confront an altered reality, one that fails to conform to current rationalist understandings of how the universe functions and provokes precisely the set of characteristic postmodern questions identified by McHale.

This questioning of worlds, placing of worlds into confrontation, and, as I will discuss below, placing worlds "under erasure" clearly is the organizing problematic of all three *Evil Dead* films. In keeping with supernatural horror films in general, in both *EDI* and *II* a confrontation is staged between the world of reality as initially shared by both characters and viewers and a world inhabited by malevolent supernatural forces. It is *AOD*, however, that comes closest to realizing McHale's characterization of the postmodernist condition as "an anarchic landscape of worlds in the plural" in that the worlds that come into conflict are not just the natural and supernatural ones, but also, as a result of the sf/fantasy device of time travel and Ash's anachronistic technology, the worlds of present and past.

All three films present what, borrowing from French philosopher Michel Foucault, one could refer to "heterotopias." As developed in Foucault's *The Order of Things* (1966), heterotopias are supplemental spaces that exist as a kind of inverted outside to culture. These can be sacred or taboo spaces, or places that house people excluded from mainstream society, like asylums. Such spaces and places are both excluded from society and simultaneously a part of it — through the logic of what Jacques Derrida refers to as the supplement, they are both inside and outside at the same time and the existence of one is necessary for the existence of the other (there must be an outside in order for there to be an inside and the "meaning" of the inside is dependent upon its difference from the outside).[22] Appropriating this idea of heterotopic spaces, McHale contends that such spaces are paradigmatic of postmodern writing, which stages heterotopias in a variety of ways including through the juxtaposition of noncontiguous spaces, the interpolation of an alien space within a familiar space, the superimposition of two familiar spaces on top of one another, and the "rupturing" of conventional associations through a strategy of misattribution.[23] It is worth noting that horror movies almost always take place in or move into heterotopic spaces and students can easily generate lists of such locations.

In *ED I* and *II*, rationalist understandings of how the universe functions conflict with what one could refer to as an inspirited world — a world inhabited by demonic forces and supernatural agents that exist outside linear time. In each film, through a kind of performative invocation, ancient demons are summoned when a tape recording of a reading of a forbidden book (the *Nyturan Demonta* in *EDI*, the *Necronomicon Ex Mortis* in *EDII*) is played. The cabin and the surrounding woods thus become a kind of carnivalesque heterotopic space through a process of supernaturalization. That the cabin is a space apart, a sort of outside to the world of waking rationality, is signaled in the first film even prior to the playing of the tape recorder. As Cheryl sketches in her room, the pendulum of the grandfather clock she is watching abruptly stops, ominously suggesting that the laws of time and space have been suspended — which is indeed the case. In *EDII*, after Ash has taken a chainsaw to the animate severed head of his girlfriend, Linda, the house itself literally comes alive. Reflecting Ash's disordered mental state, lamps cackle and sway, a mounted buck twists and laughs, books flutter, cabinet doors flap, and the room in general becomes a crazy space in which the line between animate and inanimate disappears. The cabin becomes the nightmarish underside to the waking world of reality — and here students could be asked to consider whether these events are "actually" taking place or whether they are all hallucinations.

AOD ups the heterotopic ante, so to speak, by combining supernatural horror with a convention of science fiction: time travel.[24] Whereas the clock stops in *EDI*, it winds backward in *AOD* as Ash, having been sucked into a time portal opened up in *EDII*, literally falls into the past and plummets to earth (together with his 1973 Oldsmobile) in what is presented as a fictive representation of England in A.D. 1300.[25] Through the device of time travel, past and present are overlaid upon each other, creating a kind of irrational time-space in which modern technology — chainsaws, rifles, automobiles — anachronistically compete with medieval swords and truncheons as the living battle the dead for control of the *Necronomicon* and, the film asserts, thus for control of the world.

At the center of the disordered heterotopic landscape of *AOD* (which we could, following Foucault, consider a heterotopia of time or "heterochrony") is yet another heterotopia: the cemetery, a "heterotopia of deviation," an uncanny contact point between self and other — or, more properly, a contact point that prompts the anxious recognition of the other as self. In an essay translated as "Of Other Spaces," Foucault speaks to "the strange heterotopia of the cemetery" and the way in which these problematic spaces, both sacred and taboo, now function as "the other city, where each family possesses its dark resting place."[26] In *AOD*, Ash's quest for the *Book of the Dead* takes him to the city of the dead, the cemetery, the forbidden outside to the life-world (such as it is) of medieval England. The only effective armor here is ritual — the recitation of the memorized incantation. Ash bungles the spell and, as a result, the dead rise. But what comes back first and foremost is Ash himself, Evil Ash, that part of Ash he has shot, dismembered, and buried (as apt a metaphor for repression as one can find), but which nevertheless persists and returns the moment the prophylactic of tradition is violated. And, inasmuch as we can assume that the dead buried in the cemetery are those of Lord Arthur and his people, the evil dead in *AOD* are not ancient Sumerian demons summoned from their sleep of millennia but the people themselves — their own family and ancestors. The Deadites thus become "Dead I's," us, our own, the Self, disavowed as Other, returned to destroy us. In this respect, *AOD* foregrounds the unconscious as the ultimate heterotopia, the excluded space within.

"After that, I'm history"

The time-travel conceit developed in *Army of Darkness* aligns the film with yet another device common to postmodern narrative: the alternate history. In Hutcheon's discussion of postmodernism in her *A Poetics of Postmod-*

ernism, she privileges as paradigmatic of our postmodern moment what she refers to as "historiographic metafictions," narratives that are "intensely self-reflexive and yet paradoxically also lay claim to historical events and personages."[27] These are works that demonstrate "theoretical self-awareness of history and fiction as human constructs"[28] — a central postmodern assumption that students should be prompted to consider. Her discussion in *Poetics* then focuses on authors including E. L. Doctorow, Salman Rushdie, Robert Coover, Maxine Hong Kingston, Gabriel Garcia Marquez, and others who in their works "re-write or re-present the past ... to open it up to the present"[29] and who in the process refute "the natural or common-sense methods of distinguishing between historical fact and fiction."[30] Elaborating on this idea, Marshall adds that

> History in the postmodern moment becomes histories and questions. It asks: Whose history gets told? In whose name? For what purpose? Postmodernism is about histories not told, retold, untold. History as it never was. Histories forgotten, hidden, invisible, considered unimportant, changed, eradicated. It's about the refusal to see history as linear, as leading straight to up to today in some recognizable pattern.[31]

Complementing both Hutcheon and Marshall is again McHale, who suggests that the methods through which postmodern texts "un-narrate" history or place it under erasure include "apocryphal history" and "creative anachronism."[32] Apocryphal history, according to McHale, "contradicts the official version in one of two ways: either it *supplements* the historical record ... or it *displaces* official history altogether." In either case, "the effect is to juxtapose the officially-accepted version of what happened and the way things were, with another, often radically dissimilar version of the world,"[33] thereby foregrounding the fact that accessibility to the past is conditioned entirely by textuality; as Hutcheon puts it in a phrase that it is worth asking students to "unpack": "We cannot know the past except through its texts."[34] Creative anachronism, according to McHale, results in a kind of "double vision" in which the present and the past are simultaneously in focus, each inflecting and conditioning the reception of the other.

Army of Darkness of course stages precisely such an alternate, apocryphal history. Ash is sucked into the past and lands in medieval England (complete with his anachronistic chainsaw and Oldsmobile) — but this is no England that ever existed in "real history." Rather, this is the fantasized "England" made familiar through swords and sorcery epics in which supernatural creatures terrorize man or do his bidding, the boundary between life and death is ambiguous and permeable, and magical incantations and spells function as felicitous speech-acts.[35] Beyond this, what *AOD* literalizes is the postmodern proposition that the past exists only as a product of the present (that is, that the past only exists as a result of the ways in which we conceptualize and narrativize it in the present). In *AOD*, Ash comes from the future to save the past — he is the prophesied hero who arrives to save mankind from the Deadites. Paradoxically, the existence of mankind in the past is thus dependent upon an intervention from the future. Further developing this paradox is then Ash's quip to Sheila (Ambeth Davidtz), "After this, I'm history," which suggests that Ash only assumes his place in the past by virtue of completing the circle and returning to the future.

Also of note here is that — in an especially metatextual twist — by reluctantly assuming his role as hero, Ash thereby becomes a character in a book. In *EDII*, Annie interprets a page of the *Necronomicon* for Ash that describes a "hero from the sky" who arrived in A.D. 1300 to "destroy the evil." This of course is Ash whose future is written in the past — and who by traveling into the past assumes his textualized future. In *AOD*, both past and present are revealed to be texts written from particular perspectives and requiring interpretation.

Retroactive Continuity

Not only do the *Evil Dead* films offer a reconceptualization of history, they also offer a persistent calling into question of *their own* history as each new entry in the trilogy revises the storyline. Retroactive continuity (often shortened to "retcon") refers to the deliberate alteration or reframing of previously established facts in a work of serial fiction to serve current plot needs. This most commonly involves "recasting" facts from a new perspective that changes their interpretation — as in the "it was all a dream!" conclusion. When altered events work in conformity with that which was previously stated, this is called a revision; when new facts replace older ones, this is a rewrite. The ideal retcon from a conventional perspective clarifies a situation or answers a question introduced earlier in the series without introducing new questions and revisions and this is generally preferred in Hollywood script writing rather than rewrites, which can be disorienting or unsatisfying to the spectators who have been conditioned to expect continuity.

In keeping with everything discussed about *The Evil Dead* films so far, it will be no surprise that they consciously upend conventional Hollywood cinematic expectations through their use of the explicit rewrite retcon. If the instructor has the luxury of screening both *EDI* and *EDII*, the question can then be posed as to the relationship between the two films. Close attention reveals that the first six minutes or so of *EDII* function as a condensed reprise of *EDI*, except that the summary alters the events of the original in significant ways: most notably in that rather than having five people journey to the cabin, only Ash and Linda make the trip — and while Bruce Campbell again plays Ash, Linda is now played by Denise Bixler rather than Betsy Baker. As Ndalianis appreciates, *EDII* is "preoccupied with its status as a sequel," which becomes one of the "most challenging aspects of the film's interaction with its audience."[36] The beginning of the film is a puzzle that poses a series of questions to the spectator concerning the film's status: is it a sequel to *EDI* or a remake? It is an original or a copy? Is Ash returning to the isolated cabin or going for the first time? Ndalianis concludes that "The contradictions, the plays on repetition, the undercutting of expectations, all have the effect of making us contemplate the production of generic 'meaning' and how we extract it. Rather than passively accepting *Evil Dead II* as a sequel, the film invites the audience to ask the question 'what is a sequel?' and furthermore 'what is a sequel's relationship to genre?'"[37]

The beginning of *Army of Darkness* similarly alters the end of *Evil Dead II*. At the end of *EDII*, Bruce Campbell and his Oldsmobile fall out of the sky and into the past where he blasts a flying claymation "deadite" with his shotgun and is hailed as a hero. The start of *Army of Darkness* again has Ash and the car falling from the sky, but rather than slaying demons, Ash is suspected by Lord Arthur (Marcus Gilbert) and his men of being a spy for rival warrior clan leader Duke Henry the Red (Richard Grove) and is taken prisoner. The beginning of *AOD*, like the beginning of *EDII*, "presents itself as a film that both is and is not a sequel, a narrative that is and is not a narrative continuation."[38] The obvious pedagogical question here is how do we, as viewers, make sense of these apparent discontinuities?

Multiple Lindas, Multiple Selves

As noted above, when Ash returns to the cabin/goes for the first time in *EDII*, he travels with a Linda (Denise Bixler) who both is and is not the "original" Linda of *EDI* (Betsy Baker). This difference encapsulates the interrogation of coherent selfhood that is not only arguably the hallmark of the *Evil Dead* films, but a persistent theme of postmodern theory. In Barbara Johnson's explanation of the logic of deconstruction, she observes that, while "traditionalists say that a thing cannot be both A and not-A, deconstruction opens up the ways in which A is necessarily but unpredictably already different from A."[39] This is exactly the post-structuralist logic of the *Evil Dead* films. Linda both is and is not Linda. This deconstruction of the idea of coherent, stable selfhood is then amplified when we turn to Ash, who in each of the three *Evil Dead* films splinters and fragments in very literal ways into multiple divided selves that both are and are not Ash.

In *EDI*, this fragmenting of self is visually represented by Ash reaching into his reflection in a mirror, which ripples and absorbs his hand like black water. *EDII* (having already offered a brief early representation of possessed Ash in the first ten minutes) offers a reprise and elaboration of this device as Ash's reflection leans out of the mirror and chokes him — and then in the next shot, Ash is shown choking himself. Following this confrontation, Ash's body literally turns against him as his hand, now seemingly possessed, attacks him — precipitating Ash's severing of his own hand with a chainsaw.

In *EDI* and *EDII*, Raimi presents to the spectator what one with a theoretical bent could refer to as the undoing of the Lacanian mirror stage and thus again a kind of ideological demystification. According to Lacan, human subjectivity is founded upon a fundamental form of misrecognition that installs anxiety at the center of the subject. During the mirror stage, the infant identifies with its specular image, which gives rise to the sense of an ego or "I." But because the reflected image of the unified body is at odds with the infant's lived experience of its body (a "body-in-pieces"[40] according to Lacan), this "imago" is established as an "Ideal-I" toward which the subject will perpetually strive. Put differently, this process of misrecognizing one's self in the image in the mirror creates a sense of self that is built around lack.

Particularly suggestive for this discussion of the *Evil Dead* films is Mary Klages's online gloss of Lacanian theory, in which she writes concerning the infant just prior to the moment of the mirror stage,

> At this age ... the baby or child hasn't yet mastered its own body; it doesn't have control over its own movements, and it doesn't have a sense of its body as a whole. Rather, the baby experiences its body as fragmented, or in pieces — whatever part is within its field of vision is there as long as the baby can see it, but gone when the baby can't see it. It may see its own hand, but it doesn't know that that hand belongs to it — the hand could belong to anyone, or no one.[41]

This seems a perfect description of what happens to Ash in *EDII*: after he is assaulted by his own mirror image, his body becomes incoherent and falls to pieces — and his "possessed" hand literally seems to belong to someone else. He becomes controlled by an other that seems to be simultaneously within and without — he is both mad and possessed.

As has been the case with most of the other postmodern themes addressed in this essay, *Army of Darkness* latches on to the anti-humanist notion of the "decentered subject" and develops it even more completely than the preceding two films. In *AOD*, when Ash enters the windmill, he again confronts his image in a mirror (a recurring device that students could be asked to consider not just in the *Evil Dead* films, but in horror in general). Seemingly misrecognizing the image for another person (and the image does appear to move of its own accord), Ash charges the image and collides with the mirror, shattering it into many pieces — each of which reflects a tiny Ash that then springs from the mirror and attacks him. Ash's self here has splintered into multiple antagonistic selves. Then, as though this scene were not already surreal enough, Ash is forced to swallow himself as a tiny Ash dives into his mouth to attack him from within. In response, Ash (having previously fried his face on a hot woodstove without apparent detrimental effect) pours boiling water into his mouth from a teapot.

Ash's attempt to destroy the tiny Ash within fails, however, and this sequence of events culminates with Ash literally splitting as a second Ash erupts from his shoulder. Here Ash confronts himself as doppelganger and the spectator is initially invited to consider the reflections simplistically as "good Ash" and "bad Ash." The film, however, quickly complicates this binary opposition by having "good Ash" blast his evil counterpart and remark in one of the film's many memorable lines, "Good, bad, I'm the guy with the gun." Bad Ash is then dismembered by Good Ash (in a scene essentially the same as Ash's dismembering of Linda in *EDI*) who then buries the pieces after some Monty Pythonesque banter with his doppelganger's severed head, (which interestingly seems to have acquired a Scottish accent).

Repeatedly, the postmodernism of the *Evil Dead* films is foregrounded by their persistent thematization of the decentered subject. There really is no such thing as a coherent self or identity in the films. Rather, controlled by warring forces both within and without, characters differ from themselves (Linda in *EDI* and *EDII*, Ash in *AOD* as compared with *EDI* and *II*) and literally splinter into multiple selves. Highlighting the misrecognition (*méconnaissance*) of the mirror stage, the imaginary identification with the specular image is undone by reflections that differ from the bodies that cast them and bodies that fragment into pieces. Students likely will be able to relate this anxiety concerning bodily integrity to any number of other contemporary horror films, which is a topic that can be expanded in a variety of directions to encompass issues of gender, race, and class.

Cyborgs

In the *Evil Dead* films, it is worth noting (however briefly) that the assault on bodily integrity is counterpoised by the technological enhancement of the body through mechanical prostheses. Incorporating that most postmodern of tropes, the *Evil Dead* films reconstruct Ash's fragmented body as cyborg. As famously developed by cultural theorist Donna Haraway in her "A Cyborg Manifesto," the cyborg functions as a potent metaphor for postmodern personhood. For Haraway, the cyborg undoes the nature/culture dichotomy and moves beyond traditional dualistic thinking about gender and, indeed, humanity. In *EDI* and *EDII*, as well as at the start of *AOD*, the transformation of Ash into cyborg is accomplished through the mediation of the chainsaw, which Ash actually fashions in *EDII* to fit over the stump where his hand used to be. In *AOD*, this prosthesis is exchanged for another, a mechanical hand. Subsequently in *AOD*, after mixing up some gunpowder, Ash will further extend his cone of agency by transforming his Oldsmobile into a kind of tank/car/helicopter hybrid that is quite effective in bowling over Deadites until Ash crashes the vehicle rather than pancake Evil Sheila.

One could add that this fragmentation and reconstruction of Ash's body is mirrored in all three films by various bodies that fall to pieces, subsist in different forms, and are rebuilt. This is most notable in *EDII* when Linda's dismembered form emerges spectrally from the ground and reassembles itself in order to perform a literal *danse macabre*—a form of reconstructive self-fashioning then mimicked in *AOD* by Evil Ash and the Deadite army whose disparate parts recombine for the purpose of waging war upon the living. All bodies in the *Evil Dead* films are arguably represented as cyborgized assemblages of tenuously held together pieces that undo the natural/unnatural distinction. As with the discussion of anxieties concerning bodily integrity above, the technologized body in the *Evil Dead* films presents another topic for broader classroom consideration. Is a cyborg a monster? And where does the human stop and technology start?[42]

Incredulity Toward Metanarratives

This discussion is far from exhausting consideration of the postmodern elements of the *Evil Dead* films, but the goal here is not completeness (indeed, if our postmodern moment emphasizes anything, it is that interpretation never reaches an end) but rather provocation; the objective has been to consider the films in light of several different characteristics generally associated with postmodern texts to provide a "jumping off point" for additional pedagogical conversation about postmodernism. With that in mind, there is one last postmodern aspect of these films I would like to introduce here: their ultimate incredulity toward "metanarratives."

Skepticism toward metanarratives may well be among the best known of postmodern tropes. As introduced in Jean-François Lyotard's *The Postmodern Condition*, the idea is that our postmodern moment is characterized by an incredulity toward grand narratives — abstract ideas like religion, nationalism, or science — that offer comprehensive explanatory frameworks for making sense of existence. As I have discussed above, the *Evil Dead* films persistently trouble familiar narratives about history, temporality, and identity — all truth claims in the films are put under erasure, invoked only to be revoked. Horror becomes "horror," history becomes "history," even Linda and Ash become "Linda" and "Ash." What we are left with finally is a "sequence" of films (which we can't even call a sequence because the second isn't really a sequel and the third becomes a kind of sequel that functions as prequel) that undercuts any definitive truth claims; the films finally take themselves as their main subject, playfully foregrounding their constructedness at every step and highlighting that their "meaning" is endlessly open-ended.

The place to conclude then is with a consideration-yet-to-come to be held in the classroom concerning what the films tell us about history and our historical moment, about contemporary anxieties and desires, about cinema and about genre. The purpose of this essay has been to outline some of the many ways in which the *Evil Dead* films can be considered postmodern texts. This essay, however, has skirted the larger, more important questions that still need to be asked about what this means and why it matters. Ash looks into a mirror and ends up choking himself. Movies, of course, are also types of mirrors. So what is it we see when we gaze into the *Evil Dead* films? And is there anything actually there or is it, finally, just Sam Raimi giving us something to choke on?

NOTES

1. As I will discuss below, neither *Evil Dead II* nor *Army of Darkness* can unproblematically be considered a sequel.
2. For a thorough discussion of suture, see Kaja Silverman's *The Subject of Semiotics* (London: Oxford, 1983).
3. Daniel Dayan, "The Tutor-Code of Classical Cinema" in *Film Theory and Criticism: Introductory Readings*, 4th., eds. Gerald Mast, Marshall Cohen, and Leo Brady (New York: Oxford University Press, 1992), 188.
4. Dayan, 188.
5. Brenda K. Marshall, *Teaching the Postmodern: Fiction and Theory* (New York: Routledge, 1992), 3.
6. Angela Ndalianis, "The Rules of the Game: *Evil Dead II*...Meet Thy *Doom*," in *Hop on Pop: The Politics and Pleasures of Popular Culture*, eds. Henry Jenkins, Tara McPherson, and Jane Shattuc (Durham, NC: Duke University Press, 2003), 508. I would add that this is also why censorship of the films seems so absurd — the stylized violence is so hyperbolic and patently artificial that the effect is funny, not horrific.
7. Linda A. Hutcheon, *The Politics of Postmodernism* (New York: Routledge, 1989), 1–2.
8. Brian McHale, *Postmodernist Fiction* (London: Routledge, 1987), 100.
9. Ndalianis, 514.
10. Ndalianis, 514. I think Ndalianis goofs when she says "by 1983." *EDI* came out in 1981. The interview with Raimi took place in 1983. It would make more sense to say that by 1981, when the film was released, Raimi considered Craven pop and his work real. However, this temporal confusion, as I'll discuss below, is entirely in keeping with the problematic role of time in the *Evil Dead* films, so maybe it is intentional after all. On a separate note, this observation could lead to an interesting discussion with students about what constitutes "real horror" in today's cinema.
11. Hutcheon, *Politics*, 93.

12. Linda A. Hutcheon, *A Poetics of Postmodernism: History, Theory, Fiction* (New York: Routledge, 1988), 5.
13. McHale, 56.
14. Hutcheon, *Poetics*, 11.
15. Tison Pugh takes this characteristically gendered dynamic of the horror film into account when he notes the feminization of Ash. See his article, "Queering the Medieval Dead: History, Horror, and Masculinity in Sam Raimi's *Evil Dead* Trilogy."
16. Mark Edmundson, *Nightmare on Main Street: Angels, Sadomasochism, and the Culture of Gothic* (Cambridge, MA: Harvard University Press, 1999), 10.
17. Ndalianis, 509.
18. McHale, 10.
19. McHale, 10.
20. McHale, 16.
21. McHale, 73.
22. As with the concept of *différance*, the idea of the supplement is central to Derridean deconstruction and is discussed in a variety of places, most notably perhaps in *Of Grammatology*.
23. McHale, 46–48.
24. McHale observes on page 66 that, "postmodernist writing has preferred to adapt science fiction's motifs of temporal displacement rather than its spatial displacements."
25. While the consensus seems to be that Ash falls into England, as of April 9, 2011, the Wikipedia page for *Evil Dead II* intriguingly suggests that the Ash and his Oldsmobile "land in what appears to be the Crusader-held middle-east." That would open up an especially provocative racial reading of the film.
26. This article is available online. The discussion of the cemetery can be found under "The second principle."
27. Hutcheon, *Poetics*, 5.
28. Hutcheon, *Poetics*, 5.
29. Hutcheon, *Poetics*, 110.
30. Hutcheon, *Poetics*, 93. What is interesting about Hutcheon's selection of authors and texts in *A Poetics of Postmodernism* is that, even though she observes in *The Politics of Postmodernism* that postmodernism calls into question the high art/low art and elite culture/pop culture divides, she then chooses to focus almost exclusively on what would generally be considered "highbrow" texts. (However hard it is to believe, she doesn't mention *The Evil Dead* even once!) In her own way, like Fredric Jameson who surveys postmodernism's "waning of critical distance" with dismay in his *The Postmodern Condition*, Hutcheon seems a modernist at heart.
31. Marshall, 4.
32. McHale, 90.
33. McHale, 90.
34. Hutcheon, *Poetics*, 16.
35. What this makes clear is that *EDI* and *EDII* are also in their own ways films about time travel. When the magical incantation is recited in each film, demons from the past are "awakened"—transported into the present. Through a kind of retroactive temporality, *AOD* demonstrates that, once the incantation is spoken, the cabin in the two preceding films is absorbed into the time-space of *AOD*'s alternate medieval England.
36. Ndalianis, 511.
37. Ndalianis, 512.
38. Ndalianis, 512.
39. Johnson, *A World of Difference* (Baltimore: Johns Hopkins University Press, 1987), 14.
40. Jacques Lacan, "The Mirror Stage as Formative of the I Function, as Revealed in Psychoanalytic Experience," *Ecrits* (New York: Norton, 2002), 3–9.
41. Mary Klages, "Jacques Lacan," http://www.webpages.uidaho.edu/~sflores/KlagesLacan.html.
42. Philosopher Nöel Carroll would likely answer yes to the question of whether a cyborg is a monster. In his *The Philosophy of Horror: Or Paradoxes of the Heart* (Routledge: New York, 1990), he proposes that one recipe for monstrosity is "fusion," which creates "a composite that unites attributes held to be categorically distinct and/or at odds in the cultural scheme of things in *unambiguously* one, spatio-temporally discrete entity" (43). This would seem to encompass the cyborg.

Towards a Monster Pedagogy: Reclaiming the Classroom for the Other
John Edgar Browning

Introduction: Monsters in the Classroom

From *monere* ("to warn [against]") and *monstrare* ("to demonstrate"), the term "monster" is an evolving and socially constructed category. The figure it describes embodies whatever the dominant groups in society have most feared or considered abnormal. Similarly, the term "teratology" ("marvel" or "monster" + logy), a term Humanities scholars have fashionably appropriated from outside the discipline,[1] is the "branch of biological science," according to *Webster's Revised Unabridged Dictionary*, "which treats of monstrosities, malformations, or deviations from the normal type of structure, either in plants or animals."[2] My use of this term refers to the study of monstrosity or monstrous figures. Unlike Gothic tropes, which developed in the West before cross-culturally fertilizing other regions, the idea of "monstrosity" (meant here not as a pejorative but a "person" or "condition" that deviates from what a particular society deems socially, physically, or morally acceptable) is, and always has been, universally present; that is, monsters are, for all intents and purposes, the endeavors of organized societies to classify what they deem "normal."

For this essay, I take as an organizing premise that monstrosity may easily function as a discourse on both national and global levels — a means of inquiry into the socio-politics of given cultures, denoting either what they fear to let into the interior of their social *corpi* or what they seek to expel from those interiorities. In either case, teratogenesis — that is, the production or development of monstrosities — is neither limited by national borders nor subject to the same common set of socio-cultural conditions. In line with this analysis, Judith Halberstam has noted for example that anti–Semitism and mythical bodies like that of the vampire share in a "Gothic economy" because of their mutual "ability to condense many monstrous traits into one body."[3]

Furthermore, iconic figures like Dracula, Halberstam continues, serve as "technologies of monstrosity," or programmable edifices, as it were, in which out-dated forms of otherness can be exchanged for new ones. Here and throughout this essay, I wish to emphasize the centrality of this circulative function, which allows the monster's body to transcend the superficial mechanisms and structural *principia* to which it refuses reduction. But more crucial, for the purposes of this essay, is how this adaptive, pliable quality demonstrates that monsters can be equally serviceable at making visible the larger social framework of dominative and "corrective" moral and behavioral imperatives by which particular societies construct "normalcy."

It is these imperatives that present monstrosity itself as a strategic site, to borrow loosely from the work of Eve Sedgwick,[4] for confronting and challenging the ideological assumptions both culturally and historically imbedded in hierarchal, classificatory systems. Thus, monsters make accessible the infinite potential of exposing, plotting, tracing, and in the end, unfixing the repressive/oppressive categories that precipitate marginalization. When considering the conjunction between monstrosity and the politics of identity, I find the Marxist philosophy of Althusser particularly helpful in elucidating the social use of normative imperatives. To this end, I assert that monsters can provide educators with a critical tool with which to facilitate the re-examination of cultural and historical prejudices. Although this tool is practical for classroom use — practical because monsters elicit in students both curiosity and stimulation (responses that can elude even the most skilled educators) — it is often inaccessible to students in general postsecondary education courses who lack the appropriate theoretical underpinning. Rooted in that premise, this essay underscores the notion that genres and configurations previously considered "low-brow" (like horror and monsters) are gaining increasing prominence and applicability in the classroom. At the same time, however, educators are finding themselves more and more ill-equipped to appropriate these themes for classroom use because they remain areas in which pedagogical theory is severely lacking. This chapter has therefore grown out of an overwhelming need to initiate dialogue with educators who either appropriate monstrous figures or who incorporate discussions about horror (or both) into their curricula.

In his seminal essay "The American Nightmare: Horror in the 1970s" (1986), Robin Wood sought to lay bare a general theory for navigating and interpreting the horror genre's "social significance" with the use of sociopolitical criteria for identifying various monstrous forms and categorizing the films in which they appear.[5] In what follows, I wish to build on Wood's "wild work" by attempting to equip educators, as well as students, with more practical and culturally responsive tools for not only engaging in monster theory but improving its accessibility and applicability in, as well as outside, the classroom. I shall discuss effective ways in which educators can (1) use monsters to empower students by raising their socio-political awareness, and (2) utilize a classroom praxis that fosters counter-hegemonic knowledge (that is, information that raises consciousness contrary to the *status quo*) while emphasizing student-centered "safe space(s)" in which students feel more encouraged to voice their ideas or concerns. Safe spaces — be they through open class discussions, smaller group activities, or virtual forums — are particularly helpful if the students' concerns address marginalized identities or "other" more sensitive, sub-topical issues. I therefore find it necessary to review mine as well as others' classroom experiences with teaching the rhetorics of monstrosity. Additionally, I will examine fear responses common among students in counter-hegemonic learning environments — more specifically, classrooms in which conflicted representations of monstrosity (where "good" and "evil" blur ambiguously into one another), as opposed to "classic" models (where "good" and "evil" enjoy clearly demarcated boundaries), figure prominently in lectures, classroom discussions, and student-led group activities. This chapter proceeds in accord with three fundamental areas that provide the basis of my approach: theory, praxis, and conceptual tools for students.

My discussion begins by establishing the need for a sort of meta-politics when designing a course, a section, or just a lecture around monstrosity or horror films. I also discuss the limitations inherent in both the classroom and the institution; the practical capacity for introspection and meta-political thinking outside the classroom; and, in realistic terms, the level of agency and efficacy that students entering the workforce can expect in "life after the university." My discussion then narrows to consider an article by two women of color (their term) faculty members who discuss their experiences with mistreatment by their students. I wish to add to their insightful discussion by offering possible suggestions for dissipating or disarming the prejudices and marginalization their students impose on them by introducing a theory of otherness to the students. Expanding this notion, I then elaborate upon other theoretical models and tools as well as their practical use in guiding students beyond student-teacher politics. Specifically, I describe the use of a classificatory system, or vocabulary, that students can use to engage and organize the familiar monsters and threatening images they regularly encounter. Finally, I consider the particular Gothicized terrains in which monsters appear, as well as the ways in which the positionality of given monsters is articulated in these terrains, which is visually useful to students in helping them to disassemble or "de-code" the highly politicized rhetoric through which monsters and horror films are constructed.

Because my experiences with these ideas have generally been confined to the university level, specifically in first-year composition and sophomore-level survey literature classes, readers may question the applicability of these theoretical tools and models to classes outside of the academy. However, I wish to emphasize that although my experiences have been restricted to the university, the implementation of these tools and models would be feasible in many different teaching situations, or in any environment in which there are marginalized persons, hierarchical systems of normalcy, or tales told to frighten.

Why Monsters?

"Monsters," I often tell my students, are "legitimations of power" (more specifically, *social power*) because they are in direct contrast to the "'ideal' inhabitant of our culture," one whose sexuality "is sufficiently fulfilled by the monogamous heterosexual union necessary for the reproduction of future ideal inhabitants," as Wood aptly explains, "and whose sublimated sexuality (creativity) is sufficiently fulfilled in the totally non-creative and non-fulfilling labor (whether in factory or office) to which our society dooms the overwhelming majority of its members."[6] But why tell students this? Why teach them how to break down the distinctive symbologies that are Freddy's, Jason's, Dracula's, Leatherface's, or Chucky's? The twentieth century birthed the monster in film, affording it an identity that has been as much one of fluidity as it has been one of propaganda: a story that neither space nor theme will allow me to relay fully here. However, my own experiences and observations as a student/teacher/scholar using Monster Pedagogy over the last five years will, I hope, permit me to elucidate and extend this practice beyond its more informative role in light of the *functional* relevance it also offers. While the pedagogy I propose in this chapter spends considerable time addressing the complexities of identity and marginalization with which monstrous figures are imbued — which I do in an effort to provide a *means* to identify the political, heteronormative coding of monsters and thus contest it — I first need to explain *why* I should arm students with a means to contest it.

Understanding the relativism of deciphering politically coded figures like monsters is, I argue, a necessary task not only for the student but also, as Rachel Buff and Jason Loviglio argue in "'The Inescapable Public': Teaching (During) the Backlash," for "a *successful* Cultural Studies pedagogy (emphasis added)."[7] While this more agendic pedagogical model (i.e. raising student's political consciousness) is understandably more challenging, it is nonetheless crucial for classes in which instructors desire to effect in students the possibility of change through heightened meta-awareness, what Carol Stabile calls "political awakening" in her essay "Pedagogues, Pedagogy, and Political Struggle."[8] In what follows, I will outline my Monster Pedagogical Theory (hereafter MPT) agenda, which is informed heavily by Stabile's essay, as well as Susan Sanchez-Casal and Amie A. MacDonald's "Feminist Reflections on the Pedagogical Relevance of Identity,"[9] both of which address the challenge of an agendic pedagogy in great detail.

My goal with MPT is situated as a "political project of the feminist classroom," to borrow from Sanchez-Casal and MacDonald.[10] That is, by helping "students understand more about the network of moral and political assumptions that inform their cultural identities" I thereby equip them with an effective means to "contest hegemonic knowledge."[11] Sanchez-Casal and MacDonald observe that the contentious language and assumptions inherent in sexist, racist, and homophobic claims provide "the conditions for collective, progressive knowledge-making" and therefore should be present in classrooms in which students are prompted to engage with and evaluate the politics of identity making.[12] These same conditions, I posit, are comparable to or inherent in the "monster," an evolving political space given physical, representational form — a sort of malleable public arena in which social structures deposit current ideals about deviance and alterity. To deconstruct the monstrous bodies in which such ideals about deviance and alterity flourish is, essentially, to expose them, and thus to unseat them from the power relations they inhabit. Thus, the underlying political agenda behind my self-proclaimed MPT: to help students understand and explicate the implicit role of monsters.

Crucial to the pedagogical model I use in the classroom is my avoidance of what bell hooks calls "lumping everything about race and difference together in one section" at the end of the semester.[13] It is only by re-centering "difference" in the classroom that students will begin to unlearn the tendency to differentiate as a means to marginalize. My approach to literary and filmic monsters — who, I have argued, critique racialized, gendered, sexualized, and class-based notions of social "deviancy" by juxtaposing them against putatively "normal" communities — reshapes, and (re)defines normative behaviors and hierarchies. I help students to address the mass production and intersection of these so-called "deviant" identity formations — which articulate a wide range of phobias as they simultaneously provoke fear and stimulate desire — and examine the frequency with which these identity formations have been articulated within ethnic and, particularly, sexual minority politics. This approach allows us to glimpse the social topography of what is essentially a history of stresses produced by contradictory and competing ideological discourses of which gendered, sexualized, racialized, and class-based antagonisms comprise crucial components.

As a teacher, I rely heavily upon group activities and discussions in which students situate literary and visual narratives within historical, cultural, and political contexts. Doing so allows them to begin examining and writing about monsters as expressions of cultural anxieties about race, class, sexuality, and gender. Additionally, in the course of a semester, students engage with a variety of literary and filmic texts, such as Jack London's "Samuel," Stephen Crane's "The Monster," Kate Chopin's "Désirée's Baby," Bram Stoker's *Dracula* and its cinematic retellings, Anne Rice's *Interview with the Vampire*, and a host of serial killer narratives (most recently Patty Jenkins' film *Monster*). Exposing students to multiple genres that require them to argue from various viewpoints pertaining to the relationship between monstrosity and culture promotes understanding of the unstable, fallible and yet durable nature of such formations in grappling with our collective anxieties, traumas, or aspirations across literatures, film, and popular culture.

Equipping students with these theoretical tools, and thus helping them to empower themselves by actively identifying and (re)examining the shifting moral and behavioral imperatives that resonate in mainstream culture enables them to continuously pose questions and re-think critical processes in other disciplines and workspaces. But is this enough? For students entering the workforce, "the contradiction between the democratic classroom," Stabile explains, "and a world in which they have never had any input into decision-making processes can be immensely frustrating."[14] For, although "the illusion of democracy and plurality in the classroom may be a comforting one," Stabile continues, "it does not prepare students for understanding (much less fighting against) the less-than-democratic realities of their futures" outside of American classrooms.[15] MPT does not presume to claim otherwise; for the critical lens it imparts to students is merely a beginning, one from which small ripples coalesce into small waves, and small waves into larger ones. MPT allows students, at the very least, to perceive and break down "the code," then decide for themselves whom or what they should fear. This informs their behavior and decisions and allows them "to act on the information they [have] receive[d]," thus imparting to them a greater sense of agency. Through collective struggle, the student's ability to move "beyond the immediate context of the institution," and engage with life lessons about sexism, racism, and homophobia that the university classroom cannot simulate "leads to political transformation."[16]

While MPT may not resolve all the problems a student encounters in life after the university, it does provide a coherent model for understanding and grappling with the complex constructions of identity that simultaneously privilege and oppress. More crucially, the "teacher/student division," Stabile aptly remarks, "becomes meaningless in the context of political struggle," because political (re)education, like theories of monstrosity and marginalization, "necessarily involves a continuous, collective process of learning, unlearning, and relearning certain lessons — a process in which we are all students operating with various levels of skill."[17] I therefore issue this challenge to monster theorists, instructors in horror cinema, and even literary Gothicists: Helping students to merely *understand* monsters is not enough; rather, monsters must be used to help students better understand not only themselves but each other, as a precursor to *act* and effect change.

Congealing Racist and Sexist Thinking

According to Juanita Johnson-Bailey and Ming-Yea Lee's study "Women of Color in the Academy: Where's Our Authority in the Classroom?" the positionality students afford "non-white" female faculty members in the university is one of alterity, where race and sex are constructed as hierarchical in terms of validating intellectual capacity and authority.[18] "Otherness," a condition typically at home in Gothic narratives, is a term appropriated by Johnson-Bailey and Lee to describe the very real conditions under which they are marginalized in the classroom by their own students. This "othering" has the effect of erecting "a filter or barrier," note Johnson-Bailey and Lee, "that complicates, distorts, or perhaps delegitimizes" the exchange of information and the facilitation of learning.[19] The classroom therefore becomes a "'contested terrain,'" as opposed to a safe one, where "battles for voice" ensue between student and teacher. The classroom is reflective of society as a whole, Johnson-Bailey and Lee further remark, "and is therefore representative of the hierarchical systems," like race and sex, "that order the non-academic world" as well.[20] To address the sexed and raced subordination outlined in their essay, they call for a reconstitution of feminist pedagogy, a revised set of recommended classroom practices for feminist women of color faculty members. However, Johnson-Bailey and Lee's strategies are not applicable just to discussions of color and ethnicity but extend also to other positionalities. MPT, as I intend to show, could help to expand the limits of those strategies. I do not belong to the raced and sexed demographic Johnson-Bailey and Lee address. However, as a gay male college instructor, I do belong to a demographic that has seen its own history of marginalization and humiliation, and therefore the recommendations I offer here derive not only from professional experiences, but personal ones as well.

It seems to me that Johnson-Bailey and Lee's recommended classroom practices may ultimately encounter heightened resistance from students because these practices merely ask students to trade in one set of culturally and socially specific behavioral imperatives for another, without giving them any real, conceptual reason for doing so. I contend that a pedagogy drawing on the strategies outlined by Johnson-Bailey and Lee must therefore do more than this: It must first attempt to de-/re-socialize the students by making them more aware of *how* they intuit their experiences. For this purpose, I propose introducing a model of inquiry that appropriates Althusser's work[21] on "Ideology" and its function in society. The application and effectiveness of this model are by no means definitive, but it would provide a conceptual tool enabling students to "congeal," that is, to recognize or become aware of, the social and political hardwiring with which they experience the world. In what follows, I wish to extend Johnson-Bailey and Lee's "recommended" classroom practices and techniques by discussing how these practices and techniques could benefit from this critical model.

One way this de-/re-socialization can be achieved, I posit, is by enabling students to lay bare the political infrastructure within which they function, by exposing, as it were, the network of social conditioning that continuously frames their daily lives. The experience, however, must be a personal one, consciously enacted by the students themselves in order to legitimize it and prevent the scenarios alluded to by Johnson-Bailey and Lee in which the students accuse the professors of using oppressive language and attacking white men in particular.[22] To facilitate this process, I borrow from Sally Chandler's essay "Reflective Discourses in the Classroom: Creating Spaces Where Students Can Change Their Minds," in which she articulates the conditions that promote "'safe' answers" (i.e. ways in which students use "cultural rhetoric" to maneuver around racist and sexist perspectives "in order to avoid both personal confrontation and real communication").[23] In order to deter her students from resorting to "'safe' answers," Chandler offers her students tools for "develop[ing] resources for conceptualizing, representing, and assessing various patterns for organizing experience."[24] Engaging students "in discourses different from the preferred repertoire," Chandler adds, "can broaden their resources for generating knowledge."[25] Similarly, Johnson-Bailey's and Lee's students can be provided with a vocabulary that would enable them to begin to identify and articulate the determiners of their own social consciousness, the same oppressive consciousness that inevitably leads to Johnson-Bailey and Lee's marginalization in the classroom.

Johnson-Bailey and Lee offer several general techniques for classroom use by women of color faculty that can be extended to other marginalized faculty, three of which I will address directly. Above all, it is important to note that the success of their classroom practices, in part, hinges upon what I contend is an inadequate conceptualization provided to the students, while simultaneously re-centering the faculty as "others." The first and most crucial of the techniques suggested by Johnson-Bailey and Lee is the use of "pivotal questions" to incite critical class discussions; they include, for example: "Have you ever been taught by a woman of color before? How can a teacher's gender and racial background affect the course?" and "How do you perceive us ... as instructors?"[26] However, such a "direct" approach could incite evasiveness and resort to "'safe answers."

Thus, an alternative to posing such questions, and instead get the students thinking self-reflectively about their perception of "women of color" faculty members (or other marginalized groups for that matter), could come, I suggest, in the form of equipping students with a working knowledge of what Althusser calls the "false consciousness" and the ideological framework out of which this consciousness is constructed. Helping students to understand exactly how ideology affects their everyday lives, how it evolves over time, and who has stood to benefit most from its placement encourages students to (re)consider more than just class relations, like how the politicization of sexuality, race, sex, and gender has been used over time to negotiate power relations. Attention to these matters would serve to draw focus away from the positionality of the professors as "other," and instead focus it on the actual matters at hand, like perception itself and how is influenced by cultural assumptions and "common knowledge."

A second technique Johnson-Bailey and Lee offer is the use of technology to allow students to engage in anonymous *e*-discussions on more sensitive matters — such as the students' perceptions of their "non-white" professors, thus allowing for more heightened "comfort levels" in a sort of *e*-refuge. Doing this, Johnson-Bailey and Lee contend, allows students to communicate more openly about sub-topical issues, in effect keeping the professors at a distance from the brunt of sexed and gendered "lashings out." However, again, rather than centralize themselves in these discussions (i.e. contribute to their own positionality as "others"), the professors could urge their students to consider how outside forces — like friends, family, media outlets, schools, the church, etc — have contributed to their consciousness about *how* they should feel about or perceive the things around them. A consideration of these outside forces would promote a certain level of "congealing," which in turn would prepare students for Johnson-Bailey and Lee's third technique.

Johnson-Bailey and Lee maintain that with the "understanding [of] new and contradictory knowledge" often come feelings of "guilt, anger, betrayal, and resistance to denial."[27] Therefore, the availability of "materials and activities that address both the cognitive and the affective component of the learning process" becomes crucial. However, in addition to the students' coping process, teachers must also address the students' urge to apply what they have learned and to confront it directly. For example, the students' emotions may be effectively dissipated by asking them to select rhetorical images from the internet that influence the ways people act towards, think about, make, or perceive various groups outside of their own, and to bring those images to class for discussion. I have often found that students are more receptive to this task if asked to start by examining horror film posters, or even war-time propaganda posters that appropriate monstrous forms, both of which tend to draw from subjects in which the students are generally already interested. In class, students readily volunteer to display the images they have found and point out the particular ways in which the monstrous or "deviant" configurations revealed in the images are encoded with minority politics, often leading other students present in class to discuss films they have seen as well in which the same or similar politics are at play. This redirects power to the students, giving them — if only in fleeting moments — what Althusser calls "relative autonomy" and thereby allowing them to take what they have learned and grow.

Ultimately, what I have attempted to do here is to extend Johnson-Bailey and Lee's classroom practices and techniques in a way that, based on my own experiences in the classroom, may facilitate more successfully the management of the conditions under which faculty members are typically marginalized in the classroom. The use of an Althusserian model of inquiry, as I have stated, is by no means a definitive means for accomplishing this task, but has in the past served as an effective tool in my own classroom experiences, particularly when trying to help students understand the relationship between controversial issues and how society has conceptualized monstrosity over time.

Counterhegemonic Tools for Students Across Disciplines

What Neil Larsen calls the "stripp[ing] of knowledge [in the classroom] needed even to recognize, much less independently construct, the most elementary theoretical postulate" is a condition with which university educators are all too familiar, one that is no less prevalent today (in the early 2010s) than it was in the late-1990s when Larsen wrote these words in his article "Theory at the Vanishing Point: Notes on a Pedagogical Quandary."[28] In the decade since Larsen's observation, we have, in fact, seen a continuous surge of popular/mass cultural artifacts steadily figure into both academic scholarship and college curriculum, as Mike Hill is apt to point out in his article "Cultural Studies by Default: A History of the Present," citing (as of 1993) the "ten thousand researched articles, collections, and books ... on Madonna [in English alone]."[29] Larsen's lament about the state of "increasingly 'theory'-illiterate classrooms"[30] and Hill's remarks about the amalgamatory future of Popular/Cultural Studies are particularly relevant to MPT. Like Larsen, I, too, face classrooms populated almost entirely by students who have had little or no exposure to theory or to thinking outside of heteronormativity. Therefore, what is needed — to borrow Larsen's phrasing — is a certain degree of "consciousness-raising,'" especially when discussing monstrosity, a condition that, historically, has been more inclined to invoke fear and aversion rather than sympathy and change.[31]

In order for students to be able to discern "counterhegemony," as Larsen claims, within a cultural narrative, it is not enough for them to have a *will* to do so. Rather, this *will* must be preceded by a (theory-based) "conceptual procedure,"[32] or, to extend Larsen's term further, the students must first be equipped with a set of specific, but flexible "[re]conceptual" tools. In the discussion that follows, I shall address directly three such conceptual tools: (1) *Other*-types, (2) Gothic landscape, and (3) Gothic space. These concepts have, for me, routinely served as the most helpful pedagogical tools for engaging and interpreting monstrous figures. Before proceeding, however, it is necessary to outline the essentials from previous work I have conducted on this topic.

Previously I argued that equipping students with a new vocabulary base allows them to begin the process of identifying and articulating the "ideologies" of their own social consciousness, the same oppressive consciousness that inevitably leads to marginalization. For this purpose, I proposed the use of an Althusserian model of inquiry, whose practices and techniques, though by no means a definitive measure, afford students a conceptual basis from which to begin "congealing" the social and political hardwiring through which they experience and interpret day-to-day life. For example, students need a working knowledge of "false consciousness," that is, the ideological framework out of which social consciousness is constructed. They must be able to trace how and why these ideologies have evolved over time and who has stood to benefit most from their placement and to understand how the politicization of sexuality, race, class relations, sex, and gender has been used over time to negotiate power relations. All of these relations help to initiate the process of drawing the students' focus to counterhegemonic knowledge. Not only does this redirect power to the students, giving them — if, as I stated, only in fleeting moments — what Althusser calls "relative autonomy," it initiates a sort of coping process (a condition when students are both repelled by and drawn to this new sense of separation), from which, in my experience, students quickly develop an urge to confront and re-envisage their realities. This somewhat emotional phase may be effectively dissipated through the use of certain conceptual tools, which I shall now discuss at length

The first of the conceptual tools I wish to discuss is "*other*-type," which may seem at least partially familiar to Gothicists, as well as to race theorists,

Marxists, gender theorists, or any other discipline in which marginalized groups are a particular focus. My usage of the word *other*-type is simply a more pedagogically efficient (i.e. student-accessible) way for students to cognize the notion of otherness, because it allows them to discern more easily the particular general form (or "type") of "otherness" represented in a person. For example, in many cases Dracula has been characterized in film using several *other*-types, often simultaneously,[33] such as ethnic otherness and sexual otherness; whereas with the character of Leatherface in the original *Texas Chainsaw Massacre* (1974), his use of women's make-up and, at times, feminized mannerisms (which, as Carol J. Clover argues in *Men, Women, and Chainsaws* [1992], is typical of male slashers[34]) gesture towards another *other*-type: gender inversion. Its application in the classroom functions as both a starting point for students to identify deviancy in monstrous figures, as well as a way for students to classify their findings as they initiate the process of reconsidering previously accepted notions of deviancy and normalcy. To achieve this, one method I have often returned to involves asking students to select rhetorical images outside of class that influence the ways in which people act, think, and purchase, and to bring those images to class for discussion. Additionally, we also view slides or film clips in class that demonstrate conventionally modeled *other*-types (e.g. Freddy, Dracula, or Leatherface). This is instructive because it offers a valuable way for students to sharpen their critical skills through the use of familiar examples, a precursor to venturing off to tackle more unfamiliar configurations. I have found that the ability to organize deviant configurations, as this method implies, is essential for students, particularly in the initial stages of re-considering notions of deviancy, because in addition to aiding the coping process, its usage also offers students enough flexibility that they never fully exhaust its application, either in or outside the classroom. Therefore, as the students' consciousness evolves, so too does their usage of the word *other*-type. Over time, students usually find that the propensity with which they classified (whether consciously or not) sexual, social, or racial *other*-types before enrolling in my class begins to diminish, and eventually progresses — whether wholly or in part — to more liberal notions of acceptance.

The last two conceptual tools I wish to discuss are thematically linked and are therefore grouped together. My usage of the terms Gothic landscape and Gothic space, which I liken to Larsen's "conceptual" use of genre theory,[35] is equally central to my discussion of monstrosity because the application of these terms by students accomplishes more than just allowing them to identify the wild settings within which monstrous figures are generally located. For example, Gothic landscapes in literature, although easily identified by their allocation of familiar tropes (like scary castles, old white houses, gnarly trees, deserted roads in dark forests, dilapidated buildings, etc.), are often helpful for identifying *other*-types as well. Furthermore, Gothic tropes and *other*-types are appropriated by filmic narratives, which I find to be a crucial junction, not only for the students, but for the instructor. In terms of thematically organizing my class curriculum, this junction between Gothic literature and horror cinema offers a seamless way for students to apply what they have learned from one medium to the next; for example, the Gothic tropes prevalent in literature can then be used by students to locate *other*-types in film as well.

However, whereas Gothic landscape deals primarily with the "locating" of *other*-types, Gothic space (or "Gothic *Feng Shui*," as I tell my students) is concerned primarily with the contextual positionality of *other*-types. Whereas Gothic landscape infers a centralized location (the *locus gothicus*— a physical edifice typically adorned with scary trappings and figures), Gothic space should be identified in more abstract terms, because it more or less deals with the narrative's use of distancing, separation, or orientation to help juxtapose *exteriority* (that which is *out there*) with *inferiority* (that which is *undesirable*).[36] That is, the relegation of the Gothic locus to what is generally a distantly located site, one that often evokes apprehension (e.g. Dracula's ruinous castle in Transylvania; Freddy's dreary dreamscape boiler room; the abandoned, isolated site where the horrible self-mutilation is committed in the *Saw* films, etc.), serves as a visual marker that renders the conceptual *real*.

While the more obvious use of these conceptual tools is pedagogically at home in courses on horror cinema, Gothic literature, or eighteenth- or nineteenth-century literature, their practical applicability in other disciplines in which identity politics plays a central role should be apparent. My approach to texts — whether filmic or literary — in which monstrous or marginalized figures play decidedly key roles, is resistant to dominant or patriarchal institutional practices. For example, I do not identify or locate the monsters for my students; instead, I provide the conceptual tools, so that the task of locating and identifying is left to them. The classification and categorization of "deviant" figures, and the reconceptualization of deviance itself, must be left to them to actively perform.

Conclusion

Helping students to re/consider monstrous images and representations — images that hierarchically dictate "inferiorly"-sexed, -classed, -raced, or -sexualized positionalities while legitimizing "superior" ones — must be the task of the educator. Educators who use or who are considering using Monster Theory in their curricula must not limit themselves by giving a historiography of monsters and horror cinema; instead, theirs must be a decidedly more political task. Educators must want their students not only to chronicle monstrosity, but to observe and understand its functionality within a much broader cultural framework. Monsters do cultural work, Jeffrey Jerome Cohen's seminal work *Monster Theory: Reading Culture* tells us, because the "Monster's body is a cultural body."[37] Cohen writes:

> The Monster is born only at this metamorphic crossroads, as an embodiment of a certain cultural moment — of a time, a feeling, and a place. The monster's body quite literally incorporates fear, desire, anxiety, and fantasy (ataractic or incendiary), giving them life and an uncanny independence. The monstrous body is pure culture. A construct and a projection, the monster exists only to be read..."[38]

Helping students to understand monsters using this critical lens, and to discern through it the "patriarchal institutions that reinforce negative aspects of society, such as aggressive competition, domination, hierarchies of power, and gender inequality," serves to incite students, in my experience, to *want* to begin the process of separating themselves from oppressive ideologies.[39]

This task is not an easy one, and sometimes not without repercussions. This essay has intentionally drawn from readings that approach MPT from very different angles, not only in terms of praxis, but in terms of its reception by students as well. I have argued that to teach monstrosity a/effectively, one must essentially begin by divorcing the students from the structure — that is, from the (mis)conception "that reproduces and popularizes the *structure*," to borrow from Eve Sedgwick's analysis in *Touching Feeling*.[40] My preferred method for accomplishing this task, as I have previously shown, has been to use what I have termed an Althusserian model of inquiry. Generally, however, the difficulties I have faced over the years have come not from my appropriation of this critical model, but from the reactionary emotions of the students themselves to what one might call the process of *enlightenment*. This "reaction," what Sedgwick (quoting Silvan Tomkins) might call the "fear response," is an initial fear of the awareness or knowledge of counterhegemony, which is, in my experience, followed by a temporary refusal of that knowledge. This process — the taking up of "a potentially terrifying and terrified idea or image" for as long as necessary, Sedgwick writes, in order "to burn out the fear response," notes Tomkins — is repeated, until such time "that idea or image can recur," Sedgwick continues, "without initially evoking terror."[41]

Despite these and other drawbacks that unavoidably occur, I have developed and implemented MPT with increasing success over the last seven years, across very different kinds of institutional environments — including a major doctoral research institution, a major public regional comprehensive university, a mid-sized public regional comprehensive university, a smaller private university, and an accredited proprietary institution — while enduring the emotional lashings out of my students, but in the end watching at least half grow into burgeoning critical thinkers. MPT is, to borrow from hooks again, a "transformative pedagogy," inciting transformation within the student's cultural consciousness as well as the pedagogical consciousness of the educator (36). "Difference," hooks notes, must be at the center; for it is only when "difference" is re-centered in the classroom that students will begin to unlearn the need to hierarchize themselves in relation to others. Difference is everywhere, especially in "our [monsters]," who are—after all—merely ourselves, as Nina Auerbach's seminal work on vampires aptly reminds us.

Author's Note: I wish to thank David J. Riche for his incredibly helpful comments on earlier versions of this chapter. I am also indebted to the editors of this volume for their insightful suggestions.

NOTES

1. Examples worth consideration are Jackie Stacey's *Teratologies: A Cultural Study of Cancer* (London: Routledge, 1997); Katherine Angell's "Joseph Merrick and the Concept of Monstrosity in Nineteenth Century Medical Thought," in *Hosting the Monster* (Amsterdam: Rodopi, 2008), ed. Holly Lynn Baumgartner and Roger Davis, 131–152; and Melinda Cooper's "Monstrous Progeny: The Teratological Tradition in Science and Literature," in *Frankenstein's Science: Experimentation and Discovery in Romantic Culture 1780–1830* (Hampshire, England: Ashgate, 2008), ed. Christa Knellwolf and Jane Goodall, 87–98.
2. *Webster's Revised Unabridged Dictionary (1913 + 1828)*: 1846, accessed at http://machaut.uchicago.edu/?resource=Webste%27s&word=teratology&use1913=on&use1828=on.
3. Judith Halberstam, *Skin Shows: Gothic Horror and the Technology of Monsters* (Durham, NC: Duke University Press, 2006), 88. Halberstam offers as an example of "Gothic economy" the figure of Count Dracula: "He is monster and man, feminine and powerful, parasitical and wealthy; he is repulsive and fascinating, he exerts the consummate gaze but is scrutinized in all things, he lives forever but can be killed. Dracula is indeed not simply a monster but a technology of monstrosity" (88).
4. See Eve Sedgwick, *Touching Feeling: Affect, Pedagogy, Performativity* (Durham, NC: Duke University Press, 2002).
5. Robin Wood, *Hollywood from Vietnam to Reagan ... and Beyond* (New York: Columbia University Press, 1986/2003), 69.
6. Ibid., 64–65.
7. Rachel Buff and Jason Loviglio, "'The Inescapable Public': Teaching (During) the Backlash," in *Class Issues: Pedagogy and Cultural Studies*, ed. Amitava Kumar (New York: New York University Press, 1997), 197.
8. Carol Stabile, "Pedagogues, Pedagogy, and Political Struggle," in *Class Issues: Pedagogy and Cultural Studies*, ed. Amitava Kumar (New York: New York University Press, 1997), 208–220.
9. Susan Sanchez-Casal and Amie A. MacDonald, "Introduction: Feminist Reflections on the Pedagogical Relevance of Identity," in *Twenty-First-Century Feminist Classrooms: Pedagogies of Identity and Difference* (New York: Palgrave Macmillan, 2004), 1–30.
10. Sanchez-Casal and MacDonald, 10.
11. Sanchez-Casal and MacDonald, 13.
12. Sanchez-Casal and MacDonald, 12–13.
13. bell hooks, *Teaching to Transgress: Education as the Practice of Freedom* (New York: Routledge, 1994), 38.
14. Stabile, "Pedagogues, Pedagogy, and Political Struggle," 214.

15. Stabile, 214.
16. Stabile, 217.
17. Stabile, 217.
18. Juanita Johnson-Bailey and Ming-Yea Lee, "Women of Color in the Academy: Where's our Authority in the Classroom?" *Feminist Teacher* 15, no. 1 (2005): 111–122. Among the dilemmas Johnson-Bailey and Lee faced during their early teaching careers, they focus their article around three representative incidents: "being interviewed by a student before he would consent to take our class, receiving [student] evaluations that centered on how we dared to be different and not fit the stereotypes that students had of Asians and African Americans, and coteaching with another women's studies professor with disastrous results" (111).
19. Johnson-Bailey and Lee, 115.
20. Johnson-Bailey and Lee, 115.
21. See, for example, Althusser's "Ideology and Ideological State Apparatuses," in *Lenin and Philosophy and other Essays*, trans. Ben Brewster (Monthly Review Press, 1971), 121–176.
22. Johnson-Bailey and Lee, 113.
23. Sally Chandler, "Reflective Discourses in the Classroom: Creating Spaces Where Students Can Change Their Minds," *Feminist Teacher* 15.1 (2005): 16.
24. Chandler, 19.
25. Chandler, 19.
26. Johnson-Bailey and Lee, 19.
27. Johnson-Bailey and Lee, 120.
28. Neil Larsen, "Theory at the Vanishing Point: Notes on a Pedagogical Quandary," in *Class Issues: Pedagogy and Cultural Studies*, ed. Amitava Kumar (New York: New York University Press, 1997), 85–86.
29. Mike Hill, "Cultural Studies by Default: A History of the Present," in *Class Issues: Pedagogy and Cultural Studies*, ed. Amitava Kumar (New York: New York University Press, 1997), 148.
30. Larsen, "Theory at the Vanishing Point," 83.
31. Larsen, "Theory at the Vanishing Point," 82.
32. Larsen, "Theory at the Vanishing Point," 78–79.
33. See Chapter 4 "Technologies of Monstrosity: Bram Stoker's *Dracula*" in Judith Halberstam's *Skin Shows: Gothic Horror and the Technology of Monsters* (Durham, NC: Duke University Press, 2006), 86–106.
34. Carol J. Clover, *Men, Women, and Chainsaws* (Princeton, NJ: Princeton University Press, 1992), 162.
35. Larsen, "Theory at the Vanishing Point," 84.
36. For further discussion of Gothic tropes in the cinema, see Misha Kavka's excellent treatment of the subject in "The Gothic on screen," in *The Cambridge Companion to Gothic Fiction* (Cambridge: Cambridge University Press, 2002), 209–228.
37. Jeffrey Jerome Cohen, *Monster Theory: Reading Culture* (Minneapolis: University of Minnesota Press, 1997), 4.
38. Cohen, 4.
39. Amy Spangler Gerald, Kathleen McEvoy, and Pamela Whitefield, "Transforming Student Literacies: Three Feminists (Re)Teach Reading, Writing, and Speaking," *Feminist Teacher* 15.1 (2005): 48.
40. Sedgwick, *Touching Feeling*, 94.
41. Silvan S. Tomkins, *Affect, Imagery, Consciousness: The Positive Affects*, vol. 1 (New York: Springer, 1962), 161; Sedgwick, *Touching Feeling*, 95.

When the Women Think: Teaching Horror in Women's and Gender Studies

AALYA AHMAD

In the summer of 2009, I began teaching a rather unusual course in the Pauline Jewett Institute of Women's and Gender Studies at Carleton University in Ottawa. My course "The Monstrous Feminist: Gender and the Horrific" was offered as a seminar at the third-year level, drawing a broad range of students from both within and without the discipline, including students from Psychology, Economics, English, Film and Art History, some of whom did not have much prior experience with feminist critical analysis.

The course description was as follows:

> This course examines gender and culture in relation to horror fiction and film. If horror's "formula," in the words of the late Canadian film critic Robin Wood, can be described as: "Normality is threatened by the Monster," then what "normal" and "monstrous" gender categories are available? Critics have argued that horror is exclusively for a young male heterosexual audience that delights in seeing women victimized. More recently, feminist critical analyses have appeared that problematize horror's violence against women even as they take into account the powerful complexity of women's relationships to these texts. Developing their own critical analyses, students will look at a range of theories on the topic, examining ideas of women and gender in horror from the "Female Gothic" to the "Final Girl" and beyond. Particular attention will be paid to horror texts that focus on gender issues and that are produced by women.

It is, of course, not particularly surprising that students might wish to take a horror course and horror fans can be found in any university department. However, teaching a horror course in Women's and Gender Studies (WGST) is rarely done. In fact, despite the above description, more than one WGST student who took the course claimed during the first class that they did not actually expect to be reading or viewing horror texts (to my relief, most of these students stayed after the first class).

My goal in teaching "The Monstrous Feminist" was not to "convert" WGST students into horror fans, although such conversions sometimes occurred as a by-product of taking the course. Rather, I wished to try to open up broader avenues for both horror and women's studies. Firstly, I wanted to offer horror as a viable area of scholarship and critical reflection to WGST students who might be unaccustomed to combining their feminism with cultural studies. Secondly, I wanted to encourage the discussion and development of perspectives on horror that might expand on well-known feminist theoretical analyses, a few of which, it seemed to me, have hardened into overly sweeping and dogmatic approaches that seemed to lock feminists into perpetual struggle. I wanted to explore alternative interpretations while remaining mindful of the danger of overly celebrating horror, of getting mired in its pleasures. In what follows, I will offer a discussion of prevailing currents in feminist horror criticism before going on to discuss the varied and interesting perspectives produced by "The Monstrous Feminist" students, who showed me that reflecting on these theories of horror and on horror texts themselves in the context of the feminist classroom can often engender critical reading and interpretive practices that escape the confines of "the male gaze" as first famously conceptualized by Laura Mulvey and then elaborated on by critics such as Linda Williams, whose well-known essay "When the Woman Looks" (1984) I have, of course, played on for my title. The language of the look so often applied to horror appears insufficient, given horror's range across media. Putting scopophilia at the centre of horror did not seem to me to be enough to describe what horror does with and to women and what women might do with and to horror.

The contemporary obsession with what Isabel Pinedo calls "the spectacle of the ruined body"[1] has created significant debate among feminist critics, some of whom regard horror (and the slasher film in particular) as inherently misogynistic, while others such as Judith Halberstam and Pinedo offer more celebratory interpretations of horror for women, raising intriguing questions about gender, sexuality, monstrosity and what it means to look at horror. In her classic essay "Visual Pleasure and Narrative Cinema" (1975), Mulvey argues that traditional cinema reflects men's status as "bearer of the look"[2] and "builds the way" that "a woman is to be looked at into the spectacle itself ... cinematic codes create a gaze, a world, and an object, thereby producing an illusion cut to the measure of desire."[3] This formulation of the male look as active and the female image as passive is used by Williams in order to argue that, "when the woman looks" at horror, she invariably "is punished ... by narrative processes that transform curiosity and desire into masochistic fantasy." Williams further claims that women don't look at horror because "they are given so little to identify with on the screen."[4] According to her application of Mulvey to horror film, the woman "exists only to be looked at" and has no agency, but can only hide "behind the shoulders of ... [their] dates."[5]

But who is this woman who looks? Williams' early account allows no possibility for women to engage with horror without "dates" present. Her generalization rules out many women's experiences with horror films, including my own encounter with *A Nightmare on Elm Street* (1984) during a sleepover where I cowered, not behind the shoulders of a date, but behind a heap of entangled pajama-clad legs attached to giggling, squealing female friends who pelted each other with junk food during Freddy Krueger's rampages. Brigid Cherry has conducted empirical research of such female horror fans — the ones who "refuse to refuse to look"[6] — that also critically interrogates such sweeping assumptions. Cherry's work reveals that the female horror audience tends to be "marginalised and invisible"[7] because it often keeps its viewing experience "private," with women and girls watching rented horror movies at home, as my friends and I did.

Perhaps it is such pervasive stereotypes of women's relationship to horror that discourage female horror fans from 'going public,' reinforcing the dominant notion that horror — and women — are only for men to look at. Rhona J. Berenstein's research on the marketing and reception of classic horror films has revealed that gendered fear can be performed and that horror movies are "sites of negotiation and contradiction when it comes to their portrayals of and assumptions about gender, both male and female"[8]: a finding amply borne out by my experiences teaching "The Monstrous Feminist" course. As Berenstein and Cherry have both shown in their research on female horror audiences, the widespread critical assumption that female patrons of horror films are always flinching and cowering, dragged to their movie theatre seats by their boyfriends does not necessarily stand up to scrutiny.

Following a lengthy argument that makes ample use of Susan Lurie's writing on pornography, Williams suggests, "that the monster in the horror film is feared by the 'normal' males of such films in ways very similar to Lurie's notion of the male child's fear of this mother's power-in-difference."[9] She grudgingly admits that in "a sense," women may find visual pleasure in the recognition of the monster's "similar status within patriarchal structures of seeing,"[10] a claim that she builds on in "Film Bodies: Gender, Genre, Excess" (1991). In this essay, Williams persuasively argues that horror is one of the "body genres" and that producing a response on the part of its readers and audiences is central to its discursive practice. Williams suggests that this may be why horror — a "fear jerker" rather than a tearjerker — is regarded with such suspicion;

> I suggest ... that the film genres that have had especially low cultural status ... are not simply those which sensationally display bodies on the screen and register effects in the bodies of spectators. Rather, what may especially mark these body

genres as low is the perception that the body of the spectator is caught up in an almost involuntary mimicry of the emotion or sensation of the body on the screen along with the fact that the body displayed is female.[11]

Williams suggests that the success of horror films can be measured by the amount of reaction they elicit and mentions William Castle — the ultimate "Fear Jerker": "The rhetoric of violence of the jerk suggests the extent to which viewers feel too directly, too viscerally manipulated by the text in specifically gendered ways."[12] But, despite the interesting questions about "tear jerkers" (melodrama) and "fear jerkers" that she raises, Williams's pronounced (and performed) distaste for the genre remains agonistic in her earlier work, conveying her sense of being "jerked" around by the film's narrative and imagery which remain mired in the inevitability of the psychoanalytic gaze. But does a look at the monster's "horror version of her own body"[13] necessarily "paralyze" a woman and fix the monster as the "bearer of sexual difference," as Williams asserts? In a 2001 reflection on her earlier work entitled "When Women Look: A Sequel," Williams acknowledges that the "Mulveyan paradigm" did not account for "the *pleasures*, however problematic, women viewers may take in this genre" and that the "spectatorial-viewing experience" needed to be considered.[14] Another version of the same essay, "Learning to Scream," similarly revises her earlier position and acknowledges the performative possibilities of horror. However, Williams interestingly maintains that such subversive and gender-destabilizing positions only come as a result of education, of discipline; women must be *taught* "how to look" at horror:

> I once interpreted this classic women's reaction as a sign of resistance that women resisted assault on their own gaze by refusing to look at the female victims of male monstrosity. However, this notion of resistance simply assumed a masculine monster and the displeasure of horror for female spectators. Now I am more inclined to think that if some of the women in the audience were refusing to look at the screen, then they were also, like my girlfriends and I at the early stages of assimilating a discipline that was teaching us *how* to look — emboldening us to look as the men did, in the interest of experiencing greater thrills.[15]

Horror's "guilt by association" thus seems to persistently haunt those fascinated with the field and particularly feminist critics such as the above, who describe their engagement with horror as an inherently agonistic struggle to define the relationship between their interest in the texts, and the perception that they are viewing or reading material that may not be compatible with the progressive concerns they voice. Representations of tortured and terrified women struggling with frightening men or man-like monsters are paired with the agonized writings of feminist critical theorists grappling with the genre. Horror has overwhelmingly been regarded as a male genre, its fans stereotyped as violent, pornography-addicted teenage boys and immature men, and the conventionally dominant understanding of women in horror is that they are meat for the monsters. What most current feminist approaches lack is the recognition that, while women, with a few notable exceptions, may only be in evidence on one side of the camera in film, there is no shortage of feminist horror authors, neglected though they are in purportedly comprehensive accounts of the genre. Thus, in horror, it is not always the case that the woman exists to be looked at: the woman may also be described as active and creative, a narrator, a focalized subjectivity, a fan, a student and a thinker. Cynthia Freeland points out that the "images of women" approach, focusing on what roles women play in horror films — "agents, patients, knowers, sufferers"[16] asks only a "rather simple set of questions" pertaining to gender ideology. The flip side — women's productions, performances and interpretations of horror — remains largely unexamined.

The struggle with horror's images of women undergoing violence and pain has been integral to feminist analyses of horror, even those that celebrate it. The problem that Pinedo sets herself, for example, is to untangle the relationship between horror and feminism, which has often seemed to entail a skeptical if not downright hostile approach to the former as replete with depictions of victimized women: "My short-lived response to this quandary was to boycott the genre."[17] Eventually, Pinedo, echoing Berenstein, as a formerly "closeted female horror aficionado" returns to the enjoyment of horror "in good conscience." Her task then becomes to account for women's guilty pleasure in horror through excavating the potential feminism of such horror films such as *The Stepfather* (1987). I disagree with Matt Hills's position that such self-reflexive struggles are just another bid for (sub)cultural capital within the closed circles of academic disciplines.[18] A very real discomfort over what Hills terms "position-takings" is evident, particularly in feminist attempts to come to grips with horror's pleasures. Such positions frequently take the form of an apologetic attempt to find redeeming values that validate at least a sub-text of the horror fiction in question. This makes horror particularly susceptible to Hills's "theory first-pleasure second" or "horror-as-schooling" approach described by Sean Moreland and myself in the introduction to this volume.

With Pinedo and others, I have faced the reconciliation of a taste for horror texts with feminist principles; unlike Pinedo and others, I want to resist essentializing formulations such as the following, in which she makes the case for justifying women's pleasure in certain horror films defined as "postmodern":

> Postmodern horror compels its heroes, many of whom are women, to both exercise instrumental rationality and to rely on intuition; it requires them to be ... violent

and to trust their gut instincts. As such, postmodern horror defies the Cartesian construction of reason that reduces it to instrumental rationality and pits it against emotion and intuition.[19]

However, "instrumental rationality" cannot always be so easily distinguished from "emotion and intuition" as Pinedo implies, even in a film that explicitly foregrounds and interrogates gendered binaries, as does the clever Canadian Third Wave feminist horror film *Ginger Snaps* (2000). It is equally faulty to presume that all women are going to cheer on their post–Cartesian onscreen sisters and forgo what Williams describes as the "pleasurable and self-conscious performance" of gendered feminine responses.[20] Another option may be to perform what Noël Carroll describes as a type of "endurance test," "macho rites of passage" for adolescent males.[21] Cherry points out that her research subjects, whose preferences in horror seemed gendered, seemed to also engage in "deliberate interpretive strategies to accommodate the films' representations of women, either ignoring and making excuses for what they see as negative representations or condoning feminine behaviour in strong female characters."[22]

Women may thus look at and respond to horror in a variety of different ways and for a variety of different reasons; I am suspicious of any account that outlines an essentially feminine (or masculine) response. In fact, many compelling horror fictions, which have also been created and produced by women, bypass the Cartesian binary altogether and link horrifying body with malevolent mind, offering abundant examples of what Barbara Creed calls "the monstrous feminine" rather than harried and hunted heroines. In this sense, the focus by feminists upon women not as active fans of the horror text but as passive consumers who merely "identify" with slashed victims rather than participating boisterously in horror productions and producing horror fictions of their own, serves to efface some of the most important strategies of horror texts.

Pinedo also criticizes the heterosexist and over-generalizing assumptions that inform Williams's earlier claims about audience's and women's behavior at horror movies, arguing that "Williams fails to recognize the pleasure of not-seeing." She goes on to accuse both Williams and Tania Modleski, who also equates horror with pornography, of wrongly assuming "that the female viewer derives no comparable pleasure from the contemporary horror film since female mutilation and murder figure so prominently in the genre."[23] However, Pinedo herself resurrects Williams' pornography comparison in her use of the term "carnography" and her assertion that "if pornography is the genre of the wet dream, then horror is the genre of the wet death."[24]

The word "carnography," which she attributes to Richard Gehr, is intended to highlight "this very carnality which relegates hard core and gore to the status of disreputable genres ... both are disreputable genres because they engage the viewer's body ... elicit physical responses such as fear, disgust and arousal in indeterminate combinations, and thereby privilege the degraded half of the mind-body split."[25] Again, we must ask, what happens *when the women think* about what they are looking at? What happens when they are not simply or only grossed out or terrified? What happens, for example, when they perform horror fandom or other reading/learning practices that let them venture beyond merely "degraded" physical responses by deploying their intertextual knowledge of horror and engaging critically with horror texts?

Hills notes the importance of fan autobiographical accounts of encounters with horror such as the one with Wes Craven's *Nightmare on Elm Street* that I described above. For Hills, again, this "self-account" is simply a performative bid for (sub)cultural capital, or a description of how knowledge of horror has been accumulated, a "position-taking" on the part of an ungendered or otherwise unidentified fan, which serves to distance the knowledgeable fan from "the culturally feminizing spectre of horror as fear provoking."[26] For a woman facing such specters, particularly a feminist, and even more so if she is racialized or otherwise marginalized within a culture, horror fandom may not be a comfortable fit, no matter how much theory one applies. Still, I shall contend in the next section of this essay on teaching "The Monstrous Feminist" that even if students reflecting on horror do not perform fandom, other types of "position-taking" become possible in the classroom.

In her celebrated and groundbreaking *Men, Women and Chainsaws*, Carol Clover also follows Mulvey, citing both Poe's "famous formulation" that the most "poetical topic in the world" is the death of a beautiful woman and Hitchcock's comment during the filming of *The Birds* (1963) that he would follow the advice of the playwright Sardou to "Torture the women!'"[27] With varying degrees of appreciation, as I have demonstrated above, feminist scholars have examined the gender ideologies of earlier 1960s and 1970s slasher and rape-revenge films such as *Halloween* (1978), *The Texas Chainsaw Massacre* (1974) and *I Spit on Your Grave* (1978). Clover's book has been particularly influential in the re-visioning of these sub-genres by making room in psychoanalytic criticism for cross-gender identification in the viewer's gaze at the figure of the "Final Girl," or slasher survivor. In order to explain this gender opposition, Clover resurrects Thomas Laqueur's interesting concept of a "one-sex model": "sexual difference as we officially know it — the 'two-sex' or 'two-flesh' model ... has not existed from time immemorial but is a relatively modern construction that sits, in fact, rather lightly on large sectors of the culture." This "slippage and fungibility, in which maleness and femaleness are always tentative and hence only apparent" was "displaced" in the late eighteenth century, according to Clover, with the strict division of male and female categories. Yet the retention of the one-sex model in "the popular mind" has resulted in the popular genres of horror and science fiction:

> Horror may in fact be the premier repository of one-sex reasoning in our time (science fiction running a very close second) ... The one-sex model is echoed not only in horror's bodily constructions ... it is also echoed in its representation of gender as the definitive category from which sex proceeds as an effect.[28]

Men, Women and Chainsaws is a powerful argument that modern horror cannot simply be reduced to female victimization since, in many cases, the slasher film concludes with a tomboyish kicking, screaming, fighting woman who triumphs over her pursuers, the occult film features men "opening up" to feminine forces of "Black Magic" as opposed to 'White Science," and the rape-revenge film explores the most graphic instances of "getting even." In Clover's version, however, the horror film viewer is still always gendered male, vicariously enjoying a temporary masochistic position as a slasher victim who is still always gendered female because of "her" crying and cowering. Clover cautions:

> [t]o applaud the Final Girl as a feminist development ... is, in light of her figurative meaning, a particularly grotesque expression of wishful thinking. She is simply an agreed-upon fiction and the male viewer's use of her as a vehicle for his own sadomasochistic fantasies an act of perhaps timeless dishonesty.[29]

In class, where we read two excerpts from *Men, Women and Chainsaws*, I encourage the students to question why Clover would open up such wonderful territory for women in horror by insisting that a horrified subjectivity may be fluid, only to cede it yet again to the ubiquitous, sadomasochistic male fantasy. Indeed, many of our class discussions of the Final Girl were not confined to "images-of-women" approaches that sought simply to identify which characters in the films could be Final Girls — the class often tried to problematize the concept by talking about how particular characters did *not* behave like Final Girls. Still, Clover's emphasis upon horror's dynamic effects and how its consumption may construct varying positions of identification, not to mention her exuberant, detailed and insightful readings of given films, greatly expands the range of available interpretations to feminist scholars. However, her theories continue to create lingering questions about the acceptability of such pleasures for feminists. Celebrated and thought-provoking critical feminist theoretical contributions such as Clover's are central to the field. However, theories of psychoanalytic identification focused on scopophilia that have informed so much feminist criticism on horror should be informed by a greater respect for the texts themselves and a greater concern for horror's status *as fiction*.

For example, Williams theorizes around the classic Universal films and then extends her claims to the entire field. Similarly, Creed uses Julia Kristeva's theory of abjection to discuss horror as a rejection of the semiotic order of motherhood for the symbolic law of the father — all work and no play — without ranging beyond a scant handful of films picked to illustrate her categories of feminine monstrosity: archaic mother; monstrous womb; vampire; witch; possessed monster; deadly femme and castrating mother. Freeland cautions that we should avoid such psychoanalytic determinism and pay more attention to the "individuality of critical reaction from the audience" over the generalized "viewer's allegedly primal motives" emphasized by Williams and Creed. Sources of horror, Freeland argues, are not necessarily always synonymous with the "castration anxiety" invoked by being the possessor of "the gaze," just as they are not necessarily synonymous with the gooey, pre–Oedipal stage of Kristeva's abject:

> Psychoanalytic feminist film interpretations are significantly constrained by the theoretical vocabulary and framework of psychoanalysis. Psychoanalysis is not only very internally divisive but it is far from achieving anything like general acceptance as a psychological theory ... typically in film studies, psychoanalytic interpretations are advanced a priori rather than in an open-minded spirit of testing how well they actually work.... The notion of abjection in Creed's interpretations expands to become almost vacuous. It is simplistic and reductive to understand in advance that all the varieties of horrific monstrousness we can think of or witness on film are really just "illustrations" of the "work" of abjection.... In what sense is a psychological theory of abjection "explanatory" when it becomes so broad?[30]

Freeland, along with many others in the field, regards Clover's theory of the "Final Girl" in slasher movies as an example of a deep, Irigarayan "disruptive reading"[31] of horror that resists such "psychoanalytic determinism" and attempts the same approach, as does Halberstam, with *Silence of the Lambs* (1991), a canonical text for feminist psychoanalytic horror theories. The reductive focus on psychoanalysis applied to a handful of North American films obsessively dwelt upon by feminist horror criticism tends to train its gaze further inward upon a particular type of horror film, the slasher or serial killer film, now somewhat dated, straitjacketed in its "low" cultural asylum, and thus an easy target for what Joan Hawkins has criticized as overly "literalist" feminist interpretation. Hawkins convincingly underlines the similarity between low-brow slasher films and high art's "metaphorical" violence against female bodies, arguing that the high-brow gets away with murder while all eyes are upon the low's more spectacular displays of splatter, which she calls "para-cinema."[32] The temptation to gendered readings of what Judith Halberstam has called "bodies that splatter" (punning of course on Judith Butler's *Bodies that Matter* [1993])[33] is difficult to resist, particularly as horror's plays on gender, sexuality and the body are so entertaining. Although Carol Clover includes interesting and detailed discussions of the occult film and the rape-revenge narrative in *Men, Women and Chainsaws*, the popularity of her Final Girl theory has eclipsed her work in other areas of the field and established the slasher film as (North American) horror to the exclusion of many other, potentially more interesting sub-genres and also important considerations of the role of written horror texts.

For example, one gender-based study of horror film reception by researchers Justin M. Nolan and Gery W. Ryan has yielded interesting results about what elements of horror appear to resonate most with male and female audience members. Their study concluded that "rural terror," "a concept tied to fear of strangers and rural landscapes," tended to leave lasting impressions on male viewers, whereas "females display a greater fear of family terror, which includes themes of betrayed intimacy, stalkings and spiritual possession."[34] Despite an intriguing result indicating that the female subjects of their study reported a higher fear response and the concluding connection of this result with power-control theory, Nolan and Ryan ignore anything about the texts under discussion other than that they are a collection of gendered "themes." Thus, they quote Clover's definition of the slasher film as one in which a psycho killer "slashes to death a string of mostly female victims, one by one until he is subdued or killed, usually by the one girl who has survived"[35] as if that is all one ever needs to know about slasher films. In such a study, horror texts become not only homogenized, but homo-generic; their individual features do not much matter. Clover's synopsis is therefore presented as the essential metanarrative of the slasher film. One does not even have to view the distasteful thing for oneself before moving on to the study's findings. While Clover's work on gender and the slasher film is justly acclaimed as pioneering, this brief synopsis cannot be good enough to establish and accurately measure responses to horror texts — gendered or not — without incorporating other aspects of the texts under consideration and without acknowledging that there is more to horror than slashers.

The important point that it is virtually impossible to sum up the horror genre has been made by Stephen King in his fairy-tale encapsulations of "some of the scariest movies ever made"[36] for example, in the summary of *Night of the Living Dead* (1968) which follows:

> Once upon a time a lady and her brother went to put flowers on their mother's grave and the brother, who liked to play mean tricks, scared her by saying "They're coming to get you, Barbara." Except that it turned out they really were coming to get her ... but they got him first.[37]

As King implies by this simplification, such synopses of theme and plot cannot produce sufficient understanding of why and how these movies evoke the responses that they do. Nolan and Ryan focus their research upon differentiation in gendered responses, and a certain amount of summarizing each text's individual elements becomes necessary. But considerations get lost here that ought to be vital to their study. For example, how do particular representations of the tropes of "rural" and "family" terror contribute to their respective impacts upon males and females? Does the presence of a stranger or stalker guarantee the responses they describe? Are there gendered differences in experiences of being frightened? Thus, the ability of a horror text to engender multiple, diverse and often pleasurably contradictory reactions among fans, readers and audiences by virtue of its affective and contextual elements, becomes either neutralized by scholarly distance or simply "screened out" by the critic who refuses to give these elements any "play." As Steffen Hantke aptly puts it, "[i]t is not the horror text that silences the critic, it is the critic who silences the horror text."[38]

In this process of disciplining and silencing horror texts, horror written by women, such as, for example, the terrifying short stories of Joyce Carol Oates and Patricia Highsmith, goes unremarked and unacknowledged, with the possible exception of Anne Rice whose bestselling novels have become distanced from the horror genre (Rice's own gender is less remarked on than the queerness of her vampires). So too do the more obviously horrific narratives of Shirley Jackson, Elizabeth Bowen, Suzy Mckee Charnas, Tanith Lee, Kathe Koja, Jane Yolen, Lisa Tuttle, Chelsea Quinn Yarbro, Nina Kiriki Hoffman, Melanie Tem, the Canadian writers Gemma Files, Nancy Kilpatrick and Nalo Hopkinson, as well as the Gen-X Goth splatterpunk trilogy of Poppy Z. Brite, Caitlín Kiernan and Christa Faust, to name only a few women working in the field. Written horror has, as Ken Gelder notes,[39] been completely subordinated to film in even very recent critical accounts. Perhaps this is why so much horror produced by women does not get any scholarly play as a heavier emphasis is directed toward the film industry where women are in a drastic minority on the other side of the camera. One goal of "The Monstrous Feminist," therefore, was to redirect some attention to the women who write horror fiction against the grain of much scholarship, which seems to worry endlessly and solely about horror fiction writing or filming women.

In fact, when women look beyond the obvious film categories we have been thinking about so far, all kinds of potent "monstrous-feminist" archetypes, such as Sandra Gilbert and Susan Gubar's celebrated study of the Victorian "madwoman in the attic" (1979) become available for consideration. This colorful array is considerably enriched by work on international horror films (Tombs, 1998; Schneider, 2003; Schneider and Williams, 2005) that adds such figures as the Japanese white-faced vengeful ghost or the Malaysian *penanggalan* to the pantheon of powerful female monsters. For example, one of the stories that "Monstrous Feminist" students read, Poppy Z. Brite's "Calcutta: Lord of Nerves,"[40] appropriates Hindu mythology to make a fascinatingly monstrous figure out of the goddess Kali, presiding over a post-zombie-apocalyptic Calcutta where only the dead are left to worship her. The postmodern, pubescent lycanthropes of *Ginger Snaps* (2000), the *vagina-dentata*ed protagonist of *Teeth* (2007), and the titular predatory succubus of *Jenifer* (2005) are only a few of the more recent creations that both enrich and surpass Creed's categories of the monstrous-feminine.

For this reason, "The Monstrous Feminist" course combines the study of horror film with the study of horror literature, starting in our first few classes with the notion of the "female Gothic." While the students read excerpts from Anne Radcliffe's Gothic novels, Mary Shelley's *Frankenstein* and of course Charlotte Perkins Gilman's classic feminist nightmare "The Yellow Wallpaper," we try to avoid getting mired in the vast and murky realm of the literary Gothic, proceeding as quickly as possible to more contemporary horror stories by Shirley Jackson, Angela Carter and Joyce Carol Oates as well as work by Christa Faust, Suzy McKee Charnas, Kathe Koja and Poppy Z. Brite. It is unfortunate that so many feminists remain oblivious to the work of these writers; for example, Linda Badley's study of written horror, gender and the body pays attention to the well-worn thoroughfares of Stephen King, Clive Barker and Anne Rice but ignores works such as Charnas's *The Vampire Tapestry* (1980), Brite's *Exquisite Corpse* (1997) and Koja's *Skin* (1993). Maintaining its focus on such texts produced by women, including film, wherever possible, the course challenges students to rethink their conceptions of horror as located mainly in slasher films or dominated by recent formulations of "torture porn."[41] Students therefore came to understand that horror could be defined by far more than film clichés and that literature was neither stuck in the past of horror nor merely fodder for filmic adaptation. They also realized that much feminist horror might not always make its way onto the screen.

Although the course begins with literature and theoretical readings, we also devote significant time to horror film where, unfortunately, I have far less choice as to women-produced horror but can still pay attention to the ways gender issues are tackled. The second section of "The Monstrous Feminist" asks students to work in groups to facilitate class discussions of horror films. The film selections have varied over the three times I have taught the course so far, but have included (along with discussions of their remakes): *Black Christmas* (1974, 2006), *The Hills Have Eyes* (1977, 2006), *The Hunger* (1983), *The Texas Chainsaw Massacre* (1973, 2004), *The Texas Chainsaw Massacre 2* (1986), *The Stepford Wives* (1975, 2004), *Teeth*, *Let the Right One In* (2008), *Ginger Snaps*, *Jenifer*, *Sick Girl* (2006), *Fido* (2006), *Dawn of the Dead* (1978,

2004), *Day of the Dead* (1985) and *Audition* (1999). These films and/or their remakes often feature strong, non-normative or monstrous female characters. They tend to either dwell on or raise issues important to feminists such as sexism, menstruation, pregnancy, motherhood, abortion, rape, gender trouble, and the gendered, raced or classed mapping of the body. They often contain Final Girls. They also range from comical to grueling, from slower to fast-paced, from "classic" horror to "postmodern"[42] from less gore to more. Other candidates for screening that have been suggested or that I have considered and may feature in future courses are *Resident Evil* (2002), *Tokyo Gore Police* (2008), Peter Jackson's *Braindead / Dead-Alive* (1992), the French "extreme horror" films *Inside (À l'Intérieur)* (2007) and *Martyrs* (2008) as well as the beautiful and disturbing film directed by Claire Denis, *Trouble Every Day* (2001).

Pinedo characterizes horror film as a "participatory" genre that demands interaction and occasionally uproarious engagement, reminding us that class and ethnicity are also implicated in the dictates of taste. To illustrate this, Pinedo describes her experience as a member of two different movie audiences viewing *Aliens* (1986). Following social historian Lawrence Levine, both Pinedo and Williams in "Learning to Scream" make an interesting distinction between the "boisterous audience ... a racially and economically mixed group" which "unabashedly let out loud screams, laughter, gasps, sarcastic remarks and exclamations," and

> the more affluent and white ... audience [that] quietly murmured to their viewing companions and barely let out a scream.... These two contemporaneous movie theater audiences parallel what ... Levine describes in *Highbrow/Lowbrow: the emergence of cultural hierarchy in America* as the raucous audience and the passive audience. Levine chronicles the process by which the unruly audiences of the eighteenth and nineteenth centuries were disciplined into the docile audiences of today. By the twentieth century, "audiences in America had become less interactive, less of a public and more of a group of mute receptors."[43]

Pinedo points out that most horror film audiences tend not to be "mute receptors." The responses of a raucous audience interact with and participate in that text and what diverse and indeed contradictory pleasures it may afford. Indeed, Modleski has also questioned horror's location on the Frankfurt School's divide between lowbrow "pleasure" and highbrow *jouissance*, reminding us that horror does not necessarily comfortably inhabit the prevailing taste culture's distinctions.[44] Horror film audiences may in fact illustrate the uncoupling of the pairings of *jouissance* (high culture, anti-bourgeois) and pleasure (low culture, pro-bourgeois society). For Clover, horror's pleasure for women lies in the "uncertainty" of gender identity it creates but *jouissance* may also be derived from the cultural competence that women might develop as they become empowered to gain intertextual or fan knowledge of horror. Like Pinedo, Kermode and Hills, Freeland takes the audience and the fan into consideration, citing Ed S. Tan's work on "cinephilia" and film as an "emotion machine" to argue for the distinctiveness of horror audiences as "participatory. We may clap, laugh uproariously, or otherwise respond in surprising ways to things that we recognize as allusions, in-jokes, or sight gags, while our more weak-stomached friends ... find the movie frightening or simply disgusting."[45]

As such, I bore the dynamics of our film screenings very much in mind during "The Monstrous Feminist" film section and encouraged the students to at all times feel comfortable and empowered to express and be aware of their reactions, no matter how strong, as a starting-point for analysis. One film presentation group for *Teeth*, which features rape scenes, also chose to include "trigger warnings" and bring in a representative from a sexual assault centre as a resource for the class. Students were also aware that they had the option to temporarily leave the classroom if they found a particular film or sequence too difficult to watch.

It is difficult to describe experiences of watching the films in the Women's and Gender Studies classroom but my notes on our screenings and ensuing discussions show that clearly these experiences were very different from the "date" or individualized experiences described by Williams and interrogated by Berenstein or, for that matter, the intimate screenings of Cherry's female horror fans. "The Monstrous Feminist" classroom was certainly far from docile during film screenings. Students screamed, howled, jumped and laughed at their and others' reactions. They also placed themselves into the films in a process of identification often tinged with satire. Watching *Black Christmas*, for example, students started to react visibly once the sinister caller is revealed to be "in the house," calling out: "Are you kidding me—she's not going up there!" During the prolonged death scene of the brutally patriarchal character Captain Rhodes (Joseph Pilato)—nicknamed "Captain 'Roids" by students—in *Day of the Dead*, students bellowed, "Shoot him!" They laughed raucously at the sex scenes in *Teeth* and *Jenifer*, as well as the "menstrual piss" scene in *Ginger Snaps* that featured men "unmanned" and monstrous women attacking the sacredness of the phallus and of phallic imagery. Interestingly, the students expressed mostly angry frustration with the character of one of Clover's classic Final Girls, Sally in *Texas Chainsaw Massacre*, who continually screams and moans throughout her ordeal. Rather than any form of identification, the class loudly berated her, saying "Oh come on!" "Shut up!" This seems to confirm Clover's sense that the Final Girl is a "fiction," one with which this class certainly did not agree.

As a generation largely conditioned by slashers and their parodies such as *Scream* or *Scary Movie*, WGST students also sometimes expressed audible disappointment or surprise at the slower-paced and less gory older films such as *The Hills Have Eyes*, expecting "more jumping" and shocks. Sometimes they chose to write research papers comparing remakes with "originals" that explored not only gender differences in the portrayals of the characters but the meanings and effects of the bloodier representations of violence in the newer films. The idea that remakes might reflect backlash against women often surfaced in these papers. Students also discussed the implications of the hypersexualization of women with guns in newer horror films, referring to Amazon-with-gun fetishization as "Sarah Palin feminism." Such experiences demonstrated to me that older ideas of women looking symbolized by images of terrified women cowering behind their dates might be by now hopelessly outdated.

Analyses of the films that arose during class discussions following the screenings were similarly not restricted to slotting women and monsters into formulaic psychoanalytic roles. Indeed, the students demonstrated remarkable sophistication in pointing out, for example, the raced and classed implications of gated communities and their relationship to public versus private space in films such as *Fido* and *The Stepford Wives*. Our discussions of intersectionality also considered Franklin as a disabled and gendered-feminine character in *The Texas Chainsaw Massacre*, issues of racism, colonialism and consumerism in zombie films and cross-cultural comparisons with *Audition*. However, some of the most interesting discussions applied feminist theory to the horror films. For example, students asked: could rape revenge films such as *Teeth* and *I Spit on Your Grave* (1978, 2010) be considered Third-Wave feminism or just "Hollywood's take on feminism"? The protagonist's predicament of having a *vagina dentata* in *Teeth* also spurred discussions of the Rape-Axe, a South African anti-rape device that functions as an insertable *dentata* as one student mused, "I wouldn't mind having something like that." Similarly, Clover's description of "phallic weapons" wielded by the slasher killer engendered some particularly memorable discussion of what non-phallic weapons might look like — cling wrap, water, piano wire garrotes, mouths (although vampire teeth were excluded by the students from this category as, in the words of Sean Moreland, who gave guest talks, "dental erections").

Of particular interest during our discussions were male versus female deaths. Pinedo's previously cited "wet death," for example, becomes a bit of a joke when Brenda in *The Hills Have Eyes* props her mother's corpse up as bait to lure the monstrous family's patriarch, Papa Jupiter. At this juncture, my notes show a discussion among students reflecting the idea that "the Feminine Mystique has to die in order to slay patriarchy." Students were also intrigued by the relationships between women in horror, for example, the sisterhood bond in *Ginger Snaps*, as well as by the grotesqueness of hypermasculinity. At one point, I performed for the class, rather to their shock, some of the obscenities that the possessed Regan (Linda Blair) utters in *The Exorcist* as an example of how the aggressive violation of feminine rules of decorum can be utterly monstrous and terrifying. This led us into a discussion of what types of fear might be empowering or disempowering and whether women's desire for horror can be dangerous.

Feminist pedagogy, inspired by the anti-oppression education work of Paulo Freire, has never regarded students as passive recipients of expert knowledge. Freire describes the idea that pedagogy is "an act of depositing" knowledge into passive students as the "banking model" of education and remarks that "the capability of banking education to minimize or annul the students' creative power and to stimulate their credulity serves the interests of the oppressors, who care neither to have the world revealed nor to see it transformed."[46] Women's and Gender Studies students, therefore, are routinely trained in critical thinking and active participation in the classroom just as horror audiences are active participants in horror films. Combining the two, I found that engaging WGST "Monstrous Feminist" students as facilitators and strongly encouraging them to use creativity in their presentations produced astonishing results. The film group presentations were graded partly on how much participatory engagement groups could inspire, requiring students to take full responsibility for the course material and encouraging groups to be inventive in devising ways to keep their classmates active in the seminar through the use of handouts and other interactive materials. For example, one group as part of their presentation handout for *Day of the Dead*, circulated warning pamphlets about the "life-impaired" and a survey asking the rest of the class to rank their priorities for action in the event of a zombie apocalypse, while another group presenting *Ginger Snaps* came up with a trivia contest about the film where those who provided correct answers were rewarded with a wrapped tampon (in a nod to the film's satirical association of menstruation with lycanthropy). Still another group working on *Audition* gave the class an "Audition Casting Call" quiz, which analyzed the female characters in the film and invited those taking the quiz to step into one of their roles. Other groups handed out "props" such as little mirrors and bottles of garlicky water marked with crosses during the vampire film *Let the Right One In* or "chastity rings" during *Teeth* to accompany the background research the group did on "purity balls" and the importance of virginity to patriarchal organizations in the United States, where, according to their presentation, "accepting patriarchy" becomes an integral "part of growing up."

In addition to the handouts and other materials they produced, many film groups expressed their creativity in the form of preparing snack food for the class, consulting Halloween recipes to come up with "gross-out" fare: eyeball cupcakes, "lady fingers" complete with almond nails, body-part cookies and corpse cakes, gummy worms, bloody punch, complete with a disgustingly realistic-looking hand fashioned from a rubber glove floating in the punchbowl, "blood-corn" and ginger snaps. Such creative and participatory work shows that students need not merely be passive, acted-upon recipients of a film's messages about gender. Indeed, I frequently witnessed students enacting and performing "gender trouble" in their struggle to actively define, frame and interpret the horror films they were tasked with presenting. Students put on carnivalesque drag, actively subverting and transforming gender normativity. One group presenting *Day of the Dead* included a zombie George Romero and a zombie mermaid-princess among its presenters. This group also dressed up the classroom, transforming the room into a fortified bunker — named after the course code "Bunker 3005B" — as in the film and galvanizing the class with an introductory skit where the "Monstrous Feminist Survival Brigade" harangued the group *à la* Captain Rhodes about zombie survival. Students produced artwork as well as pamphlets, including a portrait of Leatherface. Another *Ginger Snaps* group presented a slideshow of photographed *tableaux* where, like the characters Ginger and Brigette in the film, each group member staged a couple of variations on their own horror show deaths — one with her head in the oven like Sylvia Plath, another floating face down in a swimming pool. In short, "The Monstrous Feminist" students, with very little prompting from me, gave consistently outstanding horror performances that incorporated an incredible awareness of the interactions of gendered fear with social constructions of the body. I was glad to have the technological capacity, through the university's learning management system, to be able to put these bravura performances on display.

Many of these performances incorporated the satirical and subversive possibilities of horror. Thus, one of the pamphlets handed out by a *Ginger Snaps* group mimicked the earnest tone of health and sexuality pamphlets designed for adolescent girls, slyly asking: "That funny feeling inside ... understanding the transition from girl to werewolf — is it normal?" Another group created a similar pamphlet on "Signs of STW — Sexually Transmitted Werewolf," which apparently includes the "desire to strut in slow motion," parodying Ginger's self-conscious sexy walk through the halls of her suburban high school, itself a parody of the expectations on young women to act like fashion models on a catwalk.

In conclusion, I have attempted to create "The Monstrous Feminist" classroom as a site where students are encouraged to think about what it means to be fearful, fearsome, feminist and feminine, producing "monstrous" readings and performances that go against the grain of many of the conventional theories of horror. So far, these have not only been rewarding, but enthusiastically received. One of the cleverest handouts our class received was a hand-drawn "Choose Your Own Adventure" from a *Texas Chainsaw Massacre 2* group, showing the Final Girl weaving her way through a cartoon maze of formulaic choices and possibilities to "do the chainsaw dance" at the end, demonstrating how much of a cliché the slasher has come to be for students. For me, this particular handout epitomized the choices and possibilities around teaching horror in Women's and Gender Studies — there being so much more to be gained from thinking about horror in a variety of ways, rather than just looking at it.

NOTES

1. Isabel Cristina Pinedo, *Recreational Terror: Women and the Pleasures of Horror Film Viewing* (Albany: State University of New York Press, 1997), 51.
2. Laura Mulvey, "Visual Pleasure and Narrative Cinema," in *Film Theory and Criticism: Introductory Readings*, eds. Leo Braudy and Marshall Cohen (New York: Oxford University Press, 1999), 833–44, 837.
3. Mulvey, 843.
4. Linda Williams, "When the Woman Looks," in *The Horror Film Reader*, ed. Mark Jancovich (London: Routledge, 2001), 61
5. Williams, "When the Woman Looks," 61.
6. Cherry, "Refusing to Refuse to Look," *The Horror Film Reader*, 169.
7. Cherry, 170.
8. Rhona J. Berenstein, "It Will Thrill You, It May Shock You, It Might Even Horrify You": Gender, Reception, and Classic Horror Cinema" in *The Dread of Difference*, ed. Barry Keith Grant (Austin: University of Texas Press, 1996), 121.
9. Williams, "When the Woman Looks," 65.
10. Williams, "When the Woman Looks," 64.
11. Williams, "Film Bodies: Gender, Genre, Excess" in *Film Quarterly* 44:4 (Summer 1991): 2–13.
12. Williams, "Film Bodies: Gender, Genre, Excess," 5.
13. Williams, "When the Woman Looks," 64.
14. Williams, "When Women Look: A Sequel" in *Freud's Worst Nightmares*, accessed at http://www.sensesofcinema.com/2001/15/horror_women/.
15. Williams, "Learning to Scream" in *The Horror Film Reader*, 168.
16. Cynthia Freeland, *The Naked and the Undead: Evil and the Appeal of Horror* (Boulder, CO: Westview, 2002), 13.
17. Pinedo, 2.
18. Matt Hills, *The Pleasures of Horror* (London: Continuum, 2005), 15.
19. Pinedo, 25.
20. Williams, "Learning to Scream," 167.
21. Noël Carroll, *The Philosophy of Horror or, Paradoxes of the Heart* (New York: Routledge, 1990), 193.
22. Cherry, 175.
23. Pinedo, 70.
24. Pinedo, 61.
25. Pinedo, 61.
26. Hills, 77–78.
27. Clover, 42.
28. Clover, 13–14.
29. Clover, 53.
30. Freeland, 20.

31. Freeland, 14–15.
32. Joan Hawkins, *Cutting Edge: Art-Horror and the Horrific Avant-Garde* (Minneapolis: University of Minnesota Press, 2000), 195.
33. Judith Halberstam, *Skin Shows: Gothic Horror and the Technology of Monsters* (Durham, NC: Duke University Press, 1995), 138.
34. Justin M. Nolan and Gery W. Ryan, "Fear and Loathing at the Cineplex," in *Sex Roles* (vol. 42, nos. 1–2, 39–56): 39.
35. Carol Clover, *Men, Women and Chainsaws: Gender in the Modern Horror Film* (Princeton, NJ: Princeton University Press, 1992), 21.
36. Stephen King, *Danse Macabre* 179.
37. King, 177.
38. Steffen Hantke. "Shudder as We Think: Reflections on Horror and / or Criticism," *Paradoxa* 17 (December 2002), http://paradoxa.com/excerpts/17intro.htm.
39. Ken Gelder, *The Horror Reader* (London: Routledge, 2000), 6.
40. Poppy Z. Brite. "Calcutta, Lord of Nerves," in *Wormwood: A Collection of Short Stories* (New York: Dell, 1995).
41. See the chapter endnote on the origins of the term "torture porn" in the preface to this book.
42. Pinedo, 17.
43. Pinedo, 42–43.
44. Tania Modleski. "The Terror of Pleasure: The Contemporary Horror film and postmodern theory" in *Studies in Entertainment: Critical approaches to mass culture*. (Bloomington: Indiana University Press), 1986.
45. Freeland, 7.
46. Paulo Freire, *The Pedagogy of the Oppressed* (New York: Continuum, 2000), 72–73.

Acts of Re-Possession: Bollywood's Re-Inventions of the Occult Possession Film

SEAN MORELAND AND SUMMER PERVEZ

Over the course of our combined teaching experience, we have found that one of the most stimulating, controversial, and debate-provoking topics we have engaged with our students has been the idea of spirit-possession. This pedagogical observation would doubtless come as no surprise to the influential theorist of (among other things) gender and horror film, Carol Clover, who in "Opening Up," an essay which deals with what she calls the "occult possession film," observes that "the possession or exorcism plot, assimilated directly or indirectly and in varying degrees to a psychoanalytic model, is one of the most generative ones of our time."[1] The number of popular British, European, and American horror films in the first decade of the twenty-first century that ground themselves in this plot-formula amply testifies to the lasting truth of Clover's observation,[2] as does the fascination these films exert for our undergraduate students, many of them born around the same time Clover published her landmark book. However, Clover's study of gender in the modern horror film restricts itself to Western, and especially American, cinema. Our shared interest in Bollywood horror films led us to ponder the degree to which Clover's analysis also applies to the popular occult possession narratives that have increasingly been emerging from India's cinematic industry.[3] We pose this question, while considering some of the historical and cultural implications of Clover's argument, by examining three recent Bollywood occult possession films: Ram Gopal Varma's *Bhoot* (2003), Vikram Bhatt's *1920* (2008) and Mohit Suri's *Raaz: The Mystery Continues* (a.k.a. *Raaz 2*, 2009).

Through exploring the telling parallels between the narrative and identificatory structures of *Bhoot*, *1920* and *Raaz 2* and those of some of their Western counterparts, it becomes immediately apparent that these Bollywood films, like the films Clover considers, follow a "standard scheme [which] puts, or at least seems to put, the female body on the line only in order to put the male psyche on the line,"[4] using the female body as a locus for cultural crises in masculinity. However, despite the considerable stylistic allusions and pastiches presented by each of these films, we argue that the structural parallels they share with earlier Western possession films are often not so much the result of direct influence or imitation as they are the result of a shared ancestry in pre-cinematic cultural, and especially religious, narratives. Additionally, the various approaches taken by the films' makers effectively challenge traditional Indian ideas about film, particularly horror film. These varied approaches effectively interrogate and alter the gendered tropes Clover identifies, often in ways that their Western counterparts do not. Ultimately, the "opening up" of the bodies of these films' female protagonists parallels the "opening up" of Bollywood film-making to a wider diasporic and international audience, as well as an "opening up" of South Asian history and culture to new mass media configurations.

Since 1995, Bollywood films have been aimed at an increasingly global audience. The Bombay film industry in particular has recognized and capitalized on the vast potential of the South Asian diaspora, with landmark films such as *Hum Aapke Hain Kaun* (Who Am I To You, 1994) and *Dilwale Dulhaniya Le Jayenge* (The True of Heart Will Win the Bride, 1995). This process of the "opening up of the diasporic market to Hindi cinema" has been termed "Bollywoodization" by numerous scholars,[5] who argue that Bollywood "went global" by renegotiating its commodity-value and self-positioning as an "unofficial ideological apparatus."[6] This trend coincided with the liberalization of the Indian economy in the 1990s, or its move from a partly socialist economy towards free market capitalism. As Gautam Basu Thakur has argued, "Bollywood participates in the ideological construction and privileging of a new ethics of globalized living."[7] It does so not simply by reflecting the spread of new technologies in India's radically globalized media landscape, but with a neo-nationalist agenda that "reimagine[s] the relation between the nation-state and its capital-rich diaspora."[8]

It is not surprising that it is in the age of globalization that contemporary Bollywood films have, perhaps belatedly, attracted the attention of Western academics and filmmakers. Indian popular cinema has finally entered the Cinema Studies discourse, as it is now "counted as a 'valid' cultural product, an episteme worthy of the attention of the Anglo-American media."[9] This has been reflected in our respective classroom experiences both institutionally, by a greater number of courses — in part or in whole — devoted to South Asian film, and also on the part of our students, who show a greater awareness of, interest in, and desire to contemplate and discuss Bollywood films within the context of cultural studies generally. This wider international critical interest has accompanied a dramatic shift within Bollywood filmmaking itself. Rini Bhattacharya Mehta has noted that in its post-global phase, Bollywood has adopted a new paradigm which no longer depends on the East/West binary, with the West as a vague cultural signifier of moral degeneracy pitted against a morally superior East. Alert to the vast potential of the diasporic market and eager to "catch the next train to global capital," Bollywood has rearranged its orientation to accommodate an increasingly international audience.[10] Furthermore, it has participated in a renegotiation of its own commodity value on the international stage of cinematics, with new aesthetic strategies that involve modes of narration less reflective of Bombay cinema and more aligned with the conventions of both Hollywood and international *avant garde* cinema.

However, if Bollywood cinema in general has been slow in gaining the international recognition it deserves, Bollywood horror cinema has historically lagged even further behind; even with the surge of critical and popular attention that horror cinema has been internationally attracting since the 1980s, very little critical attention has been paid to Indian horror films. There are a few notable scholarly exceptions, including Pete Tombs' valuable contribution, "The Beast from Bollywood: A History of the Indian Horror Film," which provides an overview of the history of Indian horror film until the turn of the twenty-first century, and is a solid starting point both for our argument and for undergraduate-class excursions into Bollywood horror.[11] Tombs explains that it was the debut film by the Ramsay brothers, *Do Gaz Zameen Ke Neeche* (Two Yards Under the Ground, 1972) that sparked Bollywood's interest in the horror genre, from a conceptual standpoint. Written by F.U. Ramsay and directed by Tulsi Ramsay, the film, in Tombs' words,

> was not necessarily the best of its kind, but it was effectively the first of its kind. It was also a hit. Consequently, it set several precedents that Indian horror films have followed ever since. Firstly, that horror movies are generally low budget affairs. Secondly, that they follow Western models very closely with the "Indian" elements more or less grafted onto a generic plot. Thirdly, that the exploitable elements of horror make it unnecessary to have either great music or star casts; and finally, that they will be most popular with rural audiences and the urban poor and treated as rather a joke by everyone else.[12]

Tombs' essay is frank, perhaps sometimes to the point of excoriation, in its critical assessment of the production values and limited aesthetic ambitions of twentieth-century Indian horror films. However, his argument applies less to a number of larger-budgeted and more experimental Bollywood horror films produced since its publication in 2003. Indeed, to some degree this is because the horror film has not been exempt from the process of the "Bollywoodization of Hindi cinema."[13]

Despite early forays in the 1970s, it was not until the 1980s, with what could be called the second generation of Indian horror, made by filmmakers such as the Ramsay brothers (this time, Shyam and Tulsi), that India saw a wide range of popular horror films. However, the popularity of films such as *Tahkhana* (The Dungeon, 1986), *Veerana* (The Wilderness, 1988), and *Purana Mandir* (The Old Temple, 1984) was not due primarily to their mimicking of Hollywood horror conventions, but to their grounding in *Bhutavidya*,[14] the pervasive occult writings, beliefs and practices embodied in centuries of Indian religious texts, mythology and folklore. This body of knowledge and belief has been central to Indic literature for thousands of years, and the popularity of the occult horror film in India cannot be properly understood without recognizing its grounding in these traditions, as much as in the modes, tropes and techniques derived from Hollywood film.

Possession narratives in particular have a long tradition in South Asia, present in all of the region's major religions, and disseminated as popular folklore in all social strata. While pre–1995 horror films remain grounded in traditional South Asian ideas surrounding the occult and possession, they have come to increasingly mimic both the conventions and narrative modes of Western cinema, often lifting entire plots from popular Hollywood psychological thrillers and creatively modifying them to suit a Bollywood audience. In the context of horror, this shift has led to the creation of films — such as Varma's *Kaun?* (Who?, 1999) *Bhoot* (Spirit, 2003), and *Darwaza Band Rakho* (Keep the Door Closed, 2006) — that embrace recognizable Western horror conventions, narrative modes, and cinematic techniques, but which often retain very South Asian frameworks and narrative traditions. Additionally, many of these films effectively re-frame the narrative trajectories of the films they draw upon, often retaining much of their structure, while radically changing their focus and significance.

Not only is this kind of (anxiety free) influence to be expected in the "media contagion" that typifies a globalized context of capitalist circulation and consumerism, but "pursuing the best of the West" may also be, as producer/director Ram Gopal Varma has argued, a necessary strategy for success:

> There's going to be a massive change. A lot of old filmmakers are going to go out of business. Anyone who looks at a film as a formula ... who doesn't look at the totality of the film, is lost now. Anyone who follows the old prudish traditions ... is gone. And anyone who doesn't follow the West is gone. For many people in the business, their pride won't let them. But following the West is not surrendering. Following the West, the best of the West, is following originality. Western innovation is superior, and I think we're just beginning to understand that. With my films, I am targeting urban multiplexes, the sophisticated media-savvy young crowd. Frankly, I couldn't give a f— k for the villages.[15]

Varma's strategy implies a clear shift in audience, primarily toward the Westernized or diasporic South Asian. His statement also illustrates the degree to which he has been, since *Raat* (Night, 1992), determined to rewrite the proverbial playbook of Bollywood film production. His insistent, and commercially very risky, focus on the horror genre — traditionally the purview of "the rural audiences and the urban poor" — is part of his rejection of what he terms "the old prudish traditions" of Indian cinema.

In his 2003 film *Bhoot*, striking parallels to *The Exorcist* make Varma one of many Bollywood filmmakers inspired by the Western horror classic: as Tombs explains, it "was the worldwide success of William Friedkin's *The Exorcist* (1973) that sparked the interest of India's movie moguls,"[16] signaling the potential occult horror films could have for international commercial success. Its commercial viability in the West, however, was not the only factor that attracted Bollywood filmmakers to Friedkin's film. Whereas earlier, comparably successful Western horror films such as *Night of the Living Dead* (1968) or *Rosemary's Baby* (1968) failed to fully capture the attention of Indian audiences and filmmakers, *The Exorcist* succeeded in doing so. While the widespread practice of cremation made George Romero's ghouls/zombies rather a limited prospect for pleasurable terror in India, and the urbane, cosmopolitan Satanism of Roman Polanski's film similarly lacked resonance, South Asian audiences were prepared for Friedkin's transformation of religious possession into a grotesque spectacle by millennia of religious and mythical writings about the realities of spirit possession, and in particular, the existence of spirits called *bhutagraha*,[17] thought to possess the bodies of pregnant women and children.

The Exorcist also had a third important point of appeal for Indian filmmakers, as Tombs points out: "[t]he Indian censor, with a brief to protect filmgoers from explicit sex and Western ideas, would obviously find horror a cause for concern. This was one reason for using *The Exorcist* as a model. The film's story seemed tailor made for Indian tastes. The brave priest fighting an evil, multifaceted demon for the soul of a child was something that resonated with Indian sensibilities."[18] Viewed from a certain angle, *The Exorcist*'s narrative could be read as one that upholds religious traditionalism against secular modernity, suggested by its exploration of the mystery of faith, giving it a unique moral and cultural appeal for Indian audiences and filmmakers. Given *The Exorcist*'s popular appeal and sustained influence, the homage paid it by most occult possession films — in India and elsewhere — is no surprise.

However, despite their numerous parallels with and occasional allusions to *The Exorcist*, *Bhoot*, *1920* and *Raaz 2* all depart from Friedkin's film's central relationship. While a number of critics, perhaps most notably Barbara Creed, have pointed out *The Exorcist*'s emphasis on the horrors of the maternal, as it is Chris's relationship with her daughter Regan which is the primary affective focus of the film,[19] each of these Bollywood films opts instead to present the heterosexual romantic couple as its primary — and certainly more conventional — locus. Furthermore, each film performs an almost identical heterosexual division of labor (to borrow a phrase from Laura Mulvey), as it is the woman in each who becomes possessed, while it is the man's responsibility to free her from this state of possession. Due to this duplicative engendering, Clover's arguments about *The Exorcist* are for the most part readily applicable to these films, whereas Barbara Creed's equally influential monstrous-maternal interpretation of the film is less so, given the heteronormatively romantic reframing of the possession plot these films perform.

Bhoot, 1920 and *Raaz 2* invite their audiences to share in the initially idyllic relationship of a young couple in the early stages of their connubial life. More specifically, each presents us with a man providing a new home for his wife/lover; shortly thereafter, each presents her as becoming the "home" of a hostile and invasive power. In this respect, the initial narrative schema of these films is identical, and each follows the typical gender dynamics identified by Clover, who points out that "the portals of occult horror are almost invariably women," and identifies the shared basis of these films as "a girl/woman possessed by the devil and of the man/men involved in her exorcism."[20] As she aptly points out, films such as *The Exorcist* and *Witchboard* are "variants in a tradition extending all the way back to the Bible."[21] Frederick M. Smith makes a comparable point in *The Self Possessed: Deity and Spirit Possession in South Asian Literature and Civilization*, which includes a review of possession narratives in early Vedic literature. Smith also points out the relative preponderance of female "hosts," writing "more women than men appear to experience possession."[22]

The shared scriptural ancestry that informs all these cinematic narratives makes for muddy waters where questions of originality and imitation are concerned: to consider *The Exorcist*, for example, as "the original" or *only* source text for *Bhoot, 1920*, or *Raaz 2* is to distort the reality of a much older shared lineage. While there are certainly points of direct stylistic or narratological influence, the more important point is that these films all share common ancestors, and address common themes, which undoubtedly enables their horrific potential, as well as informs their international popularity.

Clover further explains that "[t]he idea of impregnation by the 'pneuma' is ancient and widespread in both learned and popular beliefs, and it turns up repeatedly in occult films in connection with the reproduction/possession complex of ideas. It plays on an equally ancient and widespread association between the vagina and the throat — an association reflected in the fantasy of the vagina dentata."[23] Clover's analysis goes on to elucidate the connection between female anatomy and domestic architecture in American possession films by returning to Freud's classic essay, "Das Unheimlich." These films, Clover explains, "take on the 'occult' in its original sense (that which is hidden, derived from Latin *occultus*, past participle of *occulere*, 'conceal'), a sense that in turn squares nicely with Freud's notion of uncanny sensations as the effect of the 'former Heim [home] of all human beings.'"[24]

Like the American films Clover considers, *Bhoot*, *1920* and *Raaz 2* revolve around associations between the universal mammalian "home" of the womb, figured in the body of the woman who, because of this "opening," is vulnerable to entry/possession, and the house (or apartment) as home, as a locus of domesticity, familial identity and social status.[25] *Bhoot* features a successful stock analyst, Vishal (played by Ajay Devgan), and his new wife Swati (played by Urmila Matondkar). Questing for the perfect home for them, Vishal thinks he has found it on the top floor of a chic twelve-story apartment building that turns out to have a tragic history. *Bhoot* repeatedly pays homage to Roman Polanski's films *The Tenant* (1976) and *Rosemary's Baby*, frequently underlining the connection between Swati's identity as a traditional wife and home-maker and her viability as a host for what is eventually revealed to be the vengeful ghost of the apartment's former resident, Manjeet (played by Barkha Madan). Swati's physical opening and Vishal's emotional-epistemological opening are both anticipated by their first sexual union after moving into the apartment, an event which immediately precedes the first apparition of Manjeet, who the audience sees malevolently observing Swati, unseen by her. This also creates a parallel between the possessive agent ("Manjeet") and the voyeur-viewer, for whom the spectacular locus of attention is, of course, Swati's body, and whatever force occupies that body. It turns out that Manjeet, who committed suicide to avoid being raped by another tenant (Sanjay, played by Fardeen Khan), has embodied herself in Swati to seek revenge for her child's death, as well as her own. At least on one level, then, *Bhoot* provides itself with a quasi-feminist subtext:[26] attempted sexual assault is avenged from beyond the grave, and a woman's identity and individuality can be put at risk by the restrictions that marriage and domesticity impose.

1920, too, revolves around a newly married couple and a young husband's quest for the perfect home for himself and his wife. Arjun Singh Rathod (played by Rajniesh Duggal) is an aspiring architect who is commissioned to turn an old, palatial *haveli* into a modern hotel when his Westernized and Catholic wife, Lisa (played by Adah Sharma), begins experiencing strange occurrences that culminate in her spectacular possession by a malevolent spirit.[27] Two architects have already been killed at the story's start, but rather than killing the third, the spirit chooses to possess Lisa instead and, much like the eponymous entity of *Bhoot*, uses her body to avenge its own death.

Whereas Swati's vulnerability in *Bhoot* is, at least implicitly, linked to her traditional role as wife and home-maker, Lisa's possession is quite explicitly connected to her Western identity; she is already foregrounded at the start of the film as abject, evidenced by her husband Arjun's forsaking of his Hindu religion and family in order to be with her. With her mixed race and Catholic religion, Lisa already fits Kristeva's definition of abjection, as "that which does not respect borders, positions, or rules," and which disturbs identity, system, and order.[28] This is emphasized during an early scene in which Arjun's father and brothers threaten Lisa, and their repeated, almost incantatory use of the derogatory word "*neech*" to describe her (translated as "filthy," with connotations of the abject) foreshadows both her fate as the victim of the film's vengeful spirit, and her husband's eventual banishment of the spirit through a religious incantation. This scene foregrounds the degree to which Lisa's possession merely amplifies her abjection, after which she comes to exemplify one of Creed's archetypes of the monstrous-feminine, the "woman-as-possessed-monster."

Finally, *Raaz 2* features a young model named Nandita Chopra (played by Kangana Ranaut), in love with a newly successful director and TV personality, Yash (played by Adhyayan Suman), who hosts a "reality show" that investigates supposedly supernatural occurrences. Although she is cautioned by her friend to take their relationship slowly,[29] Nandita eagerly moves into the apartment Yash has procured for them when she discovers her pregnancy. Whereas the primary relationships in *Bhoot* and *1920* are dyadic, *Raaz 2* revolves around a triad: Nandita meets a visionary young artist named Prithvi (played by Emraan Hashmi), who has been receiving visions of her endangerment and death, which he then paints on canvas. Nandita's eventual possession by an enigmatic spirit is thus aligned with a number of other, more mundane, transformations in Nandita's identity: conjugal life, a new domestic space, and the burgeoning prospect of motherhood. Once she has lost her unborn child, her career prospects, and her relationship, it is eventually revealed that she is possessed by the spirit of Prithvi's father, a man named Veer Pratap Singh (played by Jackie Shroff), who was murdered after learning of an American-owned chemical company's conspiracy to dump toxic waste into a specific river site, or *kundh*, used for sacred Hindu rituals, and is now seeking justice and reparation.

In all three films, "it is not just the centrality of a female body, and the interest in its passages and interiors and its capacity to accommodate alien intrusion, that mark the possession film as somehow 'feminine,' but the fact that the male psyche/body is understood in like terms, and its story is told with reference to the 'internal space' of a woman."[30] As Clover argues, in the occult possession film, "behind the female 'cover' is always the story of a man in crisis."[31] This claim proves to be as true of these Bollywood films as it is of Clover's examples of American films: all feature "'dual focus' narratives, [with] attention alternating between the story of female possession on one hand and the story of male crisis on the other."[32] The degree to which this dual focus also defines Bollywood possession films is striking, if perhaps not altogether surprising, given their common investment in patriarchal religious traditions. In light of their cultural context, however, the sub-textual focus of these films on contested masculinity has rather different effects.

According to Clover, "the possession film's psychological interest, its problem, typically resides at least as much in the significant bystander — the boyfriend, husband, doctor, or priest — who attends and struggles to understand as it does in the afflicted person herself." Clover's examples from Western horror, such as *The Exorcist* and *Witchboard* (1986), testify to this.[33] The usual "quandary of the rational male," as Clover explains, "is a simple one: should he cling to his rational, scientific understanding of human behavior, or should he yield to the irrational? To that quandary the experience of the troubled woman, however theatrical its manifestation, is largely accessory."[34] This is demonstrated equally by *Bhoot, 1920,* and *Raaz 2*, where it is the male protagonist, invariably a loved one of the possessed woman, who is offered as the point of subjective identification for the audience.[35] In all three cases, the male protagonist, initially representing the voice of reason and science, must learn to acknowledge the existence of the supernatural if he is to succeed in the exorcism of his partner.

This could not be more clearly evident than it is in *Bhoot*, where Swati's physical transformation under the influence of Manjeet is the visual cue for Vishal's psychological transformation. While Vishal learns early on about the death of Manjeet and her young son, he keeps the information from Swati, whom he is afraid might be further disturbed by it. When she learns of the apartment's dark history, and becomes angry with Vishal for his deceptive omission, he responds by belittling her for making so much out of what is, to his mind, a trivial, and harmless, part of the building's history: "Swati, just because a woman died here, should we leave this house? Every other house has deaths; that doesn't make people leave their homes. How can you believe in such superstitious nonsense?" Swati's subsequent possession by Manjeet triggers Vishal's questioning of his own assumptions regarding the occult. A man of reason and science, Vishal's initial attempts at curing Swati involve consulting a psychiatrist, who claims Swati's unpredictable behavior is the result of multiple personality disorder. Ultimately, however, Vishal is internally transformed; he finally turns to Manjeet's mother (played by Tanuja) and Sarita, a practitioner of black magic (played by Rekha), to help save Swati.

Likewise, *1920* is not so much about Lisa's progressive entrapment as it is about Arjun's shift from atheism, a position from which he can easily deny the supernatural, back to Hinduism, a religion in which possession has a long history of spiritual significance. In other words, in keeping with Clover's basic thesis about the occult possession film, Lisa's possession appears to have more to do with her husband's abandonment of his mother culture (Indian identity and Hinduism) than anything Lisa herself has done. According to Bhatt, the violation of cultural tradition in the marriage between Arjun and Lisa has been at the heart of the story since his initial conception of its plot. Asked in a pre-release interview what his new film was about, Bhatt described it as "a love story, based in the year 1920. It is about a Hindu boy and an Anglo-Indian girl, who fall in love and get married against their parents' wishes. Arjun Singh Rathod ... is an architect, who wants to demolish a haunted house and build a hotel there. His wife Lisa ... gets possessed by the spirits of the house."[36] The pending dispossession of the spirit from the house is paralleled in the film's narrative with Arjun's abandonment of his religious and cultural roots; the implication is that Lisa's possession is a counter-balancing reaction for Arjun's dispossession of his faith and traditions, enacted through his wife's body. When the Catholic religion fails to exorcise the spirit from Lisa, Arjun is forced to take matters into his own hands. It is ultimately through a series of chants from the *Hanuman Chalisa* that Arjun himself becomes the means to recover Lisa from abjection[37]; where before she was cast out, she can now be brought back, but only into the fold of her husband's recovered spirituality. In line with Clover's argument then, Lisa's body serves merely as a medium for the resolution of the male's psychological crisis: saving her requires an end to Arjun's fight with the gods and a return to his abandoned faith.

Like both Vishal and Arjun, *Raaz 2*'s Yash comes from a position of atheism — established early in the film — and must also learn to acknowledge the power of the supernatural. However, in his pursuit of global success, Yash is so insistent on his refusal to recognize the occult that he actually ends his relationship with Nandita. It is no accident that this scene takes place in a church, where Nandita feels protected from the malevolent spirit haunting her. Here, along with expressing concern that the gossip regarding Nandita will negatively affect his reputation and career, Yash tells her that God cannot help her because he does not really exist. Insisting that her problem is medical, he urges her to seek the help of a doctor. Soon after Yash's abandonment of Nandita in this scene, Vir Pratap's spirit stops his intermittent possessions of her and begins to haunt *him* instead. It is only when Yash is forced to confront the supernatural himself that it becomes evident who Vir Pratap Singh is really after: both Nandita and Prithvi are mere conduits through which the spirit can reach Yash.[38] Thus, as with Lisa in *1920*, Nandita's body is used to punish what ultimately turns out to be Yash's (in this case, literal) crime. The link between Nandita's identity as a victim of possession and her loss of identity as Yash's wife-to-be is dramatically underlined by the revelation that Yash kept the illicit disposal of the factory's pesticides, and attendant murder of Vir Pratap Singh, a secret in return for the chemical company's sponsorship of his TV show. Vir Pratap's motive is not only to have the conspiracy uncovered and expose the truth, but also to take revenge on Yash (as well as numerous others) for keeping it hidden in order to advance his own career. Nandita's body becomes the means through which the film figures Freud's Schelling-derived definition of the uncanny as what was supposed to remain hidden coming to light. Her possessed body first conceals, and eventually reveals, the psychological and cultural conflicts of which it is, throughout most of the film, also the battleground.

The Exorcist, as well as more contemporary Western possession films including *The Exorcism of Emily Rose* and *Paranormal Activity 1* and *2*, present what Creed calls the monstrous-feminine through linking the act of possession to the unconscious agency of the female bodies of their possessed, both through their visual treatments and their narrative accounts. *Bhoot, 1920* and *Raaz 2*, however, depart from this tendency insofar as they fissure their narrative rationales for the possession starkly from the visual logic they employ. Each film's narrative explicitly situates the *cause* of the possession in the realm of masculine agency, as each of the women ostensibly becomes possessed as a direct result of something her husband/male lover says or does. What is, in Clover's analysis of American possession films, a submerged causality, reflected in the films' patterns of engenderment, but not directly in their narratives, becomes in each of these Bollywood films far more explicitly expressed in the storylines themselves. For example, in *The Exorcist*, Regan's possession can only ultimately be resolved alongside Father Karras' crisis of faith. However, the film does not diegetically portray it as *originating* there; rather, it is ambiguously linked to the unearthing of an ancient pagan idol in Iraq and/or a young girl's experimentation with a Ouija board.[39] Similarly, In *The Exorcism of Emily Rose*, the ambiguity of the possessing entity's ontological status means that Emily's embodiment of monstrosity — as one who is both possessed and visibly disfigured by her possession, and as one who is hysterical (whose womb is dis-placed) and a victim of her own physiological disposition to illness — makes her demonstration (demenstruation?) of femininity inextricable from her *demon*stration of monstrosity.

The possessed women of *Bhoot, 1920*, and *Raaz 2*, then, all experience their possession — at least according to diegetic logic — not because of what they *are* so much as who they are romantically attached *to*. Swati is exposed to a vengeful spirit because she is left alone in the haunted apartment her financier husband has procured, and because of another man's earlier act of sexual violation against another woman. Lisa is possessed because her architect husband renounces cultural tradition and religious fidelity, first by marrying her, a non–Hindu, and abandoning his religion and family "for her," and second by participating in the modernization of a traditional home-structure in attempting to turn it into a commercial institution. Finally, Nandita is possessed because of her husband's corrupt dealings with immoral industrialists. This shared shift in causality means that each of these films undermines the logic of the monstrous-feminine even as it deploys it. As a result, the monstrous-feminine becomes, or is revealed as, a projection: it is an effect that men have on women, not a product of the women themselves. In an odd way, then, each of these films reveals the mystification behind the monstrous-feminine, even as it exploits it for its affective power.

Extracting the monstrous-feminine from the beloved becomes the task of the male in all three films. In keeping with Clover's analysis, the world of each of these cinematic fictions begins in a state of imbalance, as "white science" (a rationalistic, skeptical, masculine perspective) dominates. Once a spiritual entity — generally malevolent — possesses the female body, her victimization can only be overcome once an important male protagonist is "converted" to the reality of "black magic." In a certain sense, the male must be feminized — or symbolically penetrated by the existence of the world of spirit — which enables the possessing entity to be evacuated from the body of his beloved. Clover identifies this formula as being typical of possession films, which she sees as employing "two competing systems of explanation — White Science and Black Magic," terms she takes from Wes Craven's film, *Serpent & the Rainbow*. She explains that

> white science refers to Western rational tradition. Its representatives are nearly always white males, typically doctors, and its tools are surgery, drugs, psychotherapy, and other forms of hegemonic science. Black magic, on the other hand, refers to Satanism, voodoo, spiritualism, and folk variants of Roman Catholicism [...] its inhabitants are blacks, Native Americans, mixed-race peoples [...] and third-world peoples in general [...] but first and foremost, women.[40]

Such distinctions do prevail to some degree in these Bollywood possession films, albeit often in a transfigured manner, marked by the cultural differences informing their production.

Of the three, *Bhoot* remains closest to Clover's trajectory: its male protagonist Vishal must be "converted" to the world of black magic in order for his beloved wife to be saved. The film's dramatic resolution underlines this in glaring colors: Vishal's movement from rejection to an exigent acceptance of the existence of the supernatural is underscored when the vengeful spirit, persuaded to leave Swati's body, begins controlling Sanjay's body.[41] Not only has Vishal already begun to accept the reality of the world of black magic, but so have the film's staunchest representatives of masculine, patriarchal science and authority: Dr. Rajan and police inspector Liaqat Qureshi. It is only with the symbolic feminization of these resistant authority figures, or their ideological penetration by the reality of black magic, that the spirit which previously penetrated Swati can depart so she can finally find rest. Attaining this requires multiple female representatives of black magic: the maid, the exorcist summoned to Swati's aid, and Manjeet's mother, who Vishal finally contacts once having undergone the required interior transformation brought on by Swati's possession. Sanjay's death at the invisible hands of the spirit seems almost an afterthought to this balancing of the figurative books.[42]

Bhoot thus supports Clover's observation that in possession narratives, not only white science (often represented by psychiatry) but also traditional religious orthodoxy is ultimately ineffectual in dealing with the world of "black magic"; either more mystical methods, or more heterodox religious rites, are required for successful exorcism. The latter is represented well by *The Exorcist*, where the Catholic Church's prescribed *Rituale Romanum* ultimately fails to save Regan from her possessor; instead, it is Father Karras's unorthodox (but also broadly Christian) offer to sacrifice himself in her place that defeats the demon. In *Bhoot*, religion has even less of a role, since the exorcism of Manjeet is ultimately attained through her mother's *secular* powers of persuasion, or maternal love. In *1920*, however, it is Arjun's *return* to his orthodox Hindu faith that finally saves Lisa, after the folk-magic of Balwant and Catholic ritual of Father Thomas have failed to do so, thus inverting Clover's schematic in a significant way.

What makes *Raaz 2* the most interesting of the three films is the degree to which it initially slavishly adheres to Clover's schematic, but then turns the expectations of audiences familiar with Western horror films against them. Initially, the Yash-Nandita relationship very obviously parallels those heterosexual couplings at the heart of films like *Witchboard*, or, more recently, any of the *Paranormal Activity* films. Yash is a skeptic who makes his living debunking claims that there is life after death, and he insists that Nandita's salvation will be found in science and psychiatry. His presence, however, is countered by that of Prithvi, whose mystical visions reinforce the reality of the terrifying, numinous world with which Nandita has unwittingly come into contact. In this case, however, it is Yash's destruction, not his conversion, that finally allows for Nandita's salvation, thereby paving the way for a return to the conventional, heterosexual dyadic couple.

Another highly significant difference between these possession narratives and those that Clover considered (and, insofar as we are aware, every American possession-horror film produced in the last ten years) is the identity and motivations of the possessive entity. *The Exorcist* suggestively situates the origins of the evil that will take possession of Regan's body in its opening frames. Father Merrin witnesses a series of potentially mundane, but quite disturbing, events as he moves toward an archaeological dig site in Iraq. The shift of focus from this locale to the United States is precipitated by Merrin, and by extension the viewer, as he lays his eyes on the phallic statue of Pazuzu, an ancient Babylonian deity. The film's invading force, then, implicitly comes from the East, in a conventional gesture which could be called — following Creed's logic — the monstrous-oriental. In traditional Bollywood horror narratives, however, this tropic movement is often inverted, with the threatening force being portrayed as something which comes from a decadent and dangerous West — the monstrous-occidental.[43] In each Bollywood film considered here, however, it is not a generic, demonic force which possesses these women, but a volitional and (at least arguably) moral revenant with a particular agenda inspired by a sense of justice. For example, the eponymous spirit of *Bhoot* seeks retribution for Manjeet's unfair death, which results from her attempt to avoid being sexually assaulted. The possessive entity in *1920* similarly seeks revenge on the descendants of those who hung him, as well as the modern architects who refuse to preserve traditional order by maintaining the *haveli* in its original historic state.[44] In *Raaz 2* as well, Nandita is not possessed by demonic forces, but by the spirit of an outraged man who seeks revenge, specifically for the illegal and highly dangerous environmental exploitation (instigated by a white American) that led to his death, through serially killing everyone either involved in or aware of the plot to cover up his own murder.

The cultural differences that underlie these narrative disparities are considered by Frederick M. Smith in *The Self Possessed*. Smith indicates the tremendous difference between the possession narrative in Western cinema, where it is almost invariably associated with the horror genre, and in South Asian cinema, where it features in a much wider generic distribution. Contrasting the film *Paheli* (The Riddle, 2005) with the American film *The Exorcism of Emily Rose*, he writes that

> [i]n the Hindi film, *Paheli*, the wife is seduced by a *bhut* (spirit) who falls in love with her.... Almost as casually as *Emily Rose* replicates Western assumptions of selfhood and fixed identity, *Paheli* illustrates the Indian (and other Asian) recognition of selfhood as mutable, multidimensional, nonlinear and (at least in Buddhism) fabricated, a moving part among other moving parts. The *bhut* maintains his self-posesssion, his own identity as *bhut* (the wife also knows this — it's their great secret), aware that he has instigated his own construction.... We also see in *Paheli* a striking sympathy for the character of the *bhut*, a portrayal of possession that would not be possible in Western cinema, except perhaps as comedy.[45]

As in *Paheli*, the possessing entities in *Bhoot*, *1920*, and *Raaz 2* similarly gain sympathy from the audience when the motives for their possessions are finally revealed.

Nonetheless, despite these major (cultural) differences regarding the origins of evil and motives for possession, all three films include tropes of Western possession films in a manner which suggests a clear shift in intended audience. While *Raaz 2*'s retention of the traditional element of the song-and-dance interlude might suggest an intended audience familiar with and accepting of the conventions of Bollywood, both *Bhoot* and *1920* are *soi-disant* attempts to adapt the conventions of Western horror film for both diasporic South Asian and Western audiences. Although *Bhoot*'s ostensible critique of traditional gender roles may go hand in hand with its director's rejection of traditional Bollywood cinema, and his openly expressed pursuit of Western cinematic and auteurist models, this direct imitation is less clearly the case for *1920*. Nonetheless, much of the film appears to be an homage to the early British Hammer Studios-style of period Gothic: an interesting dissonance is created by its claim to be set in late nineteenth- / early twentieth-century India, while simultaneously calling constant visual attention to the spatial locus where it is shot — a palatial estate in Yorkshire, England — which Bhatt has described as "the true protagonist of the film."[46]

The invading alterity of the film's haunted estate and its (female, human) protagonist are mutually reinforcing. Geetanjali Gangoli has considered the "representations of the Anglo-Indian woman, the Christian woman, the modern westernised woman" in Indian cinema, and she argues that "in popular Hindi films [they] form a continuum of experiences and representations of a 'type' of woman, the other of the Hindu middle-class woman, the good wife and mother."[47] Gangoli identifies the most popular "representations of the vamp and the western(ised) woman in Hindi films through the 1970s to the present in at least three discrete, yet connected ways: the vamp as Anglo-Asian; as marginal Indian, yet westernised; and, the vamp as metaphor represented in the body of the heroine."[47] Despite her initially sympathetic portrayal and her lack of characteristically vampy seductiveness, *1920*'s Lisa looks back to these representations in a way that Swati and Nandita do not.

Indeed, Lisa's portrayal as a Westernized woman is largely indissociable from her status as a viable object for possession, and this portrayal is linked to *1920*s historico-political theme. The film makes it is difficult *not* to recognize in the "colonization" of a (marginally British) woman's body by invasive spirits a metonymic inversion of India's colonial history.[48] In this respect, *1920* also inverts at least one dimension of Clover's schematic by linking Lisa's vulnerability to her "white" (British, Christian,) identity, which modifies the religious terms of narrative conflict. In part because of this inversion, *1920* joins *Bhoot* and *Raaz 2* in situating possession within an Indian cultural and national matrix. In each case, the possessing entity is, perhaps ironically, an occult colonizing force from within that resists more mundane incursions of cultural imperialism from without.

Despite the presence of this matrix, if we consider the relationship between the representation of the possessed women in these films, the audiences at which these films are aimed, and the cultural conditions of their production, an "opening up" of the bodies of these films' female protagonists is suggested — one that parallels not only the "opening up" of Bollywood filmmaking to a wider diasporic and international audience, but also the "opening up" of South Asian history and culture to new mass media configurations. For instance, in contrast to Clover's claims regarding Western horror, *Bhoot, 1920,* and *Raaz 2* are not based primarily in male identification, nor intended for an exclusively male audience. While Clover claims that "[t]he cultural observer hoping for signs of change in the representation of females and femininity will find little satisfaction in the female story, the spectacular story, of occult horror,"[49] Isabelle Cristina Pinedo has argued that the "horror film speaks both to women and about them, often by articulating the legitimacy of female rage in the face of male aggression and by providing forms of pleasure for female viewers."[50] In light of Pinedo's claim, although the three films each explore a male crisis through the body of a woman, rendering her a vessel or victim to the problems of the men around her, they also suggest a new notion of womanhood that starkly contrasts previous representations of women in South Asian horror, as well as articulating an "opening up" of female independence and agency by encouraging more active female audience identification. This marks a sharp departure from earlier horror films of the 1960s, 70s, and 80s (particularly those made by the Ramsay brothers), where the locus was more markedly and exclusively the male voyeuristic gaze, and women were more uniformly presented as vamps, witches, or temptresses to satisfy this gaze.

Writing specifically of *Aitraaz* (Objection, 2004), but also of a general trend in Bombay cinema in the early 2000s, Purna Chowdhury claims that "[i]n contrast to the restrictions placed on the heroine of the nineties, the films of the next decade generate strategic rhetorical means for upper/middle-class women for asserting their presence in the local/global scenario."[51] This shift in paradigm with regards to female sexuality has occurred in tandem with Bollywood's desire to globalize and gain international audiences and recognition — one that erases the "traditional demarcating line between the vamp and the heroine in Hindi films of the pre-globalization era."[52] Chowdhury suggests that when approached from this angle, "the gender matrix of 'Bollywood' may well offer insights into the changing modalities of Indian national identity and a redefinition of what may be termed the Indo-feminine in a global cultural context."[53]

We would like to bring Chowdhury's point to bear while returning to Laura Mulvey's classic and oft-contested conception of the cinema as having "structures of fascination strong enough to allow temporary loss of ego while simultaneously reinforcing it."[54] For, while it is tempting to interpret cinematic presentations of possession as grotesque emblems of the colonization of the woman's body by the male gaze (which Mulvey sees as the master trope of Hollywood narrative cinema), it must be borne in mind that possession in Bollywood cinema, as in South Asian culture more broadly, is a much more variable and nuanced affair than Clover's paradigmatic Western possession narratives might suggest. As Smith emphasizes, in South Asian culture, "possession is simultaneously utopian and dystopian; this dialogic quality is the *sine qua non* of its body politic."[55] In light of this, Bollywood's re-openings of the occult possession narrative may present a much more capacious metaphorical model for spectatorship than either Mulvey or Clover's analyses suggest. Smith defines possession in South Asian culture — as experienced outside the realm of cinematic fiction — as being "a state of tension, of lived irony, in which dilemmas are resolved (for better or worse) because the volition of the dominant, socially hegemonic voice is reduced to the point of disappearance as another authority is expressed through the body."[56] This depiction parallels Mulvey's conception of cinema's power to produce "temporary ego loss," reinforcing the link between cases of non-fictional possession and the privileged place possession has within cinematic narratives, as a figuration of the effects of film spectatorship itself.

However, unlike Mulvey's profoundly pessimistic analysis of Hollywood film narrative, Smith's conception of possession leaves room for a great deal of variation and adaptation, and can thus be of great use to us as both a heuristic and pedagogical tool for coming to terms with possession narratives. Smith's emphasis on the variability of possession as a cultural phenomenon can provide students (in the broadest possible sense of the word) of not only Indian but also international possession films with one way to avoid the binaristic trap that often dominates ideological film criticism. In her essay "Paradoxes of Spectatorship," Judith Mayne has aptly cautioned against the impulse to categorize films "as either conservative or radical, as celebratory of the dominant culture of critical of it,"[57] and we share her conviction that there can be no "simple division between the cinema that functions as an instrument of dominant ideology, and the cinema that facilitates the challenges to it."[58] We both work to bring this recognition into our classrooms: whether we are engaging with these films as part of the international field of horror, or as part of South Asian or diasporic studies, it can be useful to counterbalance our students' (and our own) tendency to demonize or valorize cinema for the pleasures it offers, with the ideological and cultural work to which these pleasures are necessarily indexed. For Geetanjali Gangoli is surely right in her assertion, following Mulvey, that "cinema does more than reflect existing values in society. It also plays a vital role in creating, legitimising and entrenching identities."[58] However, it does so in a way that is — as Smith observes of possession as cultural phenomena — both utopian and dystopian, and which must be constantly "opened up" to acts of spectatorial and critical re-possession.

NOTES

1. Carol J. Clover, *Men, Women and Chainsaws: Gender in the Modern Horror Film* (Princeton, NJ: Princeton University Press, 1992), 65–113.

2. Examples of films made since the turn of the twenty-first century that embrace this trope are *The Exorcism of Emily Rose* (2005), *Mirrors* (2008), *REC* (2007) and, to a slightly lesser degree, its American remake, *Quarantine* (2008), *Paranormal Activity* (2009) and its sequel (2010), and *The Last Exorcism* (2010).

3. It is worth noting that this essay was sparked by such student interest. During a section of a second year English course which presents a survey of horror fiction, I (Moreland) was introducing the class to some of Clover's formulations. During our discussion, a number of students raised the question of the cultural specificity or universality of Clover's depictions of the slasher and occult possession subgenres, a question which generated considerable (and to my pleasure, generally well-informed) debate. This debate later led to a long conversation with my coauthor Summer Pervez, to whom I owe a debt of gratitude for providing my initial "crash course" in South Asian horror films a few years ago. This discussion led to a mutual resolution to collaboratively examine this, and related, questions.

4. Clover, 86.

5. Sangita Gopal, "Sentimental Symptoms: The Films of Karan Johar and Bombay Cinema," in Rini Bhattacharya Mehta and Rajeshwari V. Panharipande, eds., *Bollywood and Globalization: Indian Popular Cinema, Nation, and Diaspora* (New York: Anthem Press, 2010), 16, 20.

6. Rini Bhattacharya Mehta, "Bollywood, Nation, Globalization: An Incomplete Introduction," in Mehta and Panharipande, eds., *Bollywood and Globalization*, 1–2.

7. Gautam Basu Thakur, "Globalization and the Cultural Imaginary: Constructions of Subjectivity, Freedom, & Enjoyment in Popular Indian Cinema," *Bollywood and Globalization*, in Mehta and Panharipande, eds., 75.

8. Gopal, 18.

9. Mehta and Panharipande, 6.

10. Mehta and Panharipande, 5–7.

11. Pete Tombs, "The Beast from Bollywood: A History of the Indian Horror Film," Steven Jay Schneider, ed., *Fear Without Frontiers: Horror Cinema Across the Globe*, (London: FAB Press, 2003). Tombs briefly notes some of the reasons for this lack of attention, explaining that in India, "the term horror denotes something very specific": in short, mush-faced monster costumes, producers' busty trophy girlfriends screaming unconvincingly, shoestring budgets, negligible acting, and (often bungled) startle-scenes. These associations, of course, still cling to horror films the world over for many viewers and critics, but not to the same stultifying extent that they do for Indian audiences. In Tombs' memorable phrase, to bring up horror films in Bollywood film circles has been "almost the same as announcing that you are a half-wit." See Tombs, 243, 253.

12. Tombs, 245.

13. Gopal, 16.

14. Smith explains that *Bhutavidya* is "the *vidya* (science) of *bhutas* (existent beings), most of which are invisible or assumed to be inhabiting other beings," 472.

15. Quoted in Amit S. Rai, *Untimely Bollywood: Globalization and India's New Media Assemblage* (Duke: London, 2009), 6, 110.

16. Tombs, 244.

17. See Frederick M. Smith, *The Self Possessed: Deity and Spirit Possession in South Asian Literature and Civilization* (New York: Columbia University Press, 2006), 273.

18. Tombs, 244. Tombs' claim that *The Exorcist* has a "story seemed tailor made for Indian tastes," free of "explicit sex," has at least one notable exception: midway through the film, Regan is told by the spirit possessing her, "Let Jesus fuck you," and she proceeds to do so with a cross, followed by a command to her mother, "Lick me!." This visual is certainly sexually explicit in its presentation, even though certain actions take place either beneath the camera's frame line or partially hidden from the viewer.

19. Barbara Creed, *The Monstrous Feminine* (London: Routledge, 1993). It could be argued that this is one of the ways Friedkin's film departs slightly from Blatty's novelistic treatment of the story; while the film largely retains the juxtaposition of Father Karras's struggles with both his faith and his elderly mother with Chris's struggle with Regan's possession, it effectively amplifies the latter relationship. If our experiences of watching the film with both friends and students are any indication, for most of the film's audience, it is Chris's suffering for her daughter that most effectively grounds its grotesque effects in an emotional reality.

20. Clover, 71. Clover's observation, that the vast majority of possession victims in horror films are women, remains accurate and this tendency has even intensified, rather than changed, in the decades since her article was written. More recent examples include *The Exorcism of Emily Rose* (2005), in which the gendering of the narrative closely parallels the Anneliese Michel case on which it was loosely based, *The Last Exorcism* (2010), *Paranormal Activity* (2009), and its sequel *Paranormal Activity 2* (2010).

21. Clover, 67.
22. Smith, 68.
23. Clover, 79.
24. Clover, 109.
25. There are many uncanny parallels between the various terms in South Asian languages including Sanskrit, Pali, Hindi, and Urdu for spirit possession and the language of sexual intercourse, and both are equally inflected by notions of domination. See, on the one hand, Smith's account of such terms, which he prefaces by writing that "language after language in South Asia has terms for riding, mounting, and so on that are characteristic of possession, preponderantly women's possession" (69). And on the other, the famous seventh chapter of Andrea Dworkin's *Intercourse*, which iterates the parallels between the language of human sexuality and that of possession/domination: "*Violation* is a synonym for intercourse. At the same time, the penetration is taken to be a use, not an abuse; a normal use; it is appropriate to enter her, to push into ("violate") the boundaries of her body. She is human, of course, but by a standard that does not include physical privacy. She is, in fact, human by a standard that precludes physical privacy, since to keep a man out altogether and for a lifetime is deviant in the extreme, a psychopathology, a repudiation of the way in which she is expected to manifest her humanity." See Andrea Dworkin, *Intercourse* (New York: Basic Books, 2007).

26. This quasi-feminist subtext links *Bhoot* generically to the rape-revenge subgenre Clover considers in the third chapter of *Men, Women and Chainsaws*.

27. This malevolent spirit is eventually revealed to be the soul of a treasonous solider who was hanged outside the *haveli* in 1857, during the Sepoy Mutiny, which explicitly links Lisa's possession with India's history of "possession" by the British.

28. Julia Kristeva, *Powers of Horror* (New York: Columbia, 1982), 4, and Barbara Creed, "Horror and the Monstrous Feminine: An Imaginary Abjection," in *The Dread of Difference: Gender and the Horror Film*. Ed. Barry Keith Grant (Austin: Univ of Texas Press, 1996), 36.

29. The friend's words, spoken in English, are ironic given the plight Nandita is about to face: "I know you really love him but [...] you know, it's so important to have *your own identity* today."

30. Clover, 112.
31. Clover, 65.
32. Clover, 70.
33. In the former, the inner story is that of Father Karras' tormented spiritual crisis and awakening, and in the latter, the story is less about Linda's entrapment than Jim's transformation from a failed student (he is a medical school dropout) into a worthy friend and groom. See Clover, 85–86.

34. Clover, 85.
35. It is worth noting that, in this respect at least, *The Exorcist* deviates from the template

it also cinematically inaugurates, as it is Regan's mother, and not a husband, father, or boyfriend, who plays this mediatory role.

36. Rediff: India Abroad Interview, http://specials.rediff.com/movies/2008/jul/16sli1.htm.

37. Smith (277) notes that Hanuman is one of the Hindu deities most frequently associated with the exorcism of unwanted possessing spirits, perhaps because he is "a deity whose connections to humans are felt to be closer than those of many other deities."

38. In the film's final scenes, the spirit moves into Yash's body in order to kill him. Why Vir Pratap Singh does not target Yash directly from the start, as he does other figures like David Cooper who are also involved in the scheme, remains a mystery. A woman's body is used as a conduit for no real reason, showing adherence to Clover's "standard scheme" of the American occult possession film.

39. Regan's experimentation with the *Ouija* board involves a great deal of pushing, rubbing, and fingering—not to mention dialogic exchange with a seemingly masculine "spirit" named "Captain Howdy"—all of which surely reinforces the recognition of Clover, Creed and others that the monstrosity presented by the film is linked to the young Regan's burgeoning sexuality, at the onset of puberty.

40. Clover, 66.

41. This is as close as *Bhoot*, in this respect a supremely traditional possession film, comes to showing a male character possessed by a spirit. As mentioned above, *Raaz 2* has a similar moment at its end, where Vir Pratap's spirit leaves Nandita's body and to possess Yash briefly.

42. The fact that the occupying spirit is nominally female does little to displace the thematic Clover identified in Western possession films. However, it does show an interest in the history, agency, and identity of the possessing spirit itself which often distinguishes Hindu from Western possession narratives, a point to which we shall return.

43. In terms of its treatment of this trope, Varma's *Bhoot* differs most revealingly from both *1920* and *Raaz 2*; this difference clearly reflects the director's attitude toward both Bollywood and filmmaking in general.

44. This is a socially conservative agenda that, in effect, is paralleled by the entity's punishment of Arjun's non-traditional marriage through the possession of his Christian wife. This is an ironic turn of events, given the British loyalties of the soldier during his pre-*bhut* incarnation.

45. Smith, xvi.

46. See "Haunted House the Real Protagonist in *1920*," interview with MSN Entertainment. India Syndicate. August 9, 2008. http://entertainment.in.msn.com/bollywood/article.aspx?cp-documentid=3024229.

47. Geetanjali Gangoli, "Sexuality, Sensuality and Belonging: Representations of the 'Anglo-Indian' and the 'Western' Woman in Hindi Cinema," in Raminder Kaur and Ajay J. Sinha, eds., *Bollyworld: Popular Indian Cinema through a Transnational Lens* (New Delhi: Sage Publications, 2005), 147.

48. Gangoli, 144.

49. Clover, 105.

50. For more on the link between (post)colonial history and certain key horror film tropes, see Isabel Cristina Pinedo's *Recreational Terror: Women and the Pleasures of Horror Film Viewing* (Albany, NY: SUNY Press, 1997), 119.

51. Purna Chowdhury, "Bollywood Babes: Body and Female Desire in the Bombay Films Since the Nineties and *Darr, Mohra*, and *Aitraaz*: A Tropic Discourse" in Mehta and Panharipande, 65.

52. Chowdhury, 70.

53. Chowdhury, 51.

54. Laura Mulvey, "Visual Pleasure and Narrative Cinema," in Vincent Leitch, ed., *The Norton Anthology of Theory and Criticism*, (New York: Norton, 2001), 2185.

55. Smith, 586.

56. Smith, 587.

57. Judith Mayne, "Paradoxes of Spectatorship," in Linda Williams, eds., *Viewing Positions: Ways of Seeing Film* (New Jersey: Rutgers, 1995), 182.

58. Mayne, 176.

59. Gangoli, 145.

Beyond the Lure: Teaching Horror, Teaching Theory
Brian Johnson

A Personal Inventory

My teaching of horror fiction has always been haunted by the spectre of "theory." When I first taught ghost stories to undergraduates in an introduction to literature course, I did so alongside excerpts from Vladmir Propp's "The Morphology of the Folk Tale" (1927) and Tzevtan Todorov's *The Fantastic* (1975). The goals of this convergence were, first, to puncture my students' psychological-realist ideas about character so that they might approach it as a functional unit within the morphology of literary subgenres and, second, to get them thinking more technically about the role played by form in the production of readerly affect. One popular assignment option was for students to write their own ghost story based upon Todorov's description of either the "'pure' fantastic" or the "fantastic-marvelous" tale and to complicate it through strategic violations of some of the conventional ghost story character-functions that the class had collectively theorized after reading and comparing a number of primary texts. As this early attempt on my part to bring horror fiction into the classroom showed me, it was difficult to approach the teaching of horror to undergraduates without at the same time introducing them to fundamental questions about genre formation, structuralism, and narratology. This is in part because the genre itself can to some extent be understood as a technical exercise in the production and intensification of specific readerly affects through the manipulation of conventional motifs, narrative form, and point-of-view. But it is also because the flagrantly "popular" thrills that affect-rich texts like horror stories produce left many students — and, indeed, at the time, me too — unclear about how to talk about them, how to speculate about what, beyond their technical achievements in producing the pleasure of a good shudder, such fictions might "mean."

This question of how to discuss the "meaning" of horror fiction with undergraduates became the focus of my second, more substantial turn towards teaching horror a number of years later, this time in the context of an upper-year honors seminar entitled "Critical Approaches to the Fantastic." Here, after rehearsing a range of debates over generic definitions of "horror," "Gothic," "the uncanny," "fantasy," and "the fantastic" (and its neighbors), with reference to all the usual suspects — H. P. Lovecraft, Sigmund Freud, Todorov, Rosemary Jackson, and Noël Carroll — we moved into the kinds of psychoanalytical and politically inflected modes of interpretation that were advertised in the course title as "Critical Approaches to...." Whereas previously the focus had been on genre as a mechanism for the production of affect, now it moved increasingly towards mapping the unruliness of the genre's psychic economies and towards grasping the ideological slipperiness of its various and often conflicting treatments of gender, sexuality, class, race, age, nationality, and history — those critical coordinates that have defined the "-isms" of politically inflected literary and cultural theory for the last several decades.

What became apparent in my second stab at teaching horror through the lens of assorted "critical theories" was that, as useful as theory was for framing questions and for providing a point of entry into the interpretation of horror texts, the reverse was also true. As we worked through the theoretical perspectives on Bram Stoker's *Dracula* offered by the Bedford Critical Edition of that text, or analyzed *Alien* as a horror film alongside readings on the abject from Julia Kristeva or Barbara Creed, students were as excited about the principles of psychoanalytic cultural criticism as they were about our "primary" texts themselves. Learning about both the theory and the primary texts was, of course, an intrinsic goal of the class. But as the seminar proceeded, my then somewhat vague instinct that horror was at least as useful for teaching theory as theory was for teaching horror was repeatedly reaffirmed in ways that made me wonder about the unusually tight fit between these two seemingly quite different modes of writing and thought.

On the one hand, the differences between these two modes of discourse seem both vast and self-evident. The meta-principle of the course reinforced this sense of a gap between them, for it was concerned with teaching students to respect what Derek Attridge, in a brilliant book of the same name, calls "the singularity of literature," which is to say its fundamental resistance to the instrumental reductionism that all theoretical approaches, even very sophisticated ones, ultimately force texts to undergo in the act of interpreting them and making them speak in the service of some unfolding critical "project."[1] For this reason, I had never encouraged students to "apply" theory to the texts according to the notorious and justly derided "cookie-cutter technique" of miraculously finding what one seeks in every reading; rather, I tried to model for students how one must listen to the questions that texts themselves pose (either explicitly or by implication), learn to be attentive to how they answer — or refuse to answer — these questions, and, finally, engage in the ethical and political work of historicizing those answers, evasions, and enigmas, while also asking what they might mean to us as contemporary readers. The role of "theory" in all this, I suggested to them, was to help refine the sensitivity of our ears when listening for these textually generated questions, answers, and aporias ("what are we listening *for*?"), while at the same time making our operational assumptions explicit, thereby opening our interpretations to genuine and more searching (self-) scrutiny and debate ("how and why are we listening in the first place?").

On the other hand, despite these caveats and precautions about the pitfalls of simply imposing readings on the texts we study and reducing them to "illustrations" of whatever theoretical approach we happen to have adopted, or whatever political or aesthetic project we happen to be pursuing, I continued to be struck by the unusually fertile interplay between horror and theory in the classroom. Although they remained separate entities, defined by their own discursive rules and, at times, by profoundly incongruous ideological investments, both seemed nonetheless to enjoy similar, mutually reinforcing powers in their capacity to generate critical thought about the relation between authors, readers, texts, and the world. Thus, if my earliest effort at teaching horror was in some sense "haunted" by theory, my second attempt suggested that "hunted" might be a better way of characterizing the relationship between horror and theory in my classroom practice.

Since 2009, my teaching of horror texts has been almost fully overtaken by the theoretical impulse that has nipped at its heels since my very first attempts to discuss M. R. James and W. W. Jacobs with my students. Horror texts now constitute privileged objects of engagement in my second-year methodologies course entitled "Theory and Criticism," the general purpose of which is to prepare English majors for advanced literary study by giving them a practical introduction to theories and methods of literary and cultural analysis. As in most classes of this sort (which have become a staple of undergraduate English programs since the 1980s), its syllabus and assignments are designed with several specific goals in mind: (1) to make students more self-reflexive about their critical practices while introducing them to a range of theoretical fields and approaches; (2) to help them bridge the gap between abstract theorizing and the practical business of doing literary and cultural criticism; and (3) to provide students with a sense of disciplinary history while introducing them to the current debates over literary value and critical praxis. My aim in what follows is to explain why and how I have found horror texts so useful as a means of fulfilling such pedagogical aims, but also to suggest ways in which such an engagement with horror in the undergraduate theory classroom turns out to be more complex than it initially appears. Rather than simply providing an arbitrary sounding board for theoretically informed habits of reading, horror texts reveal a fundamental affinity with the assumptions, preoccupations, and critical orientations of much contemporary theory. For this reason, the border between the teaching of horror and the teaching of theory, like the seeping and ambiguous ontological boundaries that characterize the horror genre's ghoulish antagonists, proves to be astonishingly porous.

My argument resembles that recently advanced about a different genre by Carl Freedman in *Critical Theory and Science Fiction* (2000), wherein he traces "certain *structural* affinities" between critical theory and science fiction, arguing that "each is a version of the other"[2] and contending that their "conjunction ... is not fortuitous but fundamental."[3] Freedman's defense of science fiction as the "unconsciously" privileged genre of post–Kantian critical theory[4] usefully defines critical theory as "dialectical" and "unswervingly oppositional" in its characteristic gesture of "dissolving the reified static categories of the ideological status quo" thereby "show[ing] that things are not what they seem to be *and* that things need not eternally be as they are."[5] To the extent that Freedman's privileged categories of Marxism, psychoanalysis, and "postdialectical" (poststructuralist) thought all embrace "historical mutability, material reducibility, and utopian possibility,"[6] they, along with the numerous critiques of gender, race, and sexuality that have emerged in conversation with them, exemplify Freedman's claim that critical theory "maintains the cutting edge of social subversion even at its most rarified and abstract."[7] It is against this backdrop that Freedman aptly praises science fiction in terms first set forth by Darko Suvin as a "literature of cognitive estrangement"[8] where stylistic and narratological features fictionally replicate the cognitively estranging operations that are fundamental to critical theory's own "cutting edge of social subversion." But, as is typical of genre-based studies, Freedman's favors exceptionalism over catholicity in its estimation of the value of the wider generic landscape. Thus, it gives horror (or at least its nearest "official" generic representative, the Gothic) rather short shrift when it praises SF as the paradigmatic literature of "cognitive estrangement" but dismisses "the irrationalist estrangements of fantasy or Gothic literature" on the grounds that they "may secretly work to ratify the mundane status quo by presenting no alternative to the latter other than inexplicable discontinuities."[9] There could be no better illustration of Jason Colavito's canny observation that "[m]any science fiction scholars claim that sci-fi is a cognitive and philosophical genre while horror is purely emotional, with the implication that this is a lesser state."[10]

My own experience of reading horror has been, on the whole, closer to

Colavito's view that "horror has its own philosophy and cognitive pleasures"[11] something that has been borne out in the classroom where I have found that the estranging function of horror remains profoundly valuable as a means of awakening students to fundamental issues of direct concern to critical theory, regardless of whether or not horror can claim to rival SF in being "[o]f all genres ... the one *most* devoted to the historical concreteness and rigorous self-reflectiveness of critical theory"[12] in the arena of dueling genres and academic subspecialties.

This does not mean, however, that horror is, as Freedman maintains of science fiction, "unswervingly" oppositional; it isn't. But nor is it "unswervingly" reactionary. Jackson is correct when she argues, in her classic study of fantasy, that "[a]lthough nearly all literary fantasies eventually re-cover desire, neutralizing their own impulses towards transgression, some move towards the extreme position ... [of] attempt[ing] to remain 'open,' dissatisfied, endlessly desiring."[13] This position is echoed by Carroll's reluctance to account for the persistence of horror on any ideological ground — either that "the creations of the horror genre are always politically repressive" or that they are "always emancipatory (politically subversive)"[14] — since persuasive examples can be adduced for either case, and since, further, "many horror fictions seem too indeterminate from a political point of view to be correlated with any specific ideological theme,"[15] I argue that it is precisely horror's ideological unevenness (across texts) and ambivalence (within a single text), coupled with its powerful evocations of transgression and excess, that make it particularly well-suited to introducing undergraduates to the challenging work of reading for and against ideology that is fundamental to all forms of contemporary political criticism.

What follows is a selective overview of my course in "Theory and Criticism" that highlights the dialectical relationship between teaching horror and teaching theory, while also foregrounding several key moments in the course's meta-narrative, which is ultimately organized around teaching the debate over interpretation currently unfolding within the humanities over the nature and function of literature as such, and therefore also over how we should read it. This debate between proponents of "aesthetic" and "political" approaches to textual study emerged in the 1990s as a reaction against "political" theory's storming of the ivory tower, and has typically (and in some ways incorrectly) been understood as the defensive gesture of a beleaguered formalist *arrière-garde*. What the "ideological" study of horror helps students in my methodologies course to explore is how the polarization of this disciplinary debate into a contest between a complacent and politically naïve "formalism" on the one hand and a reductionist and aesthetically naïve mode of "ideology critique" or textual "utopianism" on the other offers us a false choice that fundamentally misconstrues the relationship between textual politics (ideology) and literary form.

Because horror texts offer such visceral and spectacular cognitive estrangements in their presentation of monstrosity, transgression, and excess, while at the same time varying widely in the manner in (and degree to) which they frame and manage these "oppositional" moments, such texts constitute an ideal proving ground for the rigorous study of how the "meaning" of any given horror text in political/ideological terms is inseparable from the specificity of its formal demands. I will elaborate this claim briefly by pointing to some of the uses to which several exemplary texts might be put in the classroom: Amelia B. Edwards' "The Phantom Coach" (1864), M. R. James' "The Rose Garden" (1911) and "An Episode of Cathedral History" (1914), W. W. Jacobs' "The Monkey's Paw" (1902), and Edith Nesbit's "Man-Size in Marble" (1893).

I. Tackling the "Whatever"

Those of us who teach literary and cultural theory to undergraduates have all, at one time or another, been greeted by three principal student objections: theory is too difficult; theory is too abstract; theory is boring. Taken together, these reservations define the parameters of the pedagogical challenge that has come to be known in academic discussion as "the resistance to theory."[16] To be sure, these are not the only objections students make to theory, and many student objections are astute, politically informed, and productive.[17] However, prior to the kinds of interventions that students make along these lines in the theory classroom, one remains confronted with the bedrock of resistance delineated by these three objections. The first two objections are cognitive: one pertains to intelligibility (comprehension), the other to utility (praxis). The third pertains to affect and amounts to an exasperated "whatever!" in the face of objections one and two. What that third objection records, in other words, is a defensive recoil from the threat of appearing "stupid," a cluster of affects that Dianne F. Sadoff usefully summarizes as "frustration, depression, intellectual and emotional overload ... [and] anxiety."[18] Such a response to encountering theory for the first time is common, for there are few intellectual challenges more dispiriting, anxiety-provoking, or potentially humiliating for bright undergraduate English majors than being asked suddenly to master texts that are difficult to understand, even after careful rereading, much less bring them to bear upon the study and interpretation of the kinds of texts that have drawn these students to the study of literature in the first place. Within this context, the dismissive "whatever" of objection three amounts to hollow bravado in the face of real anxiety, and it is this state of intellectual shut-down that is both the most immediate challenge to and the greatest opportunity for the development of a pedagogy that would excite students about theory, while at the same time training them to become better readers of the literary texts they already value.

It is specifically to tackle this "whatever" that I employ horror fiction as a lure to teach theory. Without for a moment denying the need to employ specific pedagogical methods for enabling students to gain confidence in grappling with difficult, frequently interdisciplinary, primary readings in theory and for helping them reflect on how they might employ the insights they glean from these readings to enrich their own critical practice,[19] the obvious advantage of using horror fiction to help teach theory to relatively uninitiated undergraduates is that, in the vast majority of cases, the average student's interest in reading horror fiction is inversely proportional to their interest in deciphering the obscurities of French structuralism or deconstruction. In my experience, most students are interested in horror, even if they do not identify as fans; and if they do find the stories of M. R. James and H. P. Lovecraft anxiety-provoking, it is usually in the paradoxically pleasurable sense that Carroll identifies as "be[ing] attracted by what is repulsive."[20] The ironical use of a fear-based genre like horror to teach *through* student anxiety about theory is thus of no incidental importance. By thematizing and even in some instances generating pleasurable fear, horror texts both obliquely reference and help to model (at the level of readerly affect) precisely the kind of transformation that the course is designed to enable within students themselves over the duration of the term in relation to their initial recoil and subsequent diminishing of anxiety around the "horror" of reading and working with theory.

What this means in practice is that careful reading, comparison, and classroom discussion of horror texts (often with the help of study questions) typically precedes the reading and exposition of theory. Thus, for instance, at the beginning of the course, a selection of ghost stories by Amelia B. Edwards ("The Phantom Coach"), J. S. LeFanu ("Dickon the Devil"), Bram Stoker ("The Judge's House"), M. R. James ("The Rose Garden," "Oh, Whistle, and I'll Come to You, My Lad"), E. G. Swain ("Bone to His Bone"), and Algernon Blackwood ("The Willows") furnishes students with an archive that they are then called upon to account for in generic terms. If these stories are representative of a "genre," then what are their common features? On what basis has an editor selected them for inclusion in within an anthology of *Great Ghost Stories*? How do they differ from works (like *Hamlet*, say, or *Macbeth*) that feature ghosts, but do not seem easily assimilable to this body of writing?

Working through induction and a species of "concept learning" that recalls cognitive psychologist Jerome Bruner's method of conceptualizing categories through the comparison of similarities and differences, students try their hand at becoming genre theorists[21] prior to reading selections from Vladimir Propp's "The Morphology of the Folk Tale," which employs a similar comparativist approach to determining literary forms of categorization. Thereafter, these stories become the basis for a close reading and detailed excursus of Todorov's structuralist approach to "the fantastic" and its neighboring genres, beginning with Edwards' "The Phantom Coach." The exemplary pedagogical nature of this tale is due both to the way it explicitly thematizes the "reality-testing" thesis that organizes Todorov's generic spectrum and to the way in which its narrative elements (plot, setting, character) illustrate this spectrum with a kind of diagrammatic precision that anticipates Todorov's own organization of generic differences in terms of a spatial metaphor of "adjacent realms," where "the fantastic in its pure state" is "a frontier," represented in Todorov's famous diagram "by the median line separating the fantastic-uncanny from the fantastic-marvelous:"[22]

Uncanny	fantastic-uncanny	fantastic-marvelous	marvelous

As we will see, this spectrum — because of its extremely useful attentiveness to a given story's disruptions and/or reaffirmations of "'reality' as it exists in the common opinion"[23] — subsequently becomes the foundation of the political and sociological methods of reading that we explore later in the term, methods which emphasize precisely this "structural" question of "reality-testing" in their focus on transgression, defamiliarization, and ideology.

What makes Edwards' story especially useful for teaching Todorov's distinctions between the fantastic and its neighboring subgenres[24] is its mapping of the epistemological theme of "reality-testing" onto the first-person narrator's literal movement across a symbolically freighted landscape, the nodes of which correspond directly to the three cardinal points of Todorov's generic compass:

1. the ordinary moor-side village of Dwolding where science and "'reality' as it exists in the common opinion" still hold sway and where mysterious events are explained away as merely "uncanny";
2. the isolated moorland home of "the master," a "visionary" "conjectural philosoph[er]"[25] who expounds upon the "marvelous" nature of reality after being exiled from the scientific world for his belief in ghosts; and finally,
3. the "fantastic" interstitial space of the moor itself, the space that is literally located between these two epistemologically defined loci where the protagonist ultimately has his encounter with the story's titular horror: a phantom mail coach filled with corpses in which he becomes an unwitting and ultimately credulous passenger.

As we trace the protagonist's movement — from the rational certainties of Dwolding where he is, prototypically, a "barrister-at-law"[26] to the epistemologically uncertain region of the moor itself (where he gets lost and a snow storm impedes his vision), to "the master's" house (where he takes shelter, only to be lectured by his host on the existence of ghosts and sent back out into the moors to meet the night-mail that will return him to Dwolding) — it becomes evident to students that the story's settings schematize a series of epistemological positions that the protagonist himself is in the process of navigating and that the story requires us to navigate along with him.

The intensification of motifs of obscured vision and "delayed decoding"[27] around the moments of incipient epistemological transition in "The Phantom Coach" enhance the story's pedagogical usefulness as an ad hoc allegory of Todorov's structural account of the fantastic-marvelous, the Todorovian subgenre of "the supernatural accepted" that becomes especially pertinent to our study of horror-fiction as the course unfolds.[28] The narrator's discovery of an enormous telescope on wheels in the master's barn — seemingly "the work of some self-taught optician"[29] — is paradigmatic of the subgenre's epistemological reversal, for this "huge object gauntly dressed in a dingy wrapping-cloth, and reaching half way to the rafters ... a telescope of very considerable size, mounted on a platform, with four small wheels"[30] symbolically anticipates the phantom coach — a conveyance into which the narrator eventually steps, encountering ghostly corpses and having his outlook on the nature of reality "as it exists in the common opinion" transfigured. The story, in other words, is self-theorizing: the mobile telescope and the phantom "night-mail" are metafictional tropes for the epistemologically "transporting" effect that this tale (and the fantastic-marvelous subgenre it exemplifies) is crafted to produce in readers subjected to a gradual confounding of "rational" explanations and compelled, through the accretion of evidence and suggestion, to affirm the diagetic necessity of supernatural causality in a story whose details and style are initially designed to affirm the opposite by at least paying lip-service to the notion that the focalizing characters and the implied-reader are both spiritually resident in the rationalistic epistemological enclave of Dwolding.

Students see the story's metafictional and self-theorizing dimension in the way Edwards makes the phantom coach a "night mail," so that the reader's and the narrator's epistemological "transport" becomes additionally identified with the postal tropology of message delivery. Within this context, the "message" posted by the diabolical master to the naively rationalistic society that spurned his belief in ghosts turns out, quite literally, to be the epistemologically transformed narrator himself. This connection, which makes the story into a kind of generic allegory as well as a demonstration of the fantastic-marvelous, is confirmed by the fact that the delirious narrator is identified, following his misadventures, by "the letters in [his] pocket-book."[31] He has functioned throughout the tale as a kind of letter: first misdelivered to the master's house after getting lost in a storm only to be marked "return to sender" by the master himself and sent back to Dwolding by a phantom mail coach, the experience of which rewrites his original message, turning him from a representative man of reason (a barrister) into an advocate for "the supernatural accepted." Reading Todorov in the wake of our mapping of the story's epistemological adventure, we are guided then by what we have already learned about the story's form and motifs, for what is a fantastic-marvelous tale in Todorov's account but a kind of unsettling postcard from an "adjacent" region that radically alters the reader's sense of the rules of the reality about which they have been reading?

As we examine and debate the manner in which other stories confirm, frustrate, or complicate this structure through their manipulation of action, setting, character, and narration, the first essay assignment asks students to hone their skills at structuralist close reading by unpacking the narrative and symbolic significance of what might be called threshold- or boundary-objects in the fantastic-marvelous ghost story. The pedagogical value of this exercise is first to allow students to explore how deeply the structural unity of these stories' formal construction runs, preparing them for the more complex task of mapping the ideological significance of form in the second half of the course. The study of threshold-objects also facilitates the class's transition from the spatial logic of Todorov's structuralist approach to genre to the more temporally oriented logic of psychoanalytic approaches to "the uncanny."

Threshold- or boundary-objects in ghost stories imply an overlap between the spatial and the temporal, since these artifacts, characters, and settings that function as meeting-points of greater or lesser intensity between epistemologically divergent "realms" are also typically marked by a powerful temporal inflection. Mysteriously engraved whistles, mezzotints, paintings, lockets, windows, ancient inns, even superstitious village elders — all of these narrative elements, whose function is the production of an uncanny affect in both readers and characters by virtue of their relation to the supernatural, evoke the double-structure of the fantastic-marvelous transition, condensing the spatial logic of "adjacent realms" into a concrete (or in some cases, diaphanous) figure whose ultimate referent is the epistemologically disruptive appearance of the ghost itself.

At the same time, ghost stories translate the spatial metaphor of fantastic-marvelous epistemological transformation into an uncanny structure that obeys the temporal logic of the revenant, what Freud famously identified, in psychoanalytical terms, as the *return* of the repressed; the ghost, in other words, like the uncanny threshold-objects that anticipate its arrival on the scene, organizes the convergence of epistemological "realms" around the problematic of temporality. Even if they are not always present, the preponderance of antiquarian artifacts that serve as points of supernatural cathexis in so many Victorian and Edwardian ghost stories is symptomatic of this doublestructure; when they appear, they vividly highlight the genre's structurally organizing opposition of epistemologically adjacent spaces by condensing these realms within a history-spanning artifact that makes the eruption of the supernatural into the quotidian resonate also with the notion of an uncanny return of the past.

The old oak post that is thoughtlessly uprooted by modernizing "improvers" in M. R. James' spectral satire of bourgeois vulgarity, "The Rose Garden," typifies this sort of boundary-object whose role is both rhetorically to anticipate and structurally to mirror the double-signification of the ghost itself: in both cases, the meeting of two adjacent realms (space) is made coincident with the "impossible" encounter between past and present (time). In James's story, the oak post (which, unbeknownst to the haunted protagonists is in fact a stake employed to lay the restless spirit of a Chief Justice from the era of Charles II), functions as a point of communication between the supernatural "realm" and the realm of "ordinary reality" in which the former is disavowed. It is at the post, prior to its uprooting, that an earlier generation of children had heard a ghostly transcript of the judge's bloody seventeenth-century trials; similarly, the uprooting of the post in the story's narrative present precipitates a return of this auditory phantom transcript in the bad dreams of the protagonists as well as precipitating the climactic appearance of the ghost itself.

Asking students to discuss the uprooted post as a symbol of the story's fantastic-marvelous structure complicates the dynamics of Todorov's spatially oriented generic spectrum. Compared to Todorov's original table, the post serves iconically as a new diagram showing the overlap between time and space within the generic structure of stories of this type (Fig. 1). As the uprooted post suggests, the structural logic of the story employs visual depth as its principle for demarcating the adjacent realms of a rationalistically construed ordinary reality (above ground) and an expanded conception of reality in which supernatural events become legible (below ground). Within this economy, the post functions as a symbol of both the superficial division of past and present inherent in the modern characters' historical myopia (above/below) and the deeper unity of historical totality that belies such blindness to the past when communication between the two realms is restored (staked/uprooted).

The relation between these two sets of symbolic oppositions is complex because the post's proper function within the story is boundary maintenance (exorcism), but within the original time of the laying of the ghost, the

```
┌─────────────────────────────────────────┐
│         above-ground section            │
│                                         │
│            "ordinary reality"           │
│      narrative present/ focalization    │
│                                         │
│                UNCANNY                  │
│         (supernatural denied)           │
│                                         │
│       conduit of mysterious events      │
│         epistemological hesitation      │
│                                         │
│               FANTASTIC                 │
│       (epistemological hesitation)      │
├─────────────────────────────────────────┤
│         below-ground section            │
│                                         │
│  hidden supernatural evidence for new reality │
├─────────────────────────────────────────┤
│                                         │
│   ghost originates in narrative past (history) │
│        and erupts into narrative present│
│                                         │
│              MARVELOUS                  │
│         (supernatural accepted)         │
│                                         │
│        Fig. 1 The Uprooted Oak Post     │
└─────────────────────────────────────────┘
```

upper/lower distinction would have implied a division between past and present that was functional (the "before" and "after" of the exorcism) not cognitive (ignorance of the past, disavowal of historicity). In other words, the story originally identifies the structural upper/lower division not with the historical myopia of the present that disavows the supernatural that is the target of James' satire but with precisely the opposite: the epistemologically unified world view of the supernatural-accepted in which exorcisms are a matter of course and traffic between the living world and the spiritual realm is inconvenient but not unthinkable. It is only when the post's original purpose has been forgotten that it assumes its primary Jamesian function of punishing the historically negligent, becoming, like Edwards' phantom coach, a conduit between realms for a cautionary message that reaffirms the totalization of reality under the sign of "the supernatural accepted."

Importantly, this totality is historical and not just epistemological, as the story's bemused satire of "modernizers" who are spooked by the appearance in their rose bush of a ghostly face with a specifically articulated and detailed historical pedigree makes plain. Unlike the folkloric and unnamed ghosts of "The Phantom Coach," the ghost of "The Rose Garden" is a public figure in the Court of James II, evoked in the story primarily as a photograph belonging to "the Essex Archaeological Society" and as an entry in the Westfield church registry — documents that foreground the story's thematic preoccupation with historicity itself. The post's symbolic affirmation of the unity of seemingly separate epistemological realms is thus more profoundly a statement about the necessary continuity between past and present and the dangers of forgetting history that James emblazons in the story's ironical closing caution, "*quieta non movere*" [do not disturb things at rest],[32] an injunction to respect the emotional and aesthetic power of pre-modern epistemologies that still give the spiritual reality of the numinous its due.

The shift from the pure structuralism of Todorov to the study of the convergence of temporal and spatial considerations and the symbolically loaded boundary-objects of M. R. James' ghost stories ("Oh, Whistle, and I'll Come to You, My Lad" also works beautifully in this regard) serves an important contextualizing function for many of the stories we study since students' investigations of the temporal themes of James' antiquarian ghost stories becomes a basis to discuss the matrix of cultural concerns about modernity out of which these stories emerge. Their fascinated depiction of a late-nineteenth and early twentieth-century present that is literally haunted by a "horrifying" yet also strangely tantalizing past provides an ambivalent response to these concerns. However, the focus on temporality that "The Rose Garden" thematizes so paradigmatically also suggests a more explicitly psychoanalytical understanding of ghost and horror stories drawing upon the foundational mental topographies of Freud and later theorists like Lacan and Kristeva. These topographies, like those of the ghost and horror stories we study, are at once spatial (the division of the mind into consciousness, the unconscious, and the preconscious) and temporal (since Freud's model of the psyche is organized, throughout its development, by an economy of repression — which is to say, a temporal economy of "forgetting" past experiences only to have them "return" in symptoms, pathologies, and uncanny phenomena).

As students read selections from Freud's essay on "The Uncanny" alongside its literary reference point, E. T. A. Hoffmann's "The Sandman," and Hélène Cixous's poststructuralist-feminist critique of Freud in "Fiction and Its Phantasms," our overarching goal is to think about the implications of a psychoanalytic subject (constituted by what he or she does *not* know) for the writing and reading of horror fiction. Certain stories seem to provide us, though their dramatization of madness or altered mental states, with fictional "case studies" that project the author's own intuitive grasp of the underlying assumptions of psychoanalytic theory itself—"The Sandman" and Henry James's *The Turn of the Screw* being only the most obvious examples, featuring characters whose environments seem grotesquely transformed by the play of their own unconscious projections. Conversely, we explore how stories might themselves be read as symptomatic of their author's own complexes and repressions, and how our interpretations of these stories might provide us with revealing indices of our own. As we explore these questions, we circle back to Todorov's categories, filling their silence on psychoanalytic questions by focusing on the overlaps and divergences between Freud's notion of the uncanny as a literary phenomenon and Todorov's generic categories of the fantastic-uncanny and the pure fantastic.

I begin the course with structuralist and psychoanalytical approaches to horror because as students begin to employ horror texts to explore political and sociological theory in earnest, I want them to do so from a position that already brings with it attentiveness to the literariness of these texts as complex formal structures as well as a sense of what is at stake for us as readers in experiencing the affects of horror — uncanniness, revulsion, fascination — that are characteristic of the texts we will be studying. More specifically, however, I begin with structuralist and psychoanalytic approaches because it seems to me that the false "universalism" with which these approaches are routinely condemned (that is, their tacit assumption of an analytical "neutrality" in a diagnosis of both textual and psychic structures that is in fact gendered as well as being historically and culturally particular) is actually pedagogically useful as a launching pad for the kinds of questions that will emerge in our study of the more self-consciously located interventions of feminist, queer, Marxist, postcolonial, and critical race theory that follow.

Just as importantly, from the perspective of our study of horror fiction, the "universality" of these two ways of approaching a definition of genre (through "the fantastic" or "the uncanny"), even if it is shown in the end to be in need of further nuance, carries with it the additional heuristic value of presenting the fundamentally transgressive dimension of horror — its preoccupation with transgression as both a theme and a structural condition of possibility — in the most provocatively totalizing and abstract terms. Todorov's structuralism, for instance, can be used to define horror in formal terms, particularly in its fantastic-marvelous mode, as a readerly experience of epistemological rupture that occurs when the boundaries of the secular epistemology associated with narrative realism are transgressed by the intrusion of supernatural elements implying an incommensurable position. Psychoanalysis similarly characterizes the uncanny as a discourse of transgression in which consciousness is displaced from its position of authority by irruptions of the unconscious that demonstrate the arbitrary limits what was once thought to be the preeminent ground of human subjectivity. In both cases, what Jackson calls fantasy's "preoccup[ation] with limits, with limiting categories, and with their projected dissolution"[33] is evoked—firstly at the level of form and epistemology and secondly at the level of subjectivity and affect.

Given the course's dual emphasis on the relationship between literary form and ideological meaning, on the one hand, and the transgressive impulse that subtends contemporary cultural theory in both its diagnostic and subversive moods, on the other, beginning the course with approaches that theorize horror in terms of its transgressive structure and range-of-affect is invaluable. Todorov's structuralism, while hardly beyond critique as a theory of genre, provides a broad and useful set of rubrics for understanding basic operational principles of texts that we subsequently read with an eye to sociological and political forms of interpretation and the theories that underpin them. As we move increasingly into the realm of cultural theory, moreover, psychoanalytic concepts like repression, projection, the uncanny, and abjection, both trouble and converge with the work of feminist, Marxist, queer, and postcolonial theory to help define horror as a genre or mode of unconsciously inflected aesthetic production that plays on both a subject's and a culture's repressions, desires, fears, and dark dreams.

II. The Explorations

If the "practical" emphasis of the course at the beginning of the term is on formal and structural close readings of horror stories in terms of their technical features, their manipulation of the epistemological field, and the psychical referents of their generation of paradoxically pleasurable forms of fear, anxiety, and disgust, the emphasis in the second half of the term builds upon this work, focusing upon the ideological implications of the various ways in which these stories conduct their heavily affect-laden assaults upon the epistemological foundations of "ordinary reality." As in the first half of the course, we continue to approach the study of theory and criticism through theoretical readings that are set in dialogue with works of horror fiction whose thematizations of transgression and excess are used to introduce, to illuminate, and often (as students gain confidence in reading for the politics of form) to provide counterpoints to the more explicitly oppositional politics of theory, be it feminist, queer, gender, Marxist, critical race, or postcolonial. Thus, for example, the homoerotic hauntings of "Oh, Whistle, and I'll Come to You, My Lad" and *The Turn of the Screw*, which we have already studied in the context of structuralist genre theory and the psychodynamics of hysteria and the uncanny, now provide us with an introduction to the concerns of queer theory elaborated in Eve Sedgwick's *Epistemology of the Closet*; the female monster of James' "An Episode of Cathedral History" and the female victim of Edith Nesbit's "Man-Size in Marble" present complementary case studies of masculine gender-trouble and the feminist critique of phallogocentrism; and Jacobs' "The Monkey's Paw" and Rudyard Kipling's "The Mark of the Beast" serve as introductions to the class-oriented concerns of Marxist literary analysis and the phantasms of Orientalism respectively.

As we explore the stories and begin to develop more detailed and complex readings of their politics in light of the theories that the stories themselves have introduced, we are guided by Jackson's historically minded account of literary fantasy as a discourse that is "produced within, and determined by, its social context," often "struggl[ing] against the limits of this context."[34] More specifically, we take up her challenge to "extend Todorov's investigation from being one limited to the *poetics* of the fantastic into one aware of the *politics* of its forms"[35] by drawing upon the terms, questions, and debates raised by critical theories of "difference" and translating the *epistemological* disturbances of so-called "ordinary reality" (the Euro-American, ethnocentric, phallocentric, and heteronormative world circumscribed by nineteenth-century bourgeois realism) into properly historical and cultural terms as instances of *ideological* disturbance. Therein, "otherness" irrupts into this bourgeois "reality," but in disguised form, "designated as otherworldly, supernatural, as being above, or outside, the human."[36] As Jackson points out, understanding the politics of form and the place of the other within that politics requires attentiveness to "the relation between ideology and unconscious life," since "it is in the unconscious that social structures and 'norms' are reproduced and sustained within us." It is precisely those unconscious social structures and norms that are at stake in the sense of threat that horror produces when it presents a realist frame that is systematically undermined by the appearance of external or internal forms of otherness coded as monsters, ghosts, hallucinations, or some other figure of epistemological excess that troubles received definitions of "'reality' as it exists in the common opinion."[37] For this reason, our study of "form" as the foundation of more politically oriented readings necessarily integrates psychoanalytical accounts of the structures of psychic life. These include its drives, blockages, satisfactions, compromises, and dissimulations, but also the dynamic of repression-and-return that characterizes the uncanny and the more radical dynamic of abjection that, in Kristeva's classic formulation, provides a powerful account of the overlap between psychic and social forms of exclusion and boundary-maintenance, even as it highlights the fragility and the discontents of social and ego boundaries, postulating our radical ambivalence towards the kinds of boundary dissolution and category confusion that are characteristic of horror fiction's contradictory affects (pleasurable anxiety, pleasurable revulsion), ambiguous and borderline forms (the fantastic, the fantastic-marvelous), and hybrid, liminal motifs (ghosts, monsters, boundary-objects, etc.).

"An Episode of Cathedral History" provides an especially illuminating example of the social implications of psychoanalytical structures, which I use to help teach Kristeva's theorizing of abjection. Like "The Rose Garden," the story is superficially a tongue-in-cheek cautionary tale about the dangers of "improving" renovations; in this case it is "the wave of Gothic revival" that "sm[ites] the Cathedral of Southminster," leading to the removal of a pulpit that exposes an altar tomb, freeing a monster which proceeds to terrorize the town. Structurally, the story can be read as offering the epistemological disturbance that is characteristic of the fantastic-marvelous tale, as rational explanations for the mysterious night sounds and agitated pets give way to a direct encounter with the supernatural inside the church during the story's climax. When asked to discuss what is frightening or disturbing about the monster, students immediately note the ambiguity concerning its gender since this red-eyed "mass of hair" on "two legs" is identified both as a "lamia" (a female demon) and as a "satyr" and "a thing like a man, all over hair, and two great eyes to it." The confusion evoked by the monster's nebulous gender suggests, on the one hand, the category confusions of the abject — its famous inbetweenness that "*draws me towards the place where meaning collapses*," that repulsive (monstrous) pre–Symbolic matter that the ego must expel in the process of effecting its own (ultimately gendered) "clean and proper self."

Yet the ambiguity of the monster's gender is also in a curious sense unevenly distributed, for its allusive and nominal gender contradictions are overshadowed by its evocation of the monstrous feminine in a sexualized scene in which two young boys (one of whom is the narrator) poke rolled-up choir music through a chink in the altar tomb only to have it bitten off by the monster within in a rather cheeky evocation of the *vagina dentata* motif. In the context of this misogynist tradition of demonizing the "terrifying" power of female sexuality, the unsettling discovery and escape of a female monster who has been buried beneath the pulpit in a Cathedral that is itself rumored to have been built "on a site that had once been a marsh" is a "return of the repressed" that serendipitously allegorizes Kristeva's account of the foundational abjection (expulsion) of women by the symbolic structures of patriarchal cultures anxious to safeguard male authority from the threat of maternal power. Indeed, the story's climactic scene, in which the boys' ineffectual "penetration" of the tomb is re-enacted by the men of the community (including the narrator's father) who, armed with crowbars instead of rolled-up scores, open the tomb to destroy the monster, brings the patriarchal implications of abjection into the foreground. It is not simply that the story's presentation of monstrosity exploits the effect of abjection — our revulsion before the radical confusion of categories that are closely tied to the unruliness of the pre-gendered, pre-symbolic body and its drives. It is also that the story dramatizes the manner in which, as Kristeva also argues, Western culture (represented here by the Church and the community fathers) attaches these forms of radical category confusion to women, a "hygienic" gesture that expels categorical ambiguity and feminine authority from the realm of "the clean and proper" in a fell swoop. That the story ends on an ironical and unsettling note with the escape of the monster, the spectacle of the defeated father, and the compensatory inscription of the biblical motto "IBI CUBAVIT LAMIA" on the empty tomb further underlines what Kristeva describes as the fragility of a symbolic order that is predicated on abjection since both egos and forms of culture founded upon radical exclusion require constant boundary-maintenance in the form of ritual re-enactments of the founding exclusion in order to sustain their power.

The story's dramatization of the ultimate impotence of such patriarchal rituals in a horror story focalized through a narrator on the cusp of manhood, suggests rather vividly the subversive charge that horror's exploitation of the motifs of abjection can acquire — in this case, a diagnosis of the internal weaknesses, inherent instability, and illegitimacy of a religious patriarchal culture founded upon the othering and abjection of women. This sort of reading would seem to confirm Andrew Bennett and Nicholas Royle's observation that insofar as the uncanny "concerns a sense of unfamiliarity which appears at the heart of the familiar."[38] it is akin to the Russian Formalist notion of "defamiliarization" or to Bertolt Brecht's "alienation effect" in theatre since all of these ways of talking about literature foreground its capacity to "shake our beliefs and assumptions" by estranging us from our habitual modes of perception.[39]

Yet the subversive diagnostic of masculine anxiety that James' tale seems to allegorize does not tell the whole story, for the "female" monster who escapes from beneath the pulpit where she has been safely imprisoned for centuries is summoned to chill, not to edify, James' readers, and certainly not to edify them about the nature of patriarchal oppression! The story's open-endedness with regard to restoring order does not necessarily make it less reactionary. Indeed, beyond its exploitation of cultural fears of the monstrous feminine to spook its implied reader, the story's familiar Jamesian satire of modern "improvers" might even be read as veiled or unconscious jab at early twentieth-century feminism.

As the ambiguous nature of this story's gender politics helps to demonstrate, coordinating the complexity of psychoanalytically inflected formal analysis with ideological critique requires far more than some general assignation of political valence to Todorovian or Kristevan categories. Even if horror's thematic outrages, transgressive motifs, and epistemological disruptions do in some sense perform the political work of "defamiliarization" that is foundational to any critical intervention by "giv[ing] utterance to precisely those elements which are known only through their absence within a dominant 'realistic' order,"[40] my project in the second half of the course is to get students to see that such productive defamiliarizations must nonetheless be situated within the broader formal and thematic context of the narrative in which they are embedded. As Carroll argues in his exemplary critique of attempts to define horror with reference to some ultimate generic ideology, "the question of which and how many or what proportion of horror fictions are reactionary" — or emancipatory — "cannot be settled a priori ... but requires empirical research."[41] In other words, even though horror fictions evoke all manner of ideological challenges to the status quo of the dominant order through their epistemological and psychic disruptions, there is no magic formula for evaluating the political resonance or investments of a given text. Feminist or postcolonial theory might help us to pose questions about the discursive significance of horror's picturing of monstrosity — its subversive as well as its reactionary implications — but we are ultimately thrown back upon a rigorous analysis of narrative form when we are tasked with assessing the place of transgression within the work's ultimate ideological horizon of meaning.

Two texts that are especially illustrative of the importance of form to the method of reading horror are Jacobs' "The Monkey's Paw" and Nesbit's "Man-Size in Marble"— stories which we read in the final phase of the course in conjunction with Marxist criticism and feminist theory. By now, students are expected to come to class prepared to discuss four things: (1) how they would classify the assigned story within Todorov's structuralist range of generic categories, (2) which elements of the story invite psychoanalytical readings or exhibit structural dynamics that seem consonant with either uncanniness or abjection, and (3) how "ordinary" reality and the forces that disrupt it are contrastingly characterized (according to what tropes? with what allusions and associations? invoking which displaced social categories of otherness?), and (4) whether they feel that the story in question invites the alignment of our sympathies more with the forces of order or with the forces of disruption and alterity. During our meeting, the class as a whole brings forward its initial answers to these questions, identifies points of contention, and attempts — with me playing referee at the chalkboard — to develop a coherent and persuasive reading of the story in ideological terms that brings all four factors into play.

In the case of "The Monkey's Paw," students have no trouble identifying the titular wish-granting "fetish" that is brought from India to the British country cottage of the "White" family by an elderly colonial officer as a racially marked object of Empire. But observant students also notice the manner in which the story foregrounds more proximate forms of wealth and labor, since the first of the three cursed wishes that the paw grants is the father's wish for two hundred pounds to settle the mortgage on the family home — the classically bourgeois dream of owning property. That the wish is granted in the form of monetary compensation for the sudden death of the man's son in a factory accident in which "he [is] caught in the machinery"[42] the following day further suggests that the story's depiction of apparently supernatural events invites its reading as a class allegory, an idea students have already encountered in Bruce Robbins' essay on the class fantasies of servants and governesses in *The Turn of the Screw*. From this perspective, the details of the story coalesce into a striking allegory of the consequences of capitalist exploitation whose emphasis on the seemingly "magical" quality of money to appear "as the product and yet the non-product of man" recalls Marx's description of "the riddle of the money fetish" in his notes on James Mill's *Elements of Political Economy*.[43] Within this allegory, the wish-granting "fetish" would seem to function as a symbol of the ultimate capitalist fetish: money itself. Meanwhile, the antagonistic relation between the property-owning father and the laboring son who dies in the machines — suggested by the opening chess game in which the father plays "reckless[ly]" and only belatedly notices a "fatal mistake" in his game-play[43] — can be read as allegorizing the relation between the exploitative capitalist class and the exploited proletariat, given the manner in which the father literally appropriates surplus value from the fatal labors of his son, having his wish then granted in the form of blood money paid by a firm that "will admit to no liability."[44] The manner in which the story's ironies brutally dismantle the father's naïve belief in the benign power of magical wishes powerfully suggests that the story's project is precisely to defamiliarize the fetishistic nature of money as surplus value that arrives, seemingly from nowhere, of its own accord, all the while disguising, through its abstraction, the exploitation of proletarian labor that produces it. The fetish of money, in other words, seems savagely parodied by the grotesque monkey's paw (itself suggestive of the laboring hand of the "bestial" underclass) and its tantalizing curse. The family's use of the final two wishes, first to resurrect the son and then to wish him dead again when they realize that it is his mangled corpse that will return to terrorize them, seems to reinforce such a reading, suggesting as it does the futile belatedness of bourgeois guilt.

As students discover, paying attention to formal and psychoanalytic elements of the narrative significantly blunts the subversiveness of the story's defamiliarizing edge. When asked about how they would classify the story according to Todorov's generic categories, two contending positions emerge: half the class thinks the story is an example of the pure fantastic in which readerly hesitation over whether or not new laws must be invented to account for the unusual events in question is sustained, and the other half feels confident that the story is indeed fantastic-marvelous because adequate "proof" of supernatural occurrence has been provided by the narrative to allow the reader to decide that an epistemological shift has taken place. The ambiguity of the story's form stems from its climax — the "moment of truth" in most fantastic-marvelous tales when the supernatural is encountered head on and some manner of confirming circumstantial evidence is produced to corroborate the authenticity of the visitation; if that "proof" of the supernatural in such stories contains a loophole, it is a loophole that, as M. R. James suggests, is "so small as to be unusable." In "The Monkey's Paw," however, this logic is undermined by the fact that the "proof" provided by the climactic moment is precisely the *non*-appearance of the "ghost" (the reanimated son). The granting of the first wish could be considered a coincidence; the granting of the second wish ("I wish my son alive again") is implied but not confirmed by a knock on the closed front door of the cottage; and the third wish (not uttered within the narrative, but implied by the "deserted road" that greets the couple when Mrs. White throws open the door) ironically seems to confirm the occult power of the monkey's paw by removing the spectacle of supernatural horror promised by the reanimated corpse, turning the absence of the supernatural into a paradoxical "proof" of its operation.

This paradox accounts for students' confusion over whether the story sustains or resolves the fantastic ambiguity of the exposition and rising action; but it also has implications for a political reading of the tale since the story's refusal to show either the bourgeois parents or the reader the spectacle of the horribly mangled worker-son points to a defensive limit in the story's exploration of capitalism's structural violence. It first diverts our gaze from the son by keeping him hidden behind the door, literally locked outside the protected domestic space of the bourgeois cottage. It then frustrates our gaze from seeing the mangled worker a second time by having the father literally "wish him away." Both these occlusions of vision, which forestall or subtly undermine any definite epistemological/ideological transformation, dramatize the cynicism of the capitalist (his bad-faith refusal to be confronted with the proof of the structural violence his fetishism abets, even though he, like the father in the story, believes in its existence enough to want to wish it away!); but they also implicate the story in this act of bad faith. That is because the story's ambiguous form (its refusal to grant unequivocally the epistemological/ideological shift that the spectacle of the living-dead proletarian corpse would assure) in effect repeats and affirms the actions of the father, a figure within the class allegory we have been tracing, who prefers to avert his eyes from the uncanny return of the repressed proletarian body of capitalism's structural violence, even when that body belongs to his own son.

Indeed, the manner in which the story handles the uncanny structural motif of the return of the repressed is itself telling, for it suggests further that the threat posed by the son's resurrection might be read not simply in cognitive terms as allegorizing the possibility of the capitalist's self-apprehension, but, more literally, as a figure of revolutionary counter-violence — a genuinely political "return of the repressed" represented by the revived body of the mangled worker who threatens to invade the literal and symbolic stronghold of bourgeois illusion: the family home. In this case, the "empty road" where the revolutionary subject should be standing is empty precisely because the capitalist retains his "magical" powers, but just barely — his three wishes are now used up. Revolution thus emerges as a phantasmal figure of negative potentiality at the end of the story: a utopian horizon that has yet to be made manifest.

Like "An Episode of Cathedral History," it is possible to read the diagnostic allegory of "The Monkey's Paw," including its depiction of the dominant order's defensive gestures, as an instance of subversive defamiliarization in which dominant ideology is subtly mocked by the dramatization of its own dissimulations and crises, a possibility made especially apparent in both stories by ambiguities surrounding the fate of the monster or ghost, casting doubt on the extent of the dominant order's ability to fully manage the elements that threaten its authority. In "The Monkey's Paw," however, the ambiguity is more subtle, set within a plot that affirms the horror of the other and the necessity of expelling the supernatural threat at all costs. It is after all "weak" and "irrational" mother-love that cajoles the father into wishing his son back to life, and it is, conversely, the heroic reassertion of the father's law that dispels him again in the story's final hair-raising moments.

This internal battle between Mr. and Mrs. White serves the story's reactionary organization of affect around the necessity of expulsion for it deflects the capitalist's guilt over his role in mangling the worker onto an internal enemy: the dangerously sympathetic mother who refuses to see the worker in dehumanized terms. Her insistence on the value of the "sentimental" ties of kinship over an identification with the capitalist class powerfully affirms her structural alignment with a proto–Marxist position that, as Robbins argues about Miles' refusal to dehumanize Quint in *The Turn of the Screw*, involves a "rejection of class hierarchy" and an assertion that "'others' do 'count.'"[45] In other words, despite extraordinarily suggestive evocations of social transgression and revolution, "The Monkey's Paw" still strives to dispel these subversive impulses, invoking them only to contain and manage them through the logic of its form.

Nesbit's "Man-Size in Marble" is another story that repays investigation in terms of the politics of form in ways that complement our discussion and analysis of "The Monkey's Paw," this time in terms of feminist criticism's analysis of female authorship, a topic we study in conjunction with excerpts from Sandra Gilbert and Susan Gubar's *The Madwoman in the Attic*. Starting from our four orienting homework questions, students typically begin by identifying "Man-Size in Marble" as a quintessentially fantastic-marvelous tale, and, indeed, its structure is exemplary of the form: a pair of newlyweds— "Laura" and her unnamed husband, the story's first-person narrator—leave the city for a life in the English countryside. They lease a small cottage where Laura writes and her husband paints, and the pair enjoy a bucolic several months until October, when Laura is upset by their old housekeeper's sudden resignation. As the husband learns, but Laura does not, the housekeeper refuses to stay in the house during the last days of the month because she credits legends about "the two effigies of knights in armour" who are, according to the local idiom, "drawed out man-size in marble" in a nearby church.[46]

> Their names were lost, but the peasants told of them that they had been fierce and wicked men, marauders by land and sea, who had been the scourge of their time, and had been guilty of deeds so foul that the house they had lived in—the big house, the way, that had stood at the site of [the newlyweds'] cottage—had been stricken by lightening and the vengeance of Heaven. But for all that, the gold of their heirs had bought them a place in the church.[47]

On the last day of October, these stone figures reputedly "sits up on their slabs, gets off them, and walks down the aisle, *in their marble*," retracing the path of the bier-balk along which corpses are carried to burial, all the way back to the location of their evil former dwelling to indulge their foul appetites for the duration of the night.[48] In the subsequent working out of the narrative, the husband dismisses the legend and decides against sharing it with his wife; on the evening of the last day of the month, however, he embarks on a walk to the church leaving his wife alone in the cottage; he arrives at the church to discover the effigies gone and wonders if he is mad; is delayed on his trip home and decides to return to the church to check the effigies again, this time finding them in their proper place, though noting that the hand of one of the marble knights is broken. Until this point, all of the story's events remain fantastic; finally, however, the husband returns to the cottage to discover his wife dead, clutching in her hand "a grey marble finger"—the "moment of truth" upon which the story ends where supernatural explanations are confirmed and the epistemological shift from the fantastic to the marvelous occurs.

Within this seemingly conventional structure of epistemological dislocation, Nesbit elaborates a feminist critique of the domestic relations between husband and wife that becomes evident when students begin to discuss the manner in which the ghosts are characterized and to discern the presence of unconscious motivations within the behavior of the narrator. What always amazes me about student reactions to this story is that the majority of them fail to see any fundamental difference between Nesbit's powerful male aggressors and the ghosts and monsters of writers like M. R. James, Rudyard Kipling, and W. W. Jacobs, who, in the stories we study in class, tend to reinforce normative categories of otherness by constructing their ghosts through allusions to a range of discourses of "difference" (racial, classist, gendered, etc.). Unlike the abject feminine monster of "An Episode of Cathedral History," the supernatural others of "Man-Size in Marble" subversively symbolize and defamiliarize a dominant position within the cultural order — in this case the rapacious power and structural violence of patriarchy that is concealed by the late-nineteenth-century discourse of chivalry that the knight-figures also evoke, but which the details of their story (the flagrant moral fraudulence of their "legitimization" within the church, which has been purchased rather than earned, for example) satirically demystify. Once students begin to think in these terms, the relation between the supernatural figures and Laura's condescending husband, who is fond of calling her by "pet names" like "Pussy" and "wifie" becomes all too apparent.[49]

The rapacious knights in effigy, whose names have been lost to history, function as doubles for the husband in the story whose narrative role is to make explicit the hidden violence of the gender hierarchy organizing the couple' marriage — the fact of the supernatural knights' namelessness suggesting precisely the archetypal or abstractly structural nature of patriarchy, as does the namelessness of the husband, which is set off by Nesbit's humanizing assignation of a proper name to Laura. Significantly, the story foregrounds the power struggle between the couple in their domestic relations since, on the one hand, Laura's magazine articles on folklore, not the husband's paintings, appear to support their household financially, and, on the other, the husband wishes to relocate Laura's duties within the domestic sphere when he refuses to see the loss of the housekeeper's services in the "greyest light" of "unreasonable" Laura, belittling her (quite reasonable) fears that the drudgery of housework will interrupt her ability to "work ... or earn money."[50]

The narrative's subtle depiction of the husband's attempts to regain the upper hand over his wife gains further support when students begin to discuss the place of uncanniness within the story, noticing that its fantastic-marvelous structure is overlaid with a psychoanalytic structure of "the return of the repressed," wherein the violent attack by supernatural embodiments of an unalloyed masculine will-to-dominate appears to represent a kind of unconscious wish-fulfillment on the part of the grief-stricken husband who holds her corpse in his hands and suggestively laments, "Poor child! Why had I left her? Brute that I was."[51] Why indeed? The parting condescension, "Poor child," points to an answer, and so too does the self-accusation, for the term "brute" implies a subterranean connection between his own mysteriously unmotivated decision to leave her alone on the night he has been warned about and the actual "marauders" who brutalize his wife. The husband's obscure intuition that he should wander away from the cottage — "I felt vaguely that it would be good to carry my love and thankfulness to the sanctuary whither so many loads of sorrow and gladness had been borne by men and women of the dead years"[52] — on the night of Laura's murder by supernatural agents of patriarchy strongly suggests the operations of the unconscious, as does the husband's curiously erratic memory: "It will seems strange, perhaps," he admits, "that I should have gone half-way up the aisle before I remembered — with a sudden chill, followed by a sudden rush of self-contempt — that this was the very day and hour when, according to tradition, the 'shapes drawed out man-size in marble' began to walk."[53]

In all these ways, Nesbit's tale foregrounds the powerful role of form in the analysis of ideology by exploiting the structures of both the fantastic-marvelous and the uncanny to produce a feminist counter-discourse on patriarchy in which the symbolic order itself is coded as monstrous and the human (female) "other" is its innocent victim. Thus, in the first instance, the story's fantastic-marvelous structure produces the epistemological shift that is the mechanism of the story's demystification of patriarchal ideology: read as feminist allegory, the "reality-testing" dimension of the story culminates in the formal demand that the reader recognize the horrific violence of patriarchy as a genuine reality rather than dismissing it as the mere "superstition" of aged rural housekeepers. Meanwhile, the story's superimposition of the return of the repressed onto its "reality-testing" form further nuances its feminist critique, showing how the supernatural aggressors may be understood as representing not just the husband's repressed wishes, but the structural violence of a system whose gender hierarchy is unconsciously held by individual men (like Laura's husband) who operate within it, benefit from its effects, and are thrown into crisis by challenges to its tenets, such as Laura exhibits when her bread-winning work as a writer undermines her husband's domestic authority.

Horror and the Teaching of Theory: Some Conclusions

The course ultimately asks students to reflect critically on what might be called literary criticism's ideological turn and horror fiction provides an especially useful critical object for justifying the need for such critical reflection. As George Levine writes in his survey of the changes that took place in literary criticism in the 1980s and 90s and that remain with us (Levine's "Reclaiming the Aesthetic" is one of several concluding essays we read on the debate that has emerged between "ideological" and "aesthetic" approaches to the study of literature), "a virtually total rejection of, or even contempt for, 'formalism'" has taken hold among many literary scholars, coupled with "a determination that all things are political and hence that the function of literature and of literary study is primarily political."[54] There has been, in other words, a turn *from* form *to* politics in literary criticism, the effect of which has been "to reduce critical practice to exercises in political positioning" and to denigrate "aesthetic experience" as "mystified ideology."[55] The scope of Levine's defense of the aesthetic is broader than I can indicate here, but his remarks do provide a sense of how the race for (political) theory has in some ways run roughshod over aesthetic and formalist modes of training in ways that have left our students ill-equipped to perform the very sorts of political readings that many of us ask them to attempt. As Levine persuasively argues, "cultural study *requires* the sorts of literary and formal analytical skills that have been associated with the New Criticism"—or, one might add, with structuralism.[56] To be sure, such a claim about the priority of formal analysis is far from being alien to politically inflected theory—it is central to Marxist literary criticism, as well as to feminism, queer theory, and postcolonial criticism. But if the plethora of decontextualized analyses of gender stereotypes in the many term papers I have graded on "representations of women in..." are any indication, it is a lesson that is easily lost on our students when, in our own rush to "cover" the extraordinary breadth of contemporary theory, we might inadvertently leave them with the impression that "doing" political criticism is merely a matter of identifying empowering or reactionary tropes, the parameters of which they have learned from often a very profound and detailed reading of, say essentialism and anti-essentialism debates within "French" feminism.

The advantages of teaching theory in the context of a course that integrates fiction are considerable, since teaching fiction alongside theory provides opportunities for practical criticism and in so doing foregrounds the mediating function of form. These advantages are especially numerous, however, when horror fiction is employed in this supplementary capacity, and I want to conclude by highlighting just four of its pedagogical virtues for the teaching of theory, beyond its potential to function as a lure for reluctant readers. The first, as the foregoing readings have shown, is that the flagrant excesses of the genre's transgressive figures—its monsters and ghosts and madmen—and their positioning within melodramatic narrative structures that foreground the dominant order's relation to alterity help to dramatize issues that are central to contemporary critical theory, a body of writing that in many ways emerges out of and is pre-eminently concerned with the place and claims of the other: its epistemological, ontological, ethical, and political relation to the normative center as well as its modes of self-apprehension in terms of both psyche and culture. Horror's excesses, in other words, often make its stories (or parts thereof) into rough-and-ready theoretical allegories that dramatize, in extremely vivid fictional form, the interventions made by contemporary theory from an extremely broad range of ex-centric positions.

Second, the ideological unpredictability of a genre organized around the extremely broad affect of *fear* helps train students to remain attentive to the interpretive implications of the form of any given work — both its genre and the structure of its plot. Third, the more broadly philosophical dimension of horror that stems from what Colavito identifies as horror's preeminent concern with "the role of knowledge"[57] and what Carroll sees as the tendency of some works of horror "not [to] project any ideological theme, repressive or otherwise"[58] offers an important check on the political turn that is evident in much contemporary theory and which the second half of the course emphasizes, but does not uncritically endorse. Finally, horror fiction's often politically incorrect visceral power to frighten or upset its readers has a way of "bringing home" to students the unconscious investments in sexism, homophobia, racism, or class prejudice that they may hold, giving us opportunities to reflect critically, and hopefully with some humility, upon the locatedness of our own critical practices.

NOTES

1. Derek Attridge, *The Singularity of Literature* (New York: Routledge, 2004), 7.
2. Carl Freedman, *Critical Theory and Science Fiction* (Middletown, CT: Wesleyan University Press, 2000), xv.
3. Freedman, 23.
4. Freedman, xvi.
5. Freedman, 8.
6. Freedman, xvi.
7. Freedman, 8.
8. Freedman, xvi.
9. Freedman, xvi-vxii.
10. Jason Colavito, *Knowing Fear: Science, Knowledge and the Development of the Horror Genre* (Jefferson, NC: McFarland, 2008), 13.
11. Colavito, 13.
12. Colavito, xvi (my emphasis).
13. Rosemary Jackson, *Fantasy: The Literature of Subversion* (New York: Routledge, 1993), 9.
14. Noël Carroll, *The Philosophy of Horror* (New York: Routledge, 1990), 196.
15. Carroll, 197.
16. Dianne F. Sadoff, "Frameworks, Materials, and the Teaching of Theory," *Teaching Contemporary Theory to Undergraduates*, ed. Dianne F. Sadoff and William E. Cain (New York:

MLA: 1994), 18; Diane Fuss, "Accounting for Theory in the Undergraduate Classroom," *Teaching Contemporary Theory to Undergraduates*, 105–09.

17. Fuss, for example discusses the frequently heard objection that whatever theory being discussed is merely the latest intellectual "fad," that study of its details is a waste of time — an objection that Fuss finds productive as a reminder of theory's cultural and historical locatedness and thus an index of its (salutary) built-in obsolescence (105–107). Finke describes the specific discontents that arise when teaching feminist theory; Laurie A. Finke, "The Pedagogy of the Depressed: Feminism, Poststructuralism, and Pedagogical Practice," *Teaching Contemporary Theory to Undergraduates*, 154.

18. Sadoff, 17–18.

19. My own efforts in this area have benefited greatly from Fuss's psychoanalytically inflected strategy of organizing syllabi and developing classroom practices that embrace "the principle of repetition and return" (109). Such practices — which include assigning shorter readings, working through them in class, creating "open spaces" for student discussion, and revisiting the same text several times over the course of a term — make possible what Fuss, following Jacques Lacan's model of the psychoanalytic encounter, calls "time-for-understanding"(109). Like analysis, such pedagogy directly engages "the role resistance plays in the learning process" by "acknowledg[ing] the importance of what one might call leisure time in the act of theorizing" and stimulating, via repetition, "forward progress *through* backward motion, through the hard epistemological work of recollection, rethinking, and reenvisioning" (109). In other ways, as the proliferation and popularity of literary casebooks like Norton Critical Editions and Bedford-St. Martin's superlative Case Studies in Contemporary Criticism series over the last twenty years attest, pedagogical approaches to overcoming the resistance to theory among undergraduates are now routinely focused around the intensive study of a single text from a variety of critical approaches: psychoanalytic, deconstructivist, new historicist, etc. By presenting contextual documents, overviews of critical "schools," and illustrative essays that analyze the primary text from a range of competing or complementary perspectives, such casebooks have enormous heuristic value and in my experience do help most students over the hurdle of their lingering attachment to more intuitive, unreflective, or at best purely formalistic models of literary response. The horror-theory interface in my own "Theory and Criticism" course is in many ways a version of these casebooks writ large.

20. Carroll, 160.

21. I am grateful to Cindy Donatelli, whose course on literary analysis that I took as an undergraduate at the University of Manitoba in the early 1990s introduced me to this technique and whose pedagogy has had a lasting impact on my own.

22. Todorov, *The Fantastic* (Ithaca, NY: Cornell University Press, 1975), 44.

23. Todorov, 41.

24. In Todorov's classic formulation, "the fantastic" is a "transitional" genre that "lasts only as long as a certain hesitation, common to reader and character, who must decide whether or not what they perceive derives from 'reality' as it exists in the common opinion" or whether "new laws of nature must be entertained to account for the phenomena" (41). In the case of the former, the story is "fantastic-uncanny," for it ultimately discloses its allegiance to a diegetic world that, whatever its extremes of cruelty or violence, does not violate "'reality' as it exists in the common opinion." In the case of the latter, the story is "fantastic-marvelous" because it reveals its purpose as an overturning of that "common opinion" in favor of evoking a picture of "reality" in which "new laws of nature must be entertained."

25. Amelia B. Edwards, "The Phantom Coach," *Great Ghost Stories*, ed. John Grafton (Mineola, NY: Dover, 1992), 6.

26. Edwards, 3.

27. Ian Watt, *Conrad in the Nineteenth Century* (Berkeley: University of California Press, 1979), 175.

28. The course's (non-exclusive) focus on the fantastic-marvelous is partly justified by Carroll's definition of art-horror as a genre in which the appearance of impossible monstrosity violates the natural order of things and disturbs precisely through the monster's troubling of received categories (145). But there are also pedagogical reasons for giving special emphasis to this subgenre. Although we study works of the "pure" uncanny like Poe's tales of murder, the "pure" fantastic like Henry James's *Turn of the Screw*, and the "pure" marvelous like Angela

Carter's fairytales in *The Bloody Chamber*, the formal significance of these genres is still best understood in relative terms — that is, Carter's employment of a "marvelous" mode for her feminist fairytales is at least partly significant because the radical utopianism of her feminist project of writing the body of feminine desire aims at describing the real future possibility of a (to us, now) "marvelous" world in which the "difference" of feminine desire has been integrated into the currently phallocentric nature of "ordinary reality," and has, as a result, utterly transformed the structural relation between masculinity and femininity. To write "marvelous" (as opposed to "uncanny" or "fantastic") tales of gendered transformation is thus a formal choice that resonates powerfully with the gender politics of the tales themselves. The decision to make fantastic-marvelous ghost stories a leitmotif of the term is thus pedagogical and strategic: our focus on the transition between the fantastic and the marvelous in these tales helps foreground the ways in which genre-choice in general reinforces or complicates the meaning of individual texts in relational terms — something that becomes much clearer as we move into political and sociological readings of the tales after the opening unit on genre and structure.

    29. Edwards, 3.
    30. Edwards, 3.
    31. Edwards, 11.
    32. Edwards, 80.
    33. Jackson, 48.
    34. Jackson, 3.
    35. Jackson, 6.
    36. Jackson, 53.
    37. Jackson, 6–7.
    38. Andrew Bennett and Nicholas Royle, *Introduction to Literature, Criticism and Theory* (Harlow, UK: Longman, 2004), 34.
    39. Bennett and Royle, 35.
    40. Jackson, 25.
    41. Carroll, 204.
    42. W.W. Jacobs, "The Monkey's Paw," *Great Ghost Stories*, 66.
    43. Quoted in Geoffrey Pilling, Marx's 'Capital,' Philosophy and Political Economy, Marxists Internet Archive, chapter 5, Web, 6 July 6 2011.
    44. Jacobs, 61.
    45. Jacobs, 67.
    46. Bruce Robbins, "'They Don't Count Much, Do They?': The Unfinished History of *The Turn of the Screw*," *The Turn of the Screw*, Henry James, ed. Peter G. Beidler (Boston: Bedford / St. Martin's, 2004), 342.
    47. Nesbit, 129.
    48. Nesbit, 128.
    49. Nesbit, 129.
    50. Nesbit, 163, 127, 162.
    51. Nesbit, 127.
    52. Nesbit, 135.
    53. Nesbit, 132.
    54. Nesbit, 133.
    55. Levine, 378.
    56. Levine, 379.
    57. Levine, 385.
    58. Colavito, 3.
    59. Carroll, 198.

A Raven's Eye View: Teaching Scopophilia with Dario Argento

K. A. Laity

"There's nothing gratuitous about my films."—Dario Argento

The films of Dario Argento offer a unique opportunity for introducing students to the vexed concept of scopophilia in the horror genre. Laura Mulvey's influential essay "Visual Pleasure and Narrative Cinema" retains much of its power despite criticism and complication by a variety of theorists, including the author herself. Mulvey's essay offers a way to talk about the visual characteristics of the film medium. These characteristics often seem obvious and yet students (particularly in English courses) generally have difficulty articulating visual specifics as they feel more comfortable discussing narrative and plot. While they tend to balk at the frankly biologically determinate characteristics of Freudian analysis, they do tend to respond enthusiastically to the chance to fight the camera's desire to disappear and explore Mulvey's explicitly political aim that "destroys the satisfaction, pleasure and privilege" of the implicitly male and heterosexual gaze.[1]

At the center of Mulvey's discussion — and key to unlocking the particular and knowing technique Argento employs as director — are three gazes, simultaneously voyeuristic (deriving sexual pleasure from watching) and scopophilic (simply loving to watch). As Mulvey details the three levels of watching that make up the scopophilic lens,

> There are three different looks associated with the cinema: that of the camera as it records the pro-filmic event, that of the audience as it watches the final product and that of the characters at each other within the screen illusion. The conventions of narrative film deny the first two and subordinate them to the third.[2]

The "naturalness" of the third view makes the camera and the audience disappear, which is why students have difficulty locating it until jarred from their rapt engagement in the "reality" of the film. Filmmakers want the audience to be flies on the wall, unselfconscious of their own scopophilic gaze. That absorption leaves us "obsessively subordinated to the neurotic needs of the male ego" as embodied in the camera's gaze according to Mulvey.[3] Students readily accept the gendering of the camera, but resist the notion that their own gaze conforms to the culturally constructed gender.

Argento's films explicitly embody the notion of the lens as active male gaze upon his largely passive (and conventionally attractive) female victims. The director proves to not only be conscious of this Freudian filter but actively enhances it by often using the camera's eye to mirror the viewpoint of the killer and his own black-gloved hand as the instrument of death and torture. The positioning of women as endangered viewers forms a central part of the narrative tension in many of his films, perhaps most vividly in *Opera* (1987), where steel needles taped below her eyes force the protagonist Betty to watch her boyfriend's murder and her would-be protector, Mira, is dispatched for looking through a keyhole while demanding the killer reveal himself. This essay focuses on using key films— *Opera*, *Suspiria* (1977), *The Bird with the Crystal Plumage* (1970)—to explore Mulvey's key concepts, but also to offer critiques of unidirectional readings of "gaze" which can be explored with other works in Argento's corpus as well as with horror films in general.

Students resist the notion of woman as provoking a castration anxiety through her "lack of penis," but they do quickly acclimate to the fetishizing of the female form before the camera's hungry (and presumably heteronormatively male) gaze, "active/male and passive female."[5] They resist, too, the notion of the woman's body "as bearer of meaning, not maker of meaning"[6] because they know there are female directors and also they are aware of the increasing commodification of male bodies in capitalist culture and reject harsh binaries of gender even though they may accept patriarchal assumptions about gendered behavior without much question, i.e. "naturally" everyone recognizes attractive women, without connecting it to "the active power of the erotic look."[7]

However, as Carol Clover notes in *Men, Women and Chainsaws*, Mulvey's strict binary of the lens into either "sadistic-voyeuristic look, whereby the gazer salves his unpleasure at female lack by seeing the women punished" or "a fetishistic-scopophilic look, whereby the gazer salves his unpleasure by fetishizing the female body in whole or in part" leaves out a third possibility: masochism. Clover turns to D. N. Rodowick who "has suggested that Mulvey's concern to construct a sadistic male subject led her to overlook the masochistic potential of fetishistic scopophilia."[8] Clover also invokes Kaja Silverman, who "argues that in the scenario of the primal scene ... the seeing child is, at the level of identification, not master but victim of the situation."[9] The "child held captive within the crib is controlled — indeed, overwhelmed" by the display. While students might resist such a shame-centered approach to the primal sexual scene, they will recognize the captive and terrified position of the horror audience in this analogy—helpless to escape, only able to close their eyes, which may make their situation worse given the usually skillful employment of sound in horror films.

For Clover, the horror film offers a particular opportunity to explore the masochism that Mulvey overlooks. "There are horror passages that would seem to position the spectator at least temporarily as an assaultive gazer," Clover acknowledges, pointing to the killer's-eye camera beloved of slasher films, but she considers these to be in the minority, for "the real investment of the genre is in the reactive or introjective position, figured as both painful and feminine."[10] This slippage happens much more in the horror genre, Clover argues; mainstream films allow the heteronormative male gaze to reign untroubled, but the specific focus on fear in horror films complicates that authority. The body under siege becomes feminized whether it is the victim onscreen or the audience member in his seat. As Clover puts it, "To ask, at this level of enmeshment, where male ends and female begins is somewhat beside the point."[11] The horror audience finds this slippage perfectly normal (while non-fans find it and the genre troubling). Many horror directors, too, find it untroubling. Argento seems to find delight in provoking these quick shifts in the scopophilic gaze from the desiring active male to the helpless victimized female although not always with characters who fit the expected voyeuristic gender, as Argento's camera slips from the marauding male to the suffering female victim.

Linda Williams picks up on this fluidity and suggests another reading of the monstrous that seems to fit both Mulvey and Argento. In "When the Woman Looks" Williams points out that "a key moment in many horror films occurs when the monster displaces the woman as site of the spectacle" which links the two not in an abject sense, but in terms of their power.[12] She connects to Susan Lurie's establishment of the power-in-difference of the mother to the boy in the familiar Freudian scene of discovery usually read as castration anxiety. For Williams, horror monsters reveal that "looked at from the woman's perspective, the monster is not so much lacking as he is powerful in a different way."[13] The gaze, which attempts to control the female through fetishizing, may give way to fear at being overwhelmed by the monster. "The woman's look at the monster offers at least a potentially subversive recognition of the power and potency of a non-phallic sexuality"[14] one which renders the sadistic voyeur's gaze into that of a masochistic victim. Brigid Cherry takes this notion even further, arguing that far from accepting the stereotypical cowering stance, women who enjoy horror films often "refuse to refuse to look" in "an act of defiance" that finds pleasure in the monster's power-in-difference.[15] Cherry argues that "female viewers of the horror film do not adopt purely masculine viewing positions,"[16] complicating further the notion of scopophilia and gender.

Clover notes John Ellis' observation in *Visible Fictions* that "the crucial dynamic of the war or male action film is the 'notion of survival through a series of threats of physical mutilation, to which many characters succumb. It is a phantasy that is characteristic of the male.'"[17] There is an overlap of sadistic scopophilia and masochistic pleasure that cannot be safely gendered either male or female but allows for slippage between binary gender norms. We cannot be certain that any rules remain beyond the obvious pleasure the horror film provokes — but for whom and how? As Judith Butler would doubtless argue, this is a classic case of "gender trouble." Isabel Cristina Pinedo evokes that link in her discussion of slasher films in *Recreational Terror*, concluding:

> What makes gender trouble so suitable for the horror genre is its commitment to transgressing boundaries. Horror blurs boundaries and mixes social categories that are usually regarded as discrete, including masculinity and femininity. Thus the surviving female is coded ambiguously, as "feminine" through her function as object of aggression and abject terror personified, and as "masculine" through her exercise of the controlling gaze and ability to use violence.[18]

While Pinedo, like Clover before her, focuses on the "Final Girl" survivor, we could apply the same slippage of gender and consequently scopophilic pleasure to the audience of horror films, which exhibits this same alternation without much fuss. Most students, however — not being genre fans — find the gender slippage problematic at best and in many cases, distinctly troubling.

Initially, Argento seems to uphold many gender norms in his work — the focus on beautiful women for scopophilic pleasure, for example, or the exaggeratedly clichéd portrayals of gays and lesbians. He also seems at times to recognize the slippage that occurs in the observer of horror film. In conversation with Maitland McDonagh, speaking about the process of writing and filming, Argento gives a description of his state of mind while creating films that sounds as complicated as these intersections of gendered scopophilia and masochistic pleasure: "I approach that madness [of making a picture] as something dangerous and I'm afraid, but also I want to go to it, to see what's there ... to embrace it. I don't know why, but I'm drawn."[19] The director's words echo uncannily the female horror film fans that Cherry interviewed, their desire for the monstrous and their fear combine with a contrary desire for power. "I love all my killers," Argento asserts, agreeing that it's the reason his hands often do the work of the killer.[20] While literally becoming the hands of the killers in his film seems to be an uncomplicated usurpation of the sadistic-voyeuristic role, there's also a masochist desire to embody or at least embrace the monster, too, given the complex reversals Argento also includes within the narratives. Many students reject out of hand that masochistic desire as it does not fit with conventional morality. They can see the attraction of the monster's power, but not the vicarious thrill of the suffering.

An early scene in Argento's *The Bird with the Crystal Plumage* (1970) offers a moment that demonstrates succinctly the slippery nature of scopophilia in the director's films. In this pivotal scene, blocked writer Sam Dalmas (Tony Musante) happens upon what appears to be a murder taking place in a starkly lit art gallery as he walks through the darkened city streets. After nearly being hit by a car as he crosses the street, Dalmas looks up to find the scene changed. As McDonagh describes it,

> It seems that he is about to lose his status as surrogate voyeur — the logic of the filmic space (the gallery is across the street, Dalmas is moving toward it) dictates that he is about to become part of whatever event is taking place within. But that's not what happens. Dalmas passes through the first set of glass doors and is trapped: he has been made doubly a spectator. The inner doors keep him separated from the woman bleeding within the gallery while the outer doors set him apart from the action on the street, the action of which he was a part only seconds before.[21]

Dalmas faces the additional frustration of seeing a man passing by whom he finds to be literally deaf to his cries for help. His position mirrors the slippage of scopophilia typical in Argento's films. The sadistic scopophiliac becomes trapped by his own desire for pleasure and once captured, must helplessly enjoy the vicarious masochistic revel that replaces the desired image.

As McDonagh suggests in her précis of the film, Dalmas moves from active voyeur to suddenly passive potential victim without missing a beat. His aroused curiosity in the apparent murder results in him (?) being put on display for our pleasurable anticipation, a movement from active to passive, coded in Freudian gender roles as a move from male to female. The beseeching look of Monica Ranieri (Eva Renzi), coupled with her outstretched and bloodied hand, presents a typical image of a female victim in trouble, but one Dalmas remains powerless to assist. The audience's gaze becomes trained on his figure as he moves futilely around his see-through prison. As McDonagh notes, "even after the police arrive and open the glass doors, Dalmas remains where he is; he ventures into the gallery only at Inspector Morrosini's behest."[22] He seems frozen, uncertain of his proper role, turning his gaze both inside and out, but painfully aware that he is on display.

His confusion about where to center his gaze causes Dalmas to forget an important clue in what he has seen. The camera's eye shifts with the character, unable to maintain certainty, so the audience too gets thrown off balance. All three levels of looking shift. This fact encourages the audience to read the scene in the expected fashion: woman as victim, displayed in her abject suffering. Argento's black gloves, a metonymy for the serial killer stalking the streets of Rome, add to the visual cues for the gendered assumption that the killer must be male. The surprise revelation at the end of the film — the killer is Monica Ranieri — finally triggers the incongruous memory that Dalmas has suppressed, as he realizes what he saw was not what he assumed he saw. Ranieri's husband — the figure in the black gloves and raincoat — had been trying to fend off his wife's attack, not to kill her. Argento cheats the audience slightly — *they* never saw that version of events — but there's enough weight from the traditionally gendered reading to persuade the audience that they would have drawn the same conclusion. Students accept this reading and seldom question Argento's manipulation of the original scene.

In a film that lacks the mature, vivid style of his later films' surrealism and operatic visuals, Argento nonetheless introduces this fluidity for the scopophilic gaze with seeming unselfconsciousness. The rest of the climactic scene continues these gender reversals. Dalmas' shock at the realization that the "victim" is really the killer becomes amplified by Ranieri's raucous laughter at him. Her physical revelation offers the display of a striptease but none of its invitation. Dalmas holds up the phallic knife, but her laughter renders it impotent. When the action moves from the blackness of the locked room to return to the shocking white of the gallery, the audience's gaze swings from Dalmas' surprised and fearful face to the spiny *objet d'art* about to crush him to Ranieri's triumphant face. Once more Dalmas becomes trapped and abject, the camera sweeping his nervous expression as it peeps from under the sculpture like a lover under the covers. No longer requiring her masculine plumes, Ranieri strips off the gloves and mackintosh to approach the helpless victim. The camera switches back and forth between her gloating and Dalmas' repeated cries. While she bloodies his hand with a cut, Ranieri seems to see no need to employ the phallic knife and instead decides to climb up on the sculpture the better to crush him with its pointy protrusions. The camera returns again and again to Dalmas' suffering face, his nostrils flaring, his breath coming in gasps, before flashing to Ranieri's triumph. Surely the masochistic pleasure of the scene derives from the hope that rescue of the coded-feminine hero will come in time to save him, which of course it does. That the key scenes take place in the scopophilic wonderland of an art gallery only emphasizes the pleasure of looking as a central motif. The masochistic pleasure of Dalmas' suffering serves as the centerpiece. Students resist this reading until we step through the scene slowly, sometimes frame by frame, pointing out these details.

The slippage between the types of visual pleasures occurs in all of Argento's films, but a couple of key examples will show how Argento manipulates the three looks (camera, characters, audience). In the opening scenes of *Suspiria* (1977), the now legendary soundtrack by Goblin creates a sense of unease during the credits despite the somewhat cartoonish font used. In the American version of the film, a male voiceover explains why Suzy Banyon (Jessica Harper) has come to the German dance academy, but our first image of an airport arrivals board conveys the same basic information. The camera pans down to an entry way heavily infused with red light. Argento uses color masterfully here. Suzy steps out of the red light and into the audience's scopophilic view. The scene jumps to a crowded hallway. The red light has departed, but Suzy is flanked by a woman in a red top to the left and another in a red pantsuit to the right, while a third figure in a red jacket lurks in the background. Suzy herself is dressed in white, which, like a movie screen, reflects the colors around it. The sickly green of the two signs matches the improbably green pants of the figure in the red jacket. Argento mentions on the commentary that this color scheme reflects his impressionistic memories of Walt Disney's *Snow White*. As Anna Powell puts it, "Argento's lurid, saturated colors lack nuance and assault the sensorium in their perverse mimicry of the Disney cartoon spectrum."[23] Alerting students to the importance of color in the film generally prepares them sufficiently to catch the thematic trends, which build well in discussion.

Suzy's isolation focuses the camera's lens and the audience's eye firmly upon her form. The alternating levels of sound of the Goblin theme help create a further sense of unease as Suzy heads toward another set of double doors, reminiscent of Dalmas' prison. The hiss of the doors opening — heightened by the camera's focus on the mechanics that make it happen — signal the crossing of the threshold into the strange world of the Tanz Akademie. The red of the print on the doors and the reflected green signs part to allow Suzy to explode into the windy night. The wind picks up her scarf and hair and added light frames her body, accentuating her shape and provoking a normative fetishizing gaze. Stepping out in the driving rain to hail a cab, the wind and the rain reveal Suzy's body and leave her looking vulnerable. Her face reinforces that identification. The airport around her seems bereft of people and each taxi that passes makes her seem more forlorn. The camera keeps its distance, reminding the audience of the color theme with green and red lights scattered throughout the mise-en-scène.

When she finally secures a taxi—asking in vain for help with her luggage—the refuge it provides appears distinctly suspect. As Suzy wipes rainwater away from her face, red light caresses her palm, suggestive that she will be in danger. The deep blue lighting emphasizes her almost ghostly face and her large eyes. The cut to the driver presents him only in profile as a burst of white light hits the windshield, the wipers reflecting the red and blue, while

Suzy's pale face shows up in the rearview mirror. Unlike the lingering gaze on Suzy, our glimpses of the driver sandwich him in the corner of the screen, suggesting there is nothing much in it for the male gaze to find pleasure. Suzy seems to shrink as she tries to communicate with the driver as the camera angles slightly down toward her. Pressing the written address up against the window between them, she and it are once more bathed in garish red light.

As the taxi drives Suzy to her destination, the reflections of garish red and blue permeate her figure in the back seat, although long shots of the car moving through the streets reveal no possible source of the colors. A cut-away shot to an apparent river-swollen river with plumes of water like ejaculate pouring forth, is followed by an even closer shot of the spraying water before the camera returns to Suzy bathed in color once more. The disorienting scenes of blackness and garish light reflect on her skin and emphasize her looking ineffectual and puzzled. Asking how long it's been raining like this, she finally gets the grudging answer, "Half an hour." The camera shifts to overflowing drains in the street, casting doubt on the cabbie's word and encouraging the audience to be even more fearful on Suzy's behalf. As the vocals on the soundtrack whisper "witch!" the taxi's headlight peeps through a forest of trees without visible branches (although a strange silhouette appears briefly on the trunk of one tree). Approaching the Akademie, the camera reveals its red exterior, inviting the audience to connect it to the garish crimson light that has attached itself to Suzy from the start. The camera's eye seems to mirror Suzy's mobile gaze as she approaches the building, although it does not offer any assurance that it actually looks out from the taxi by incorporating visible signs.

When Suzy steps out of the car, asking the driver to wait, the camera's gaze returns to the audience's viewpoint so we can see the taxi, Suzy and another woman in the door of the Akademie, talking to someone out of sight. Eventually we learn this is Pat Hingle (Eva Axén) and the camera's attention soon moves to her plight. Having set up a heteronormative scopophilia with Suzy, the camera easily moves the audience's focus to Pat, who's dressed in a suspiciously obvious red and blue. The camera moves from Suzy's gaze upon the fleeing Pat to see her arrive at a building with red accents on the outside that give a fleeting impression of dripping blood. As Pat enters the building, we see a riot of color — red and blue once more — in the stylized Art Deco interior. Pat halts in the lobby on the red tiles, looking very small, and turns her gaze up. The camera appropriates her gaze to stare up at the colorful glass that crowns the lobby with geometric shapes.

Crossing the lobby, Pat gets onto the lift accompanied by the shrieking soundtrack. The elevator's floor is also red and a ruby-like red pyramid signals its upward ascension. The repetition of the vermillion palette in concert with the increasingly harsh wails on the soundtrack create a strong tension, the expectation that blood will be spilled. The camera returns briefly to gaze up at the stained glass ceiling, accompanied by an ominous chord. The scene cuts to Pat, welcomed by her friend who tosses a towel to the dripping figure. The room is blue with white accents, the two women also in white, tying them visually to our image of Suzy and encouraging the same pleasurable gaze.

As the two women discuss Pat's situation, the camera moves back and forth between them, trying to disappear as the audience vicariously joins the conversation. However, Pat's face appears bathed in blue, signaling her danger. Taking refuge in the bathroom, the camera watches her stare blankly as if nonplussed by the sudden color change: grey and white Escher-like images of birds and a wall that almost looks pink. The sudden eruption of the wind through the window causes Pat to cower in terror, her face suddenly bathed in blue, as her friend closes the window once more. The camera has moved outside, looking voyeuristically through the window at the two women, suddenly drawing back to reveal lingerie drying on a line, inciting more opportunity for a heteronormative gaze of pleasure.

Moments later after Pat has locked the door after her friend departs, the camera jumps back to frame her through the window in a long shot filled once more with red and blue light, the black slip on the clothesline focusing the audience's gaze on Pat who appears beside it, looking at the camera. While the voices wail on the soundtrack, the camera creeps closer, provoking a sadistic pleasure of stalking the young woman who moves uncertainly out of the frame. The camera cuts to inside once more to reveal Pat looking nervous and watchful. Her gaze darts around the room as if to find the source of the music the audience hears. She creeps closer to the window to see the same lingerie blowing in the blue night's light. As she approaches the window, her image appears in the window meshing with the billowing slip. She walks away from the window, but glances quickly over her shoulder, uncertain, walks a few more steps and glances back again. This time the camera cuts to reflect her gaze at the window.

The camera's movement acts to draw her back to the window again and she gazes wildly into the darkness as the camera fixes on her abject fearfulness. The focus moves from watching Pat to duplicating her view on the lingerie. She picks up a lamp, which only emphasizes her frightened face in the reflection in the glass as the camera stares at her. A last switch to her point of view leaves the audience staring out onto the blue-black night (or is it the slip?) where a pair of eyes looks back at Pat and the audience. The camera's focus seems intended to make the audience jump, but our identification with Pat's gaze is broken when she continues to peer into the darkness and the camera returns to watching her do so. The unbearable strain of expectation finally shatters along with the window as a very hairy (read: masculine, although we find out a different truth later) arm breaks through to grab Pat's neck, dashing her against the other pane.

When the camera moves again, it is to take up a position outside with the aggressor gazing upon Pat's agonized face as the hand thrusts her up against the glass. Her open mouth and distorted flesh lends itself easily to the sadistic voyeur's scopophilic gaze. From here on, the camera moves between Pat's predicament and her friend's terror as she pounds on the door, then leaves the apartment to pound on a neighbor's door, crying "murder." The sadistic pleasure of the camera's gaze lingers on the frightened women, highlighting their conventional attractiveness and their physical jeopardy. Almost immediately, we see Pat stabbed in the torso by a male hand. The location seems to have changed to a room we later see in the Akademie, but this change seems random and the focus of the audience will likely be on the imperiled Pat, who doubles over groaning from the blow. Longer views of her friend still begging for help mirror the long shots of Pat in the bathroom, the small lighted image at the center of the frame surrounded by darkness. Cutting back to Pat we see her struggling as the murderer stabs her again, the scene bathed in blue light. After another brief glimpse of her friend, we return to the collapsed Pat, bathed now in both blue and red light.

The hairy masculine arms carry out the elaborate murder that includes forcing the dying Pat out onto the stained glass ceiling, an abject figure for the sadistic scopophilia of the camera's lens. She pants and moans in a parody of sexual congress as the disembodied hands stabs her again and again, until suddenly the camera cuts to the gaping hole in her chest, smeared with fluorescent red blood, which exposes her still-beating heart. While the scene extends the parody of the sexual act, the audience faces a dilemma of identification. The garish display removes the traditional signifier of beauty (the female body) and replaces it with a part of that whole. According to Mulvey, this ought to lead to fetishizing, but the horror of the moment and the exposure of what ought to be internal (the heart) forces the audience back into the fearful gaze of the trapped Pat. While the scene offers the possibility of appropriating the sadistic gaze of the killer, the camera's quick movements make it less likely that identification and the general ambience of the film—the lighting, the sound and soundtrack—will encourage the reading of masochistic suffering with the murder victim rather than with the murderer. While it may not completely destroy the "satisfaction, pleasure and privilege" of the heteronormative male gaze, the film expects the audience to have a mobile flexibility of identification and gaze that appropriates a shifting sense of gender identification. While students resist acknowledging these shifts at first, with some coaxing they become proficient in identifying those them and carry the sophistication over to other films.

Argento's 1987 film *Opera* has a similarly complicated relationship with scopophilia. Its fascinating opening shot offers us a view of the opera house interior reflected inside the eye of a raven, which blinks as we gaze upon it. This disconcerting mirroring of the watcher being watched puts the audience into an uncomfortable space immediately. The impassive eye of the raven does not offer the usual cues we expect from human features. In fact, the audience may only recognize the creature once the camera pulls back to reveal the bird perched in the auditorium while the simple title appears. The disconcerting start continues as we follow the departure of the diva, unnerved by the same raven. While the camera trails in the (mostly unseen) diva's wake, it is presumably *not* her view. The audience sees the other character reacting to her angry departure but does not see her and remains off balance, unsure. The long tracking shot of departure is broken by a long view of some of the ravens, again gazing impassively, which the diva's parting words suggest must be part of her discomfort with the role. As she heads out to the street, the camera takes in the gathering crowd, eager for a sight of the star. However, she's immediately dispatched by a passing car and her role passes to the ingénue Betty who becomes the scopophilic object of the film. The ravens' gaze provides an unusual starting point for a film that is all about looking.

One of the most famous images from Argento's work involves Betty and complex gazing. After her triumphant first performance, Betty and her boyfriend Stefan enjoy a quiet evening in bed. The cavernous Baroque interior makes the sudden appearance of Betty, sitting up in bed, incongruous, but her naked form presents an obvious opportunity for fetishizing pleasure. While the appearance of Stefan complicates the heteronormative pleasure, Betty's flesh clearly remains the focus even as the conversation details her inability to perform sexually. As he turns away to get dressed, explaining that the place is a museum and belongs to his uncle, the viewer can make the connection between Betty's body and the art on the walls, much of it mirroring her nude frame.

When Stefan once more faces Betty, he's wearing pants but no shirt. The camera's lens lingers on him for a time, disturbing the usual assumption of a desiring masculine gaze by focusing it on the display of male flesh. As he pads off to make tea, the camera returns to Betty but she begins dressing, frustrating the anticipation of prolonged focus on her nudity. A shift to a long shot viewing Betty as she gazes to where Stefan has disappeared seems disorienting at first, the feeling increasing as a sound like a heart thumping fills the soundtrack. The camera mimics the movements of Betty's gaze as she looks, perhaps, for the source of the sound. Suddenly a black-gloved hand reaches from behind her to clasp her mouth shut, tipping her head back as she gasps, then screams and tries to remove the hand. As she falls back senseless, the murderer quickly places a bandage over her mouth while the camera looks on. The position of the audience is again in question: they're not seeing through the killer's eyes, but they are seeing Betty once more displayed before them in a traditionally scopophilic manner. The sadistic controlling gaze seems to be encouraged as we watch the murderer tie her hands together and then observe the helpless Betty struggle on the bed from a medium long shot, which allows the viewer to be a little more remote from her suffering.

This distance allows the transition to a viewpoint close to (though not precisely) the killer's gaze as Betty is displayed before the camera, her abjectness clear as she's forced over to the pillar and tied in a standing position. The rope presses into the flesh of her neck, enticing a sadistic response of pleasure. Each encircling length of the cord emphasizes her body and her vulnerability. The murderer shows Betty the tape with its row of needles before attaching them below her eyes to force her to watch Stefan's murder. She flinches away from the sight, doubtless afraid of the harm they signify, but the implacable killer patiently places them along the lower lid of her eyes and the camera moves right in with an extreme close up of Betty's twitching eye. Then it moves to an *even closer* close up from the side of Betty's eye, making it possible to see the needles approaching. Next the camera shifts to a slightly different angle so the needles look as if they are about to stab Betty directly in the eyeball. For the audience, this disorienting sequence makes identification with any one gaze difficult to establish. It's hard to imagine any audience not squirming at the proximity of needles to the soft surface of the eye; the sadistically voyeuristic gaze that would be possible at a distance becomes difficult to maintain up close where the vivid suffering of the victim compels identification. Longer shots observing the murder in action as he ensures that the needles are in place alternate with close-ups again showing Betty's darting eyeball encased by the row of needles. The audience does not have the luxury of distance for long. By this point students tend to squirm uncontrollably and find it impossible to maintain distance from the victim's point of view.

To emphasize her vulnerability, the murderer shows Betty her own eyes in a compact mirror. The audience receives a doubling of the troubling image, isolating the iconic eye in the frame of the small mirror. Immediately afterward the close-ups return to Betty's eyes, the needles now adorned with drops of blood from her inadvertent blinks, heightening the sympathetic connection. As the action returns to the broader stage, the camera moves back, returning the possibility of the sadistic gaze as Betty helplessly struggle to warn Stefan as he tries to re-enter the room, but the camera continues to cut to close-ups of Betty's terrified gaze and the blood-covered needles, finally looking out from Betty's point of view through the prism of the row of needles.

Once more identification with the victim becomes the only possible gaze.

When the camera shifts away to observe Stefan finally breaking through the doorway, the student audience is likely to retain Betty's panicky outlook even though we are not seeing through her eyes as indicated by the needles. The camera moves behind Stefan as he discovers Betty, so we can gaze upon her, but almost at once returns our point of view to something approximating hers as we focus on Stefan's torso. His confusion and Betty's struggle to warn him are untied as we once more return to a close up of Betty's eye with even more blood on the needles. Her sclera is also shot with blood now, too. The focus on the single body part seems to discourage fetishizing, instead encouraging identification. After another long shot of the confused Stefan, the camera returns to a direct Betty's-eye view before bringing the two figures together in a single shot, the blood and tear-stained Betty shaking her head violently just before the gloved hand of the killer stabs Stefan just below the jaw.

The camera cuts from the phallic jut of the blade in his mouth to its mirror, the blood-covered needles before Betty's wide-open eyes. The gushing blood from Stefan's wound as his body opens up around the knife blade inscribes him with a femininity that offers a chance of returning the normalized sadistic or fetishizing gaze which is frustrated by his masculinity. Even as he lies splayed on the floor, helpless beneath the thrusts of the killer's blade, the camera returns again and again to Betty's captive gaze where tears and blood intermingle. The flurry of blows create numerous openings in Stefan's flesh and the scene is awash in his blood, but the trail of blood from Betty's eyes highlights her suffering more poignantly. The killer holds up Stefan's head to display his accomplishment to Betty, and we return once more to her point of view, looking out from the prison of those needles, as we are doubtless meant to do. The killer's final statement, denying Betty's frigidity, accompanied by a rough caress of her clothed body, fails to return authority to the sadistic voyeuristic gaze because we continue to be presented with the painful image of Betty's eyes. Although the murderer cuts her bonds and flees, and Betty removes the needles before she finishes removing her restraints, the forced masochism stays with her character and with the audience who has bonded with her through being forced to share her outlook.

The iconic image of Betty with her eyes forced open by the row of needles (McDonagh's book features it on the cover) surely reflects the pleasurable masochism of the horror fan's gaze. While the heteronormative gaze of pleasure may typify many films, the fluid nature of horror films assures easy slippage between very different kinds of scopophilia, not all of which uphold the traditional gender binaries. The films of Argento in particular explore the many openings for unconventional gazes which reward closer examination at all three levels.

NOTES

1. Laura Mulvey, "Visual Pleasure and Narrative Cinema," *Issues in Feminist Film Critics*, ed. Patricia Evans (Bloomington: Indiana University Press, 1990), 28–39.
2. Mulvey, 39.
3. Mulvey, 39.
4. Mulvey, 27.
5. Mulvey, 29.
6. Mulvey, 29.
7. Mulvey, 28.
8. Carol Clover, *Men, Women and Chainsaws: Gender in the Modern Horror Film* (Princeton, NJ: Princeton University Press, 1992), 206.
9. Clover, 207.
10. Clover, 211–2.
11. Clover, 218.
12. Linda Williams, "When the Woman Looks," *The Horror Film Reader*, ed. Mark Jancovich (London: Routledge, 2002), 61–66.
13. Williams, 64.
14. Williams, 65.
15. Brigid Cherry, "Refusing to Refuse to Look: Female Viewers of the Horror Film," *Horror: The Film Reader*, ed. Mark Jancovich (London: Routledge, 2002), 169–178.
16. Cherry, 176.
17. Quoted in Clover, 220.
18. Isabel Cristina Pinedo, *Recreational Terror: Women and the Pleasures of Horror Film Viewing* (Albany, NY: State University of New York, 1997), 84.
19. Maitland McDonagh, *Broken Mirrors/Broken Minds: The Dark Dreams of Dario Argento* (New York: Citadel, 1991), 242–3.
20. McDonagh, 245.
21. McDonagh, 53–4.
22. McDonagh, 54.
23. Anna Powell, *Deleuze and Horror Film* (Edinburgh: Edinburgh University Press, 2005), 142.

The Hulking Hyde: How the Incredible Hulk Reinvented the Modern Jekyll and Hyde Monster

Lance Eaton

Introduction

In any classroom, as the topic turns to monsters, one thing becomes evident: Monsters change. Evolve might be a better term; no type of monster can stay the same when audiences demand variations and creators take liberties. These discussions about monsters invariably conclude that monsters evolve, but the specifics of how they do so are not always so clear. Students often weigh in with classicist views that the original *Frankenstein*, whether book or film, is always better and everything else is an unoriginal rip-off. Other students find themselves drawn to the modern renditions of zombies, feeling that the voodoo zombie or even the Romero zombie seems rather silly. These conversations, like many others about literature, films, comics, music, and other arenas, often play out as competitions of who can make the best argument and, through that, acquire a larger stock of cultural capital.

These discussions frequently miss acknowledging how the monsters' progeny often become sufficiently influential in their own right to morph the purpose, meaning, and capacity to horrify of the original monsters. Monsters, like humans, evolve, but do so in *bricoleur* manner, borrowing from and copulating with other monsters to develop modern monsters that more effectively evoke the audience's fears. As Jeffrey Jerome Cohen explains in *Monster Theory: reading culture*, the monster always comes back.[1] The second half of that truth is that monsters must often breed with their offspring and other monsters in order to attract new audiences. This hybridization always takes place at the crossroads of our cultural fears and desires, the source of contemporary retellings of traditional horror narratives.

The character of Dr. Jekyll/Mr. Hyde fits under the archetype of the human body-transformation monster. In these narratives, the fear of the monster manifests in its often-uncontrollable transformation from something human to something inhuman. The classic example of the transformative monster is the were-creature, in particular, werewolf. The contrasting nature of this archetype as it shifts from benign to harmful is a major theme within Robert Louis Stevenson's novella. The narrative's tension grows significantly when Jekyll reveals that his transformation into Hyde is no longer voluntary, but that he needs the secret elixir to return to his "normal" state as Jekyll.

Jekyll/Hyde also evokes the evil-double archetype, as Hyde, according to Jekyll, embodies all the emotions and desires that Jekyll wishes to remove from himself. Rather than have separate bodies, the evil double is bounded into its counterpart. Though the novella makes clear that Hyde is not Jekyll's evil double, but rather that Jekyll voyeuristically enjoys Hyde's actions, the diverse range of representations of *Dr. Jekyll and Mr. Hyde* since its 1886 publication, often develop Hyde as an evil double. As a result, the Jekyll/Hyde has become its own archetype that blends this evil-double monster with the body-transformation monster.

This essay considers one among many ways in which the Jekyll/Hyde archetype has changed over the last 125 years through intertextual renderings. The purpose is to understand how later versions, particularly Marvel Comics' *The Incredible Hulk,* have served to restructure the ways in which creators (novelists, comic creators, scriptwriters) tell stories containing the Jekyll/Hyde archetype. In the contemporary narrative landscape, monsters utilizing the Jekyll/Hyde archetype are prominent, especially within serial killer narratives such as the Hannibal Lecter and Dexter series. I will discuss the serial killer strand towards the conclusion of this essay, insomuch as it has been influenced by the physically monstrous Hyde strand, which is my primary concern here. More particularly, I will explore the tendency for Hyde-inspired characters to become increasingly physically monstrous while simultaneously shedding their villainous natures, becoming redemptive anti-heroes or tragic heroes.

This essay initially positions and discusses Hyde within Stevenson's text and the 1931 film adaptation to highlight and emphasize his villainous nature. Next, it explores Marvel Comics' creation, uses, and re-renderings of the Incredible Hulk in comics, television, and film over the last 50 years, finally exploring three contemporary renderings of Dr. Jekyll and Mr. Hyde found in the graphic novels, *League of Extraordinary Gentlemen Volume I & II*, Volume I's film adaptation, and the 2007 BBC television miniseries, *Jekyll.*

The focus on intertextual development has several uses for the classroom.

Focusing on this arc of influence can be central to understanding how genre develops. Making sense of the intertextual development provides a more meaningful class discussion when looking at modern renderings of classic monsters. For any course in horror, it provides students with a solid foundation for reconsidering the creative process (their own or others'), the evolution of monsters, and the reasons why archetypal monsters are re-presented as well as why some succeed or fail in scaring audiences. It also improves the analytical frame for students, enabling them to encounter any horror narrative and better appreciate the present and past context for such pieces.

This essay uses the Incredible Hulk as the central vehicle to understand Hyde's transformation in narrative. However, there have been other Jekyll-/Hyde-inspired narratives that have played a role in contemporary re-interpretations of Jekyll/Hyde, such as Alfred Hitchcock's *Psycho* (1960) and Jerry Lewis's *The Nutty Professor* (1963). The former influenced the sexual transformation Jekyll/Hyde undergoes in *Dr. Jekyll and Sister Hyde* (1971) and *Dr. Jekyll and Ms. Hyde* (1995) while the latter influenced more comical and child-friendly versions such as *Jekyll and Hyde ... Together Again* (1982) and the animated film *Dr. Jekyll and Mr. Hyde* (1999). This article does not aim to be the only approach to discussing contemporary Jekyll/Hyde narratives, but rather to provide educators with one particular way of tracing a monster's development. The development of this strand aids students in understanding the multiple ways that a singular narrative or monster can work. In this instance, the Jekyll/Hyde narrative shapes the construction of *The Incredible Hulk*, which significantly changes how contemporary culture tells the Jeykll/Hyde stories. Such monster narratives have great interdisciplinary potential since the instructor can develop lessons around offshoots of the narrative in such areas as cultural studies, gender studies, film history, literature, and popular culture.

Hyde'n Appearances

Before getting into any classroom discussion about the novella *The Strange Case of Dr. Jekyll and Mr. Hyde* it is useful to probe students about what they know about Dr. Jekyll and Mr. Hyde; questioning their perceptions about physical descriptions of Dr. Jekyll and Mr. Hyde works particularly well. While some students know that Frankenstein is the name of the scientist, not the monster, in Mary Shelley's novel, it is rare that any student will know Hyde is "pale and dwarfish" and "gave the impression of deformity without any nameable malformation."[2] Instead, their answers will tend to present Hyde as a large, evil, hulking mass. Jekyll by contrast is understood as a slim weakling, often described as good or nice but meek and diminutive. Generally, students perceive Jekyll to be young, though age rarely comes up directly; they believe his impatience and impetuousness lead him to take the potion. This conversation primes students to be aware of appearance, age, and other characteristics of Hyde as they read the text. The disconnect between their expectations and the actual characters provides a clear opportunity to talk about why they see Jekyll as weak and Hyde as monstrous. Clearly, their perceptions are influenced by modern retellings of Jekyll and Hyde. Whether students have been influenced by the classic *Looney Tunes* episodes "Hyde and Hare" (1955) and "Hyde and Go Tweet" (1960), the recent cinematic Hulk films, or other narratives of physical transformation, they understand Hyde to be a large and beastly monster. Why is that the case?

There are several interconnected reasons for these perceptions of physical form. One is that visual storytelling has dominated the twentieth and twenty-first centuries. Over the last century and a half, mainstream audiences have increasingly privileged visual formats.[3] The early magazines with drawings (and eventually photographs) seduced readers away from texts without images. Newspapers hired out comic strip artists from one another in the late nineteenth and early twentieth century to sell more papers. Children and teens bought millions of comics monthly in the 1930s and 1940s and went to many movies, leaving less time for reading purely textual material.[4] It is no wonder that numerous visual adaptations of Stevenson's hit novella were produced. Indeed, the first dramatic adaptation, a play, was produced within months of the novella's initial publication.[5] Over the years, well over one hundred visual renditions of Jekyll and Hyde in film, theatre, comics, and even video games have been produced for mass consumption.[6]

For each rendering of Hyde to distinguish itself from others, the creators must provide some significantly novel re-presentation of Hyde, through a version that differs physically, psychologically, or in both of these ways. There is a tendency within horror for this shift to become increasingly base and malignant, particularly when coupled with the demise of the Hays Code within film, the elimination of the Comics Code, and television rating systems allowing room for more violence, sex, and gore.[7] The cumulative effect of these changes increases Hyde's vicious nature and violence. In the novella, Hyde is directly responsible for one death (Sir Danvers Carew), but that soon turns to two in the 1931 Rouben Mamoulian film (Ivey and Brigadier-General Sir Danvers Carew), and by the 2007 BBC mini-series, he slaughters dozens of men and women.

In the same vein, the physical transformation from Jekyll into Hyde must become increasingly dynamic and visually evocative. From early on, the transformation scene was a paramount moment in the film, both because it suggested the degree of monstrosity that emerged and also because it illustrated the technological skill and investment of the filmmakers. There is a need to make this transition torturous, frightful, and prolonged in order to distinguish the film from previous versions and emphasize Hyde's monstrosity. For instance, the 1931 film focuses on the changing facial features and hands during the transformation. The 1996 adaptation of the novel, *Mary Reilly*, a retelling of Jekyll and Hyde by Valerie Martin, provides a transformation through special effects in which Hyde grows out of Jekyll's body, becoming larger while Jekyll's body rescinds into Hyde's newly formed body.[8]

The other reason narratives have descended into a monstrous rendering of Hyde lies in Stevenson's description of the character. In describing Hyde, Stevenson heavily relies on the reader's imagination to make Hyde look repulsive, but for visual depiction, Stevenson's approach is problematic.

> Mr. Hyde was pale and dwarfish, he gave an impression of deformity without any nameable malformation, he had a displeasing smile, he had borne himself to the lawyer with a sort of murderous mixture of timidity and boldness, and he spoke with a husky, whispering and somewhat broken voice; all these were points against him, but not all of these together could explain the hitherto unknown disgust, loathing and fear with which Mr. Utterson regarded him. "There must be something else," said the perplexed gentleman. 'There is something more, if I could find a name for it. God bless me, the man seems hardly human! Something troglodytic, shall we say? or can it be the old story of Dr. Fell? or is it the mere radiance of a foul soul that thus transpires through, and transfigures, its clay continent? The last, I think; for, O my poor old Harry Jekyll, if ever I read Satan's signature upon a face, it is on that of your new friend."[9]

Hyde's unnamable "malformation" and Utterson's inability to pinpoint his feelings of "unknown disgust, loathing and fear" regarding Hyde create the effect of something haunting without pinpointing what is so repulsive about Hyde. The description above, as well as others throughout the text, emphasize the fact that Hyde's abnormality is not something clear and precise. People's angered and frightened reactions to Hyde speak to a negative feature of his appearance that is not explicit. For a textual audience, this tactic works well, since readers can import whatever they particularly care to think of as being subtly grotesque about Hyde.

The textual description of Hyde creates challenges for a visual narrative. The visual depiction requires a specific and singular rendering of Hyde, whereas the textual one allows for as many versions of Hyde as there are readers. Given a single chance to present Hyde to many people, the creators must use elements to depict Hyde that make him most repulsive to the widest audience. Therefore, visual renderings continually grant Hyde less human appearances.

Within the classroom, instructors can highlight the above passage and challenge students to explore what Stevenson meant or ask them to clearly describe what Hyde looks like. Eliciting different students' descriptions will yield a variety of different Hydes, illustrating the complexity and power of Stevenson's prose. The discussion can be further developed by addressing how just this specific element (i.e., Hyde's appearance) creates such different interpretations, thereby demonstrating how the adaptation process is much more problematic than students may believe. This discussion allows students to move away from a fixation on textual fidelity in adaptations, since it becomes apparent that such fidelity is not realistic in some ways. From here, the instructor can lead students to the aforementioned reasons for Hyde's variations in visual media, discussing particularly influential adaptations that connect their original perceptions of Hyde (e.g., large and hulking) with Stevenson's physical presentation. The major adaptations that bridge this gap are discussed in the following two sections.

EARLY TRANSFORMATIONS

Previous dramatic, radio, and cinematic adaptations notwithstanding, Mamoulian's 1931 *Dr. Jekyll and Mr. Hyde* stands as a good starting point, given its connections with the other popular monster films of the 1930s.[10] Mamoulian's film provides the earliest and strongest predecessor to modern renderings, delivering a Hyde that is repulsive in his transition, his appearance, and his actions. Fredric March (the actor who played both Jekyll and Hyde) gasps, grunts, and twitches alongside a mixture of camera effects and blended transitions to make the conversion quite remarkable for the time in which it was produced. Hyde is physically presented as a man with kinky hair on an almost cone-like skull, thick lips, protruding jagged teeth, dark skin (in contrast to Jekyll's pale complexion), and hairy hands, coding him as ape-like in a manner consistent with the novella. These elements are coupled with his increasingly apelike actions, which include climbing trees, leaping fences, skillfully outmaneuvering police, and scaling bookshelves to evade them. His actions also become more repulsive as he desires, forcibly takes, abuses, and dispatches Ivy (a lower-class, uneducated prostitute with a pale white complexion) and then attempts to violate Muriel (an educated, upper-class, sexually innocent fiancée to Jekyll). In his final brutal act, Hyde canes to death Brigadier-General Sir Danvers Carew, an upper-class white male that represents all that is proper in the Victorian London setting.

However, for an American audience in the 1930s, Hyde can be read also as African American.[11] If his physical markers are not enough to signal his "darker" nature, his first words exclaimed are "Free! Free at last!" with a rising fist, evoking an African American spiritual song.[12] He also curses Lanyon and Carew as "hypocrites" and "deniers of life," which speaks more to implications of enslavement than scientific endeavors — people that have lorded over his work (Lanyon) and his love (Carew). He follows his exclamation with the stretching of his arms as if his hands had been bound together. The racial tension of the 1930s was strongly present within U.S. culture. The first feature length film, *Birth of a Nation* (1915), and even the first talking film, *The Jazz Singer* (1927), both fixated on race. Debates around evolution (and our descent from apes and Africans) also took shape during this time, including the famous Scopes Trial in 1925.[13] The 1910s and 1920s witnessed an increased membership of the Ku Klux Klan.[14] In the same year the film played across the country, the Tuskegee Institute began its infamous experiments wherein 399 African American males suffering from syphilis were left untreated for decades for the purposes of medical experimentation.[15] Even if Hyde were not coded as African American, he would still come across as evil within the film. However, the racially charged context of the 1910s-1930s make his racial coding equally important because he is the earliest American version of Hyde steeped in cultural fears and anxieties.

The film *Dr. Jekyll and Mr. Hyde* also provides three clear moments where Jekyll and Hyde's sizes are significantly different. The first scene occurs after Hyde kills Ivy but cannot transform back to Jekyll without his potion. Through a letter, he convinces Lanyon to get the ingredients and meet Hyde at Lanyon's house. When Hyde appears requesting the ingredients, Lanyon demands to know that Jekyll is safe. At gunpoint, Hyde takes the formula and returns to Jekyll before Lanyon's eyes. The camera shifts to a tall candle burning, and through a dissolve, quickly burns down several inches, thereby indicating that time has passed. The shrinking of the candle is carried over to the shrinking of Jekyll. As the camera returns to Jekyll and Lanyon talking, Jekyll is positioned in an oversized chair, making him appear small in stature. This is aided by Lanyon's desk and chair, which are positioned visibly higher than Jekyll, making him look even smaller. If this scene emphasizes the shrinking of Jekyll, the second scene emphasizes the growing dominance of Hyde. The scene comes right before the film's climax, after Jekyll has rejected Muriel. Believing himself damned from Hyde's murder of Ivy, Jekyll leaves Muriel's house but stops outside the window. Upon listening to Muriel cry, the transformation occurs; for the first time in the film, this transition clearly marks a Hyde that is taller than Jekyll. The body grows taller and broader than Jekyll was a few seconds prior. This transformation contrasts with previous ones in which Hyde appeared smaller. The final moment comes minutes later when Hyde is fleeing the Carew estate with police pursuing him. As he turns into an alley and continues running past the screen, the lighting is positioned to show his shadow growing larger and larger with each step. As one of the last images that the audience sees of Hyde, this leaves a lingering impression of

Hyde as bigger than previously conceived. Through these three scenes, the lasting impact on audiences is that Hyde is bigger than Jekyll.

This larger Hyde impacts later renderings of Hyde, which can be seen as early as Warner Bros.' 1942 Looney Tunes cartoon short "The Impatient Patient," in which Daffy Duck finds himself consulting "Dr. Jerkyl" for a cure for his hiccups. Dr. Jerkyl takes a formula and transitions from a small timid doctor into large oafish man with protruding teeth, i.e., a Hyde that reveals the influence of the 1931 film. In the classroom, instructors can address the 1931 film in several ways. They can require students to view the film and discuss the film's elements with pointed questions to lead to the above discoveries, or they can just go over the main points about the film while showing some screen shots to illustrate how the film visually morphed Hyde. Regardless of whether the 1931 film is viewed in its entirety, instructors should make certain to address this particular presentation as it fills the necessary gap between pre–Hulk versions and post–Hulk versions of Hyde that is essential.

HULKING HYDES

The conversation now turns to Marvel Comics' *The Incredible Hulk*. Debuting in May 1962, the Hulk has proven the strongest influential narrative on the development of Hyde as a large bestial creature. He has appeared in over 3500 individual comic book issues, while also being the focus of two feature-length films, three television series, three made-for-TV movies, two direct-to-DVD animated movies, and several video games.[16] Hulk has culturally captured American and international audiences and served as an ongoing narrative focal point for the Jekyll/Hyde motif for over fifty years. Given this abundance of representations, many students think of Hyde as a hulking mass and some contemporary adaptations of the character have produced Hyde in a manner that reflects the Hulk's influence. In explaining the transition to students, it becomes necessary to not only discuss the Hulk as it relates to Hyde but to recognize the other cultural forces at work, which made Hulk more relevant than Hyde in the 1960s, a time situated in the midst of the Cold War, with people still feeling the fallout from World War II.

The Hulk was originally modeled on the character The Thing from Marvel Comics' *Fantastic Four*, another character straddling attraction and repulsion. Creators Jack Kirby and Stan Lee had created The Thing as part of the team but appreciated the concept of a self-hating superhero enough to use it for *The Incredible Hulk*.[17] However, Lee has said that two of the major influences in creating the Hulk were *Dr. Jekyll and Mr. Hyde* and *Frankenstein*. It becomes clear that the transformation from Bruce Banner to Hulk evokes the visual transformation scenes from any prior Jekyll and Hyde film; however, the final product, the Hulk, visually references Boris Karloff's iconic version of Frankenstein's monster with its heavy brow and large, flattened head. The powerful influence of James Whale's *Frankenstein* also changes audience perceptions of the Hulk. Modern films and television series have emphasized a Hulk that is simplistic, rage-driven, and lacks linguistic capabilities beyond saying things like "Hulk smash!"[18] However, in the first six-issue run of *The Incredible Hulk*, the Hulk could speak in clear (although often short) sentences and used the first person instead of the third person when referring to himself.

The mixture of Hyde and Frankenstein's monster offers a useful lesson to students in understanding that even though the Hulk is a Jekyll/Hyde monster, the influence of other monsters still weaves into how Hyde is depicted in the modern texts. To emphasize this point, instructors might want to provide side-by-side shots of both the Hulk and Karloff's Frankenstein for students to draw comparisons. The comparison primes the students to look at all modern monsters (or narratives for that matter) more critically, trying to connect the present with the past.

The cover of *The Incredible Hulk #1* marks a good starting point for discussing the Hulk. Under the comic title, a caption reads, "The Strangest Man of All Time!!" The use of the word "strangest" connects to the full title of Stevenson's novella, *The Strange Case of Dr. Jekyll and Mr. Hyde*. Adjacent to this is a large question mark, functioning as a caption containing the text "Is He Man or Monster or…" in the curved line of the question mark and "Is He Both" in the period below. The question is largely rhetorical; the Hulk is clearly a physical monster. The gawking and pointing by characters in the background make this clear. However, since it is bounded within the question mark, the question suggests that Hulk is not necessarily monstrous in effect; after all, he is not actually doing anything violent.

The cover features a blonde-haired man with glasses and white lab coat standing in the center. Around him, wavy lines indicate his transformation into the large monster that stands over him bare-footed and in tattered clothes. The effect, as noted by Adam Capitanio, is that it resembles a mushroom cloud billowing forth from the man. This interpretation is justified upon reading the first part of the comic.[19]

On the first page, a full-page panel displays the Hulk, touted as a "Half-Man Half-Monster." The story starts in a laboratory with the "genius," Dr. Bruce Banner preparing to test his "gamma bomb." His colleague, Igor, berates him for not sharing his knowledge in case something goes wrong, but Banner rebuffs him; he is so confident in his work in that he states, "I don't make errors, Igor!" If Igor questions his scientific aptitude, General "Thunderbolt" Ross, the military leader protecting the lab, calls Banner a "milksop" for being too cautious and wasting his time. The General is also the father of Betty Ross, Banner's romantic interest.[20] After Betty and her father leave, Igor pleads one more time for Banner to divulge the secret, getting a bit rough with him. Banner's parting words to Igor are, "You know how I detest men who think with their fists." He launches the test but then runs to the testing field to protect a trespassing teenager, Rick Jones. Banner risks his life and saves Jones by receiving the brunt of the gamma radiation. Upon being hit, Banner screams, which continues for hours. Placed in confinement, Banner and Jones wait to see if they will die. But as night approaches, Banner becomes increasingly agitated and the Geiger counter starts crackling as he transforms into the Hulk for the first time. In the Hulk form, he swats Jones aside, saying, "Get out of my way, insect!" He breaks through the wall and smashes a jeep full of soldiers attempting to stop him. He considers the soldiers, "Men! More little men!!" He continues to escape, deciding he has "To get away — to hide..."[21]

This opening story provides several noteworthy points. The obvious point is that Banner, like Jekyll, is a leading scientist, working in an area that Igor describes as "too dangerous." Igor's challenge to Banner's work contrasts neatly with Jekyll's "scientific heresies" according to Lanyon.[22] However, Banner's masculinity is also called into question by the General. As a military leader with a daughter, the General proves he is both powerful and potent, an alpha male, whereas Banner wears a laboratory coat and lacks evidence of any potency. The fact that Betty comes to his defense further illustrates Banner as weak. Grounds for insufficient manhood can also be found within the novella, when Utterson raises questions about Hyde's relation to Jekyll, believing Hyde to be "the cancer of some concealed disgrace."[23] Utterson's judgment of Jekyll's "wild" youth is contrasted with Utterson's "fairly blameless" past.[24] Like Banner, Jekyll lacks a certain respectability despite being a doctor.

The Hulk, like Hyde, is physically distinguishable from Banner. He speaks in full sentences much like Hyde. Also, Hulk carries a disdain for Banner that is akin to Hyde's. Upon seeing a picture of Banner, Hulk exclaims, "Fool! I am glad it happened!! I'd rather be me, than that puny weakling in the picture!" In looking at the picture, Hulk, a creature who thinks with his fists, doubtlessly feels like Hyde in that, "he resented the dislike with which he was himself regarded [by Jekyll]."[25]

The Incredible Hulk took the Jekyll/Hyde monster in several new directions. First, it shifted the science from chemistry to physics to meet the fears and anxieties induced by the creation of nuclear power and ensuing Cold War. The power of the atom was ambiguous. Though acceptable and even beneficial in the hands of the U.S. and its allies, the power was deeply feared when in the hands of the Soviets. The Hulk himself was ambiguous since he was a wild card, controlled by neither the United States nor the Soviet Union.[26] Second, the Hulk's creation comes from Banner's self-sacrifice to save Jones. This deviates from Jekyll's desire to split his pure and impure personas.[27] A further complication is that though the Hulk is perceived as a villain within his world, the reader perceives him to be an anti-hero at worst and even a hero in other situations, such as when as he saves the individuals, the U.S., and the planet, from various monsters, aliens, Soviet and other foreign threats. Preserving life becomes a central dynamic for the Hulk creation story within all its manifestations in comics, film, and television. These two distinctions have staying power within the Hulk narrative that influence and change how the contemporary Jekyll and Hyde narrative is told. The first element, physics, evolves into genetics in the twenty-first century adaptations. Most interestingly, the self-sacrificial aspect of Banner is turned into a self-sacrificing Hyde within modern adaptations.

So, where does the leap from a self-sacrificial Banner to a self-sacrificing Hyde occur? The answer can be found in the live-action television series, *The Incredible Hulk* (1977–1982). The series provides several key pieces connecting the comic book version of Hulk with the contemporary renderings of Hyde that this paper will examine after explaining the key points of the pilot episode, "The Incredible Hulk," directed by Kenneth Johnson. In this episode, Dr. David Banner has been lamenting for a year, figuring out why he failed to save his wife, Laura. While driving down a country road, a blown out tire sends their car careening off the road and rolling over several times. Banner escapes the car and tries to lift the car to save his wife but cannot do so, and she dies. He spends the following year interviewing women, elderly men, and other people who appear (or at least are culturally suggested to be) less powerful than him, all of whom were able to save their loved ones through calling upon inhuman strength at the height of an accident. He discovers the "gamma" levels in his blood failed him that day and gives himself a high dosage of gamma radiation to induce the strength that he lacked. He takes a higher dosage than expected, and this turns him into the Hulk whenever his emotions become escalated. While driving home from the experiment, Banner's car gets a flat tire, and he attempts to fix it. Injuring himself in the process, Banner morphs into the Hulk for the first time. While roaming the countryside as the Hulk the next morning, he comes upon a young girl who is frightened by his appearance and falls into the nearby lake. Looking to help, the Hulk grabs a broken tree to put into the water for the girl to grab. At this moment, the father appears and believes the Hulk is attacking the girl, so he shoots the Hulk. The Hulk eventually returns to being Banner, who finds protection in Dr. Elaina Marks, a colleague. The two work on Banner's condition, trying to find a cure until a series of events leads to the fiery destruction of the laboratory and Hulk enters to save Marks. She dies shortly after and Banner must go on the run since he is presumed dead and the Hulk has been publicly denounced as the perpetrator.

This episode provides a major shift worth emphasizing. First, Banner severely lacks a strong sense of masculinity. He is incapable of saving his wife even though old men and women in similar circumstances prove strong and powerful enough to save their loved ones. At one point, he even blames his mother, "My mother always said, 'Don't get angry.'"[28] This strikes an interesting chord of concerns about American identity (and by proxy, masculinity) in the late 1970s after the loss of Vietnam, Watergate, and the rising tide of feminism. Banner becomes a bigger "milksop" than previously, since he seeks out the gamma rays to compensate for his inabilities, rather than sacrificing himself and exposing himself to gamma rays to protect another person's life. The self-experimentation brings Hulk into closer alignment with Stevenson's novella since Banner, like Jekyll, seeks to improve himself (and to some degree, purify himself, with physical weakness being understood as a sign of male impurity). However, it is this lacking masculinity in Banner that means the Hulk will continually risk and sacrifice himself on behalf of others. This occurs in the first episode where he goes into a fire to save Marks, and it carries through to the conclusion of the series, a television movie, *The Death of the Incredible Hulk* (1990), where he is killed while pursuing the villains who have done harm to his friends. Present within the TV series more so than the comic (at least initially), this theme of an insufficient man becoming hypermasculinized and willing to die for good people is rethreaded into the Jekyll/Hyde narrative.

In classroom discussions of the Hulk's influence on Hyde, it is important to provide access to the original comic (reprinted numerous times) or even watch, in part or in full, the pilot episode of the TV series. The aforementioned discussion of the Incredible Hulk #1's cover is important, but students will also need to see the initial constructions of the Hulk, since their perceptions of the Incredible Hulk will also be tainted by recent versions.[29] Understanding Hulk's initial construction in comics and the switch occurring in television makes clearer the readable influences Hulk has on Hyde, transcending just physical appearance.

The Hydes of Hulk

The Incredible Hulk's influence on contemporary renderings of Hyde can be clearly identified and discussed within both the comic (1999) and the film (2003) of *The League of Extraordinary Gentlemen*, *Hulk* (2003), and the BBC mini-series, *Jekyll* (2007). Though there are other Jekyll/Hyde adaptations that could be included here, such as the film *Van Helsing* (2004), these three provide the clearest discussion that can be addressed within a classroom without having to deviate into other tangents.[30]

Alan Moore's *The League of Extraordinary Gentlemen* serves as a Victorian mash-up of classic adventure and horror fiction from the worlds of H. Rider Haggard, Robert Louis Stevenson, Bram Stoker, Jules Verne, H. G. Wells, and many others. At its center, a team of Victorian characters must save England from near destruction.[31] The team includes Allan Quatermain, Mina Murray, Griffin (the Invisible Man), Captain Nemo, and Dr. Jekyll. Jekyll and Hyde's origin is based upon the novella with some occasional hints that the report is missing key pieces. Much like in the book, readers first meet Hyde, not Jekyll. Quatermain and Murray encounter Hyde while resolving a rash of murdered prostitutes in Paris on the Rue Morgue. Hyde first appears as a large behemoth, whose frame and height is larger than the door through which he is squeezing. He holds Quatermain up with a single hand that is bigger than Quatermain's head. He speaks in clear sentences with the occasional grunt. However, the characteristics and skin color of Hyde in this work clearly evoke the ape-like qualities that Stevenson includes. With a brownish hue and visible hairiness, Hyde has a large jaw with fangs and feet that can grasp things. However, Hyde is bigger than any ape or human. An explanation for his ballooning size comes in the second series when Hyde, after brutally slaughtering a traitor within their group, explains to Captain Nemo, "when I started out, good God, I was practically a ****ing dwarf. Jekyll, on the other hand, is a great big strapping fellow. Since then, though, my growth's been unrestricted, while he's wasted away to nothing. Obvious really. Without me, you see Jekyll has no drives and without him, I have no restraints."[32]

The explanation provided makes some narrative sense but has its limitations. It comes with the second series, published in 2002, two years after the end of the first series. This lag in time makes the explanation feel more like backtracking than actual intentionality on Moore's part, particularly when coupled with Hyde's character arc through the series. Hyde's self-reported lack of restraint is dubious. Within the first series, he is willing to fight with the rest of the members of the League in order to save London, be pardoned for his crimes, and thus be able to live in England. The second series positions Hyde as a brutish but still self-sacrificing hero. To stall the invading aliens, Hyde launches a singular attack on an alien tripod and causes it to explode, which ultimately kills him. This sacrifice resembles those of the Hulk, who continually sacrifices his life and his safety to protect people he cares about and the world in general. No matter how much of a brute the Hulk becomes, he always comes back to saving the humans that hate him. The Hyde of Stevenson's novella has no such redemptive qualities. He hides within Jekyll or kills himself to avoid facing the consequences of his actions. Yet, Moore's Hyde aligns more closely with the Hulk as a self-sacrificing, brutish behemoth with a weak male counterpart than with Stevenson's Hyde.

Obviously, the film of *League* (2003), directed by Stephen Norrington, takes its lead from the comic series in presenting Jekyll and Hyde as more akin to Banner and Hulk. During the first two thirds of the film, Jekyll fights with Hyde, who appears in mirrors and other reflective surfaces demanding to be released from the cage of Jekyll's mind. But when Captain Nemo's submarine suffers an internal bombing that jeopardizes the crewmembers and the League, Hyde and Jekyll set aside their differences to save the ship. Jekyll willingly becomes Hyde and Hyde saves everyone. Jekyll is nevertheless still skeptical of Hyde, stating, "Let's not make a saint out of a sinner. Next time he may not be so helpful." But Hyde continues to become saintlier. In the climax of the film, the team assaults an arctic fortress, where the villain, M, is poised to mass-produce nastier versions of the team members with plans for world domination. Hyde arrives just in time to witness a soldier take the entire potion instead of the smaller dosage that he uses. This dosage turns the man into a beastly creature significantly larger and more deformed than Hyde himself: a massive hunchback with dark, slimy skin. As a point of contrast, this monster can palm the entirety of Hyde's head and shoulders. Clearly outsized, Hyde takes a beating for the next several minutes of the movie, occasionally getting in a good shot but mostly distracting the monster from attacking the others, who would stand no chance.

This Hyde clearly parallels the Hulk. Physically, he looks more human, akin to the Hulk with his disproportionately large upper-body, but much less apelike than Moore's rendering. Hyde is sought after by the authorities (The League) and his brutish nature and past crimes are, if not completely forgiven, at least temporarily forgotten since his strength is much needed. The narrative arc of Hyde as self-experimenter-turned-monster, threat, and savior is mirrored by both recent film adaptations of the Hulk, *Hulk* (2003) and *The Incredible Hulk* (2008). The 2003 Hulk film actually appeared three weeks before *The League* film, making the comparison all the more notable. *The League* versions, both comic series and film, illustrate a Hyde character that is shaped as much by the Hulk as by Stevenson's novella. Hyde is more physically powerful and beyond normal human size; he is loathed by the characters within the story but not necessarily by the audience, and he ultimately redeems himself through his fighting.

A redemptive Hyde who is needed to fight a greater evil makes sense in the 2000s. In the contemporary world of the September eleventh attacks and the U.S. invasion of Iraq, the idea that some men need to do immoral things in order to prevent a more disastrous event appears to resonate with an audience much more strongly than the simpler moral dichotomy presented in Stevenson's novella. Hyde represents the necessary but ethically complex measures a person or society must take for protection. This too works more strongly with the *Incredible Hulk* comic, which was situated around the question of atomic power's role in the Cold War politics of the 1960s.

It seems appropriate to end this exploration of Jekyll and Hyde with the 2007 BBC mini-series, which is a complicated narrative that deserves more attention than the scope of this article allows. This six-hour TV series brings the narrative of Jekyll and Hyde to the contemporary world by presenting Jekyll as a real person and Dr. Tom Jackman as his descendant. Upon discovering Hyde, Jackman hires someone to watch over him and even restrain him when Hyde is present. As in earlier incarnations, Jekyll and Hyde prove antagonistic; each dislikes the other and finds ways of harming or interfering with the other. However, the company Jackman formerly worked for, Klein & Utterson, seeks to understand and use the power of Jackman's transformation for its own gain. The company orchestrates plans to capture Jackman and his family. Rather than remaining separate, Jekyll and Hyde merge their identities to save their family. In merging with Jackman, Hyde's already established power grows exponentially, and he is capable of hacking computer systems with his mind and singlehandedly eliminating an entire squadron of specially trained combat soldiers. The series ends with Tom as a unified person, his family saved, and Klein and Utterson nearly destroyed. It deviates from the giant-sized Hyde, but clearly invokes the strength of the Hulk and strongly relies upon the redemption element so present in modern Hyde narratives that stem from the Hulk.

Though the series avoided physically distorting Hyde, it did significantly increase Hyde's powers. Hyde has superior strength; he singlehandedly slays two lions. He has hyper-reflexes as well as other superhuman abilities that Hulk lacks. More importantly, however, Hyde is a redemptive character, almost more so than the Hulk. Hyde, like the Hulk, becomes the hero of the narrative despite his sadistic and violent actions in the first arc of the series, which include drug use, prostitutes, murder, and general mayhem. He stops fighting with his other half and sacrifices his singular identity to merge with Jackman. In merging, Jackman/Hyde fights the extensive forces of Klein and Utterson to save Jackman's family, with little likelihood of surviving. Thus, Hyde "out-hulks" the Hulk in performing a double sacrifice. Superpowers and redemption through self-sacrifice prove to be central characteristics within the Hulk versions of Hyde, but these are largely missing from adaptations solely reliant upon Stevenson's novella.

For teaching purposes, incorporating the BBC series into a discussion of the Hyde/Hulk model can be challenging. Its length and complicated plot does not lend well to classroom viewing or explanation. However, if Hyde and Hulk have been discussed in the context provided herein, it may be useful to briefly point to the series and challenge students to explore the series on their own.

Conclusion

The focus on how Hulk was derived from Hyde and how Hyde turned into the Hulk provides one means of exploring the contemporary renderings of Stevenson's archetypal figure. Given the numerous adaptations and variations of Jekyll and Hyde since 1886, there are many different variations worth considering, as with any monster archetype. However, saying that monsters change over time through a complicated mixture of narrative adaptations and cultural forces does not provide students with a critical understanding of the process. Students are often aware on some level of pattern changes within monster archetypes, but they usually need a clear and detailed example to illustrate the pattern. This article can be used to provide a specialized knowledge of a particular archetype and the pattern of change that recreates the monster for modern-day audiences. Learning about the archetype and how it becomes what it is today is important, but so too is encouraging students to be aware and search for such patterns in any monster archetype they may encounter.

This proves useful for any course in horror, but this lesson is one worth presenting even in other courses such as popular culture and literature more broadly, since it helps students understand how interconnected their modes of entertainment are, be they books, comic books, video games, films, or TV series. To understand how and why Hyde operates as he does in the television miniseries, *Jekyll*, it proved necessary to connect Stevenson's novella, Mamoulian's film, Lee and Kirby's comic, Johnson's pilot episode, Moore's comics, and Norrington's film. The cross-representation provides an interesting look at how cultural forces shape and are shaped by the forms of storytelling afforded them — certainly, a point useful for many courses.

NOTES

1. Jeffrey Jerome Cohen, *Monster Theory: Reading Culture* (Minneapolis, Minn: University of Minnesota Press, 1996), 4–6.

2. Robert Louis Stevenson and Katherine Linehan, *Strange Case of Dr. Jekyll and Mr. Hyde: An Authoritative Text, Backgrounds and Contexts, Performance Adaptations, Criticism* (New York: Norton, 2003), 17.

3. Nicholas G. Carr, *The Shallows: What the Internet Is Doing to Our Brains* (New York: W.W. Norton, 2010).

4. Randy Duncan and Matthew J. Smith, *The Power of Comics: History, Form and Culture* (New York: Continuum, 2009), 24–32.

5. Raymond T. McNally and Radu Florescu, *In Search of Dr. Jekyll and Mr. Hyde* (Los Angeles: Renaissance Books, 2000), 166–167.

6. Robert Louis Stevenson Website.

7. Chip Selby, *Tales from the Crypt from Comic books to Television* (Reistertown, MD: CS Films, 2004), Joseph Maddrey, and *Nightmares in Red, White and Blue: The Evolution of the American Horror Film* (Jefferson, NC: McFarland, 2004). See also the documentary film based on the latter book and bearing the same title directed by Andrew Monument (New York: Kino Lorber, 2010), DVD.

8. *Mary Reilly*, directed by Stephen Frears (Columbia Tristar Home Entertainment, 1995), DVD.

9. Stevenson, 17.

10. *Dr. Jekyll & Mr. Hyde* (1932), directed by Rouben Mamoulian. While Adolph Zukor's silent film, *Dr. Jekyll and Mr. Hyde* (1920), is the usual starting point for discussing cinematic adaptations, since it is well-preserved and the first cinematic feature-length film in the U.S., it proves not as relevant for this article. Hyde appears as a small statured hunchback along with long, almost skeletal fingers. The long fingers when held in frame with his head emphasize his deformity since the hands appear out of proportion to the head. He is clearly distinguished from Jekyll and looks haggard and devious but not particularly repulsive or frightening. Other films released just prior to Mamoulian's film include the Universal Studies *Dracula* (1931) and *Frankenstein* (1931). It is also the first talking Hyde, which proves of interest as it also helps to track the development of a less-verbal Hyde.

11. I use the term "African American" as opposed to "African," though the distinction is complicated. This was a film made in the U.S. but clearly positioned in London in the 1800s.

12. "Free at last, free at last; I thank God I'm free at last; Free at last, free at last; I thank God I'm free at last." "Free at Last," Official Site of Negro Spirituals, accessed August 1, 2011. http://www.negrospirituals.com/news-song/free_at_last_from.htm.

13. Interestingly, the film on the Scopes Trial, *Inherit the Wind* (1960), will star Fredric March as the prosecutor arguing against evolution while Spencer Tracy would be the defense lawyer arguing for the right to teach evolution. While both actors played the Jekyll/Hyde character, March's Jekyll/Hyde was much more based in (albeit spurious) discussions of evolution than Tracy's approach.

14. "Issues of Race in the 1930s," in "Urban and Urbane: The New Yorker Magazine in the 1930s. Accessed on August 1, 2011. http://xroads.virginia.edu/~ug02/newyorker/race.html.

15. "U.S. Public Health Service Syphilis Study at Tuskegee," Centers for Disease Control and Prevention, last modified June 15, 2011. http://www.cdc.gov/tuskegee/timeline.htm.

16. This refers to productions in which Hulk was featured in the title, but the character has appeared at different times in the various made-for-DVD Marvel animations such as *The Ultimates* and *Next Avengers*, and cartoon series such as *X-Men: Evolution*, *Spider-Man*, and *Fantastic Four*.

17. Eventually, this would be the same motif for Spider-Man as well. See Adam Capitanio, "The Jekyll and Hyde of the Atomic Age: The Incredible Hulk as the Ambiguous Embodiment of Nuclear Power." *Journal of Popular Culture* 43 (2): 249–270.

18. This comes about largely from the live action TV series which will be addressed later.

19. Capitanio, 254.

20. This interestingly parallels the relationship dynamic within many of the theatrical and film versions of Jekyll and Hyde, where Jekyll's love interest has a father (often military and aristocratic) who berates Jekyll.

21. Stan Lee and Jack Kirby. *The Incredible Hulk*. Marvel Comics 1: 1 (1962), 1–6.

22. Stevenson, 20.

23. Stevenson, 18.

24. Stevenson, 18–19.

25. Stevenson, 61.

26. The Hulk would regularly fight Soviets (including Igor, who was a Soviet spy) and Soviet-inspired monsters, alien races, etc; however, his partnering with any U.S. forces was always temporary and tenuous.

27. Though given the context of the nuclear, Banner was still playing with splitting; it just happened to be atoms, not parts of the self.

28. The echo of Norman Bates could be heard in this refrain, perhaps?

29. In any serial narrative, particularly superhero comics, the character changes by degrees and at different times, different aspects of the character are emphasized. For instance, there are story arcs of the Incredible Hulk's series where the Hulk has been fully blended with Banner (Banner's intelligence; Hulk's body, together as one) as well as physically separated.

30. For instance, to cover Hyde within *Van Helsing* means having to also touch upon the direct-to-DVD simultaneous release of *Van Helsing: The London Assignment*. However, that avenue requires substantial more discussion than can be allotted for this essay.

31. In the first series, it was rival gangs; the second series, it was the alien invasion of *War of the Worlds*.

32. Moore, Alan, Kevin O'Neill, and Ben Dimagmaliw. 2003. *The League of Extraordinary Gentlemen. Volume II*. La Jolla, CA: America's Best Comics, LLC.

Critical Thinking on the Dark Side

Lisa Marie Miller

In the spring of 2010, I finally set out to teach the course I had thought about for years. Critical Writing, the second required course at my institution, covered critical thinking and argumentation, interaction with readings and the ultimate application of these to writing, all centered around a theme of the instructor's choosing. My choice was the paranormal. The title referred to unusual and perhaps "unprovable" aspects of life and death that were generally thought to lie outside the realm of traditional scientific investigation and discussion. Having always been interested in this topic myself, I had noticed that others found it especially engaging. Students would always get into lively, fascinating discussions when readings touching on "death" were our subject. Beyond this, I had also noticed that conversations about life after death or psychic ability often became gratifying intellectual debates, bringing out the best in the participants.

I have encountered many books over the years that model the same skills, presenting the cogent arguments on different aspects of paranormal issues and revealing the higher level, abstract thinking to which such philosophical, theoretical and scientific discussions take the reader and writer. For example, *Immortality*, edited by Paul Edwards (Prometheus, 1997), provides readers with the thoughts of classical thinkers and contemporary critics on the topic of surviving death. *Is There Life After Death?* by Robert Kastenbaum (Prentice Hall, 1984), takes a no-nonsense look at the issues by introducing various points and problems associated with the idea of ghosts, telepathy, etc., through a combination of evidence, critical examination and further speculation. To supplement "real life" accounts of the near-death experience were articles from *The Skeptical Inquirer* that took the anecdotal claims in hand and offered possible medical explanations. In the face of startling accounts or even personal experiences in addition to the explanations of science, with abstract reasoning and speculation capable of pointing both ways, it was up to the individual thinker to decide; no "facts" could automatically silence either side. I saw here a perfect vehicle for enhancing critical thinking and writing skills in college students who, with few exceptions, would welcome a good discussion of the "uncanny," typically more of a "dorm" topic than the subject of their required readings, papers and class discussions.

I had proposed this critical thinking/writing course several years earlier at another school which, unlike my present affiliation, allows instructors to choose their own themes and had a select group of topics but required proposals for new additions to the list. Students I polled showed a great interest and desire to take this course and I had outlined all of the critical thinking benefits. I noted the timeliness of this example of a "New Age" topic as well as the prevalence of its detractors in what was nevertheless still a largely "scientific" era. A renewed interest in the unseen, the magical, the supernatural, a curiosity about things such as ghosts, crystals and witches was granting some respect to unusual phenomena in a society accustomed to relying upon the clarity of the scientific method and to celebrating its medical and technological achievements. People spoke of goddesses and spells, and the Gothic became a current trend alongside the latest medical research and computer advances. Concepts such as life after death and hauntings reappeared as a staple of the media in both fictional and documentary forms. This movement was in full swing in the 1990s, when I submitted the proposal. In an informal survey, nine of my twenty-five critical thinking students would have "strongly" preferred my proposed class, entitled "*Claims* of The Paranormal," to the other course offerings in the area and an additional three, while not sharing the degree of eagerness of the other group, would also have taken the class. Thus, half of my class, only one among many critical thinking classes in the college, would have elected to take the course I envisioned rather than the usual varieties of this requirement that advertised themes centering around specific decades, biographies or gender issues. In addition to the lively debate this topic tends to engender among students, I also emphasized that these students would need to rely upon good argumentative skills and constructive use of data when making claims on either side, whether they sought to defend the ghost or prove it a figment of the imagination. Finally, I included a list of four possible texts for the course, two of which were clearly from the side of "science and reason" as well as Kastenbaum's *Is There Life After Death?* The latter, in its focus on both sides of each issue and in the thoroughness of its approach was, as I explained, itself, a model of good critical thinking. I was excited about presenting what I felt was a wonderful addition to the current list of critical thinking courses, one that students also, I came to realize, wanted me to initiate and one that I knew would engage them in rigorous critical thinking while holding their interest.

Yet, the proposal was rejected because, as stated to me, it was feared that the students would "talk about paranormal things." This rejection of the paranormal as a topic is a pure case of bias, representative of a prejudice against the paranormal that appeared to exist within academic circles. The fact that it was the thinking and not the subject matter that served as its material that was important was being forgotten. Students compose papers on everything from tattooing to celebrity diets for writing classes with their teachers' approval. The subject of the paranormal, it seems, incurs more resistance. Despite rare offerings in parapsychology in some university catalogs over the years, the study of the paranormal, even as a springboard for discussion, has been looked upon with disdain. Part of this stems from fear, the fear of what "talking about paranormal things" will involve. Some immediately conjure up images of fanatics and charlatans, of the "fringe element," who fly in the face of reason and fair argumentation. Yet, it is not merely eccentric shopkeepers peddling tarot cards and incense or the subjects of television's spooky, sensationalistic trends who represent those interested; numerous doctors, scientists and psychologists also venture seriously into such investigations of the darker corners. While the initial connotation of "darkness" here may have been one of our fear and ignorance before the mysteries of death and the unknown, it has seemed to mutate in the academic world to an automatic association with the backwardness of the "Dark Ages." Even if we proceed, perhaps unfairly, to label some individuals as paranormally crazed weirdos, should we exclude all serious discussion on such topics? A sensationalized talk show segment entitled, "I Was a Three-Headed Trisexual Transsexual Transvestite" does not preclude serious classroom discussions of gender and sexuality. The supposed signal from the star Vega in the film *Contact* elicits both serious SETI investigation and a renewed search for Elvis. Our fear of fanaticism and chaos in society throws the ghost out with the otherworldly bathwater. Admittedly, this is a valid concern and I have addressed it by explaining to the class that, with all due respect for everyone's particular faiths, or lack of them for that matter, topics must be discussed *apart* from religious justifications, which are based on faith. Although faith may be valid in students' individual lives, it is not at issue in a critical thinking class; in order for God to be cited as a source, a case would first have to made for God's existence, as all do not consider this phenomenon a "given." In any case, it can be done; the "spirit" can be discussed in the language of logic. As a case in point, the question of our survival after death must be discussed, according to Kastenbaum, with the utmost respect for the rules of logic and reason. A.J. Ayer further explains how an afterlife can exist without a deity.[1] When discussing the paranormal, religion need not dominate nor even enter into a discussion.

Still, the fear of bringing the "dark side" into the critical thinking classroom remains a free-floating one, a fact that one must recognize in order to satisfactorily counter it. Throughout my teaching experience, I note that professors tried to avoid assertion based on religious belief. It seemed to follow, from their point of view, that they also would reject what they saw as equally unproven ghost sightings and near death experiences. Even within the humanities, the scientific method increasingly appeared as perhaps the highest and possibly the only means of ascertaining reality. For those academics holding such a view, serious study would necessitate statistics rather than attention to something like personal sightings of spirits and the possibility of life after death would sound too much like the purely religious concept of "heaven." In my own graduate school experience, affective responses to literature were rare among professors and the frequent motivation for students pursuing higher level degrees in the field today appears to be not the love of an art form but the desire to use artistic materials in the service of the social sciences. Even among those not ruled by this particular cast of mind, a bias sometimes still seems prevalent against the study and discussion of the paranormal in intellectual circles. As chair of the Horror division for a regional conference, I once planned a panel discussion on the topic of "Life After Death," with presenters on opposite sides of the issue. Although I was permitted to organize the panel, the conference program chair revealed doubts about the viability of the entire venture because there was "no proof" on the topic. Another humanities professor, who had referred a student with an excellent paper on children and ghost sightings to my Horror area nevertheless referred to the student's interest and good work as a proclivity toward "those" kinds of topics. When we teach literature and film of any genre, among the richest and most valuable class experiences are the discussions about issues raised by the works themselves. In the same way that studying a Victorian novel or a contemporary graphic war film can engender lively talk about feminism or war in general, a course that explores horror films and literature should not squelch students' natural ventures into where these works lead.

Beyond issues of literary and film technique, discussion of the viability of actual paranormal traditions and possibilities is often at the heart of studying classic works of horror. An ambiguity may often be at the core of a ghost story or a "haunted house" film, leading students inevitably into the realm of discussing the paranormal per se. Could it possibly have been an actual ghost that the protagonist has seen? Are there alternate explanations? Why is this film director's rendition particularly effective given what we see as possible in terms of the paranormal? As in classes based upon other, more accepted subject matter, questions will arise touching upon students' own life experiences, thoughts and beliefs about the content. The horror classroom or conference area should be no exception. When I encountered such reactions to the inclusion of the topic of the paranormal in intellectual venues, as with the department chair who reported the committee's response to my proposal, the tone was almost always one of hesitancy or even embarrassment, as if, on some level, the academic community was aware that this was an unfounded and biased reaction.

The position of automatically excluding the paranormal will therefore not appear widely and openly asserted; it is evidenced in encounters like the ones I have described above, the recognition of biased presentations even in critical thinking textbooks, which are supposed to present opposing sides as ultimately neutral material for strengthening argumentative skills and in the relative absence of this kind of topic from syllabi. Although my conference area included horror in its customary genres of literature and film, it also welcomed academic discussion on issues concerning the paranormal. The often graphic and sometimes shocking presentation displays accompanying the horror papers were greeted with full acceptance and no sneers by the academic community and enlightening conversation about wonderful presentations that nevertheless spoke of gory murders, severed limbs, vampires and werewolves, was expected. Such aspects of horror and the supernatural existed in the realm of imaginative film and literature, the world of Halloween costumes, but the attempt to discuss the ghost in reality, at a conference covering every topic from Food to Fantasy Literature, provoked at least some question. My Horror area included cultural phenomena relating to the paranormal and my proposed panel on life after death was something of a "spinoff" of this. Still, it was not the topic's fittingness in relation to the conference theme of popular culture that was at issue, but what was seen as its general lack of suitability.

It is not merely avoidance of the wild fanatic or religious follower but also this sense of the paranormal in general as an enemy to all that critical thinking stands for that we can detect here. Deemed unscientific and therefore anti-intellectual, the paranormal considers occurrences that appear to defy the scientific method and of things that are beyond our senses threatens, in its detractors' eyes, to set chaos loose and hurl us back into the Dark Ages. Students are envisioned as merely sitting around the classroom trading ghost stories, with everyone either converted or destined to become a "believer." An ignorance about the methods of parapsychology and perhaps an avoidance of such topics in non-fiction literature, as well as the customary absence of such a topic from what I have seen in years of writing class themes that included such course topics as sports, medicine and the 1920s has fueled the academy's misconception that the paranormal is "abnormal." The parent of one student in my paranormal class reacted with disbelief that his son's time and tuition money would be spent on a topic like that.

Gary E. Schwartz, professor of both medicine and psychology, anticipated such academic resistance as he embarked upon what he calls his "secret research project,"[2] a scientific study using medical technology to examine the idea of an afterlife. In 2002, he noted that no major research institution had a formal research program investigating the possibility of the survival of consciousness after death and that "most campuses" would reject this in the same way that Galileo's first heliocentric proposals were scorned.[3] After he had published his findings in 1997, he admitted: "It is one thing to publish a paper in a scientific journal, quite another to bring the research into a university as a formal project."[4] Despite the fact that, occasionally throughout history, even hallowed universities such as Harvard had conducted similar research, Schwartz still fretted over how to present a proposal that would most likely elicit department laughter and undermine his perceived professional status.[5] Although topics categorized under the "Paranormal" are not only interesting but also employ the respected academic pillars of scientific and sociological analysis, they are relegated to a "lesser" status and even considered frivolous. They are considered the stuff of superstition, which human intellectual evolution took millennia to overcome. In this sense, ghosts and goblins are not only mere material for children's tales but a dangerous throwback to less enlightened times. Carl Sagan's antidote to what he sees as the ignorance of his paranormally infested times is subtitled "Science as a Candle in the Dark." Sagan, at least, engaged these ideas in his intelligently written book, but much of the academy, although seeing itself as intellectually "liberal," nevertheless, displays its close-mindedness in failing to take a fair look at this subject and in dictating what topics were appropriate to discuss in an academic environment.

Although seeing itself as progressive, the academic world can often be slower to change than society itself. It was especially ironic that my proposal for the Paranormal course was rejected at this time. Sectors of the academy that viewed the paranormal as something too "different" ignored the fact that this current of thought was now all around them. Pushing the reaches of imagination and of scientific discovery led us to the fascinating uncertainties of the cosmos and the subatomic world and, not surprisingly to a renewed interest in the paranormal world, as well. This was the time of the "New Age" that not only reawakened interest in such topics but also elicited Carl Sagan's *The Demon-Haunted World*. The motivation for Sagan's 1997 counterargument was apparent with the other side so powerfully in the air. A program from a late 1980s meeting of the annual Whole Life Exposition in San Francisco elicited Sagan's dismay at "tens of thousands of people" attending meetings on crystals, goddesses and the violet flame.[6] An article appeared in *The New Statesman* of 1996 entitled "Generation X-Files: The Psychic Schools Have Never Been So Busy."[7]

Although originating in previous decades, the New Age movement, with its emphasis on spirituality and healing, gained force in the 1980's and 1990's. A new preoccupation with untapped powers of the mind and body and the possibilities of something beyond our ordinary experience that reflected a newfound connection with the universe manifested in a reawakening of religious belief in general, a discovery for many of the "enlightenment" of Eastern spirituality, a newfound involvement with activities such as yoga and channeling and even a new interest in astrology for some. Images of angels and references to "goddesses" were woven throughout mail order catalogs and the various artifacts of contemporary culture. Sagan notes what he sees as a disturbing resurgence of "pseudoscience" during this time: "Over the years, a profusion of credulous, uncritical TV series and 'specials' on ESP, channeling, the Bermuda Triangle, UFOs, ancient astronauts and the like have been spawned." He claims that, furthermore, these are all skewed toward promoting the paranormal.[8] People had consulted oracles and fortune-tellers throughout history, but now the Psychic Friends' Network and Psychic Hotline[s] were widely broadcast and easily available.

Ghosts and vampires had always been a part of our lore and literature and those with media access would certainly have seen a few paranormal-themed films in their lives. Now, near the end of the 20th century, the supernatural did not make its appearance mostly in the 2 A.M. television movie listings, but among the offerings of prime time entertainment. It was difficult to escape the unseen or the uncanny when turning on the television, whether it was *Highway to Heaven* (1984–1989), *Sightings* (1992–1997), *The X-Files* (1993–2002), *Touched by an Angel* (1994–2003), *Buffy the Vampire Slayer* (1997–2003) or *Charmed* (1998–2006). This spirits did not weaken with the new millennium and continued into the following decades with *The Ghost Whisperer* (2005–2010), *Medium* (2005), John Edwards' psychic displays on *Crossing Over*, a plethora of documentary-style ghost hunting shows the Harry Potter phenomenon and, of course, the current "Vampire" explosion. Even the imaginative works of popular culture reflect current interest and trends, especially where we witness a proliferation of certain themes. A proliferation of books and television programs featuring paranormal protagonists and themes reflects cultural preoccupations and this, in turn, engenders curiosity beyond the purely imaginative realm. Interest in *Twilight* and *True Blood* brings forth interest in actual vampire lore and cults, just as *The Ghost Whisperer* and *Crossing Over* not only made their debut in a receptive climate but also spurred discussions of real life ghost stories and psychic ability.

The New Age emphasis on the uncanny has not disappeared; it seems that the spirits are still with us. Interestingly, "the percentage of Americans today who take astrology seriously is larger than the percentage of people who do so in the Middle Ages."⁹ Perhaps, as academic circles see that intellectual pandemonium has not ensued as a result and that paranormal topics are still a part of our popular culture for the time being, at least, they will gradually find their place in the curriculum not only in discussions of film or literature but also in an unbiased way as a tool for critical thinking.

Although the ghosts did not go away, unfortunately, at the time, my course proposal had to. Thus, students were being prevented from addressing a key preoccupation of renowned critical thinkers of both the past times and our present day. John Stuart Mill's classic discussion of the pendulum swing of ideas and the valuable contributions of each swing toward the ultimate goal of truth was obviously being unheeded as students were encouraged to ignore the recent swing toward New Age ideas. Sex, racism and politics were all fine to discuss in our modern, open age, but the purportedly liberal-minded academy's selective brand of censorship made the paranormal taboo, even though its questions got to the very essence of life itself and have been discussed by the greatest minds throughout the ages. Plato, Lucretius, Descartes, Locke, Kant, William James, and more recently, Anthony Flew, A.J. Ayer and Roger Penrose have explored the nature of consciousness and its relation to the physical body; *Immortality* is a collection of discussions from the likes of the above. It is the millennia-long continuing discussion to which Jeff Belanger, author of *The Ghost Files*, invites us.¹⁰ Those who converse about the "paranormal" are in such good company because it is a core topic of humankind, universal in its import and appeal.

In its very universality, the paranormal actually fosters the appreciation of diversity aimed at by other, more "acceptably" themed courses since it is not specific to things like race, gender or nationality and joins students as equally qualified members of the human race, confronting questions of the unknown. While retaining and sharing the cultural traditions and experiences that contribute to their identity, the students experience the effects of a richness of culture that comes into play. Students learn how the Spanish Catholic grandfather and the Chinese dorm mate each have their own experiences and traditions relating to the topic. The class enjoys hearing of and examining the lore of diverse cultures while also seeing how essential human questions and experiences unite them. Their underlying similarities loom larger as their cultural distinctions fade somewhat before their questions about extraordinary human powers or immortality. Men and women, students of Eastern and Western descent, alike, defend psychic ability or contest the validity of witches. Rising above the social issues of their time, issues nevertheless significant but dependent upon social and historical context, they are joined by their encounter with the ageless, trading ideas with classic ancient philosophers and eminent contemporary scientists. Naturally, socially and historically placed themes are of enormous impact but the fact that discussion of the paranormal actually brings students necessarily to another level of discussion is important to recognize in light of the frivolity and lack of value apparently attributed to it.

Unfortunately, though, these students were being forced into the dark by this academic fear of discussing the "dark side" and of allowing students to shine their own light upon it. Ghosts belonged in Gothic literature or film courses, it seemed, and had no business appearing in critical thinking/writing as all things paranormal obviously had no place in serious intellectual discussion. The fear that anti-intellectualism would reign clouded the recognition that such prohibition was, itself, anti-intellectual. The university, above all places, should be a place of critical expansion, not prejudiced against any particular area of discussion. As a look at the great minds of the ages attests, both supporters and critics of the paranormal display intellectual prowess but even if a topic were, in itself, capable of calling forth the worst argumentative errors among students, it would still be valuable. If reason and logic are lacking, if the claims are faulty and the data unsatisfactory, there would still be good material here for the critical thinking course. The goal is not to convert students to acceptance of specific positions, but to examine the merits of these positions critically. It is not considered, assuming for the sake of argument that ghosts are in fact, these pernicious anti-intellectual pests, as the various reactions I have received seem to attest, that the best way to exterminate them would be to subject them to critical thinking and expose them for the fantasy that they are.

Paranormal critical thinking/writing courses and textbooks generally have his latter take in mind and we might be tempted to applaud them for at least bringing the topic of the paranormal into discussion. Yet, textbooks such as *How to Think About Weird Things*, by Theodore Schick, Jr. and Lewis Vaughan (McGraw Hill, 2008) or *Paranormal Claims: A Critical Analysis*, ed. by Bryan Farha (University Press of America, 2007), although good texts in some ways, seem to already have arrived at the conclusions that students should be encouraged to reach, as they seem to "expose" the paranormal rather than treat it as an open critical topic. It must be acknowledged that they nevertheless do display insight in recognizing the value of the paranormal as a critical thinking topic and they sometimes do employ rigorous critical thinking techniques that students can emulate. Still, in these texts, rigorous techniques seem ultimately directed more toward using critical thinking specifically to debunk the paranormal. *Paranormal Claims*, dedicated to Carl Sagan, in its general critical thinking section begins with an excerpt from Sagan's *The Demon-Haunted World*, entitled, "The Fine Art of Baloney Detection" and is followed by Michael Schermer, founder of the Skeptics Society, on "Why

Smart People Do Weird Things." Although the articles included in *Paranormal Claims* are worth reading, the aim of the book appears to be to use them to subject "pseudoscientific" claims to its framework of rationality.

How to Talk About Weird Things delves more deeply into issues of perception and epistemology, concepts which are very useful to the critical thinking student. It attempts to distinguish good and bad reasons for belief and cites its purpose as neither to debunk nor advocate any claims but rather, to acquaint the student with the proper means to utilize principles of critical thinking applicable to any future topics. Refreshingly recognizing, "thinking about weird things ... brings us face to face with some of the most fundamental issues in human thought,"[11] the book does an admirable job of devoting space to such elements as deductive and inductive reasoning, premises and fallacies and looks closely in Chapter 2 at the idea of "impossibility." Yet, despite its rigorous attention to principles of critical thinking, if we look at the section on ghosts, although the book asks important questions and would be excellent reading for a paranormal-themed critical thinking class, it furnishes an example of material on the anti-paranormal side. This material would be vital to the discussion but not the only necessary component of that discussion. This nevertheless thoughtful and interestingly written examination of "ghosts" proceeds point by point ultimately to dismiss the idea of them: "ghosts are mental constructions, not external existents."[12]

While providing valuable readings on one side of the issue and even, in the case of the latter, vital information on critical thinking skills, neither textbook provides the approach I sought. In a way, these books exemplify the attitude encapsulated by John Chaffe's simple descriptions in *Thinking Critically* (Houghton Mifflin, 1994), of two contrasting pieces on astrology: the critic of astrology, according to Chaffe, writes a "carefully reasoned and detailed description," while the pro-astrology piece is described merely as a "spirited defense."[13]

It is important to realize that a class cannot satisfactorily challenge ideas and exercise critical thinking skills unless it is presented with relatively compelling material on all sides of every issue. I therefore selected my textbook of choice, *Paranormal Phenomena* (ed. Karen Miller, 2008), from Greenhaven Press's Opposing Viewpoints Series. The book's layout, itself, provided a model for what the students needed to do. For example, selections entitled "Ghosts Are Compatible with Scientific Principles" and "Ghosts Are Incompatible with Scientific Principles" appeared in sequence. In juxtaposing contrasting opinions without an opinionated, guiding narrator, it was suggested that the student was given the burden of ascertaining the truth and that the goal was finding the right pathway through the use of good critical thinking skills.

To utilize these skills to the utmost, the student needs to approach material with an open mind. In his introduction, Kastenbaum rightfully notes how the sharpest thinking avoids shutting out ideas that differ from one's own.[14] Similarly, Belanger's book, which I added to my syllabus in my second version of the course, asks readers to "bring an open mind" as well as "skepticism," rather than automatically believe everything they hear, see or read.[15] They must free themselves from the "baggage" of their particular backgrounds and beliefs, for the enemy is neither ghost nor scientific objector but a "rigid belief system" that contrasts the picture of "inquiring minds hungry for knowledge."[16] In class, we discussed the open-mindedness that true skepticism entails. One day we sat in a circle and tried to apply such an attitude to the various "ghost encounters" that Belanger includes in *The Ghost Files*. Our version of "telling ghost stories" was different from the old fear I had to contend with regarding "talk about paranormal things," for each tale was subjected to the students' votes of belief, nonbelief and undecidedness. Our discussion about the spirits was lively and enlightening as students' own attempts at open-mindedness were reinforced by hearing the views of their classmates; the usual "detractor" who did not know what to make of that particular detail or the ghost advocate who nevertheless found another explanation for what the "haunted" had experienced. It was an open forum for open minds.

The same quality which talk of ghosts and goblins lends to intellectual expansion also leads to the prejudice against it. The very factor that often disqualifies the paranormal from serious consideration as an intellectual topic, its supposed lack of "proof," is the very thing that forces students to rely on abstract reasoning to a great extent, to reach for possibilities, to settle upon qualifications, even to reflect upon the nature of epistemology itself. The art of speculation is not merely the province of spirit hunters, but also of science. Contemporary theoretical science revels in uncertainty, unpredictability and the unknown and unseen regarding everything from elementary particles to the fabric and fate of the universe. Some of our reading in *Paranormal Phenomena* addresses the anti-intellectual loyalty to belief systems that sometimes characterize scientists' adherence to certain paradigms. In any case, if detractors of the paranormal would uphold science as their contrary model, they must be reminded that true science welcomes new data and science continually discovers new things; its book has not been and never can be finished. Belanger reminds us, for example, that "the concept of ghosts goes against our *current* (emphasis added) understanding of physics, what we currently can prove. Science has not yet satisfactorily probed 'the realm of death.'"[17]

It is thought "non-intellectual" to discuss what may not even exist or what may not conform to laboratory procedure. Yet, many topics discussed in critical thinking classes fall outside this strict domain of science. This is true wherever students speak about human motivation and actions. Theories and assumptions are accepted in psychology and elevated to the level of predictions extended with a measure of certainty to the general population, when nothing may exceed the human psyche in individuality. Few college discussions deal with scientific laboratory methodology and students energetically share their views on human rights and freedoms with appeals to personal experience, offering their own policies and predictions. Readings in our textbook also interestingly showed how statistical successes in paranormal studies sometimes exceeded the numbers necessary to effect medical policy, such as deeming a drug satisfactory. Actually, laboratory studies and attempts to subject the paranormal to hard scientific investigation are quite pervasive and often entered into our class discussion.

Still, there is the position that scientific paraphernalia and attitudes may not necessarily be adequate to the task of validating the paranormal. Herein lies more of the richness of the paranormal-themed critical thinking course as we are led to discuss *how* we "know" something, what constitutes knowledge. Students suddenly think about what they have not considered before, the very nature of epistemology. Our first paper, in which the students merely recounted and argued their position on a personally experienced "paranormal-seeming" event, allowed room for the validity of "knowing" in terms of a sense, of inner experience and surety but this very "feeling" had to be defended critically and compared to other kinds of knowing. "How did this constitute *knowing* to you?" they were asked, in effect, and "Can you discount other possible explanations that may have influenced your sense of knowing?" Belanger notes how belief and knowledge are actually both a part of the truth[18] and we examined his ideas as he delves into the very nature of perception: how we know, how the brain and senses can be heightened to increase our perception, the reliability of memory and how the brain physiologically assists memory in traumatic situations.[19] Even these high level psychological and scientific concepts were not merely passively received in our class but were up for discussion, for students debated how memories can also be embellished or even forgotten. Our habit of eliminating other "possible explanations before we could claim we "knew" the truth was also put to the test and its merits examined: did the existence of another possible explanation automatically negate the first? We saw that it was important to consider alternate explanations but, beyond this, that the mere existence of another possibility did not necessarily invalidate all others. We coined a running joke that served as a paradigm for this concept, the model of the lights that flickered over the unfortunate uncle's portrait just before his death — faulty bulbs or otherworldly communication? We discussed whether a discovery of an actual electrical glitch *necessarily* negates a possible paranormal explanation and whether a "spirit" could possibly interact with the material world and perhaps effect such a change in the bulb or wiring. Student opinions varied, of course, as one would expect from a critical thinking class and "the lights flickering over the uncle's picture" became our code for such epistemological dilemmas.

How can we have students discuss what cannot be proven? By having them discuss *possibilities* critically. Is something impossible or not and, if not, *why* not? Is it *probable*, is it *unlikely* and, most importantly, *why*? It is the "possible" survival of death that is the subject of Kastenbaum's superb critical study. Likewise, my students focused ultimately not upon whether ghosts existed but whether ghosts were possible; not on whether there was an actual psychic but whether there could be such a thing as psychic ability. In my initial poll, students sometimes noted for themselves the suitability of the subject matter for critical thinking. As I observed earlier, they thus joined company with some of the greatest thinkers of all time, such as Plato, Descartes and Kant, who also chose to discuss these "unprovables," as it were. The unknown or even the "unknowable" is not synonymous with the unworthy.

The unknown is what encourages the abstract thinking that comes with speculation. Speculation may lead us to think of the afterlife as a computer state, as does mathematical physicist Frank J. Tipler in *Physics and Immortality*, who urges us to see "the human brain as nothing but an information processing device, the human soul as nothing but a program being run on a computer called the brain"[20] or 17th century philosopher, Henry More, who speculates upon the connection of the soul with a "hyperthickness in the fourth dimension."[21] In my critical thinking/writing class, students used their powers of abstraction to consider whether the "near death experience" equaled an "after death experience," whether surviving death necessarily equaled immortality, and whether a "ghost" could eventually fade away out of existence. They thought about whether establishment of the fact of survival would automatically imply *universal* survival; perhaps different "spirits" would have different survival abilities, drawing analogies with the various strengths and talents of living individuals. Thus, students were redirected from chilling stories about ghosts appearing by the bedside to abstract considerations of the purposes of immortality and the possibility and viability of a second death. Life after death was only one of the topics that led us into such vibrant and intellectually intense discussion, which would also serve as a model for argumentation in written assignments.

There is certainly something intellectually rigorous in going beyond facts to abstract conceptualization. With the subject of the paranormal, students are forced to do this repeatedly. While discussions centering around paranormal topics may employ factual evidence in the process, they cannot be closed ultimately by actual proof of the "factual" kind. Although experiential "proof" may be accumulated by paranormal supporters, mere experience is still open to interpretation and may often bring forth simultaneous alternate explanations. The students must rely upon their own powers of thinking and judgment. In my initial survey, students who preferred the other critical thinking offerings often focused in their comments upon acquiring information about human rights in other countries, for example, or looked forward to hearing about people's experience with gender issues. For this same reason, others might have said that they were interested in learning about the 1920s, another course theme. This is not to suggest that abstract thinking and philosophy are not a part of such studies as well. Plato discourses on politics and community and Mill speaks of the need for human liberty and equality. Generally, though, as my classroom survey shows, students taking historically or sociologically themed courses, who may nevertheless utilize their critical thinking skills rigorously in such courses, often sign up for them with an interest in learning about and focusing upon the historical and sociological information and often, their assignments can be made to rely heavily upon these. Research is, of course, an important part of education and even of a critical thinking course, but it is not the most important goal of such a course.

The implication here is not that such courses should not exist or that they do not have immense value for critical thinking, but rather that it is ironic that the paranormal theme, with its necessary focus upon abstract thinking and likeliness of developing these skills would actually be considered *less* valuable. Even the student who chose the paranormal-themed course because she liked to hear about ghosts and witches would find that she would be compelled to do a lot of thinking about very "deep" and abstract concepts in the class. Most students choosing such a class would also be bringing with them a *curiosity*, a desire to question and to hear other opinions; their personal experiences on the "dark side" notwithstanding, they realized that, where this topic was concerned, they were all essentially clueless as to the answers to these very mysterious questions. Our own thought processes and ability to delve into logic and possibilities are the significant factors in such a course. The paranormal theme, with its tendency toward the abstract, aims more surely at developing higher, abstract skills. One student perceived this, noting how critically discussing the paranormal would be more "challenging" because the theme is so "abstract." Although highly interesting to students, which is also an important quality, the topic is, in fact, very challenging and many readings in the field take a philosophical angle, either wholly or in part. The *Paranormal Phenomena* selection from Susan Blackmore titled, "Evidence for Paranormal Phenomena Has Not Been Found," discusses the concept of our world view and concepts of the self.[22] A selection by Martin Plimmer and Brian King discourses on the relation between interconnection and coincidence.²³ Class conversations get to the core of issues such as the nature of reality and the meaning of identity. While any topic may be raised to a level of abstraction, the paranormal, of necessity, is inherently at that level sooner when it is a subject of critical discussion. The training in abstract thinking that it offers should not only eliminate any prejudice against a paranormal-themed course, but actually emphasize the value of such a course.

It was not, however, only abstract thinking that we drew upon, but also a great deal of information. The students provided material for fair and open discussion from their own experiences with psychics, precognitive dreams, déjà vu and the assorted inexplicable and also drew from the knowledge and beliefs of their individual cultures. Some contributed information from popular culture about youth vampire cults. One semester, the class happened to include an actual paranormal investigator, who owned his own ghost detecting equipment, several biology majors and a former funeral industry worker. Class materials also included literature. We read stories touching on death, magic and apparitions, such as Katherine Anne Porter's "Magic," D.H. Lawrence's "The Rocking Horse Winner" and the ghost story "The Shut Room" by Henry S. Whitehead which led us to discussions about the uncanny, the possible and the powers of consciousness, in these works and in the universe at large, and we looked at poems that dealt with the uncertainties beyond the grave such as Walt Whitman's "On the Terrible Doubt of Appearances" and Tom Molito's "Cosmic Simplicities," which parallels our lack of pre-birth and after-death knowledge.

Still, all the information we processed and discussed, and the material we considered in our approach to various "paranormal" conundrums included more than literary pieces or students' own stories and expertise. Much of this other material we used, the material from our textbooks and other assigned readings, was potentially very difficult. We read Susan Blackmore's physiological exploration of the near-death experience as a phenomenon of the dying brain. This was an account that dealt with the nature of the visual cortex, the effects of oxygen deprivation and the loss of inhibitory activity, ultimately leading us to consider the validity of her proposition that the pervasiveness of the "near-death experience" stemmed not from its being a paranormal phenomenon but a physical, human one. We looked at theories of communal behavior[24] and electromagnetic fields.[25] We learned about temporal lobe stimulation engendering "visions."[26] We examined the incompatibility of ghosts with the laws of physics and considered whether non-physical beings could walk on a floor.[27] In turn, we considered the prospect of different dimensions and planes allowing this to happen. We studied the idea of consciousness itself, reading about wave and particle theories and about the difference between "phase space" and "real space" in relation to the location of consciousness lying within the brain or outside of it.[28] Facts and propositions from science and psychology always came into play. Our readings in *The Ghost Files* also introduced us to the idea that a ghost is not simply a ghost, for there were, according to Belanger, nine possible explanations for what a "haunting" actually might be, including an impression on a location, a "time slip," a thought projection, and the result of "colliding dimensions." We even learned about the folklore surrounding the vampire and the scientific explanations of after-death phenomena offered to discount it in Paul Barber's *Vampires, Burial and Death* (Yale, 1988). Still in the realm of the possible, we nevertheless acquired a great deal of "information" along the way.

The students were trained to read these authors critically, to agree or disagree where they saw fit, and to know the reasons for their own responses. They noticed comments about experiments not being properly controlled or phenomena needing to be investigated further, granting at times their support and sometimes their suspicion. Thus, they interacted with both abstractions and with difficult information in this course.

The course, therefore, lent itself not only to the enhancement of critical thinking and reading skills but also good research skills. The topic of the paranormal takes the student all over the library, as it touches upon many different disciplines. Students could hunt down psychology articles on how psychics prey upon human weakness or perhaps biological or medical information about death and the brain. They might have been led to consult sociological studies of group behavior in their mission to discover the validity of telepathic response. In their own research, they used books, articles, interviews, surveys and online sources. They learned how to pursue a topic of interest within a course theme. Thus, I received a final research paper on Houdini the skeptic's paranormal leanings as well as one exploring our inherent attraction to the idea of vampires. The research process was sufficiently practiced with the paranormal theme and, incidentally, one can learn to do citations with a source about a ghost sighting as much as with anything else, just as one can obviously learn good critical thinking among the ghosts.

In many ways, it actually seemed best to be among the ghosts. Chaffee defines critical thinking as "an active, purposeful, organized" cognitive process that we use to "carefully examine" both our own thinking and that of others in order to clarify our understanding."[29] It is erroneous and unfair to assume a paranormal-themed course cannot yield this process and it would be heinous to realize that it can do this and yet prohibit it by preventing the students from "talk[ing] about paranormal things," as stated in the reaction to the course proposal I had submitted years before. That proposal had emphasized how my course's highly interesting subject would nevertheless enhance critical thinking skills, showing students, as I explicitly stated, "how they must hold fast to the principles of good argumentation and cogent critical thinking in order to assert their claims." Thus, even though the academy at the time did not seem to be convinced, I was, which is why a decade later, at another institution, I proceeded to prove them wrong when I finally had the opportunity to teach the course. Armed with my chosen text from the *Opposing Viewpoints* series, with Belanger's *Ghost Files* added the subsequent semester, when I taught the course a second time, I set out to emphasize to my critical thinking class that there are different sides to every argument, that we must recognize faulty arguing, lack of evidence, the distinction between points of view, that "skeptic" and "believer" alike must be open to these tasks and even to resisting their self-imposed labels.

The importance of considering the "other side" recently emerged with special clarity when I encountered a former student of the class who greeted me with enthusiasm. At the time of our class, she had already explained to me that our treatment of the other side of an argument had given her a wonderful skill that she was employing successfully in her other classes. Now, she added that the intellectual rigors of our class had made her pursue law school! Attention to the all-important "contrary view" had been the trademark of our class. A mere glance at out various reading materials, alternations of *The Ghost Files* with readings from Carl Sagan's *Demon-Haunted World*, Kastenbaum's *Is There Life After Death?* (recommended as an ancillary text) and our main textbook, itself, *Paranormal Phenomena*, reflected the two-sided nature of things. The works, themselves, explicitly warned against prejudice and one-sided thinking. Sagan focuses primarily on the dangerous comfort and sense of power through paranormal belief while Belanger addresses the problems of bias and close-mindedness among believers and skeptics alike[30] and enlightens the reader with an entire chapter on the true, open nature of skepticism.[31] He expresses well the problem of essentially non-critical approaches on both sides of the divide:

> One of the problems with some in the scientific community is that they have turned the noble pursuit of science into a belief system and they are not open to new data on a given subject because it does not fit into what they had previously accepted as fact. And that is not just science.... There are some who have accepted that there are ghosts, and they believe that just about everything that knocks, bumps or squeaks is supernatural. That is also foolish.[32]

Thus, in my critical thinking class, the students were always challenged, both in our class discussions and in my commentary on their papers with the "What about *this* then?" A student's friend claimed may have claimed the experience of a ghostly "vision," but what mental and physical state was she in at the time? Another student may have suggested that the Lotto numbers in someone's "precognitive dream" represented nothing but coincidence, but how would that student account for the unusual vividness of the dream and the red circles around the four numbers that actually came out winners? They learned that things were not as simple as they may have seemed and that one must always look at other possibilities, a practice that became a habit in our discussions. In the first semester, we had two pro-paranormal bookends seated at either end of the class, as well as a "skeptic" (who later declared his skepticism about being a skeptic), who could always be relied upon to discount paranormal claims as we discussed various topics. The class, however, eventually came to hear the reservations of the paranormal proponents and the concessions of the "skeptic." They saw that one did not have to join a "camp," but could switch sides with different discussions. Also, things were not merely "two-sided," for we also needed to examine the validity of separate thoughts *within* an argument about ghosts or psychics.

Thus, we learned another aspect of the "other side" phenomenon, the intricacy of qualifications and distinctions. John Beloff notes how, even if there is a paranormal element at work with respect to mediums and even the near-death experience, that does not necessarily point to "life after death," due to problems such as the nature of the other world and the fact of evolution.[33] Similarly, we asked whether a "true" psychic could ever be wrong, i.e., could psychic ability be actual but not always reliable. Does "exposing" a fake psychic discount all psychics? We discussed John Randi's still unanswered million dollar 1996 challenge for someone to prove the existence of the paranormal[34] and questioned whether the paranormal can be subjected to the kind of "proof" methods Randi seeks or, as Belanger describes it, "the rules of physical science as we know it."[35] We considered in our discussion of telekinesis whether the account of bent utensils in the kitchen drawer revealed uncontestable support for the phenomenon or holes in the teller's story.

Familiarity with the thoughts and data offered by the other side was very important and enriched both our class discussions and student assignments. Interestingly, according to my anonymous post-semester survey of student opinion, the students' own positions did not finally deviate from their original levels of belief in the paranormal. Although all students did not complete the survey, an overwhelming majority rated their present belief in the paranormal between the numbers 4 and 7, or equally, between 5 and 8 on a 10 point scale, with 10 representing the greatest belief in the paranormal. Most students who noted a change in their level of belief only changed on average an amount of approximately 2–3 points. There was more change in the direction of the paranormal end but this can be deemed both predictable, in their exposure to their classmates' "real life" documentation of events and acceptable, since an anti-paranormal bias had most likely characterized their education than the reverse; thus, the slightly pro-paranormal shift in many students may actually represent an "adjustment." What students gained, however, was not so much the belief or non-belief in ghosts as a richness to their thinking, an ability both to consider propositions and to find the fallacies within them. Neither the all-out "skeptic," according to the popular definition, nor the staunch believer were favored as models. The goal was to look at things in a new way, utilizing the skills of critical thinking, and utilizing them with a sense of one's own authority to do so.

These skills and the sense of authority were emphasized in their written assignments. Students wrote papers that drew upon their own personal experience, their critiquing of art, and their responses to books and articles. They learned that one subject can draw upon many different disciplines and saw that they must not be afraid to look for answers in various places, whether science, psychology or folklore and, importantly, within their own minds and experiences. Our first assignment, in its focus on a personal "paranormal" experience, exercised their descriptive skills as they recounted the event and their critical skills as they discussed how they finally viewed the event, attending to other possible interpretations as they proceeded. The second involved analysis of the paranormal content of a fictional film in terms of either the content's believability as paranormal phenomena or the film's success in portraying paranormal content believably. Students, for example, chose to examine such films as *Paranormal Activity*, *Poltergeist* or even television series such as *Charmed*. The assignment thus continued our debates about paranormal possibilities while giving practice in critiquing art. Our third short assignment involved choosing the nonfiction paranormal article or account that one "most believed" and explaining why, thereby strengthening the students' critical reading skills and emphasizing the fact that there were various degrees to which one could "accept" another's position. For the final paper, a longer research assignment, students were free to present an argument, supported by research, on any topic within the paranormal realm. Besides the important critical thinking skills fostered by these assignments, students were reminded of their own authority as critical thinkers as well as their own authority to choose topics *within* assigned topics that suited them. They were even free to write their final paper, if they so chose, on why the paranormal was not a good subject for critical thinking!

The students did, however, see the value of the topic as a critical thinking tool and, as a whole, got a great deal out of the semester, as revealed even by those who answered my post-semester survey in both classes. Their response to whether the course helped with their critical thinking and reading skills was very positive. There were references to "think[ing] outside the box," "a fresh sort of abstract thinking," "broaden[ing] horizons," learning to develop arguments convincingly, engendering a lot of thought on a topic, evaluating one's own thinking process, putting things in perspective, learning to back up opinions with evidence and, of course, many comments about learning to look at both sides of an argument and playing a rigorous game of devil's advocate. Over 90 percent of those who responded felt they received these benefits. One student remarked how he/she could not see how the topic of the paranormal would help foster critical reading/thinking skills! The responses were also generally responsive with regard to how the class topic helped with critical writing skills, noting that the papers involved "deep thought" with attention to avoiding self-contradiction, the need to "really analyze" and think abstractly, a close consideration of the "meaning of words," a "need for sound judgment," thinking about many factors concerning a topic before forming an opinion on it, imagining examples of the opposite viewpoint, thinking "from all angles" without "prejudgment" and using "intensive research to support abstract opinions."

When asked directly whether or not they felt this topic was a good one for a critical thinking class, the response was, again, very positive, citing how it was perfect "because unproven," very conducive to arguing both sides, how it led students to think more than usual and see things in ways they never had before. They cited the subject's complexity and thought-provoking quality, its freedom from "socially restricted answers," and even noted at times that it was more "difficult" than other subjects because it was abstract. "The sheer controversy surrounding the course material pushed me to think outside the box extensively and comprehensively," wrote one student and another confessed: "Though at first I may have thought a class on the paranormal seem[ed] crazy, it turned out to be an excellent topic for critical thinking." These students, in this particular institution, had not been aware of the class theme when they signed up for their section of this required course. I then asked them if they would have taken the class had they known. Of the students who responded to this question, 87 percent said yes, most of these checking, "yes with enthusiasm." The students, as a whole, definitely found the topic interesting and many added emphasis with "very" or an exclamation point when asked. They were obviously interested, for their discussions continued well after my class when they were gathered together with each other or their friends on campus, as they reported. Some students were thrilled with the opportunity to think about things they "never got to converse about before."

Of course, there will always be some students, as with any topic, who do not particularly enjoy discussing this one or who may find topics that often touch so closely upon death disturbing. Even with respect to classes that focus upon horror, there might be individual students who believe that ghosts and vampires are to unreal for them to discuss seriously, even in the imaginative realm or students who feel uneasy being immersed for a semester in stories and films dealing with themes relating so explicitly to death. There are always those who would rather not see a horror film and those who would rather not discuss some aspects of the paranormal, either in general or because of current circumstances in their lives. That is quite understandable but it must be realized that, if the theme were advertised in the course catalog alongside the section, these students who might not sign up would have more than enough others who would vie for their seats. One or two students found our discussions a bit frustrating because we never finally proved something but most found them interesting, challenging and helpful: "I thought they were fantastic. They challenged my ideas and stimulated my mind;" they were "very mentally stimulating;" they were also described as "robust," explorative" and "very intense ... a good learning tool." One student remarked how the different opinions made for good discussion and that these discussions were interesting because this was something not talked about all the time. It was wonderful that they could acknowledge intellectual skill in various comments rather than respond according to the side the speaker was on: "...people came up with bright ideas." Similarly, students looked forward to entertaining the various ideas presented in the readings and did well with completing the reading assignments for class. They also tended to see the value in the assigned papers, finding them challenging and useful in fostering their critical thinking skills. The students likewise appreciated the freedom they were given in the papers as well as the interesting quality of the topic that was, to quote one respondent, "unlike most academic papers," and another, who described having the feeling of "wanting" to write the paper rather than a sense of being required to.

I was understandably glad that I had followed my convictions and eventually put a proposal to teach critical thinking through the paranormal into practice. Students not only found the course interesting and refreshing but also described the intellectual benefits that they had received in exercising their minds over on the "dark side." They learned to address the other side in their papers, tapping their own mental powers to muse on possibilities and to isolate distinctions and qualifications. Ultimately, they saw themselves as possessing the power to grapple with both scientists and those claiming to be the paranormally "gifted." Class discussions were vibrant and the students' main complaint one semester was about wanting a "field trip."

Still, although I heartily recommend the use of this subject as a wonderful teaching tool, there are some possible liabilities of which one should be aware. Discussions can become so intense that they may take up a great deal of class time as students emerge with one good response to the paranormal after another. This is what we want in critical thinking but if writing is an aim of the course, the needs of students with poor skills can necessitate devoting specific sections of classes to basic writing technique. This can be done, however, with sample organization of points about psychics or precognitive dreams, for example, and ghosts can easily find their way into grammar, as we discuss what is wrong with: "The hauntings was the scariest anyone had ever seen." Students may also sometimes feel uncomfortable criticizing a classmate's very personal story centering around a loved one's death, for example, but many students do learn how to treat such issues diplomatically and with sensitivity, without sacrificing their critical opinion.

Another point involves the tone of the class. Even the most rigorous intellectual discussions can take place within a class that makes students comfortable with a "lightened" atmosphere. The instructor may soon notice, however, that the "jokes" may fall too easily upon the ghosts — snickers about the noise behind the classroom door, or the temporarily misplaced lecture notes. It is much easier, perhaps, to joke about the material of the "believers" than the opinions of the detractors. It may also involve a kind of ingratiating gesture when one chuckles about the ghosts rather than the stubbornness of the non-believer in a course that we may fear, on the surface, looks as if it is favoring and promoting the paranormal. This aspect of classroom humor may, in fact, be harmless, but if engaged in too much in this lopsided fashion, may give the impression that the paranormal side is less valid, at least to some students. Finally, it can sometimes get a bit disconcerting sitting alone grading a stack of papers on apparitions and Ouija boards, not because the papers will necessarily disappoint but because the floors may creak and the pipes may make noise; having spent so much time in the paranormal-themed class, one will not be sure just what to make of it!

Some students may, in fact, have emerged from this class still not knowing what to make of certain topics we covered. Some may have tempered their original positions with points on the other side, while others may have envisioned a future in which what they see as the other side would reveal itself to be one part of a larger truth. Although there are many variations and divisions, the basic "two" sides are not perhaps as divided as we might think. Carl Sagan notes how science is a storehouse of wonder and mystery in everything from biological organisms to the outer reaches of space. We may be familiar with science's extension into the distance to find extraterrestrial life through SETI, or the quirky, surprising behavior of particles documented by quantum physics. Some even believe that, through quantum theory, science is meshing with issues of the paranormal and that some answers might lie in this common ground. Theories about wormholes and multiple dimensions sometimes appear in discussions about ghosts. Even *Star Trek's* strictly logical and scientific Mr. Spock's great powers of mind include a talent for telepathy. The different "sides" may not be as separated as we may at first believe.

The important thing, however, that the students came away with from the class was the ability to keep learning to be open to new information and new thought, to be content for the moment to believe, not believe or be unsure, for educated "confusion" is also a valid, intellectually honest state. Generally, students would come to employ their critical powers to present a point of view, but with some attention to the fact that there were, in fact, other views on this topic and that they needed to address them.

Through their intellectual travels into graveyards and haunted houses, my students did emerge as better critical thinkers, sometimes continuing their discussions among themselves apart from my class, sometimes revealing that they were now applying what they learned during our class to their more mundane subjects. Yet, they received all of this in an interesting package. "Where else could I talk about ghosts?" one student happily exclaimed. If we could only lessen the academic fear of talking about ghosts in the classroom, our students might be given the gift to go and talk about anything.

NOTES

1. Paul Edwards, ed. *Immortality* (New York: Prometheus, 1997), 273.
2. Gary E. Schwartz, *The Afterlife Experiments* (New York: Pocket, 2002), 6.
3. Schwartz, 15.
4. Schwartz, 27.
5. Schwartz, 28.
6. Carl Sagan, *The Demon-Haunted World* (New York: Random House, 1995), 208.
7. Cited in Karen Miller, ed., *Paranormal Phenomena: Opposing Viewpoints* (Detroit: Greenhaven, 2008), 82.
8. Sagan, 374.
9. Theodore Schick, Jr., and Lewis Vaughn, *How to Think About Weird Things: critical thinking for A New Age* (New York: McGraw Hill, 2008), viii.
10. Jeff Belanger, *The Ghost Files* (Franklin Lakes, New Jersey: Career, 2007), 11.
11. Schick and Vaughn, x.
12. Schick and Vaughn, 280–288.
13. John Chaffee, *Thinking Critically*, 4th ed. (Boston: Houghton Mifflin, 1994), 250.
14. Robert Kastenbaum, *Is There Life After Death?* (New York: Prentice Hall, 1984), 8.
15. Belanger, 11.
16. Belanger, 11,19.
17. Belanger, 15–19.
18. Belanger, 15–19.
19. Belanger, 19–27.
20. Frank J. Tipler, *The Physics of Immortality* (New York: Doubleday, 1994), 10.
21. Clifford A. Pickover, *Surfing Through Hyperspace* (New York: Oxford University Press, 1999).
22. Blackmore in Miller, 33.
23. Martin Plimmer and Brian King in Miller, 77–81.
24. Miller, 59–70.
25. Miller, 135–136.
26. Miller, 52–55.
27. Miller, 93–97.
28. Miller, 129–137.
29. Chaffee, 1.
30. Belanger, 19.
31. Belanger, 143–150.
32. Belanger, 19.
33. Tipler, 259–268.
34. Belanger, 146–148.
35. Belanger, 148.

"Inside ... *Doesn't Matter*": Responding to *American Psycho* and Its Dantean Agenda
Miles Tittle

> *My personality is sketchy and unformed, my heartlessness goes deep and is persistent. My conscience, my pity, my hopes disappeared a long time ago (probably at Harvard) if they ever did exist. There are no more barriers to cross. All I have in common with the uncontrollable and the insane, the vicious and the evil, all the mayhem I have caused and my utter indifference toward it, I have now surpassed. I still, though, hold on to one single bleak truth: no one is safe, nothing is redeemed. Yet I am blameless.*[1]

Introduction

Blending reader response theory with classroom analysis, this chapter focuses on the pedagogical usefulness of Dantean analysis in teaching Bret Easton Ellis's 1991 novel *American Psycho*. Dante's writings can be used to highlight the coping strategies that characterize public and student reaction to Ellis's visceral post-modern novel. The extent of Ellis's use of Dante has been largely overlooked and is unlikely to be independently recognized by students, yet public resistance to Ellis's satire in the form of accusations of obscenity and dismissive condemnation becomes newly meaningful when the relationship between his work and the *Divine Comedy* is given closer attention.

Dante's medieval critique centers on the need for separate yet equal temporal and religious powers to lead society, and the dangers of a spiritual leader possessing great economic influence and political worldliness. In *American Psycho* the imbalance is reversed: the rich and powerful are taken as ethical or spiritual models. This lack of pastoral leadership steers society's desires towards the material and superficial, away from spiritual and ethical values. Söderlind has called Ellis "the allegorist of that place where the heart [of the nation] used to be,"[2] and the author's dissection of the physical and moral anatomy of his characters not only reveals the emptiness in them and their mimetic society, it challenges readers to find their own way out of Bateman's world.

Patrick Bateman's murderous behavior is an extreme symptom of the unstable state of his society, but even his crimes are readily overlooked and tolerated as long as they remain unverified and deniable by those around him a response that many university students partially recreate in their efforts to determine Bateman's reality. Illuminating the subtle details of the text and its gestures towards Dante reveals a complex ethical agenda, at odds with assumptions of simple black satire and gratuitous sexualized violence. The length to which Dante was willing to go in describing the horrors and blasphemies of his *Inferno* reminds students that, even in classic canon texts, shocking narratives can support educational purposes and moral integrity. Yet the final decisions must be made by the readers, and the active engagement of class discussion crystallizes the space between *meaning* and *significance*. Students exposed to disparate interpretations of the text (particularly in the sense of authorial intent and media reception) realize the inherent ambiguity of crucial aspects of the novel, and move into a dynamic exploration of significance a collaborative effort to create meaning from the horrors of Bateman's narrative.

Receptions

"I look forward to your lectures on American Psycho. *I am halfway through currently, and this book is proving to be one of the most difficult, jarring pieces of fiction I have ever read"* [student email 2009].

Now that undergraduate classes are largely made up of students born after Ellis's novel was first published two decades ago, their casual knowledge of the initial furor generated by *American Psycho* is almost as unlikely as their familiarity with Dante. Fortunately there are several articles that give efficient overviews of the controversy.[3] Both Donna Lee Brien and Jack Miles notably point out that if Bateman's crimes had really occurred, the morality of the graphic descriptions might never have been widely questioned: lurid accounts of true crimes are perennial big business for publishers. For a fictional account to be attacked as "a how-to novel on the torture and dismemberment of women,"[4] is startling, given that such true-crime accounts are so pervasive (indeed, it is those factual accounts of atrocities that Bateman constantly refers to in conversation with his co-workers). Ellis himself used such accounts of real serial killers as research sources for Bateman's inventive atrocities.[5] In one sense, *American Psycho* was vulnerable precisely because it was a work of fiction, so the author's intent and moral rationale in creating this story could be attacked. Many critics, however, chose to confine themselves largely to contemptuous descriptions of Ellis's abilities as an author, dismissing the novel as puerile trash.

In my own classroom, we read samples of the critics who condemned and excoriated Ellis at the time of the novel's release, including some who openly admitted to not having read the novel.[6] Ellis was branded a vile pornographer and a vulgar writer, faced boycotts and death threats, was dropped by his publisher, saw his books banned and restricted in Canada and Australia, and even suffered the dubious shame of being banned from the opening of Euro Disney.[7] Even some of its defenders saw the novel as potentially dangerous to society. This information divided student opinion on the question of an author's moral obligation to the public. The likelihood of *American Psycho* contributing significantly to violence against women was not given much credence by most of my students, but some felt that a more subtle poisoning of attitudes towards women in certain types of vulnerable readers was a strong possibility.

The media controversy, which began even before the novel's publication, surrounds it to this day, and students must consider the role of this extraordinary reception in shaping attitudes towards the text. This can assist them in recognizing the role their own reactions play in choosing between the possibilities offered by Ellis, and the usefulness of supplementary information in structuring epistemological fields that can be intelligently explored. Reader-response and reception theory as pedagogical tools do make students more active learners, encouraging individual and subjective interpretations, but they must be informed with supplementary material and subjected to academic rigor. Discussions that elicit individual responses from readers, by triggering their background and experiential knowledge, reveal the emotional stakes in the struggle for control of the text's significance. These individual responses do not fully comprise meaning, but they are factors in determination.

Classroom debate, for instance, often centers on the persistent and important theory that all of Patrick Bateman's crimes are merely his fantasies. This attempt to rewrite his horrific actions to a somehow safer interiority is a strategy that reflects the oblivious attitudes both of *American Psycho's* other characters, and of those critics who wanted the novel to go unread. The rendering of the novel into a highly restrained psycho thriller movie[8] was a similar exercise in controlling and confining the text, suggesting Bateman's crimes might exist in a doubly fictitious space, and reinforcing his assertion that "inside... *doesn't matter.*"[9]

Classroom exploration of Bateman's unreliable narration reinforces this textual ambivalence, and deconstructing this process and its motives reveals our uneasy and paradoxical attitudes towards horror literature and film in modern times. Anxiety about the body as a site of conflict and pain has replaced the spiritual concerns often foregrounded in Gothic literature, and the specters of rape and torture, rather than Dante's fear of damnation, affect reader processing of Ellis's novel. Exploring the collaborative construction of meaning helps guide this pedagogical strategy: students focus on the social impact and reception of *American Psycho*, contrasting it with the novel's apparent intent by analyzing anxiety and rejection in the critical and popular response, movie adaptation, and their own classroom discussion. Using student responses, including the major arguments used in my class to reject Bateman's crimes as actual narrative events, I show my classes how readers consume and tailor the narrative to suit their needs.[10]

In order for students to understand the role Ellis's novel played in intensifying global debate on ethics, censorship, and obscenity in fiction, they require more than a summary of the media firestorm that greeted the novel, or a cursory explanation of the 1980s, a decade most of them are too young to remember. They need enough context to give them confidence in shaping original interpretations. In recent years I have provided three major areas of supplementary information when my undergraduate classes first encounter *American Psycho*. First, experiencing the rest of my course, as a historical survey of horror fiction, allows students to compare Ellis to the horror genre's traditions; second, an overview of the novel's reception, with some discussion of the social and political climate it satirizes (best discussed together, since the relationship between the individual and the public is of such importance in both cases); and third, a discussion of the parallels and divergences from Dante's *Inferno* (and to a lesser degree, the rest of the *Divine Comedy* and *De Monarchia*). With those elements unpacked by initial lectures, class analysis and discussion become more insightful and rewarding. Indeed, several students who initially cursed me for requiring them to read such an appalling book went on to write papers based on their own interpretations, offering reflections such as the following:

> This book is so messed up. The time it took me to read all the other novels was under a day, but for this it took me a week and a half due to the content and when I finished I was filled with this ineffable feeling of horror and anxiety (or as Patrick Bateman would say, a "nameless dread") and then I had nightmares. So *naturally* my innate inclination is to write an academic paper on a novel that messed me up for a few days! [student email 2011].

It is hardly surprising that horror novels have often met with strong opposition, contempt, and censorship. As with pornographic novels, the visceral response the genre provokes is in fact one of its yardsticks of success, and a horror novel that doesn't shock or appall is in one sense not doing its job. However, the media-stoked controversy that made the novel into a bestseller blurs the line between Bateman and Ellis, and between fictional crime and real crime. Such blurrings were a cultural hallmark of the 1980s in North America, where the danger presented to public thought and behavior by books, records, movies and games was constantly being debated and exaggerated. Television evangelists and pundits managed to convince many people that heavy metal songs could compel listeners to commit suicide, that role-playing games could lead to devil-worship and murder, and that Madonna's belly button threatened decent "family values."[11]

These ideas are not rejected by Ellis's text; they are central to it. Bateman is himself a slave to media, not only when deciding how to dress or where to eat, but when determining business ethics (as with his love of Donald Trump) and human morality (his fascination with famous serial killers). The lack of interiority makes all the characters in Bateman's world simply distorted mirrors of what they read and see around them, but his obsessive personality magnifies both the influence and the distortion. In this, as in all things, he is an exaggerated parody of his time. The final scene marking the end of the 1980s era, as Bateman, Price and their friends watch President (and actor) Reagan's duplicity revealed on TV, implies that even the president's influence on the country has been profoundly deceptive. If surface is the only reliable truth, then a lowest common denominator of perception and opinion determines reality. Similarly, Ellis's motivations and the popularly known 'truth' of his writing seems to have been largely determined by public opinion and media agendas, so the intent of *American Psycho* is difficult to extricate from the impression that precedes it. Yet analysis revealing parallels between it and Dante's canonical text re-situates students and other critical readers by revealing other aspects and uncharted meanings, and by challenging popular interpretations with evidence of authorial intent.[12]

On a larger scale, the Dantean approach had implications in my classroom because it helped change students' perceptions of horror fiction from being a genre concerned exclusively with entertainment and consumer gratification to one that could engage with popular society in a deeply critical and satirical manner, and which could sustain complex political or philosophical agendas. Harsh criticism and censorship seems to arise from a fear that literature and film has strong persuasive or corruptive potential (otherwise, why bother trying to control it?); but if a document can corrupt, it can also teach and enlighten. Only the nature of the power the text is imbued with is questioned, and the ambiguity of exact authorial intent does not detract from the fact that censorship greatly empowers a text by giving it a particular societal status as a dangerous and potentially transformative experience. Censorship is in one sense the highest compliment a work of fiction can be given, the antithesis of being called meaningless. Some of my students reacted more strongly to *American Psycho* once they had learned about its notoriety. The novel's original reception seemed to imply that it was meant to cause a strong reaction and was, in a sense, *worthy* of it. Student comments often used the claims of journalists as their starting point, debating more directly with the media critics than with the text. Similarly, the class debates about whether or not an imaginary character killed other imaginary characters in his imagination highlight the degree to which the text provokes the kind of emotional response and rejection that caused its infamy in the first place. The question of where textual meaning could legitimately be constructed was applied to the role of Ellis's novel in society and to the nature of its debated moral significance. Situating *American Psycho* as a work influenced by Dante had a salutary effect on its reception in my classroom, because it suggested at least circumstantial evidence might exist that the work had a moral agenda equal to its touted immorality.

Framing Dante[13]

Bateman is obsessed with a physical purity of appearance but alienated from humanity on a personal level. Unable to comprehend the interior realities of other human personalities or feel empathy, he publicly follows the minutiae of his social group rituals while secretly violating the most fundamental laws of human society. In Ellis's original manuscript notes for Bateman's narrative voice, he cautioned himself to "omit metaphors, similes, anything where Patrick Bateman can see something as something else, because everything is too surface-oriented for that to occur."[14] The novel at first seems merely a bitter and excessively lurid satire of 1980s materialism, lacking in moral structure or depth: at least, that was the media consensus when it was released. Yet Ellis's trivial world owes much to Dante's deeply allegorical and spiritual literary vision from seven centuries ago.

American Psycho's social intent mirrors and even parodies Dante's, besides referencing it as a partial model for Ellis's plot. The Dantean elements are warped and obscured, but the works are (on one level) both cautionary tales exposing the apathy and horrors inflicted by society on itself, and speculations on the spiritual cost of inhabiting such a world. The precise motivations underlying Patrick Bateman's acts of violence, though subtle, are present in the text, and are rooted in his inability to balance the irrational values and social cruelties of his environment. Ironically, the novel caused the author to be accused of contributing to that social cruelty himself and the book was widely proclaimed as a corrupting document rather than an exposé.[15]

In my undergraduate horror fiction classes, our work on Ellis's novel begins with a brief overview of the *Inferno* to provide the context and grounds for comparative analysis (since virtually none of my undergraduate students have read the work). Dante's masterwork is many things, with personal revenge and political propaganda high on the list. Yet *The Divine Comedy* also combines its social critique with a profound and complex search for religious authority, and a strong argument that society as Dante knew it was unbalanced because of the consolidation of spiritual and temporal authority.[16] Studying Dante alongside Ellis emphasizes the degree to which each text is meant as a condemnation of its contemporary society, and, significantly, a condemnation of the reader who finds her or himself refuting the narrator's assertions in a defense of humanity's inherent morality. Societal privilege and lack of personal identity are connected in the worlds Bateman and Dante inhabit: the financial ruling class holds enough authority to impose its own ethics without any moral or religious foundation. Norman Mailer wrote that "*American Psycho* is saying that the eighties were spiritually disgusting, and the author's presentation is the crystallization of such horror"[17] but the implications of the text extend far beyond such specific satire. Indeed, with Dante's attempt to guide his society back to a proper reception of the fundamental guiding text of the Bible by virtue of his own writings, the consequences of textual misinterpretation seem infinite, including destroyed social orders, or the damnation of immortal souls. Dante shows that "spiritually disgusting" human behavior has been around much longer than Mailer suggests (since the two authors have such an overlap in their critical agendas), but unlike his predecessor, Ellis does not have enough faith in anything to offer a definite solution to an eternal problem.

Dante shows the eternal fates of those caught in the infernal, purgatorial, and celestial machinery that rules the universe, thereby demonstrating the principles by which the only flawed sphere (our terrestrial one) should likewise be governed. Only during the brief time humans inhabit the earth and exercise free will may any alteration be made to their fate (even Purgatory is an inevitable process: all souls laboring on the purgatorial mount know they will eventually reach Heaven, whereas the damned souls in Hell are forever barred from that grace). The span of mortal life, then, is crucial for Dante: it provides the only opportunity for humans to learn enough to save themselves. For those born into a society that has lost its way, that teaches materialism and false values, the task is that much harder, and the likelihood of damnation greater. In such times, the responsibility of spiritual and temporal leaders is enormous, as the damage done by their corrupting examples may have eternal consequences.

Like Ellis, Dante examines the social aberrations that he judges as the spiritual consequences of unethical leadership. The *Comedy*, polysemous as it is, contains a scathing critique of the consolidation of theocratic and earthly power by Boniface VIII, and Dante's treatise *De Monarchia* (written alongside the *Comedy*, and in many ways a continuation of some of its fundamental arguments) directly attacks the pope's claim that his authority could supersede the Emperor's in secular matters. Dante views the pontiff and emperor as the soul and body of humanity, leading them towards spiritual and earthly satisfaction respectively. Therefore they must always be present in separate and equal positions of authority, or the resultant imbalance will have a devastating effect on the society they govern. This imbalance is the explicit state of affairs in *American Psycho*. The need for temporal and religious powers to lead society is unmet in Ellis's vision. Moving further into the text, my students could see the analogy purposefully breaking down as Dante's afterlife (highly regimented, and reflecting the perfect orderly divine will) is contrasted with Bateman's vision of a chaotic existence, followed by a meaningless death.

American Psycho is more than unruly or unreliable: all epistemic stability is suspended, and neither Bateman nor the reader can readily determine identity, reality, or find stable ground on which to build a critique, moral or otherwise. As Michael P. Clark notes, "the ceaseless slippage of signifiers" makes it impossible to establish coherent identities, let alone an absolute moral code.[18] Bateman's Manhattan is worse than Dante's Hell, where, terrible though it is, everything functions in an orderly fashion as decreed by a supreme authority. As one of my students pointed out, there is no uncertainty left in Dante's afterlife; the truth is obvious. Bateman, who calls his reality "a private maze ... an isolation ward,"[19] can't be sure if he is damned or not, and his actions are in one sense an attempt to provoke any governing powers that might exist into revealing themselves, so he can finally have proof that his transgressions are meaningful. Instead, he sometimes doubts that they've actually occurred.

In my classes, students are invited to compare Bateman to the serial killers he idolizes, and his fictional memoirs are studied in light of clinical definitions of sociopathy and personal accounts by real killers to heighten awareness of the paradoxical verisimilitude of the surreal narrative.[20] Discussions of the limits of individual empathy and the possible effects of exposure to Ellis's writing reveal that students are divided on many points, not least whether the novel's supposed allegorical and satirical aspects excuse or provide "redeeming value" for its grotesque excesses. The most visceral reactions are not dependent on foreknowledge of the public controversy: before our class discussion had even begun, more than one student told me they had thrown their copies across the room in horror and disgust. Some refuse to finish reading the book, while some find another way to disarm the text: like Bateman's lawyer Harold Carnes, they simply refuse to believe his confessions. The novel contradicts itself in enough details that those who have an emotional stake in Bateman being deluded and harmless may attempt to extrapolate the disturbing sections of the text as false narrations. The ensuing debates highlighted the reader's role in defining fictional world and revealed some of the particular fears and anxieties at work.

Throughout my in-class surveys of two centuries of horror fiction, from Matthew Lewis's *The Monk* to *American Psycho*, the changing anxieties of each audience are constantly revisited and society's attitudes towards several fundamental aspects of existence (mortality, religion, sexuality, transgression) are discerned through the popular fiction that reflects those mores. Modern horror plays havoc with both epistemic coherence (a sense that our systems of beliefs are justified) and with constitutive coherence (what is true or correct may be established from the internal connectedness of a text). Since Bateman remains largely unpunished or exposed by the novel's end, a reader cannot easily support both conditions: either Bateman is lying, in which case the novel's already fragile logical consistency is quite shattered, or he is telling the truth, in which case he threatens a fundamental moral code by his intolerable immunity to consequence. In Dante's world, both the narrative voice and the execution of divine justice are utterly reliable. Though his enemy Boniface VIII was still alive as Dante wrote, the fact that he will burn in the Inferno is predicted by another damned pope (Nicholas III), and finally confirmed by Beatrice in Heaven.

The persistent argument that Bateman merely imagines all his crimes has also been used by critics, so students are in good company on either side of the debate. John Walsh blames the ambiguity on the author, saying that "Ellis blurs many lines in the narrative between Bateman's fantasy and his 'actual' killing sprees."[21] This ambiguity is a strong point of connection with Dante, according to Ezra Pound's interpretation of the *Comedy*'s journey:

> It is therefore expedient in reading the "Commedia" to regard Dante's descriptions of the actions and conditions of the shades as descriptions of men's mental states in life, in which they are, after death, compelled to continue: that is to say, men's inner selves stand visibly before the eyes of Dante's intellect, which is guided by classic learning, mystic theology, and the beneficent powers.[22]

Pound also complains that his contemporaries paid too much attention to the *Inferno* at the expense of *Purgatorio* and *Paradiso*. He argues that Dante's Hell is the state of humanity dominated solely by passions, no longer governed by intelligence or restraint, and asserts that a "sense of irony" in the reader would best clarify the meaning of Dante's sojourn in Hell.[23] Pound sees Hell as the self-imposed state of one's existence and the *Inferno* as a satire on the human behavior that defines Hell. Hope can only be found at the gate of Purgatory, and the desire to better oneself must begin before death. Contrition is useless once a soul has condemned itself.[24]

Dante treats allegorical representations of humanity's mental states as an objective reality for the sake of art so he might better articulate the depravity of those still alive. Ellis, too, uses a certain chaotic unreliability that anticipates his later works. Such negative capability is difficult for readers to learn, the more so when they are students with a vested interest in certainty of analysis. When Bateman seemingly returns in the 2005 novel *Lunar Park* to participate in faux autobiography by stalking the character Bret Easton Ellis, the line between fiction and nonfiction has become even more obscured. This metafictional strategy, however, is no more than Dante himself did almost seven centuries earlier, beginning with real events in his life and taking his fictional counterpart through experiences that could only be true on a symbolic level.

The Dantean crisis of humanity's inability to withstand temptation shifts to New York City in 1987, where an elite group indulges the greedily excessive acquisition of wealth, possessions, and status. In this world sexual relationships are blunted by jaded appetites and drug-induced apathy, and tainted by constant fear of AIDS and homosexuality (the two are almost synonymous in the vague ignorance of Bateman's crowd) into a blurred region of anxiety. Heterosexual conformity, and being *au courant* in choice of fashion are essential; dining on absurdly exotic foods in trendy restaurants is essential to maintaining status; and a perfectly maintained physique is a sign of personal power. For the reader, anxiety lies in one's reaction to the novel and the implications of that response. Arousal and disgust, curiosity and rejection, are deeply tied into self-image. Just as Bateman is horrified at the idea of being aroused by another man, many students seem to have a great deal invested in not feeling anything but disgust at Bateman's rapes and murders: an anxiety Ellis exploits by shifting suddenly during graphically detailed sexual encounters to mutilation and murder, tying arousal and horror together intimately. Yet as Bateman spends most of his waking hours obsessing over the looks, fashions, and sexuality of other men despite his fervent heterosexuality, the reader's fascination with his murderous sexuality continues. Mark Storey has written of Bateman's crisis of post-modern masculinity and self-fashioning of identity from other men; connecting it not only to his dissections of other humans, but pointing out the postmodern instability of meanings is so profound that the crisis of masculinity (what it means to be male at the end of the twentieth century) can only be resolved in a fictive space. Bateman attempts to affirm and define his gender role by frantically memorizing and adopting vague social/media constructions, and by real or imagined acts of physical transgression that exaggerate and parody the limits of masculine identity.[25]

My students agree that Patrick Bateman seems to have everything temporal anyone could reasonably want (youth, health, beauty, sex, riches) but he is as despairing and vicious as a trapped wounded animal. The closer those of Bateman's circle live to power and wealth, the more profound their lack of spiritual individuality has become: as with the proverb about it being easier to pass a camel through the eye of a needle than for a rich man to enter Heaven, there is a dangerous cost to the material success of the Manhattan elite. One student suggested that the absence of a coherent vision of the supernatural amongst his readership requires Ellis to situate both Hell and Purgatory in Bateman's world. Amongst a people without faith, "hell" can only exist as the shared construct of warped ideologies that imprison individual psyches, poisoning simultaneously from within and without. By killing beggars, prostitutes, and poor racial minorities, Bateman destroys victims of the economic disparity that his kind perpetuates, but his self-indulgence amounts merely to a more direct and overt exploitation and consumption of these groups than that of his peers. Hell must exist on Earth, because Wall Street is made up of its nobility. My students easily grasped the social critique, but it was further mentioned that the wealthy also financially support those same prostitutes, real estate agents, cab drivers, maids, and so on. The poor have no option to separate themselves from the wealthy, even for self-preservation, and the wealthy live without moral guidance or growth. There is an exception, however. Only one character does undergo a dramatic shift in moral attitude, during a mysterious absence: Timothy Price, Bateman's Virgilian mentor.

Virgil

The most obvious Dante reference is the first line of Ellis's novel: "ABANDON HOPE ALL YE WHO ENTER HERE," scrawled in blood-red lettering on the side of the Chemical Bank near the corner of 11th and First in downtown Manhattan, as Patrick Bateman's cab symbolically crosses the threshold into Hell, or the business district of New York. These words, the final of the nine lines engraved over the gates to Hell in *Inferno*'s Canto III, are first viewed by Bateman's co-worker Timothy Price, who is as close to a Virgil as Bateman will get during his sojourn in Hell (Bateman calls him, "the only interesting person I know"[26]). At first glance, Tim Price seems a particularly odd excuse for a Virgilian guide, at least from a moral point of view. His behavior and conversation quickly establish him as a much more cynical character than Bateman, but this is intentionally misleading. Price certainly loves to lecture Bateman and his circle about the shallowness of their clique, and seems to be the only person capable of inspiring lust in the otherwise Halcion-numbed

Evelyn, Bateman's titular fiancée. Bateman's flawed Virgil, however, soon abandons all affairs, and his friend, in a mysterious manner.

One night, Price gets Bateman into Tunnel (a real NYC nightclub from the late 1980s), and in an updating of Virgil granting Dante access past the various borders and sentries of the Inferno, provides Bateman with drink tickets and two VIP basement passes, but he ultimately deserts his charge. Price becomes obsessed with the old train tracks running through the lowest level into an underground tunnel by the dance floor. After a little cocaine and vodka, he suddenly announces that he is "leaving... getting out" to find what lies behind the blackness. He climbs the railing, champagne flute in hand, and with a hearty cry of "Goodbye!...Fuckheads!" he runs into the darkness of page sixty-two, not to reappear until sixteen pages from the end of the novel. The explanation I offered my class is that Price, at the lowest physical place visited in the story, somehow recognizes that he is at the floor of Hell, the Ninth Circle, where the only exit is to climb the Devil's very body through the center of the earth until he emerges by the Mount of Purgatory. Virgil takes his charge with him, and so Dante becomes the first living man to walk the length of Hell and escape. After many demons and damned souls assure him that there is no exit, he is nonetheless safely guided by Virgil past the Devil and through the center of the world, emerging to see the stars.[27] Yet Price goes alone, whether from selfishness or because he understands that his friends could not make such a pilgrimage with him. The others belong in Hell, something Bateman himself rarely tries to deny. Indeed, when Price has vanished down the dark tunnel, the only concern voiced is Craig McDermott's worried question, "Does Price know about a VIP room that we don't?"

When Price finally walks back into Bateman's office many months later, he has been through his purge and come as close to heaven as an unredeemed soul can, but like Virgil in *Purgatorio*, has had to return to the Inferno in the end. Bateman has no understanding of where Price has gone or how he has changed, but he does see a smudge on his forehead, and suspects nobody else could see it.[28] The smudge is a reference to the seven Ps of the penitent that Dante has removed one by one as he ascends the purgatorial mount, and to the cross of ashes marked on worshippers' foreheads on Ash Wednesday for the Lent season. Virgil never wears these marks, since he is only a guide, but Price went alone to his purgatory and seems to have been at least partially rehabilitated. This detail was one of the most convincing in establishing Price's Virgilian identity, from my class's perspective, since no other explanation for the smudge that only Bateman can see could be offered.

It is worth noting that *American Psycho* seems to take place over a two-year period, from April 1987 to April 1989, and that Price ironically returns on Valentine's Day (Feb. 14, 1989), only six days after Ash Wednesday (which fell on Feb. 8 in 1989). In his short time with Bateman prior to his escape, Price does express some mild disgust at the shallow inhumanity of the lives and relationships of the social elite he rubs shoulders with (though he is also disgusted by anyone poor, fat, non-white, homosexual, etc.). When he returns from, in his words, "making the rounds" (perhaps the rings of Mount Purgatory), however, he displays a new level of disgust and disbelief at the evil of the world, especially while watching Reagan testifying about the Iran-Contra affair on TV, in the novel's final (and most important) scene.

> Price looks away from the television screen, then at Craig, and he tries to hide his displeasure by asking me, waving at the TV, "I don't believe it. He looks so... *normal*. He seems so... out of it. So... *un*dangerous."
> "Bimbo, bimbo," someone says. "Bypass, bypass."
> "He *is* totally harmless, you geek. *Was* totally harmless. Just like *you* are totally harmless. But he *did* do all that shit and *you* have failed to get us into 150, so, you know, what can I say?" McDermott shrugs.
> "I just don't get how someone, *anyone*, can appear that way and yet be involved in such total shit," Price says, ignoring Craig, averting his eyes from Farrell. He takes out a cigar and studies it sadly. To me it still looks like there's a smudge on Price's forehead.
> "Because Nancy was right behind him?" Farrell guesses, looking up from the Quotrek. "Because Nancy did it?"
> "How can you be so fucking I don't know, *cool* about it?" Price, to whom something really eerie has obviously happened, sounds genuinely perplexed. Rumor has it he was in rehab.[...]
> "Oh brother." Price won't let it die. "Look," he starts, trying for a rational appraisal of the situation. "He presents himself as a harmless old codger. But inside..." He stops. My interest picks up, flickers briefly. "But inside..." Price can't finish the sentence, can't add the last two words he needs: *doesn't matter*. I'm both disappointed and relieved for him.[29]

We will return to this scene later, but for now the conversation can be juxtaposed with Bateman's speech near the beginning of the novel at Evelyn's birthday party, where he spouts an incredible montage of politically correct views. Price "almost spits up his Absolut" when Bateman says with a straight face that the government should "control mergers and big corporate takeovers."[30] Bateman has a vague sense of the irony of what he is spouting, but is not paying enough attention to his own words to truly appreciate it. He's simply parroting social agendas he's read, the way his friends quote vacation brochures verbatim when asked how they spent their holidays, or quote *GQ* when asked about their tastes in fashion. Price, by contrast, has been through a fundamental "rehabilitation" and is now struggling to express a concept that is so newly important, yet alien to his former self, that he cannot find the words to frame it. My students noted the way Price sees Bateman after his return (calling him "a madman... an animal. A total animal," "a real nut"), and how he tries to make Bateman react to the Reagan situation in some thoughtful way.

Beatrice

With graphic depictions of extreme violence towards women causing the most fervent objections to the novel, the question of what lies at the heart of Bateman's murderous misogyny is inevitable. After connecting Tim Price to Virgil, the fragmented and apostate candidates for Dante's ideal Beatrice need to be identified. Bateman fails at redemption, I suggested, partly because his Virgil deserts him, and his Beatrice never comes. In Dante's tale, despite having walked into Hell to intercede on Dante's behalf, she awaits him beyond "the fire that refines" at the top of Mount Purgatory, in the Earthly Paradise. Perhaps, as some students felt, Bateman is incapable of experiencing actual love, so the connection is impossible: since the inability to connect meaningfully to other people is the core horror of Ellis's novel, it is hardly surprising that romantic relationships are unsustainable. But perhaps Bateman's ideal woman is just another surface, a Galatea that never becomes real.

The *Inferno* quote that begins the novel is almost immediately obscured by a bus advertisement for *Les Misérables*, featuring a young girl's face.[31] The musical posters use a detail of the illustration "Cosette" by Emile Bayard, from the original 1862 edition of Hugo's novel. The face and the Dante allusion are juxtaposed in a reflection of Virgil and Dante's discussion of Beatrice's great love for Dante. The pure heavenly love of Beatrice for Dante begins and sustains the journey of the *Comedy*, but here the ideal woman's image is just a poster, using an engraving from an antique novel: there seems to be no living Beatrice for Bateman. This absent Beatrice can be seen as the root of Bateman's horrific relationship with the opposite sex. Bateman ironically misidentifies Cosette, the illegitimate daughter of Fantine and Tholomyès, as the privileged daughter Eponine during his several allusions to the musical throughout the text, including an incident where he kisses her face on a bus stop poster.[32]

The innocent Cosette in the poster is a Beatricean child, pre-pubescent and showing few hints of the beauty she will later become (like Beatrice Portinari whom Dante first met and fell in love with in the *Vita Nuova*, she was eight and Dante nine), and obviously poor and bedraggled. She is nothing like anyone in Bateman's life, and his attempts to fill her place with living women are awkward and disastrous. His so-called fiancée Evelyn is having an affair with his mentor Timothy Price, in a seeming parody of Beatrice's descent to Hell to beg Virgil to intervene and educate Dante on her behalf, so his soul might be saved. Evelyn and Bateman have no real feelings for each other at all, not even basic lust. Their fumblings in bed are a comedy of errors, due largely to fear of disease and Evelyn's perpetually drugged state.[33]

Bateman's secretary Jean, perhaps the most important woman in the novel, survives her time with him mainly because he finds her utter misunderstanding of his nature and "lack of defense" towards him "oddly unerotic." There seems to be a level of disconnection from reality that immunizes a few of Bateman's acquaintances from him: in Evelyn's case, her prescription-drug stupor; in Jean's case, her childlike naiveté; and for Luis Carruthers, his fawning adulation. In each case, the result is an utter fearlessness, which renders Bateman impotent, and this resembles Beatrice's scorn for the dangers of Hell. On his date with Jean, he has brief sensations, glimpses that suggest a reality beyond his perceptions but, as with Price's mysterious absence, the implications of beginning to believe in love or reason are terrifying to Bateman. Several moments with Jean arouse sensations and feelings in him that he is not accustomed to, and they make him desperately uncomfortable. Jean's affection occasionally seems to almost reach a soul deep inside Bateman, but he always draws away:

> she embraces me and this time exudes a warmth I'm not familiar with... but my embrace is frozen and I realize, at first distantly and then with greater clarity, that the havoc raging inside me is gradually subsiding and she is kissing me on the mouth and this jars me back into some kind of reality and I lightly push her away. She glances up at me fearfully.[34]

Bateman's old college sweetheart Bethany, an unexpectedly vivid character who briefly enters the novel, dies horribly at his hands as punishment for having surpassed him socially: she has her own Platinum American Express card, and her fiancé Robert Hall, an old college rival of Bateman's, is now chef and co-owner of Dorsia, the restaurant where Bateman cannot get a reservation.[35] Bethany has several Beatricean aspects: she is an ex-girlfriend from Bateman's past, and he wronged her in their past life (Bateman remembers how she took him to lunch at Cambridge and, "her arm in a sling, a faint bruise above her cheek, ended it all"[36]). Like Beatrice, she has passed out of Bateman's hell, but returns, seemingly out of concern or desire for him. The horrible racist scrawl of a poem Bateman hands her in the restaurant parodies Dante's courtly love sonnets.[37] Unlike Beatrice, who tells Virgil she does not fear to walk in Hell because she is a blessed soul of the Empyrean and so beyond any reach of evil, Bethany is still human and vulnerable, and once Bateman has run out of pathetic attempts to impress her, ends up mutilated with a nail gun and tortured to death because she went alone with him to his apartment. Her downfall is perhaps in thinking Bateman can be saved, that he is worth redeeming.[38]

Bateman's vision of humanity avers that "no one is saved, nothing is redeemed."[39] If he believed otherwise, he would despair; only through refusing to believe in purity, goodness, or the possibility of heaven can Bateman shield himself from the knowledge that such things are forever beyond his reach. His attempts at confession, his efforts to be caught or at least to be recognized as dangerous and important, are all useless because he is simply confessing to other damned souls who mishear his words in a comedy of errors and ignore them. When Bateman says, "this confession has meant *nothing*," he is echoing the sentiment of the Dantean lines uttered by Guido da Montefeltro in *Purgatorio*:

> If I thought my answer were given/ to anyone who would ever return to the world, this flame would stand still without moving any further./ But since never from this abyss has anyone ever returned alive, if what I hear is true,/ without fear of infamy I answer you."[40]

Circles

Bateman's secret lair is in an abandoned apartment building in Hell's Kitchen, where he dissolves bodies, but his proper place in the infernal pit, by Dante's geography, would be the Seventh Circle, the prison of violent souls. Its entry is guarded by the Minotaur, and it is divided into three rings. The Outer ring holds those violent against people and property, who are immersed in Phlegethon, (described in classical sources as a river of fire, but here composed of boiling blood). In the Middle ring are the suicides, transformed into gnarled thorny bushes and trees and tormented by harpies. The Inner ring holds the violent against God (blasphemers), the violent against nature (sodomites), and the violent against order (usurers), all lost in a desert of flaming sand with fiery flakes raining from the sky. My class compared this to Bateman's bleak vision:

> Where there was nature and earth, life and water, I saw a desert landscape that was unending, resembling some sort of crater, so devoid of reason and light and spirit that the mind could not grasp it on any sort of conscious level and if you came close the mind would reel backward, unable to take it in. It was a vision so clear and real and vital to me that in its purity it was almost abstract. This was what I could understand, this was how I lived my life, what I constructed my movement around, how I dealt with the tangible. This was the geography around which my reality revolved: it did not occur to me, ever, that people were good or that a man was capable of change or that the world could be a better place through one's taking pleasure in a look or a feeling or a gesture, or receiving another person's love or kindness... Reflection is useless, the world is senseless. Evil is its only permanence. God is not alive. Love cannot be trusted. Surface, surface, surface was all that anyone found meaning in ... this was civilization as I saw it, colossal and jagged.[41]

The fact that sodomites also inhabit the same circle as the murderers in Dante's *Inferno* may help explain why Bateman cannot escape the comical romantic attentions of his co-worker Luis Carruthers, who worships Bateman for his physical beauty, just as many women in the novel seem to. Carruthers, like Evelyn and some of Bateman's dates, mistakes Bateman's attempt to strangle him in a restaurant washroom for a sign of affection and confesses his love, leading to some very awkward and dangerous moments. Bateman finds himself inexplicably unable to murder Carruthers, but he encounters and viciously murders another gay man and his dog soon after an incident where Carruthers embarrasses him publicly.[42] There is a rumor that Tim Price's absence is because he's receiving treatment for AIDS in a private clinic, though that story is likely made up by Bateman to upset Evelyn (as mentioned earlier, homophobia, magnified by the epidemic, pervades the entire narrative).

East Hampton, where Bateman and his fiancée go for a vacation and stay in the absent Tim Price's house, corresponds to Limbo: the peaceful home of the best of the damned. Bateman is unable to commit any serious crimes there[43] and finds the place unbearable, despite the fact that his overwhelming violence provoked the vacation in the first place:

> Life remained a blank canvas, a cliché, a soap opera. I felt lethal, on the verge of frenzy. My nightly bloodlust overflowed into my days and I had to leave the city. My mask of sanity was a victim of impending slippage. This was the bone season for me and I needed a vacation. I needed to go to the Hamptons.[44]

Evelyn has the keys to Price's house "for some reason," (i.e. the affair Bateman suspects earlier in the novel) so they stay there. The house, four stories on the water with many gable roofs, reflects the castle that houses the noble pagans in the first circle of the Inferno, "an exalted castle, encircled seven times by towering walls, defended all around by a fair stream."[45] Here Bateman "really [tries] to make things work" with Evelyn, participating in every newlywed Hallmark romantic activity possible, from breakfast in bed and fresh flowers to late-night skinny-dipping and gourmet meals with champagne.[46] With no genuine emotion to sustain the activities, however, things soon decline and Bateman finds himself wandering the beach in the middle of the night eating handfuls of sand and microwaving jellyfish, while Evelyn reverts to a diet of "dietetic chocolate truffles," talking only about spas and cosmetic surgery. Bateman analyzes his own reactions, noting that his "depersonalization was so intense, had gone so deep, that the normal ability to feel compassion had been eradicated, the victim of a slow, purposeful erasure."[47]

Evelyn has quite probably gone through this entire romantic scenario before with Price in this same house, so her quick reversion to boredom may not just be due to her blasé sedated state. When Bateman finds himself standing over Evelyn in the hours before dawn, with an ice pick in his hand, waiting for her to open her eyes, he decides they have to return to the city, the lower rings of Hell, where he can safely indulge his desires among the other damned souls. When I asked my students why Bateman doesn't simply kill Evelyn at this point, only one answer was suggested: it would be too easy. Evelyn simply doesn't inspire enough emotion in Bateman to make the prospect of her death very interesting. Similarly, Bateman finally breaks up with Evelyn when watching her try to eat a urinal cake coated in chocolate which he has presented to her in a restaurant proves "an anticlimax, a futile excuse to put up with her for three hours."[48]

Since Bateman is unable to derive any satisfaction or joy from conventional interactions, he takes desperate measures to understand humanity on a material level. His killings, described in such gory detail, are dissections, alien autopsies: doomed attempts to comprehend a race he feels no meaningful connection to. Closely watching the moment of death is always a disappointment to him. Bateman recognizes his intricate stratified society as a place that denies the development of individual selfhood, but his experiments do not uncover or salvage a meaningful personal identity, they merely reveal a sick animal aspect.

Bateman's acts do go largely unnoticed, and there are strong hints that there are others like him in Manhattan: the Evian bottle poisoner who has killed 17 people, the "young stockbroker recently arrested and charged with murdering a young Chicano girl and performing voodoo rituals with, well, various body parts."[49] Out of all of Bateman's brutal attempts to assert a unique identity, only one succeeds: his narrative to the reader. At the novel's end, nothing can be satisfactorily resolved, so my students, like the critics and scholars before them, attempt to do so through rationalizations, interpretations, and condemnations. Like Bateman's "scary drawing which looks like this,"[50] the narrative requires reader intervention to be made coherent or significant.

Ellis contrasts with Dante's quest for redemption by writing the story of a man refusing to contemplate the cost of fixing his diseased, unbalanced internal state, asserting instead that his psyche is an inevitable mirror of the world that has shaped him. But Bateman is a flawed and incomplete reflection of his society and the cracks that appear in his worldview constantly undermine his denial of a worthy external reality. The Dantean structure of the novel provides the mechanism through which these cracks appear; by referencing the primary tale of redemption and consequence in the Western tradition, Ellis betrays his protagonist and invites the reader to somehow find a resolution. The only ally we have in this endeavor is Timothy Price, who failed as Virgil early in the narrative, but who returns to gesture at something beyond the closed circles of Bateman's hell.

When Price walks back into Bateman's office after his long absence, Bateman is afraid for a reason he can't name because he knows that Price has grown in some manner, accomplished something that Bateman is unable to do himself. Price has an ability to change which Bateman lacks and the ability to apprehend what he might change into. In that final scene at Harry's, still wearing his mark of the penitent, Price seems to see clearly for the first time, and realizes there is something rotten inside of Bateman, as there is beneath Reagan's façade. Bateman silently finishes Price's thought with his own despairing attitude, claiming that what's inside is irrelevant (and yet, Bateman feels partially relieved for Price when he does not finish his thought). Price was struggling to say that the *inside* is what matters, but Bateman and the others are incapable of understanding such a statement. On another level, the debate frames the question of where meaning is constituted between the interiority of a text and the exterior public role it plays. Price is inviting us to find a meaning in Bateman's narrative that Bateman insists does not exist; this is the role my students must also play.

The novel ends as it began, with Bateman reading a sign without attempting to explain the words: "THIS IS NOT AN EXIT." As the framing answer to ABANDON ALL HOPE YE WHO ENTER HERE, this implies an error in direction. Perhaps the tunnel through which Price vanished months ago is the only true exit. Bateman, unlike Price, or Dante, stubbornly insists that all experience is meaningless, because he is terrified of acknowledging what his experience might really mean, that he abandoned all hope long ago. However, next to him is Price, whose new humanity begins to undermine Bateman's narrative by arguing that there actually is something valuable, lost beneath all surfaces: societal, human, or textual. This assertion can guide students through a particularly complex and disturbing novel to a deeper understanding of how textual meaning is constructed, and even to an apprehension of something much harder to articulate: the multifaceted social role of horror literature.

NOTES

1. Bret Easton Ellis, *American Psycho* (New York: Vintage, 1991), 377.

2. Sylvia Söderlind, "Branding the Body American: Violence and Self-Fashioning from The Scarlet Letter to American Psycho." *Canadian Review of American Studies* 38:1 (2008): 63.

3. Julian Murphet, *Bret Easton Ellis's American Psycho* (London: Continuum, 2002) provides a good overview. Also see Donna Lee Brien, "The Real Filth in American Psycho: A Critical Reassessment," *M/C Journal* 9.5 (2006), and Jack Miles, "Imagining Mayhem: Fictional Violence vs. 'True Crime,'" *The North American Review* 276.4 (December 1991): 57–64.

4. Tammy Bruce of NOW (National Organization for Women) (*New York Times* February 18, 1991).

5. Jaime Clarke and Bret Easton Ellis, "Interview with Bret Easton Ellis" *Mississippi Review* 27.3 (Spring/Summer 1999): 77.

6. Roger Rosenblatt, "Snuff this Book! Will Brett Easton Ellis Get Away with Murder?" *New York Times Book Review* 16 December 1990, 3, 16; John Leo, "Marketing Cynicism and Vulgarity," *U.S. News & World Report*, 3 Dec. 1990, 23.; R.Z. Sheppard, "A Revolting Development," *Time* 29 Oct. 1990, 100.

7. Matthew Tyrnauer, "Who's Afraid of Bret Easton Ellis?" *Vanity Fair* 57.8 (August 1994): 70–3, 101.

8. In 2000. The movie, directed by Mary Harron, might be more accurately termed a black comedy.

9. Ellis, *American Psycho* 397.

10. S.R. Horton, "The Institution of Literature and the Cultural Community," *Literary Theory's Future*, ed. Natoli (Urbana: University of Illinois Press, 1989). The term "consumption" is also relevant here, because some critics have connected reader-response to a capitalist assertion of the buyer's right to actively determine the nature and meaning of anything they consume. "[R]eader response criticism, which arrived in the early 1970s with a liberating 'power to the people/readers' whiff about it, can in retrospect more easily be seen as a subtle version of consumerism" (281). An unpleasant or horrifying text is unusual in that by giving the reader what he or she seems to desire, they are foisting an unpleasant experience on them.

11. One hardly knows where to begin referencing the spirit of the 1980s, but I recommend Tipper Gore's 1987 bestseller *Raising PG Kids in an X-Rated Society* (Abingdon Press, 1987) as the most striking example of the particular right-wing/family values–based American hysteria of the day. I have read excerpts out loud in class to great interest and amusement.

12. University students encounter a course novel differently than an independent reader because their motivations are different: they are being compelled to read the book (or at least are aware they are expected to as part of their academic responsibilities); they expect some kind of merit, whether complexity and depth, historical importance, or some other reason, to justify its inclusion on a syllabus; and they have a vested interest in comprehending the novel, as their grades depend on being able to provide some sort of insightful observations on the text. Even if they are reading a novel they would — or have — read for fun, the dynamic inevitably changes once the pressure of classroom discussion and course credit is involved.

13. While revising this paper, I have encountered a blog that makes several of the same observations about Ellis's use of Dante: *Correlated Contents* by "Michael" (apparently Michael Lutz, a graduate student at Earlham College in Richmond, Indiana). Though his conclusions (and use of *Macbeth*) are not similar to mine, I mention it here. http://correlatedcontents.com/. I am, however, directly indebted to the careful editing and suggestions of Sean Moreland and Aalya Ahmad for the final form of this chapter.

14. Clarke and Ellis. "Interview."

15. The reception of *American Psycho* has been well covered. See especially Julian Murphet's *American Psycho: A Reader's Guide*, Rosa Eberly's *Citizen Critics: Public Spheres*, and Robert Love's "Psycho Analysis" *Rolling Stone* 601 (4 April 1991): 45–6, 49–51. In my classroom, I provided a sampling of the media and critical vitriol by asking students to read Donna Lee Brien's "The Real Filth in *American Psycho*: A Critical Reassessment."

16. Dante Alighieri, *Inferno*, trans. Allen Mandelbaum (Berkeley: University of California Press, 1980). For Dante, the physical presence of Lucifer in the centre of the earth was the ultimate reason for human error, but the corruption of the church was its worst earthly manifestation. In Dante's day the forged Roman Imperial decree known as *The Donation of Constantine* (*Donatio Constantini*), supposedly written by Constantine I, was not yet revealed as fake. Constantine had supposedly granted Pope Sylvester I and his successors dominion over the entire Western Roman Empire (including Italy) in gratitude for curing Constantine's leprosy and baptizing him. Since Leo IX in 1054, popes had begun using the document as evidence that the Holy See owned its empire in both religious and earthly respects. In *Inferno*, Dante laments, "Ah, Constantine, what wickedness was born and not from your conversion from the dower that you bestowed upon the first rich father!"(Canto XIX 115–7).

17. Norman Mailer, "Children of the Pied Piper," *Vanity Fair* (March 1991): 125.

18. Michael P. Clark, "Violence, Ethics, and the Rhetoric of Decorum in *American Psycho*" in *Bret Easton Ellis: American Psycho, Glamorama, Lunar Park*, ed. Naomi Mandel (London: Continuum, 2011), 29.

19. Ellis, *American Psycho* 342–3.

20. Along with discussions of how sociopaths are identified and profiled, I invited interested students to examine the entries in *Fifth Nail* and *Fifth Nail Revelations*, blogs by American convicted serial killer and sex offender Joseph Edward Duncan III, and to compare the tone and personality traits depicted in those journal entries with Bateman. http://5nrevelations.blogspot.com/.

21. John Walsh, "Review: Psycho Killer, 'Qu'est-ce que c'est?'" *Transition* 100 (2008): 159.

22. Ezra Pound, *The Spirit of Romance: An Attempt to Define Somewhat the Charm of the Pre-Renaissance Literature of Latin Europe* (London: J.M. Dent & Sons Ltd. 1910), 117.

23. Pound, *The Spirit of Romance*, 126.

24. Pound, *The Spirit of Romance*. "Thus the 'Commedia' is, in the literal sense, a descrip-

tion of Dante's vision of a journey through the realms inhabited by the spirits of men after death; in a further sense it is the journey of Dante's intelligence through the states of mind wherein dwell all sorts and conditions of men before death [...] In the second sense I give here, the journey is Dante's own mental and spiritual development" (116).

25. Mark Storey, "'And as Things Fell Apart': The Crisis of Postmodern Masculinity in Bret Easton Ellis's *American Psycho* and Dennis Cooper's *Frisk*," *Critique* 47:1 (Fall 2005): 57–72.

26. Ellis, *American Psycho* 22.

27. Dante's emergence to the stars ("stella" is the last word of *Inferno, Purgatorio*, and *Paradiso*) is also referenced in the final image of another of Ellis's novels, 1998's *Glamorama*. Victor Ward is in Milan, looking at a mural of "a giant mountain" (Purgatorial Mount, the sight that greets Dante as he emerges from the tunnel), and he experiences sensations of falling and moving upwards simultaneously. "The stars are real./ The future is that mountain" (546).

28. Ellis, *American Psycho* 384.

29. Ellis, *American Psycho* 397.

30. Ellis, *American Psycho* 15–16.

31. Ellis, *American Psycho* 3. Later, Bateman mistakes a college girl reading Sartre for a beggar. "Her face looks too young and fresh and tan for a homeless person's; it makes her plight all the more heart-breaking" (85). Caught up in his romantic interpretation of the moment, he leans over her, "eyes radiating sympathy into her blank, grave face" (86) and drops a dollar bill into her full coffee cup. Her irritated reaction panics Bateman into awkward stuttering and hallucinations.

32. Ellis, *American Psycho* 150.

33. Serial killer Jeffrey Dahmer used Halcion, the prescription drug to which Evelyn is addicted, to sedate his victims.

34. Ellis, *American Psycho* 265.

35. The restaurant name, interestingly, derives from Val d'Orcia, a beautiful region of Tuscany, whose name means "valley of life (or nature)" though the spelling and apostrophe is altered to make the word meaningless. After pretending to be someone else in order to get seated, and subsequently being kicked out of Dorsia, Bateman finally has a romantic dinner with Jean at a restaurant named Arcadia, the Greek equivalent. It is tempting to consider the elusive Dorsia as the transplanted Eden-garden ringed by fire atop Dante's purgatorial mount. In *Purgatorio*, Dante is only able to find the courage to pass through the flames when Virgil reminds him that Beatrice awaits on the other side.

36. Ellis, *American Psycho* 211.

37. Ellis, *American Psycho* 233.

38. It is notable that Bethany makes her appearance shortly after another girl from Bateman's past, Alison, who had come close to death at his hands during a sadistic sexual weekend several years before. Upon meeting Bateman she glares at him as if he was "the opposite of civilization or something" (208) and quickly leaves.

39. Ellis, *American Psycho* 377.

40. Dante, *Inferno* xxvii. T.S. Eliot uses this as the epigraph to "The Love Song of J. Alfred Prufrock."

41. Ellis, *American Psycho* 375.

42. Ellis, *American Psycho* 164–66.

43. Bateman does, however, drown the black Chow puppy he had bought Evelyn earlier in the visit. Evelyn, who names the puppy NutraSweet, "didn't even notice its absence, not even when I threw it in the walk-in freezer, wrapped in one of her sweaters from Bergdorf Goodman" (282).

44. Ellis, *American Psycho* 279.

45. Dante, *Inferno* Canto IV 106–8.

46. Ellis, *American Psycho* 280.

47. Ellis, *American Psycho* 282.

48. Ellis, *American Psycho* 337.

49. Ellis, *American Psycho* 275.

50. Ellis, *American Psycho* 306.

In the Dark of Your Own Psyche: Jungian Theory and Horror

J. A. White

It is as difficult to analyze horror as it is to analyze comedy. The act of analysis tends to expose the elements of the genre in such a way that the most memorable themes, the most haunting characters, and the most insidious effects are lost in a sea of rationalization. The success of a good horror movie depends upon the viewer maintaining a paradoxical position of knowing and unknowing. This position essentially operates on two levels. First, it requires the "suspension of disbelief" to which Coleridge refers as a condition for enjoying poetry,[1] or, as Torben Grodal notes, "the ability to suspend belief caused by seeing, hearing, and imagining"[2]; in addition, it reflects the interaction between conscious and unconscious states of the viewer's mind, acknowledging that the viewing experience activates unconscious associative responses so that even though the viewer knows the monster in the movie isn't real, he or she may feel that *something out there* may be waiting afterwards, plotting his or her demise. However, a detailed critical examination of such a movie upsets this state, removing those non-quantifiable elements which appeal to the viewer and replacing them with a catalog of plot points, characterizations, and techniques. It dissolves the mysteries which define the genre and replaces them with objective facts; it resolves the viewer's fears. But if we turn to Jungian, or archetypal theory, the task of analysis becomes pleasurable because one can illuminate key themes, characters, and dramatic effects without eliminating the mysteries which made them successful in the first place.

The purpose of using Jungian theory is to uncover the methods a filmmaker uses to manipulate the viewer on both conscious and unconscious levels, enabling him or her to induce reactions based on characters and events analogous to the viewer's own experiences, and to draw the viewer into the world of the movie by encouraging him or her to identify with the hero—

but to understand and perhaps even empathize with the monster as well. Noël Carroll has a specific term for the cluster of emotional settings and reactions which operate within the viewer's psyche: "art-horror."[3] Distinguishable from reality-based horror largely because it is pleasurable rather than traumatic, Carroll acknowledges that a viewer shares in "the emotional responses of the positive human characters to the monsters in works of horror."[4] For example, he notes the many ways protagonists react with disgust upon seeing the monster — shrinking from its touch, screaming, treating it as an impure, un-natural thing — and acknowledging that a monster, by definition, violates the natural order by virtue of its existence. An understanding of this dual affect — the viewer's identification with the hero, along with an ambiguous apprehension of the monstrous unknown — enables students to discuss why one movie may be terrifying while another leaves them howling with laughter. Jung helps students to uncover what makes scary movies scary without sacrificing their fear and abhorrence of the monsters therein.

Jungian theory is especially useful in teaching film to undergraduates. Film, after all, is a potent form of visual storytelling. Carl Jung, his students, and followers analyzed religious, folkloric, and mythical works in a number of cultures.[5] They found that people living in different times and geographical locations and more notably, cultural groups who had had no contact with one another tackled the same themes using similar images. In uniting this work with his experience psychoanalyzing patients, Jung posited that within every mind there was an inherited repository of information about family, the stages of life, about what it means to be human: the collective unconscious. This psychic structure "consists of the sum of the instincts and their correlates, the archtypes."[6] Archetypes are expressed through universal images that recur in literature and the arts worldwide; Jung theorized that they represent "certain instinctive data of the dark, primitive psyche...real but invisible roots of consciousness."[7] He compares the archetype itself "to the axis of a crystal about which material clusters,"[8] and this allows cultural and personal material to cluster about the core of the archetype. Especially relevant to the relationship between the archetypal figures in a fictional story in any medium is the fact that a person recognizes the presence of the archetype first in another person, in projection; this means that a monster is scary because the viewer's understanding of the monster results from an unconscious combination of archetypal material with the monster's characteristics as they appear on the screen.

Major archetypes discussed by Jung include the shadow, archetype of the negative or evil within; the anima or animus, the contrasexual archetypes of femininity or masculinity within; the Self, the archetype of wholeness; the mother, who can appear as nurturer or destroyer; the wise old man, a paternal/mentor figure; and the child, symbol of innocence.[9] In keeping with Jung's observations regarding the accumulation of cultural and historical material about the archetype, Jung's students as well as later writers have updated the list over time, reflecting the fact that images may erupt or increase in prominence as cultures change.[10] A horror movie has traditionally chronicled a male hero's encounter with the archetype of negativity called the shadow, as occurs in *Frankenstein* (1931) and *Dracula* (1932). However, as James Iaccino points out, contemporary filmmakers have made use of other more recently identified archetypes in creating brilliant variations on the theme. Thus heroine Laurie Strode (Jamie Lee Curtis) functions as caregiver/martyr in *Halloween* (1979), and Sigourney Weaver's Ripley both signify the Amazon-warrior in the *Alien* trilogy.[11]

Jung's student Erich Neumann also identified a master myth, the *monomyth*, which encompassed the three major themes of the sacred tales, folktales, and myths he studied; the story sequence is populated by archetypal images.[12] Of the chapters he identified — the creation myth, the hero myth, and the transformation myth — the most popular is the hero myth.[13] Today, visual storytellers, and in particular, purveyors of horror continue to reinvent the hero myth, each endowing its simple structure with culturally specific and ultimately, personal psychological material. Continuity in the presentations of image and story by different filmmakers provides an important means whereby students can recognize links and engage in comparisons, developing their critical thinking skills and gaining an appreciation for both the unique and the traditional in film presentation.

In humans and higher mammals, fear essentially arises from the need for self-preservation. "In the early mammalian environment of evolutionary adaptiveness, disaster could strike fast and without warning, primarily through hunting predators...[humans] required a perceptual system to identify threats and a *reflexively wired* motor system to move the organism away from the danger."[14] This basic system has evolved into what is called today the fear module, located in the amygdala. One of its distinctive traits is that it is immune to conscious cognitive control. Jung referred to the impulses towards action caused by these or other perceptions connected to self-preservation as *instinct*. "Instincts are typical modes of action, and wherever we meet with uniform and regularly recurring modes of action and reaction we are dealing with instinct, no matter whether it is associated with a conscious motive or not."[15] Even today the fear module operates without one's conscious intervention. The old, old fears of the species have not faded away, although new fears have taken root beside them. Does the sound of footsteps behind you on a lonely, dark street create the impulse to run? Is that smell of smoke from an uncontrolled fire or a burned roast somewhere in the apartment building? While we, as a species, have survived by accessing our abilities to gather, assess, and react to information, our primal impulses are more immediate and operate below the level of conscious thought. Thus we cross the street to get away from a potential threat before we consciously realize we have begun to do so; and by the time the word "FIRE!" comes to mind, we are already standing in the hall thinking about whether to pull the alarm. These regions below the threshold of consciousness are those to which a good horror director makes a direct appeal. One paradoxical pleasure of viewing horror is that one can feel terrified, yet still be willing to remain in his or her seat and find out what happens next — in effect, overriding the fear module's command to flee. This odd, yet pleasant sensation is a basis for art-horror.

"Here There Be at Least One Monster": The Hero Myth and Filmic Structure

An engaging horror movie encourages the viewer to participate vicariously in the heroic quest undertaken by the movie's protagonist. Joseph Campbell, the editor of Jung's *Eranos* lectures and a co-founder of the Bollingen Series through which Jung's collected works were published, wrote extensively on the hero's pursuit of the quest — the *departure* from the familiar, the *initiation* generated though the successful defeat of the monstrous Other, and the eventual *return* of a transformed hero to his communal roots — resulting in the hero's induction into the world of experience.[16] Students encounter this story's structure many times in their early lives, as it parallels Aristotle's ideal dramatic structure and is in use worldwide by storytellers in media and the arts.[17] As preschoolers, they may encounter this structure first in cartoons or stories, and then throughout childhood in television shows and films. Typically, by the time they encounter this structure for the first time in a formal classroom, they have already internalized its elements. To test this hypothesis, one might request that each student write a short exercise describing the plot and themes in his or her favorite movie, or better yet, describing the sequence of events which unfolds during a one-hour crime drama such as *Law and Order*. Another way to test what a student knows, especially when a few class members may not have been allowed to watch television as children, is to ask the students to write a creation myth. In any case, the students' writing will share some commonalities: the stories will have a beginning, middle and end and follow a linear plot; they have a quest, whether it may be the protagonist's resolution of a problem, his or her defeat of the antagonist, or the resolution of a conflict between the two; and the ending will have a definite conclusion. Most students know this structure well. In addition, when students are assigned a story which disrupts this narrative, or offers a multiplicity of voices, they may find it difficult to follow or even proclaim it boring; hence anecdotal recollections concerning students who prefer the straightforward monster story in *Beowulf* to the multi-theater, non-linear *Odyssey*.[18]

The hero's story also metaphorically replicates the process of achieving psychic wholeness Jung called *individuation*. "It is the goal of our psychological development and in metaphysical terms amounts to God's incarnation."[19] In order to complete the process, the ego, or willful "I," must confront and make peace with the major archetypal figures in one's psyche. If the image, and therefore material contained therein, remains repressed, the host personality cannot progress in his or her quest for self-knowledge; in other words, if a person refuses to allow the material into consciousness and refuses to acknowledge that the projections he experiences are in fact products of his own psyche, he or she will remain "stuck" in place, psychologically speaking. In creative works that illustrate the heroic quest, the hero represents the ego: the hero-ego then progresses psychologically with the resolution of each individual conflict. Each confrontation represents another initiation, a completion of a lesser quest: thus, while Odysseus' main quest, for example, is to return to Ithaca, the episode in which he defeats the Cyclops is representative of a mini-initiation, for it is here that he disturbs his own universe with unnecessary boasting. A student-friendly analogy to this double structure lies in the structure of the average survival videogame; *Resident Evil* or *Dead Space* players must survive low-level, yet potentially lethal attacks by a boss on each level in order to reach the final boss and complete the game by killing him.

In most horror films, the monster is readily identifiable as an image reflecting the shadow archetype. The shadow encompasses those psychological characteristics considered undesirable by the ego and the society in which its host personality lives. "The inferiorities constituting the shadow…have an emotional nature, a kind of autonomy, and accordingly an obsessive, or better, possessive quality." Recognizing the shadow, which takes a great deal of effort, according to Jung, involves "recognizing dark aspects of the personality as present and real."[20] The archetype, as image, also embodies the objects of our fears. As Stephen King notes, our most vulnerable point concerns the universal fear of mortality, or Self-obliteration.[21] Jason Voorhees, Michael Myers, and Leatherface all bring that fear into consciousness. In addition, however, the monster taps into cultural and, ultimately, personal anxieties. King suggests that while the fear of mortality permeates all good horror, British, Continental and American movies in particular reflect anxieties about sex and desire.[22] Other cultures express their anxieties through horror as well. Asian horror, in particular, reflects cultural anxieties about one's place in the afterlife, as well as a rigid morality that demands vengeance on behalf of innocent victims. Thus *Shutter* (2004) brings forth a spirit who returns to avenge her own death;

The Heirloom (2005) tells the story of a whole family of ghost guardians, or soul caretakers. Ultimately, the horror film may represent the ongoing battle between eternal good, or the life force, and eternal evil, or death; between the culturally defined moral man and the embodiment of a culture's morally suspect characteristics; or between an individual and his or her own unwanted drives. Sometimes, it invokes all three battles simultaneously.

In the silent masterpiece *Nosferatu*, for example, the vampire Count Orlok functions as a cultural shadow. From 1917 to 1920, a vicious influenza pandemic claimed roughly 100 million victims across the world. Despite the successes of Joseph Lister and Marie Curie, among others, in developing measures for preventing and fighting infection, families, towns, and major cities all lost many of their most productive citizens, as the disease tended to hit younger, stronger people. In the United States, for example, "the death rate for 15- to 34-year-olds of influenza and pneumonia were 20 times higher in 1918 than in previous years (Taubenberger)."[23] A year after the pandemic, in 1921, F. W. Murnau, one of the fathers of Weimar-era expressionism, adapted Bram Stoker's *Dracula* for the silver screen. With the nerves and memories of many raw from life changes wrought by the plague years, Murnau introduced the tale as "a chronicle of the Great Death in [the fictional city of] Wisborg, 1838," and redefined the character based on Count Dracula as Count Orlok, "Nosferatu," or "The Undead": a man not only responsible for the deaths of those upon whom he feeds, but also responsible for the introduction and spread of the plague in the town. No character was better suited to prey upon the conscious relief and unconscious anxieties of those who had witnessed the efforts of science and medicine to bring the real-life influenza pandemic under control. The premise of the movie was guaranteed to disturb its intended audience, as it suggested that occult influences could revitalize the pandemic and render modern scientific advances powerless against the scourge. The film remains one of the better psychic or metaphorical records of the effects the plague years had on the world following World War I.

Tension between the hero-ego and the shadow raises the anxiety level of the viewer, thereby contributing to the emotion of art-horror, so a filmmaker will usually draw boundaries simultaneously along two axes: the axis of opposites, which shows how hero and monster differ from each other, and the axis of kinship, which shows how the hero or heroine has a background, personality, or goals similar to that of the monster. In the movie *Friday the 13th* (2009), for example, director Marcus Nispel has set up this paradoxical situation. Jason Voorhees is the insane son of an insane killer, commanded by her after death to avenge her murder; he is the predator, and any teen who visits Camp Crystal Lake is potential prey. His eventual nemesis, Clay Miller, has come to Camp Crystal Lake on family business as well, but his goal is to preserve life, not to take it; he has come to search for his sister, who has gone missing up at the lake. However, Clay's back story allows the viewer to discern parallel backgrounds between the hero who in Campbell's terms will answer the call to adventure, Clay, and the monster himself, Jason Voorhees. Both are orphans; both are outsiders in the teen world circumscribed by the movie; both depend on family for sustenance, lose their closest female relatives, literally or figuratively, and become enraged when the rest of the world fails to respect their mourning. Of all the teens who arrive at Crystal Lake, an observant viewer would choose Clay as the one who will step up and vanquish the monster.

The anima or animus figure may also invade the horror film as a purely negative entity, preventing the hero-ego from embracing life experience. The male hero tends to experience the anima. In her maternal aspect, the anima may overshadow the hero's ego, keeping him close in a protective role, yet, as Jung suggests, keeping him also from life. In addition, she may also play the role of evil seductress, perverting the natural process through which the mother and adult son become separate psychic entities. Along with Jung's discussion of the anima as an entity of "compensation...and solace for all the bitterness of life," he qualifies his thoughts with these words: "She is the great illusionist, the seductress, who draws him into life with her Maya...Because she is his greatest danger she demands from a man his greatest, and if he has it in him she will receive it."[24] Thus, decades later in an animated and heavily rewritten version of *Beowulf* (2009), Grendel's mother, played by Angelina Jolie, seduces the hero, and their offspring, the dragon, becomes Beowulf's greatest enemy.

Interestingly, the female hero can serve as anima to the teenage male audience. Carol Clover's theory of the Final Girl suggests that both male and female audiences identify with the woman who suffers, yet persists, plans, and perhaps even sacrifices her health for the sake of vanquishing the monster.[25] Noting that "The image of the distressed female most likely to linger in memory is the image of the one who did not die: the survivor, or Final Girl," and describing the gender fluidity of the character—she may have a masculine name, "show more courage and levelheadedness than her counterpart,"[26] yet fill the soundtrack with utterances that suggest hysteria—Clover argues that the film's structure draws the male viewer into the film experience in such a way that he subconsciously identifies and sympathizes with the woman. Although her argument is Freudian in perspective, it also suggests that the male viewer recognizes or projects his own anima onto the screen: she is masculine enough to trigger the viewer's identification, yet claims a helplessness or softness through utterance—especially in the first acts of the movie—that she also appeals to the male desire to witness submission. It also explains logically why movies such as *Halloween* (1979) and *The Texas Chainsaw Massacre* (1972) have remained popular for decades, though the male characters outside of the major shadow figures (Michael Myers and Leatherface, respectively) are largely forgettable.

Conversely, the animus figure acts primarily as a companion to a heroine in a film, but he can also be an antagonist if his primary association is with the heroine, as opposed to the larger community or zeitgeist. In his paternal aspect, he may function as a guardian; however, he may also function as the immoral or amoral "inner male" of the female hero-ego. His behavior tends to represent a political action, in that it expresses an expansion of female gender roles into those of a traditionally male domain and promises a certain kind of freedom to the woman who expresses it. Of course, in horror, it may well represent these ideals gone wrong. For example, as noted below, the character Candyman in the 1992 movie of that name functions as the heroine Helen's (literal) racial animus; a vampiric figure with a desire for revenge, he comes to represent her pain and anger as well as his own. Unfortunately for those around them, that rage turns to murder.

The ego–Self confrontation tends to occur during the final battle, if indeed it is a battle at all. Because there is such a variation of expression of this conflict, it rarely figures in classic horror movies, which tag the monster as Other and present the hero as necessarily superior. This makes sense, as Jung suggests that "the ego is, by definition, subordinate to the self and is related to it like a part to the whole."[27] If this type of confrontation has an artistic home, it is in the world of psychological suspense, where twin-ship, real or implied, leads to an implosion of the ego. *Dead Ringers* (1988) and *Apartment Zero* (1988), for example, while extremely unnerving, are more readily defined as psychological thrillers rather than horror movies.

It is important to remember that in the hero's story, the relationship between the hero and those archetypes which appear as monsters is often symbiotic. This is reflective of Jung's position on the relationship between the ego and the various elements of its host personality. According to Jung, the ego does not recognize these characteristics first as a part of oneself, but in projection: a friend who is always late to dinner hates the fact that her best friend is always late to special events; a brother who is always asking to borrow money hates the fact that his sister needs a few dollars to tide her over until her next paycheck. In horror, this association is reflected in a shared kinship between hero and monster. The monster's existence is necessary for the hero to become heroic, and the hero's existence is necessary if the monster is to be contained.

In an engaging horror movie, however, the hero is not the only one to take a journey; the monster, too, has been taking his own journey, often long before his presence is introduced. The filmmaker may explore his ancestry, creation, or development, or all three; as a result, the viewer is forced to enter into a disturbing psychic state of being in the know about the observable and objective, yet having the essential bits of knowledge linger just out of reach. "Locations of fright" occur when the journeys of hero and monster collide. It is at these intersections that we can recognize the sum of the series of Jungian events which help to define the horror film: the hero-ego's departure from the familiar and the comfortable and movement towards the acquisition of experience; the hero-ego's recognition of the monster(s) as shadow, and his or her recognition of the fact that in terms of identity and psychic movement, the hero-ego and shadow are destined to do battle with each other; the hero-ego's confrontation with the shadow archetype; the final defeat of the shadow; and the hero's return to the familiar after his initiation into the world of experience.

Shadows of an Age: Teenage Angst and Primal Fear

The 2009 horror film *Friday the 13th,* an enormously entertaining entry in the franchise, provides a recent example of a towering shadow figure informed by cultural tropes. Director Marcus Nispel and Derek Mears, the actor who plays Jason in the 2009 version, have taken bits and pieces of the Jason character from several of the previous films and added a twist of their own, transforming him from a vengeful, yet somewhat robotic serial killer into a sadistic outdoorsman who, as Bill Gibron notes at Filmcritic.com, manages to be both "more aggressive and animalistic" than any other version of Jason who has roamed the *Friday the 13t*h franchise.[28] Although he shares a hideous, malformed visage with other versions of the character, this Jason is intelligent, resourceful, and manipulative. In an interview with Horror.com's Staci Layne Wilson, Mears emphasizes that "you really see Jason thinking and planning in this one, setting people up... people invade his space and he fights back."[29] By providing the back stories for the major characters, and allowing them to present their quests to the audience, director Nispel presents two stories in this movie — the hero's story and the shadow's.

Jason is a character who, in another place and time, would have been bullied by this same group of young adults. As Mears points out, "He's a victim. He represents those people in high school who were different, the ones with [a lisp] or the hair los[s], the outsiders and the misfits. Being rejected by society and the beautiful people. We're not allowed, socially, to lash out and get our revenge, but Jason does, albeit in a poor way..."[30] Thus Jason represents everything that these cliquish, hedonistic teens dread becoming — and already fear that they are. He is, indeed, their shadow.

The horror of the film grows out of the situation that the teens are being stalked not by a mindless monster, described by critic John Fallon as "dumb and psychotic"(Joblo.com), but that they are being tortured and killed by a clever, although insane entity.[31] Jason is a self-taught survivalist; he has set up a complex network of bunkers and tunnels underneath the land surrounding the house he and his mother shared. He can and does appear and disappear in a few seconds' time, moving quietly, like a tracker, and then vanishing through any one of a number of manhole-sized trap doors. As strange as this arrangement appears to be, it gives him an extraordinary advantage in planning and executing the crimes he commits. From a practical and psychological standpoint, it gives him power over his prey, for no one can see him unless he allows them to do so. Practically speaking, he kills again and again before the survivors think to call for help; psychologically speaking, he gives the impression of being a tremendous and indefinable force, simply because no one can describe him or figure out whether he is acting alone. As long as Jason leaves the survivors in the dark about his size, his intentions, and his numbers, their terror will continue to increase.

The film also exploits age-old tensions between the wealthy people who purchase property in beach or forest communities and the working-class people who live in those communities year round. Jason and his Crystal Lake neighbors must suffer the consequences of an annual summertime takeover by boorish invaders and their children. Jason certainly represents the teens' collective shadow, a nightmarish and elusive figure whose primary purpose is to avenge his own rejection by society; but the teens also represent the community's collective shadow — arrogant, materialistic figures who appropriate the land for their own pleasure and self-aggrandizement. The complexity of the film lies partially in its initial ambivalence towards Jason's actions, an ambivalence expressed openly by one of Jason's neighbors. Yes, he's brutal and even sadistic — but the teenagers he dispatches with such passion are troublemaking outsiders who fail to consider the consequences of their actions, thanks to their collective sense of privilege. This fact adds to the political dimension of the film, as it places him in a bizarre role — protector of the local residents and the community's integrity.[32]

Of the multiple protagonists who populate the movie, two in particular stand out as potential heroes: Trent de Marco (Travis Van Winkle), the teen who brings an Escalade full of victims to his rich parents' three-bedroom cabin at the edge of Crystal Lake, and Clay Miller (Jared Padalecki), the working class teen, who has come to Crystal Lake to search for his missing sister Whitney (Amanda Righetti). A chance meeting between the two at a gas station initiates the competition; however, Trent's boorishness and lack of concern for Clay's plight suggest that of the two, Clay will be proven to be the worthier of the two men. This impression is strengthened by the fact that, as noted earlier, the more we learn about Clay, the more he seems to resemble Jason. Both are poor kids thrust into a wealthy environment; both are treated shabbily by people who cannot empathize with them. Yet the most important element that differentiates them from everyone else in the movie, as we find out eventually, is that both have lost their mothers. As the story progresses, it becomes clear that Clay and Jason are paired. It therefore makes sense that Clay steps up to rescue his sister; it also makes sense that Whitney will become a variant of Carol Clover's Final Girl.

Interestingly, the one local who winds up with a fatal case of blood loss does so after attempting to investigate his employer's attic, where, stoned and paranoid, he decides to go in search of the thief who's been stealing the old man's kerosene. Instead he discovers Jason, who appears and dispatches the young man with little hesitation after he commits the offense of reacting with disgust to Jason's hideously malformed face. This scene, as Carroll's taxonomy dictates, essentially allows the viewer to identify Jason as a monster; the viewer's disgust, shared with the character, engages the emotion of art-horror.

As brief as this scene is, it gives the viewer a clear sense of why Jason is who he is, for it tells us that his sense of himself is derived from experiences associated exclusively with rejection and abandonment. Without Mother there to soften the emotional blow, Jason must protect himself as best he can. More importantly, at this point, he is the young man marked physically and emotionally, steeped in loneliness, and deprived of either blood family or chosen family, that the teens who come to Crystal Lake actively seek to avoid becoming. He is, indeed, their individual and collective shadow.

However, there's no "zombie" Jason here, no dispatching whirlwind of unbridled, unfocused energy. Instead, he is focused, determined, and very, very angry — angry enough to plot against his victims and indulge again and again in premeditated murder. Jason's native intelligence also shines through during some of these scenes. In one heart-wrenching scene, Jason corners the token African American teenager, Lawrence (Arlen Escarpeta), who, in a testosterone and THC-soaked moment of courage, has run out to the storage shed to help bring his dying friend Chewie (Aaron Yoo) back into the house. As Lawrence escapes Jason's clutches and begins to run back to the house, Jason reaches down and picks up an axe, which he then hurls end over end, hitting the teen in the upper back and apparently severing his spinal cord. As Lawrence screams pitifully for his friends to help him, the teens remain inside, fighting with each other about leaving the relative safety of the house to rescue their pal. Ultimately, before they decide what to do, Jason kills the young man. Jason's intentions can be summed up in Clay's admonition to the group: "Stay here! He wants us to come outside. He's using your friend to lure us."

Jason's apparent defeat at the hands of the rescued sister and her brother encapsulates all that he is, and all that they are. Clay fights Jason in a brutal bout of hand-to-hand combat. Whitney distracts Jason by calling his name and offering him the locket, as a girlfriend might. "Jason," she says softly. It's okay. Come on." Clay and Whitney together form a family unit and not a romantic one: like Jason, they are motherless; unlike Jason, they have each other. It is important that a family and not a romantic couple defeat Jason because the one great lack from which Jason suffers is a lack of family; having had only voyeuristic experiences at Camp Crystal Lake, he does not have the maturity to understand what it means to have a mate. While Whitney deals the final blow, her victory is not without male agency. Whitney takes Jason's machete and runs him through, but only after Clay has managed to wound him.

A repressed archetype, however, won't stay under the surface. In the final scene of the movie, the viewer sees Clay and Whitney consign Jason's masked, chained corpse to the depths of Camp Crystal Lake. However, as she weeps and he pontificates, the inevitable happens. As the viewer listens to Clay's voiceover, there is a static underwater shot of Jason's body suspended vertically in the water. The focus shifts briefly to the mask floating down to the bottom of the lake; then, abruptly, the camera switches to deck level, where the viewer sees Jason burst out of the water and grab Whitney, his beloved. The shadow, in the final analysis, triumphs.

When one considers Jason's plight in Jungian terms, the problem is clear: Jason has grown up with an ego whose complements have been underdeveloped, due to his limited interactions with other humans. The shadow has appeared and overwhelmed the ego, which has not been strengthened as it usually is during the teenage years. The net result is that Jason is all shadow, all the time; he represents death and destruction. John Fallon singles out this character because he is neither stupid nor purposeless in his actions; yet it is precisely his intelligence and reasoned rage that makes him appear so dangerous to the audience. Jason, as he appears in the 2009 entry of the franchise, is a shadow figure made expressly for an American teenage audience.

When a Shadow Isn't: Helen's Outraged Animus

The 1992 film *Candyman* is notable for the singular way it combines elements of a standard vampire legend with an expression of liberal frustration over the way that African Americans have failed to thrive following the supposed attainment of full citizenship during the 1960s and 1970s. An insightful look at race relations in America, the movie is the product of collaboration between two Englishmen: the writer Clive Barker, whose focus is often the horror within the human psyche, and Bernard Rose, director of *Paperhouse* (1988). In it, a young graduate student, Helen Lyle (Virginia Madsen), decides to investigate the real story behind an urban legend concerning the Candyman (Tony Todd), an African American vampire and son of a slave, who will kill anyone who stares into a mirror and calls his name.[33] Like an observer who alters the measurement of a particle by merely watching, however, Helen's active pursuit of the truth brings the entity into existence. There is murder, mayhem, and the kidnapping of a perfect baby boy; but at the same time, there are also questions. How much, if any, of this story, takes place in Helen's mind? Is she a victim, or does the story unleash something powerful and ugly within her own mind? What happens when Helen's story and the Candyman's story collide? Finally, considering the film from a pedagogical point of view, does one teach that there is a one-to-one correspondence among character, theme, and archetype in a film, or is it possible for one figure — Candyman — to represent one archetype on a personal level and another archetype at a cultural level?

A number of feminist critics have addressed issues they believe to be at the center of the movie, but most focus on the issues surrounding miscegenation and the positioning of the black man as Other. Judith Halberstam complains that "Helen's character stabilizes under the sign of the white woman victim... in the context of 20th century Gothic, race becomes a master signifier of monstrosity, and when invoked, it blocks out all other possibilities of monstrosity."[34] Kim D. Hester-Williams, who examines the treatment of black subjectivity in contemporary science fiction and horror films, asserts that "[b]ecause the monster in the film is a black man — and, again the son of a former slave — it seems clear that we are to beware of all that Candyman signifies. And what he most powerfully signifies is the memory of American slavery."[35] While Isabel Cristina Pinedo categorizes the film as an example of "race horror," which she defines as films set in an urban area "that code the monster as racial Other associated with a powerful and savage religion,"[36] she is one of very few to recognize that both Helen and Candyman are depicted as monstrous, and argues that this alone is ground for a subversive reading of the film. "Is there not some pleasure and sense of power to be gained, at least by female and black audience members, from seeing the power in these violent figures?"[37]

Candyman, the entity who haunts the halls of Cabrini Green, Chicago's notorious high-rise housing project, functions as a vicious and destructive shadow figure; but he also represents the self-hatred felt by so many young

African American men who are trapped in the ghetto with nowhere to go. His history reveals the reason for both his acting out and the misdeeds of his spiritual descendents; in his original incarnation as the genteel and talented son of a slave, he is metaphorically castrated and sadistically murdered by the father of a young white woman with whom he has fallen in love. Neither his privileged upbringing nor artistic talent can shield Candyman from certain death once he has violated a social taboo based on "European myths about the aggressive, violent, and animalistic 'nature' of black sexuality...fabricated...by the phallocentric anxieties and fantasies of the all-powerful white 'master.'"[38] It is not surprising that the Candyman appears in the urban African American community, nor that his murderous impulses are satisfied there. Institutional racism and economic hardship have divided residents of places like Cabrini Green throughout the country into two camps: those who cause fear and those who suffer it. Candyman is thus an African American shadow image, denied freedom and prosperity and driven to self-destruction.

Candyman in some ways represents the spirit of the community at large: "I am the writing on the walls," he says to Helen when they first meet, "the whispers in the classroom. Without them I am nothing, so now I must shed innocent blood." Indeed, his words indicate that he owes his continued existence to the unspoken feelings and ideas of the community: the frustration and rage only vaguely expressible by those who write on the walls; the eternal isolation which neglected schoolchildren, like young Dick Gregory in "Shame," express in their whispers and notes behind the teacher's back[39]; and the menace of drugs, assault and gunfire which lurks in the halls and apartments of the projects—the menace from which young mothers like Ann Marie, mother of the baby kidnapped by the Candyman, want to protect their children. Candyman's words also suggest that it is these things which give him life, and by extension, these things which define the urban African American *Zeitgeist*.

However, the screenplay also studies the interplay among race, class and gender as it allows the Candyman legend to spill out into the film's reality. Once we recognize this fact, we must then ask a number of questions. Who is the story really about: Helen, the Candyman, the academics at the University of Illinois, or the residents of Cabrini Green? How important is it that Helen is an anthropologist and not a city planner or architect? Is there a reason besides the obvious romantic angle that Candyman attaches himself to Helen? Most importantly, why does the mirror image become personal to Helen, when Candyman first seems to be the shadow image of the whole African American community?

The answer is that while Candyman does indeed function as a shadow for the whole community—a fact reflected in the way a gang lord appropriates his name as a means of exerting control over Cabrini — the movie emphasizes his attachment to Helen. For one, Helen is responsible for bringing Candyman into his present-day corporeal existence. One of an interracial pair of graduate students doing a thesis on urban folklore, as well as an incarnation of the woman with whom Candyman had fallen in love, she first brings him into an earthly existence through her disbelief. As an academic, she presumes that there is no truth to the stories she investigates; deaths attributed to Candyman, she believes, are murders committed by gangsters. Indeed, when she and her African American colleague, Bernadette Walsh (Kasi Lemmons), are first driving towards Cabrini Green, Helen reminds Bernadette that they have a chance to make a name for themselves, now that they will be investigating "an entire community [which] attributes the daily horrors of their lives to a mythical figure." After an encounter with the brute who has adopted Candyman's name — a chance meeting during which the faux Candyman brutalizes her with the hook he carries — it seems that she has spoken the truth. But later, the real Candyman appears in her territory, a university garage far away from Cabrini, and speaks to her: "I came for you," he says in a chilling voice. "You doubted me...you were not content with the stories, so I was obliged to come." His connection is to her and not just to the community at large.

The first act of the movie is meant to show the audience how Helen negotiates an academic world dominated by stratification. Helen and her best friend Bernadette are bright and ambitious women, yet as graduate students, they belong to the bottom caste of her department. In addition, they clearly inhabit a man's world. Helen is especially competitive because she needs to prove herself to her husband, Trevor, a professor who has a taste for undergraduate women, and who is threatened by the quality of his wife's work, and her thesis advisor, Professor Purcell, perhaps even more than she needs to complete her degree. But Trevor has no respect for his wife. He flirts openly with an undergraduate in Helen's presence and sabotages her research by giving a lecture which will create biases on the part of her research subjects. Professor Purcell is no better. Their attitudes are clear: she is "playing at" being an academic, not becoming one. Their gender biases are strong, and she seems unable to change their ways. This setup will lead her, as hero-ego, to a psychological place where, theoretically, the animus will erupt to express her pain and set her free. However, she is asked to exchange one type of victimhood for another, and the solution to that dilemma is literally washed in blood.

Candyman is essentially a mystery story. The Candyman kidnaps a baby and then commits a hideous series of murders. Or is Helen the one responsible? As the plot unfolds, Helen gradually changes from the relatively powerless woman she first appears to be in her husband's lecture hall to a woman capable of murder, and her association with the Candyman is directly responsible for this change. The animus erupts; Helen appears more powerful than any of her colleagues would have imagined, albeit in a hideously corrupt way; the primary man in her life grows to fear her and is in fact forced to take her very, very seriously. Having assumed he knows what she is thinking and what she wishes to accomplish, he is put into a situation where he must acknowledge that she is at the center of a great mystery.

In the first of three separate murder scenes, someone kidnaps the child of a woman Helen has befriended at Cabrini, Ann Marie, and kills the woman's Rottweiler. Shortly before, in a deserted level of the university garage, Helen has had her first encounter with the genuine Candyman. Appearing in broad daylight, he calls her name softly from the opposite side of the level and waits for her to react. "Be my victim," he asks, as if this were a pleasant invitation. At first fearful and revolted by his physical presence, his anachronistic attire and a makeshift, bloody hook replacing his severed hand. Helen protests, arguing that she has to leave; but we see her resolve weaken as she is soothed and gradually mesmerized by his rich baritone. Eventually she faints; but then, abruptly, the setting changes and Helen wakes up covered in blood at Ann Marie's apartment, meat cleaver in hand. In a quickly unfolding sequence, Helen discovers the Rottweiler's butchered remains; learns Baby Anthony is missing; defends herself from his hysterical mother; and surrenders to police. Seconds later we learn that Helen has been taken in for questioning — and, in a scene which hints that she is receiving the same treatment as Candyman once received, we witness her humiliating strip-search at the hands of a stone-faced matron. She is arrested, but released after an overnight stay in jail — and a vision of Baby Anthony in a makeshift manger somewhere in Cabrini Green.

As the bizarre process of empowerment continues, Helen encounters the Candyman in her apartment; he chases her by simply appearing before any exit she attempts to access and blocking her escape. "I have the child," he tells her, and then, a proposition: "Come with me and be immortal," he says in a voice both lush and threatening. He wants to reclaim the family he lost nearly 200 years before and be with them forever. This strange entity, in his twisted way, offers Helen a version of ideal womanhood as it existed in his time: it includes a beautiful baby and eliminates a straying, disrespectful husband. It does, however, violate natural law, as it requires Helen to become a vampire who will thrive on blood and never die; it also requires that she couple with an entity whose decayed torso is filled with bees. In addition, as a representation of Helen's animus, his logic is straightforward, and eliminates such worrisome reality-based elements as an involvement in felony kidnapping and the fact that the actual woman he loved has been dead for almost 200 years. While Helen is clearly terrified and grabs a knife to protect herself from him, it is interesting that her "talking vision" has offered her an archaic version of an ideal life, one that requires her to simply be. At this point, we might remember how Candyman met his original Helen: she posed for him as he painted her portrait. We can also say that Trevor and Purcell have so little respect for her that they would not care if she simply didn't exist. Bernadette, however, has another type of ideal life to offer: a professional life of academic and intellectual accomplishment as an anthropologist, immortality granted by publication of academic volumes which are used for research long after their creators have died, and a personal life which values friendship and mutual support. Helen's doubts and ambivalence towards Trevor make her vulnerable to some kind of influence by the Candyman; it's not a matter of what she does want, but what she doesn't want from the men in her life.

As animus, then, the Candyman's appearance makes a twisted kind of sense. In pursuit of her academic dream, Helen has been dismissed by her husband as well as her supposed mentor; drawn to research that places her in the most dangerous project in Chicago, and threatened by a gang whose leader slams her into unconsciousness with a meat hook. The perfect academic life, it seems, belongs to her husband, but may not belong to her; in her quest for his respect, and that of her mentor and colleagues, Helen has placed her life in jeopardy and still not yet been recognized for her work. Maybe her efforts are not worth the paper her future thesis is to be printed on...and Candyman, revolting as he is, does offer her an outlandish and fantastic kind of freedom. It is unfortunate, Helen thinks—or is it the Candyman's thought?—that Bernadette stands in the way. Seconds later, when her husband walks in, Helen is lying on the floor, bloody knife in hand, and her best friend has been brutally murdered in the next room. What's notable about this scene is the fact that Helen seems to know Bernadette's death is inevitable; upon hearing her friend knock on the door, she utters a warning, but in a voice Bernadette clearly cannot hear, a voice conveying both resignation and grief. At least some of the audience may hear Simon Oakland's voice in its collective head, explaining, "It was *Candyman* killed the girl." Maybe there is a Candyman, but maybe Helen is insane.

A third murder takes place in the asylum where Helen has been transported to await evaluation and trial. The succession of scenes suggests that the Candyman does not exist outside of Helen's psyche. Earlier, she has been restrained on a gurney, and cowered as Candyman floated above her, invisible to her attendants watching on closed circuit video. "He's here," she screams in the otherwise deserted room. A month later, Helen is sitting in a psychiatrist's office, hands strapped to the arms of a wheelchair. The psychiatrist, Dr. Crane, is talking to her about the murders, but she rejects his words; in the clearest indication that she believes the Candyman to be a living entity, she tells the doctor, "I know no part of me is capable of that!" Suddenly, a shrewd look crosses her face. "Candyman!" she says in a quiet, urgent voice, and waits. A moment after, the psychiatrist suddenly grunts, and the Candyman appears behind him, his hook impaling the doctor like a dagger. "You are mine now," he says to her as he slashes her bonds, allowing her to escape.

The plot, however, cloaks these murders in ambiguity. For one, Helen is always found by authorities at the scene, covered in copious amounts of blood, holding a knife or meat cleaver, devoid of any knowledge of how she arrived there. The precipitating cause, too, is suggested to the audience, but not to the movie's characters: we know that Helen has had an encounter with the Candyman immediately before each crime is committed, but no one else in the movie can see him, and all forensic evidence leads back to Helen herself. The depth of their connection is reflected in the fact that it is never absolutely clear that she is innocent. In fact, during the one scene where the audience might question Helen's ability to kill anyone, as her hands are bound to the wheelchair in which she sits, the point of view is such that, when we see Dr. Payne killed by Candyman, we could easily be looking at a whole episode taking place inside Helen's head. Kirstin Thompson comments on the destabilization of credibility triggered during the hospital sequences: "This is the place where the spectator is left…consequently, the narrative may be unreliable—it may be the visual product of Helen's psychotic overidentification with Candyman. By extension, when Candyman is visible to us, our vision may not be trustworthy and may imply an unconscious spectatorial identification with Helen's psychotic subjectivity."[40] The only thing we do know is that the rage and vengefulness the original Candyman, Robitaille, felt, and perhaps still feels, is the same rage and vengefulness we can attribute to Helen Lyles, who is emotionally thwarted at every turn when she tries to gain recognition for her intellectual attributes—in other words, when she tries to defeat the limitations placed on her by others in society and maintain trust in her own sense of worth.

Candyman's most hideous crime, significantly, a crime attributed by the homicide detective in charge of the case to the drug dealer, is the castration-murder of a six-year-old boy. The story is that the boy, shopping with his mother, was allowed to go to the public restroom alone, and never returned. Far from gratuitous, the crime reflects the role of Helen's animus in the life of the community—and the fact that it is out of control. It has adopted an expanded role. Instead of studying the community and becoming protective of it, Helen's animus, reflecting the image of the active woman as "uppity" and aggressive in her territorial claims, destroys the community from within.

It is for this reason that she must seek redemption, a redemption attainable through her rescue of the kidnapped baby.

At the same time, however, there is a recognition by the youngest members of the community that Candyman and all that he represents is alive and destructive and must be eliminated. They light the bonfire which nearly kills the baby. They destroy Candyman as he pleads for Helen to come back to him, but Helen saves Baby Anthony, whom Candyman had kidnapped, and whom he has buried under the debris that will become a pyre. Crawling on hands and stomach, protecting the child with her body, Helen emerges from the pile, living just long enough to hand the child back to its mother. She thus redeems herself and gains a measure of immortality by performing the most maternal of acts: saving a baby. Her heroic story, like the legend of Candyman, will be told by the members of the community for decades to come. Her return to her own community lies in the fact that future scholars will study her story, just as she arrived at Cabrini to research the stories she has heard. The cycle is complete.

While the final scene in the movie takes place after Helen's death, it provides perhaps the best evidence that both propositions are true: that the Candyman does, in fact, exist, and that he functions as Helen's animus. It gives the audience one last look at Trevor — dead in the bathtub — and his undergraduate lover, Stacy, standing nearby with a knife in her hand, screaming like a banshee. In one brutal act, Candyman — or perhaps Helen's ghost — avenges the wrongs that Trevor has committed against his wife. For Helen this act functions as one last utterance of rage and power; her animus has finally crushed her main source of emotional pain and his rival as well.

Thus *Candyman* reveals itself to be a combination of two intertwined narratives: that of the hero, Helen Lyles, and that of her nemesis, Candyman; in the process it both makes a political statement concerning the deterioration of life in the urban African American community, but tells a second story about a woman who is seduced by her own rage and dies making amends. The cultural shadow, therefore, also functions as a personal animus.

Practical Applications

As noted earlier, film is storytelling. Teaching film analysis involves an adaptation of modes of literary criticism, through which one may discuss the sociohistorical contexts of a film, the characters' actions and motivations, the screenwriter's use of language and direction, and the structure or structures of the screenplay as it translates into film. In addition, however, the film professor must teach the medium, introducing such technical aspects of film as background, lighting, the number and types of shots, and encouraging the appreciation of editing, the musical soundtrack, and other post-production elements which together sustain the film's mood and produce emotional reactions in the viewer. Most importantly, a look at the director's vision and his or her implementation of the same will be included in a discussion of any individual film. How then does one add Jungian analysis into the mix?

For undergraduates, the following questions are meaningful, as they ask students to consider the general process of filmmaking.

(1) At the time and place in which the film was made, what historical events were taking place, and how did these events impact the country's constituents in horrific ways? They may be encouraged to research major disasters or political events which occurred during the time period in which the film takes place — the flu pandemic which begat *Nosferatu*, for example — or they may be encouraged to read current news sources and compare them to the types of monsters which are currently popular. This discussion leads in turn to an identification of the collective (national) shadow, a sometimes ill-defined evil that lurks at the back of everyone's mind, often fueled both by the media and by storytelling within the community. The evil within a film is often a metaphorical or personified representation of this unquantifiable threat to the community whose citizens are making or viewing the film. For example, the original *Friday the 13th* was released in 1980. While the preceding decade had been relatively quiet in comparison to the tumultuous years of the 1960s, there were four stories which resonated in American consciousness around that time: those of serial killers Kenneth Bianchi (the Hillside Strangler) and David Berkowitz (Son of Sam), and two terrorist attacks, both of which occurred on the other side of the world: the Olympic Village siege in 1972, and the Iranian hostage crisis, which began in November 1979 when Iranian students took 66 American hostages in Teheran. Political murders were still occurring offshore, far away from American soil, but meanwhile, people were killed while sitting in their cars, stopping for gas, doing their jobs on foreign soil — and for no discernable reason.[41] American audiences were thus "primed" for a horror film in which, like *Halloween* two years before, the storyline involved the intrusion of unstoppable violence and indefinable evil into everyday life. They were especially primed for the fact that there was no obvious, identifiable killer in the first *Friday the 13th*.

Thirty years later, a series of terroristic tragedies have created a different America, and director Nispel has given us an updated version of monster-as-serial-killer in his 2009 update of *Friday the 13th*; he references 21st century American anxieties and fears in revealing the nature of his monster. While the events of 9/11 permanently destabilized American attitudes towards the indestructability of the country's population centers, and xenophobic citizens suddenly became wary of the Muslim families already living among them, other events in recent American history betrayed a genuinely insidious problem: white American men who engaged in acts of domestic terrorism after adopting politically extreme views. Ted Kaczynski, the "Unabomber," killed 3 and injured 23 over a period of 25 years, until his brother became suspicious and alerted police; Timothy McVeigh, a Gulf War veteran influenced by the militia movement, took 168 lives in the bombing of the Alfred P. Murrah federal building, including those of 19 children; Eric Alan Rudolph planted a series of bombs in the Atlanta area between 1996 and 1998, killing two people and injuring over 120.[42] Rudolph eluded police for over five years, using his survival skills to hide out in the mountains of North Carolina. All of these men had survivalist backgrounds: while Kaczynski aligned himself with a leftist movement, McVeigh and Rudolph were said to have ties to right-wing, white-supremacist movements. Jason's methods of dispatching his enemies, his abilities to move efficiently in darkness and to thrive in the forest, and his underground bunker, a hideaway located below his mother's house, reflect Nispel's attempt to locate him in the rural American survivalist tradition.

(2) What is the hero's quest? Is defeating the monster the whole of the quest, or does the monster's killing serve a larger purpose and fulfill an ultimate quest? In terms of characterization, students should get used to analyzing individual characters in terms of the technical aspects of the film in order to resolve questions of how each character fits into the Jungian master play. Besides the obvious question — which characters get the most screen time? — other questions invite students to see the relationship between technical and storytelling components. Which are seen in wide shots, as part of the environment, and, when directors use a variety of shots, which are seen predominantly in close-up? Which characters appear repeatedly paired or oppositionally in the same frames? Which are linked in tracking shots? How are characters lit? In a horror film especially, are there differences in the ways the heroes and monsters are lit? Does any one character or pair of characters repeatedly retreat into darkness or emerge from it? The answers to these questions establish the relationships between the protagonist as hero and antagonist as shadow, anima or animus.

In terms of the screenplay, students might ask themselves how the language of each character helps to establish the hierarchy of the larger group onscreen. Does the hero's use of language establish him or her as a hero, or do heroic actions alone convey his importance to the viewer? What does his or her dialogue tell us about his relationship to the monster? How does the dialogue establish the oppositional relationship between the hero and the monster? If the hero is female, does she use language differently? Is she given to utterances other than words, thus drawing attention and sympathy towards herself, and establishing herself as the Final Girl? Students should also learn to notice and remember whether the monster uses language. If so, is his language limited in vocabulary? Juvenile? Does the monster only communicate nonverbally? When hero and monster appear together, are words exchanged? Can we tell that their personalities and moral characters are similar or oppositional, or do we learn that only through their action? Finally, is there a disconnect between the language used by the hero or the monster and his or her actions? Such a disconnect may bring us closer to the subconscious actions and motivations of each character, and tell the viewer that sworn enemies are as similar as they are different. This is a hallmark of the hero-shadow pairing.

(3) Which characters are recognizable as archetypes? The first question to ask is which characters are recognizable as types, but the second and more important question to ask is whether they exist solely in relationship to the hero—in the hero's constellation, one might say—and allow him or her to develop as a human being? For example, in *Candyman*, the men in the story exist in order for Helen's psychological development to be realized. Without a Helen, there would be no Candyman in the present time of the film. She draws him into her constellation. In *Friday the 13th* (2009), there is a houseful of teenagers under siege, but only three matter—Clay, who is searching for his sister; the sister, Whitney, whom Jason is holding hostage; and Trent, who is trying to maintain control of his parents' house, the location of Jason's carnage. In older films such as *Frankenstein* or *Dracula*, pairings are created between hero and monster, but other characters are drawn into that circle in positive or negative ways. If we consider the hero's encounters with the characters who represent the major archetypes, we find that those are the encounters which either change the plot trajectory surrounding the hero, or change the hero's psyche, adding to his motivation or his pain, or sometimes both.

Jungian theory works in the humanities/film classroom for two reasons: for one, it offers a response to students who argue that they can't relate to any older film, or, indeed, any film which fails to reflect their own experiences, as it places universal processes of conflict and growth into a structured context; in addition, it offers a means for students to create their own hyperlinks and develop a facility for making connections between films, between genres, and between classic film or literary works and more contemporary cultural phenomena they might find enjoyable. Finally, it leads students to an ultimate question: what does their love for certain films teach them about themselves?

Notes

1. Stephen King, *Danse Macabre* (New York: Gallery, 1981), 104.
2. Torben Grodal, *Embodied Visions: Evolution, Emotion, Culture, and Film* (New York:

Oxford University Press 2009), 101. Other studies which examine psychological and physiological processes through which film engages the viewer include Greg M. Smith's *Film Structure and the Emotion System* (Cambridge: Cambridge University Press, 2003) and Noël Carroll's *The Philosophy of Horror, or, Paradoxes of the Heart* (London: Routledge, 1996).

3. Carroll's discussion in philosophy distinguishes between natural fears and the fear a viewer feels upon watching a horror movie.

4. Carroll, 24.

5. For more information, see *The Collected Works of Carl Jung* (Princeton, NJ: Bollingen, 1953–71), Erich Neumann, *The Origins and History of Consciousness* (Princeton, NJ: Bollingen, 1970) and Neumann's *The Great Mother* (Princeton, NJ: Bollingen, 1972). Joseph Campbell's work has continued this tradition: some of his findings appear in *The Hero with A Thousand Faces* (Princeton: Bollingen, 1972).

6. Carl G. Jung, "Instinct and the Unconscious," In *The Portable Jung*, edited by Joseph Campbell (New York: Penguin, 1976), 57.

7. Carl G. Jung, *Archetypes and the Collective Unconscious 9,i* (Princeton: Bollingen, 1981), 161.

8. Jung, *Archetypes*, 187.

9. In *Archetypes* 9, where Jung discussed the major archetypes of shadow, anima, and Self (in "Aion: Phenomenology of the Self"), he also explored the child archetype (in "Psychology of the Child Archetype"), and the Mother archetype (in "Psychological Aspects of the Mother Archetype").

10. Carol Pearson has identified a number of archetypes important to contemporary man or woman; James F. Iaccino discusses these archetypes in relation to film in *Psychological Reflections on Cinematic Terror: Jungian Archetypes in Horror Films* (Westport CT: Praeger, 1994) and *Jungian Reflections within the Cinema: A Psychological Analysis of Sci-Fi and Fantasy Archetypes* (Westport CT: Praeger, 1998).

11. Jung's colleague Toni Wolff was one of the first to expand Jung's pantheon, so to speak; unhappy with Jung's focus on the mother, and his consistent return to the maternal basis of the anima, she expanded the notion of the feminine anima to include the amazon, hetaira (medium), and seductress. Irene Claremont de Castellejo summarizes Wolff's findings in "Woman as Mediator," in Molly Tuby, ed. *In the Wake of Jung: A Selection from Harvest* (London: Coventure, 1983). Pearson and Iaccino honor Wolff's efforts.

12. See *Origins* for an explanation of the sequence.

13. The monomyth today is usually equated with "The Hero's Journey," thanks to Joseph Campbell's use of the term exclusively in association with the hero myth.

14. Arne Ohman and Susan Mineka, "Fears, Phobias, and Preparedness: Toward an Evolved Module of Fear and Fear Learning," *Psychological Review*, Vol. 108, No. 3: 2001, 483–522.

15. *The Portable Jung*, 54.

16. For discussion, see the first three chapters of *Hero with a Thousand Faces*.

17. Syd Field, whose *Screenplay: The Foundations of Screenwriting* (New York: Delta, 2005) has been the authoritative text on screenwriting for decades, invokes Aristotle regularly.

18. My students have been particularly enthusiastic in discussing why Robert Zemeckis's *Beowulf* didn't work as well as the original poem. Disruption of the story's original structure was one concern.

19. *Psychology and Religion: West and East*, 2 ed. (Princeton, NJ: Princeton University Press), 157.

20. *Portable Jung*, 145.

21. King, *Danse*, 71.

22. King, *Danse*, 70ff.

23. Jeffery Taubenberger, et al., "Initial Genetic Characterization of the 1918 'Spanish' Influenza Virus," *Science* 275 (1997): 1793–96. Quoted in Molly Billings, "The Influenza Pandemic of 1918."

24. *Portable Jung*, 150.

25. Carol Clover, *Men, Women, and Chainsaws: Gender in the Modern Horror Film* (Princeton, NJ: Princeton University Press, 1992), 38. Barbara Creed's discussion of the monstrous feminine in *The Monstrous-Feminine: Film, Feminism, Psychoanalysis* (New York: Routledge, 1993) is another example of a Freudian approach which gives clarity to the concept of the anima.

26. Clover, 36.
27. *Portable Jung*, 142.
28. Bill Gibron. "Friday the 13th" AMC Filmcritic.com.. http://www.filmcritic.com/reviews/2009/friday-the-13th/, accessed March 2, 2011
29. "Derek Mears: On-Set Interview." Horror.com, accessed November 23, 2011. Http://www.horror.com/php/article-2238-1.html.
30. Mears, Interview.
31. John Fallon. "Friday the 13th" Joblo.com, http://www.joblo.com/arrow/reviews.php?id=1295, accessed November 23, 2011.
32. Oddly enough, Jason's neighbors aren't afraid of him. As one woman says when Clay knocks on her door seeking information, "Summer people come…bring trouble. He just wants to be left alone, and so do we!"
33. Kirstin Moana Thompson, in *Apocalyptic Dread: American Film at the Turn of the Millenium* (Albany: State University of New York Press, 2007), discusses *Candyman* as a film that is partly about storytelling, and notes that "Sociologists, workers, psychologists, students, professors, and city dwellers all have different frameworks for understanding the story of Candyman. These competing understandings, which frame or foreclose the story as myth or as "totally true," underscore the film's interrogation of dread and (dis)belief, and the different ways in which these become connected to storytelling as a form of national memory"(61).
34. Judith Halberstam, *Skin Shows: Gothic Horror and the Technology of Monsters* (Durham NC: Duke University Press: 1995), 5.
35. Kim D. Hester-Williams, "NeoSlaves: Slavery, Freedom, and African American Apotheosis in Candyman, The Matrix, and The Green Mile," *Genders* 40 (2004), http://www.genders.org/recent.html.
36. Isabel Cristina Pinedo, *Recreational Terror: Women and the Pleasures of Horror Film Viewing* (Albany: State University of New York Press, 1997), 7.
37. Pinedo, 131.
38. Isaac Julien and Kobena Mercer, "True Confessions: A discourse on images of black Male Sexuality," in *Brother to Brother*, ed. Essex Hemphill. (Boston: Alyson, 1991), 169.
39. "Shame" is a powerful autobiographical short story focusing on the daily humiliations of being a poor child in an uncaring or patronizing school environment.
40. *Apocalyptic Dread*, 76.
41. "1970–1979 World History." http://www.infoplease.com/ipa/A0005252.html.
42. Rosenberg, Jennifer. "1990's Timeline." http://history1900s.about.com/od/timelines/tp/1990timeline.htm.

Skins and Bones:
The Horror of the Real

John Edward Martin

> *"No live organism can continue for long to exist sanely under conditions of absolute reality; even larks and katydids are supposed, by some, to dream. Hill House, not sane, stood by itself against its hills, holding darkness within; it had stood so for eighty years and might stand for eighty more. Within, walls continued upright, bricks met neatly, floors were firm, and doors were sensibly shut; silence lay steadily against the wood and stone of Hill House, and whatever walked there, walked alone."*—
> Shirley Jackson, *The Haunting of Hill House*

> *"Our heartache poured into one another like water from cup to cup. Each time I told my story, I lost a bit, the smallest drop of pain. It was that day that I knew I wanted to tell the story of my family. Because horror on Earth is real and it is every day. It is like a flower or like the sun; it cannot be contained."*—Alice Sebold, *The Lovely Bones*

Modern horror, to be effective, must be *real*. It must be manifest, experiential, and inescapable by the usual means of covering one's eyes, thinking happy thoughts, or muttering desperate prayers. Unlike the shadowy, half-imagined terrors of the gothic or the fantastic chimeras of the supernatural, much modern horror is neither imaginary nor fantastical — it is disturbingly concrete and inextricable from the mundane world of the everyday. In fact, it is sometimes synonymous with the mundane and the everyday. Edgar Allan Poe shows us, in the opening of "The Fall of the House of Usher," that horror comes not from the dream of the reveler upon opium — those often fruitful and pleasurable sources of Romantic imagination — but from "the bitter lapse into everyday life — the hideous dropping off of the veil."[1] It is the grim and inescapable *reality* of the structure — its presence, its solid mass, and its sickening atmosphere — that, for the narrator, gives the House of Usher its hideousness, just as it is Roderick Usher's hyper-sensitivity to the material world that gradually twists his more delicate intellectual and imaginative faculties past the brink of insanity.

Similarly, it is under such conditions of "absolute reality" that Shirley Jackson's Hill House goes quietly "mad," taking its occupants along with it.[2] Eleanor Vance, like Roderick Usher, is a sensitive who finds the stark realities of her life (not just at Hill House, but prior to her arrival there) too much to consciously or unconsciously bear, and her ultimate confrontation with them is, quite literally, a car-wreck. Nothing, it seems, is more horrifying or destructive to our sensibilities than seeing the world for what it really is. Susie Salmon learns a similar lesson in *The Lovely Bones*, when her idyllic childhood of middle-class suburban comfort is shattered, not by vague, unaccountable terrors or demonic forces, but by a quiet and unassuming neighbor, Mr. Harvey. It is only afterwards, when removed from the world she once knew — into a fantastical afterlife where dreams hold sway — that Susie understands that "horror on Earth is real and it is every day."[3] Like flowers and sunlight, it is natural, and bursts forth with its own living, if not always life-affirming, energy.

These examples are just brief illustrations of the larger concerns of this essay: to examine the ways in which horror, as an aesthetic mode or sentiment, is bound to an experiential perception of "the real"— one that engages our physical sensations, feelings, emotions, and primal intuitions, as much as our rational consciousness or our speculative imagination.[4] To say that modern horror is "realistic," mundane, or everyday, is not to say that it is any more comprehensible to the rational mind, or any less shocking to our sense of normalcy, decency, or moral order, than the gothic or the fantastic. What allows horror to enter the usually safe and predictable confines of "the real world"— at least as we perceive it — is precisely its ability to disrupt and destroy those assumptions of normalcy and moral order, not to mention our illusions of physical safety and mastery of the world around us. Horror makes us aware that "reality" may not be what we think it is, that its grounding may lie beyond our limited perceptual or cognitive abilities, or that its rules may not be what either our rational scientific theories or our religious and philosophical doctrines have taught us to accept as truth. It presents us with the disturbing possibility that what we experience as everyday reality is itself the product of a diseased imagination that is incapable of directly confronting what it only intuits through dreams or religious visions or works of art. When those illusions of reality begin to crumble in the face of some undeniable physical monstrosity, then we see that it isn't the monster that is unreal — it is *we* and our world of symbols, laws, and boundaries that lack substance. The monster is *not* a symbol, and it knows no laws or boundaries; it cannot be banished by fleeing to reality, because the monster *is* the real.

At least since Poe, horror writers, artists, and film-makers have wrestled with the need to represent the experiential reality of horror in a way that can evoke its concrete origins, effects, and consequences, even while working within the symbolic and imaginative limitations of artistic expression. While some have preferred to retreat entirely into the world of fantasy and the supernatural, as a way of emphasizing the irrationality and wonder of horror (its sublime aspect), and others have chosen to explore its psychological depths and permutations (its gothic aspect), what Poe and his descendants in horror bring to the genre is an abiding interest in and understanding of the concrete, bodily experience of horror that causes us, as readers and viewers, to recoil in disgust or cringe in pain at the sight of that which refuses to be contained by the page or screen.

The difficulty, of course, is that both literature and film rely on those psychologically and socially constructed meanings — including language itself— for their form and expression. Short of literally striking their audiences in the face — an idea not completely renounced by purveyors of increasingly realistic sensory technologies like 3-D and virtual reality — artists in all genres still face a seemingly insurmountable barrier between what can be *said* or *seen*, and what horror, in its truest manifestations in experience, actually *does* to those who encounter it. That barrier, between "reality" as we are capable of perceiving and conceptualizing it, and "the real" that we can only intuit or traumatically experience, has been explored most thoroughly by theorists in the psychoanalytic tradition of Lacan and Kristeva.[5] And yet, as I will argue below, many of the insights provided by Lacanian analysis were already perceived and expressed in the literary work of Poe, and more concretely, in that of H. P. Lovecraft, who offers us one of the most cogent theorizations of modern horror and the limitations of language as a medium for expressing its reality.

But even if literature and film ultimately fall short of the reality of horror, I believe that there is another route to understanding and revealing its implications. The pedagogical situation of the classroom — of "teaching horror" — can offer opportunities for engaging with "the horror of the real" in even more complex and effective ways than merely reading or viewing horror through artistic media. If, in fact, "horror on Earth is real, and it is everyday,"[6] then it is likely within the range of most readers' direct or indirect experience. Indeed, I've found that students almost can't resist their own compulsions to draw on that experience when discussing horror texts — because the reality of horror is always a personal one. But if we also think of "the real" as a more evasive, incomprehensible level of experience that resists rational or imaginative attempts to disavow or contain its presence — the Lacanian assumption — then it is one that may require the tools and techniques of the analytic or therapeutic setting to fully appreciate or understand.[7] Through a combination of traditional reading and interpretation of horror fiction and film texts, individual reflection and storytelling, shared experiences of horror, and experiments in the conversion of "lived horror" into written or visual form, we can begin to conceptualize and analyze those "terrifying vistas of reality" that Lovecraft identifies as the source of all our greatest fears, but also some of our most sublime and pleasurable experiences (what Lacan and Kristeva might call its *jouissance*).

These pedagogical approaches require a word of caution: Evoking personal horror, either through discussion or artistic production, comes with risks that any teacher, like the writer or the therapist, must be aware of and responsive to. This is, of course, true of any pedagogical setting or subject, but it can be particularly challenging for teachers of gothic and horror literature. As we approach whatever is "real" in the representation of horror, we should be especially cautious about what we ask students to do or say in the classroom, keeping in mind that there are limits to our roles as teachers and mentors. Even so, I think there is a great deal to be learned from students in these situations, as much as from the texts, or the instructor's own theories and preconceptions.

Discovering "the horror of the real," then, can be seen as a collective project — one that evokes comparisons to the two epigraphs that open this essay. Like the motley, but intrepid cast who gather at Hill House to investigate its "conditions of absolute reality," reading horror requires its own specialized setting — one that involves physical presence, controlled isolation, a degree of intimacy, and a willingness to be open and intellectually honest. We should try, though, to take effective precautions against the potentially dangerous, or at least disturbing, influences of such an atmosphere. Self-destructive surrender to "whatever walks there" needn't be the price of our curiosity, as it was for Eleanor Vance. Hopefully, the result will be more like Susie Salmon's healing catharsis — "Each time I told my story, I lost a bit, the smallest drop of pain" — or at least, a recognition of the natural place and function of such stories in coping with the everyday horrors of human experience.

Real Horror

> *The time has come when the normal revolt against time, space, & matter must assume a form not overtly incompatible with what is known of reality—when it must be gratified by images forming* supplements, *rather than* contradictions *of the visible & mensurable universe. And what, if not a form of* non-supernatural cosmic art, *is to pacify this sense of revolt— as well as gratify the cognate sense of curiosity.*—H. P. Lovecraft, "Letter to Frank Belknap Long, 22 February 1931"[8]

Horror is a revolt against reality. It is also a revulsion brought on by our encounter *with* the real. These are the two insights that connect the Gothic Romanticism of the late eighteenth and early nineteenth centuries to the modern horror of the twentieth and twenty-first centuries. And it is the fiction and theory of H. P. Lovecraft (largely inspired by his literary master, Poe), supplemented by the psychoanalytic insights of Freud, Lacan, and especially, Julia Kristeva, that brings the shadowy, religion-haunted, and often sentimentalized nightmares of an earlier age into contact with the skeptical, materialistic, and science-obsessed sensibilities of the modern era. The result is an understanding of horror that acknowledges its reliance on language, imagination, and cultural forms (particularly, gothic and supernatural forms) for its *expression*, but also its material origins in something more primitive, animalistic, and physiological — that is to say, its grounding in "the real."

In several of his letters, and more systematically, in his seminal essay, "Supernatural Horror in Literature" (1927), Lovecraft lays out his own theory of a "cosmic horror" that is at once infused with supernatural and fantastic elements — " the normal revolt against time, space, & matter" — but ultimately grounded in something more intrinsic to human biology and psychology: a primitive fear of the unknown, or what he calls, "the sense of outsideness." In the letter to Frank Belknap Long cited above, Lovecraft defines the role of "outsideness" in literature as, "the aesthetic crystallization of that burning & inextinguishable feeling of mixed wonder & oppression which the sensitive imagination experiences upon scaling itself & its restrictions against the vast & provocative abyss of the unknown."[9] This sense of outsideness, he suggests, is derived from a combination of "the natural physical instinct of pure curiosity" and "the galling sense of intolerable restraint" experienced by all human beings when faced with their physical and perceptual limitations. Intellectual, emotional, and imaginative longing, frustrated by natural limitations, gives us the intuitive sense of powerful forces "outside" of ourselves that ultimately control our destinies. Or perhaps, he also suggests, it is *we* who are "outside," and *they* who are real and tangible. Either way, our awareness of this "outsideness" provokes a profound experience of existential horror.[10] The conjuring of supernatural or fantastic forms to represent this unexplainable "abyss of the unknown" is, in essence, a revolt of the human imagination against its vague intuitions of a reality too vast or unapproachable for the psyche to represent or signify through its usual mechanisms.

In "Supernatural Horror in Literature," Lovecraft traces the literary history of horror from its origins in classical mythology, medieval fairy tales, and folk traditions, through the Romantic and modern eras (the early twentieth century). There he argues that while superstition and religion may be the cultural origin of many of our expressed fears and beliefs in the supernatural, these feelings persist into the era of modern science and reason through "an actual physiological fixation of the old instincts in our nervous tissue, which would make them obscurely operative even were the conscious mind to be purged of all sources of wonder."¹¹ We can have horror in the absence of superstition or religion precisely because it operates independently of those cultural forms — it is grounded in our physiology, in our "instincts" and "nervous tissue."

For this reason, what Lovecraft calls "cosmic horror" must address the physiology as well as the psychology of the reader — it should evoke the psychic longing for forbidden knowledge or experience, but also the crushing limitations of the human mind and body that torment us with those unimaginable realities that lie beyond our grasp. To accomplish this, Lovecraft takes a lesson from his master, Edgar Allan Poe, in echoing the sentiment — expressed by Poe in, among other things, "The Philosophy of Composition" — that, "Atmosphere is the all-important thing, for the final criterion of authenticity is not the dovetailing of a plot, but the creation of a given sensation."¹² Sensation or effect, rather than rational narrative, emotional satisfaction, or moral truth, becomes the hallmark of both Poe's and Lovecraft's peculiar brand of horror. But it is not sensation merely for the sake of sordid "thrills"— Poe would always seek to distinguish his work from those lesser sensationalist writers of the popular periodicals of his day, just as Lovecraft often renounced his own affinity with other "pulp" writers of his era. Instead, both men see sensation as the most effective tool of the writer who wishes to evoke the material origins and consequences of true horror (or beauty, passion, love, or whatever other "effect" the writer wishes to create). Sensation, more than ideas, connects us to the reality of horror.

But the sensation of fear is only part of the overall effect that horror evokes — the other part is that alienating sense of "outsideness" that separates humanity from the true objects of our longing or our fear.¹³ Early horror writers, particularly those in what Lovecraft calls the "romantic, semi–Gothic, quasi-moral tradition" of the late eighteenth and early–nineteenth centuries, often lack this quality of "outsideness" because of a persistent "human element," that is, the tendency of the Romantic writer to take "a definite stand in sympathy with mankind and its welfare."¹⁴ Placing the heroic or tragic individual, or the writer's own humanistic or religious values, at the center of their writing, Romantic authors often fail to recognize the *inhuman* and *amoral* quality of horror — or, at least, our perception of its inhumanity and otherness. Lovecraft's own "cosmic fear," on the other hand, presents humanity and its concerns as irrelevant and futile in the face of unknown forces that operate beyond our intellectual and moral judgment. Horror, he suggests, is inherently opposed to *idealism* in all of its typical Romantic guises. Horror, in fact, resides in the failure of idealism to provide coherent meaning.

And again, it is Poe who Lovecraft sees as the first artist to comprehend this distinction and use it to create legitimate horror:

> Poe…perceived the essential impersonality of the real artist; and knew that the function of creative fiction is merely to express and interpret events and sensations as they are, regardless of how they tend or what they prove — good or evil, attractive or repulsive, stimulating or depressing — with the author always acting as a vivid and detached chronicler rather than as a teacher, sympathizer, or vender of opinion.[15]

By removing the moralistic and sympathetic concerns of the typical Romantic writer, Poe, in effect, establishes "a new standard of realism in the annals of literary horror."[16] In this case, the reality of horror is conveyed through the recognition that what is real remains "outside" of human perception or judgment — it is beyond good and evil, and can't be made to conform to the humanistic fantasies of its author or readers. This troubling recognition, as much as the material presence of the monster or supernatural force, is what gives horror its power over the mind and body of its victims.

Of course, "realism" is not a term typically associated with the strange and macabre fictions for which Poe is generally known: the gruesome and awe-inspiring figure of Death gliding through the halls of Prince Prospero's castle; the terrifying return of Ligeia in the body of her living rival, Lady Rowena; or the unnatural life and cataclysmic collapse of the House of Usher. Yet, while acknowledging that Poe is adept in the use of the fantastic, the bizarre, and the supernatural — poetic elements which add vividness and beauty to his writing — his real gift, as Lovecraft sees it, is his mastery of "the very mechanics and physiology of fear."[17] Lovecraft notes the "scientific skill with which every particular is marshaled and brought into an easy apparent relation to the known gruesomeness of material life."[18] Indeed, all of the tales cited above, and most of Poe's other fictions, revel in the physicality of his horrors, and present them with almost clinical accuracy and scientific objectivity. Take for example, the opening paragraph of "The Masque of the Red Death":

> The "Red Death" had long devastated the country. No pestilence had ever been so fatal, or so hideous. Blood was its Avatar and its seal — the redness and the horror of blood. There were sharp pains, and sudden dizziness, and then profuse bleeding at the pores, with dissolution. The scarlet stains upon the body and especially upon the face of the victim, were the pest ban which shut him out from the aid and from the sympathy of his fellow-men. And the whole seizure, progress and termination of the disease, were the incidents of half an hour.[19]

Here, we not only see the horrifying physical devastation and progress of the disease, but also its inevitable consequence: to be "shut…out from the aid and from the sympathy of his fellow-men." Horror, as Lovecraft insists, removes us from the social and moral world of Men, and leaves us to suffer its very tangible agonies and terrors all alone. Descriptions such as this one reveal the material and organic, as well as the inhuman and amoral, nature of fear in Poe's writing, and lead Lovecraft to conclude that, "Poe's weird tales are *alive* in a manner that few others can ever hope to be" [his italics].[20]

It is Poe's tradition of "living" horror — not the more genteel, romanticized, and moralistic Gothicism of contemporaries like Hawthorne and Irving — that Lovecraft credits for the emergence of modern horror, and which he traces through the work of later American writers like Ambrose Bierce, Fitz-James O'Brien, Robert Chambers, and one of Lovecraft's own much-admired contemporaries, Clark Ashton Smith. It can also be seen, he suggests, in individual works by authors not typically associated with the horror genre, including Henry James's *Turn of the Screw* and other ghost stories, Charlotte Perkins Gilman's "The Yellow Wallpaper," and in much of the short fiction of Mary E. Wilkins. More importantly, Lovecraft finds it in his pantheon of "Modern Masters," all British, with whom he claims direct kinship and influence: Arthur Machen, M.R. James, Lord Dunsany, and Algernon Blackwood. As different as these writers are from one another, in both style and temperament, what they share is a clear skepticism of the easy idealism and sentimentality of their Romantic predecessors, as well as the pervasive influence of literary realism and naturalism which operates, in the case of a writer like Bierce, through the emphasis on sharp, sometimes gruesome, physical detail, vivid sensationalism, and an almost cold emotional detachment from the suffering of his characters. In a writer like James, on the other hand, sympathy and idealism, while present in many of his characters, often serve as only a superficial cognitive defense against more disturbing undercurrents of psychic dissolution and despair. It is the intuition of "outsideness," as Lovecraft puts it,[21] that ultimately overwhelms the cultivated sensibilities of the Jamesian protagonist.

But it is in Lovecraft's own work, and in those writers who come after him, that Poe's "living" horror finally becomes ascendant in American literature. It survives beyond its Romantic origins, through the rise of literary realism, and into the modern era, largely because it is grounded in those material realities — including biology and the physical, psychological, and social sciences — that these later generations accept as the foundation of most, if not all, human behavior and ideation. After Darwin and Freud, not to mention the devastations of the Civil War and World War I, most Americans could no longer doubt their basic animal natures or the power of the material world and larger social forces to shape human destiny. But accepting those realities and understanding or controlling them are two different things — and in our failure to master the ultimate sources and drivers of human existence, we again experience that sense of "outsideness" that Lovecraft sees as the foundation of "cosmic horror."[22] If anything, our acceptance of materialism and objective science only moves us closer to the recognition of our own helplessness and insignificance in the face of a horrifying reality that lies beyond our limited capacity for control. The narrator of Lovecraft's "The Call of Cthulhu" perhaps puts this dilemma most succinctly:

> The most merciful thing in the world, I think, is the inability of the human mind to correlate all its contents. We live on a placid island of ignorance in the midst of black seas of infinity, and it was not meant that we should voyage far. The sciences, each straining in its own direction, have hitherto harmed us little; but some day the piecing together of dissociated knowledge will open up such terrifying vistas of reality, and of our frightful position therein, that we shall either go mad from the revelation or flee from the deadly light into the peace and safety of a new dark age.[23]

The irony here, of course, is that science and reason have, until this moment in history, been the principle weapons defending us *against* supernatural horror and all its imagined evils — but only because we believed that horror resided in those fantastic forms and mythic sources. Freed of medieval superstition, religious myth, and Romantic idealism, we might imagine that the shadows of the invisible world would be exorcised and dispelled once and for all. But Lovecraft, here and in his other tales, reveals that it is precisely because of science's capacity to disrupt our "placid island of ignorance" and instead reveal "terrifying vistas of reality" that we are now on the verge of something truly horrifying — a direct knowledge of "the real." The most "human" reaction, he suggests, is not to rush forward into such realms of reality, but to either go mad or "flee from the deadly light into the peace and safety of a new dark age."[24]

Where, then, do we turn? If horror exists at the extreme limits of both imagination and objective inquiry, then what hope do we have of escaping it? Perhaps the answer is to avoid those extremes, and maintain our placidly ignorant psyche somewhere within the mundane limits of our everyday, socially constructed, and carefully policed world of symbolic meanings and cultural forms. This is precisely what psychoanalysis suggests that the Ego, operating under its own "reality principle," seeks to do: to construct and maintain a functional world of meanings, somewhere between the primitive drives and impulses of the Id, and the cultural and moral demands of the Superego. By sublimating both fear and desire into forms that are more accommodating to what we believe to be "reality," we can avoid the feeling of "outsideness" that Lovecraft posits as the origin of true horror.

Like Lovecraft, however, Freud finds the stability of such illusions of normalcy and control — manifested in everything from our belief in a coherent "self" to our grandest cultural narratives of religion and national identity — to be tenuous at best, and prone to the same horrific disruptions as the idealism of the Romantics or Lovecraft's "placid islands of ignorance"[25] to which even the so-called "realist" clings. Indeed, it is Freud's theories that carry Poe and Lovecraft's legacy of real horror into the modern world.

The Horror of the Real

> *"There looms, within abjection, one of those violent, dark revolts of being, directed against a threat that seems to emanate from an exorbitant outside or inside, ejected beyond the scope of the possible, the tolerable, the thinkable. It lies there, quite close, but it cannot be assimilated. It beseeches, worries, and fascinates desire, which, nevertheless, does not let itself be seduced. Apprehensive, desire turns aside; sickened, it rejects."*[26]

Julia Kristeva's seminal book, *Powers of Horror: An Essay on Abjection* (1982), offers a remarkably similar analysis of the origins and effects of horror to that of Lovecraft, albeit through the lens of Freudian and Lacanian psychoanalysis. Kristeva, too, sees at the root of horror an intolerable intuition of "outsideness"—of being separated, perhaps for our own good, from something primal and formless, but undeniably concrete and "real"; something that "fascinates desire" but also repulses and sickens us with its otherness. But where Lovecraft often looks outward, into the cosmos and its boundless mysteries, for his "terrifying vistas of reality," Kristeva looks inward, towards our most primitive levels of consciousness and physical instinct. There she discovers and names the monstrous reality that ultimately confronts us with its horror: the abject.[27]

The abject is theoretically related to what Freud called "the uncanny"— the disturbing feeling of familiarity and strangeness that, he believed, was at the root of most successful horror fictions, but also many real neuroses and phobias.[28] For Freud, the uncanny represents some disavowed or repressed aspect of the psyche—a traumatic memory, an inappropriate desire, or an uncomfortable identification—that manifests itself in strange feelings of fascination and repulsion, compulsive thoughts or behaviors, the imparting of human qualities to inanimate or dead objects, or strange delusions of "doubling" or pursuit by one's own shadow, reflection, or mysterious twin. The uncanny is, in essence, a vague and sublimated *recognition* of ourselves in the monstrous other; thus, its repulsiveness and horror. Kristeva's abject, on the other hand, is "different from uncanniness, more violent too, abjection is elaborated through a failure to recognize its kin; nothing is familiar, not even the shadow of a memory."[29] The abject is a deeper, darker feeling of estrangement than the uncanny, with more primitive origins and more dangerous implications.

Building upon Lacan's descriptions of the earliest stages of infantile consciousness and identity formation — in which our sense of a cohesive "self" emerges out of a series of (mis)recognitions, projections, and eventual symbolic identifications — Kristeva suggests that prior to any mirroring or imaginative self-formation comes an earlier, more traumatic and terrifying encounter with what she, like Lacan, calls "the real." For Lacan, the real is simply that aspect of the primitive psyche connected to basic animal nature — the body, the instincts, our responses to the material world — that were once indistinct from the infantile psyche, and prior to any recognition of self and other. The real represents for him a lost paradise of undifferentiated being, governed solely by the pleasure principle and accessible, if at all, only in the most basic responses of the id, but never representable in the symbolic world of language, or even in the imaginative space of dreams. Indeed, he says in *The Four Fundamental Concepts of Psychoanalysis* that, "Is not the dream essentially, one might say, an act of homage to the missed reality — the reality that can no longer produce itself except by repeating itself endlessly, in some never attained awakening?"[30] The real is "never attained" because it exists outside of the psyche's imaginative and symbolic functions, which define the only "reality" to which the differentiated "self" ever has access.

Kristeva, however, suggests that the process of differentiation begins earlier than Lacan's "mirror-stage," and through a more painful and terrifying separation from the real than he might suggest. Before the psyche has come to recognize itself or to form those imaginative identifications that will eventually lead it into the symbolic world of language, *the body* begins to separate out that which can and cannot be a part of itself — namely through physical expulsion, feelings of revulsion, and rejection of whatever fails to bring pleasure or comfort. This separation of what cannot be assimilated or even acknowledged by our primitive psyche becomes the foundation of "the abject," a permanent, yet un-representable element of experience that is both present and functional in our later development, but forever evading the cognitive boundaries of meaning:

> familiar as it [the abject] might have been in an opaque and forgotten life, it now harries me as radically separate, loathsome. Not me. Not that. But not nothing, either. A 'something' that I do not recognize as a thing. A weight of meaninglessness, about which there is nothing insignificant, and which crushes me. On the edge of non-existence and hallucination, of a reality that, if I acknowledge it, annihilates me. There, abject and abjection are my safe-guards. The primers of my culture.[31]

Here, Kristeva echoes the sentiment of "The Call of Cthulhu" in acknowledging that our tenuous grip on "reality" as we know it — through the symbolic constructs of "culture" — rests on a foundation of something "radically separate," a "weight of meaninglessness," "a reality that, if I acknowledge it, annihilates me." The abject is the "primer of our culture" because without it and its separation of what cannot be a part of us, our culture, as well as our sense of self, would collapse in the horrifying encounter with... *something*.

Why is the abject so incompatible with symbolic meaning, language, and culture? It is because the abject exists prior to these things, in opposition to them, and refuses to be constrained by their rules and boundaries. It is, Kristeva tells us, "what disturbs identity, system, order. What does not respect borders, positions, rules. The in-between, the ambiguous, the composite."[32] This is why it is related to both Freud's "uncanny" and Poe's "perverseness"—two other "composite" sentiments that disrupt identity and order. And this is precisely why the abject was rejected from the psyche to begin with—expelled as waste, purged like a poison—because it couldn't be contained by the body or the mind. Although it is a natural part of us, and necessary to our existence (if only by its expulsion), the abject is, to our way of perceiving, *inhuman*. When we experience certain powerful sensations anew—repugnance, disgust, revulsion, perversion—we feel the reverberations of that earlier primitive instinct to flee or reject, to deny what cannot, *must not*, be real. The abject and the feelings it elicits thus become the early warning system for all existential threats to our sense of self and the social realities that we've constructed: "abjection notifies us of the limits of the human universe."[33] Again, we see the conjunction of Kristeva's inner exploration with Lovecraft's cosmic awareness of that sense of "outsideness" that threatens our most desperately held notions of reality.

But there is something else in the abject that Lovecraft seems only obliquely aware of, but which is at the heart of Kristeva's understanding of horror, and that is our *longing for it*. This longing is not the same as desire, which requires a recognizable object, and operates according to a symbolic logic; the longing for the abject is more adequately described by the term that both Lacan and Kristeva designate as *jouissance*—the pleasure of excess, of transgression, of unrestrained passion. As Kristeva says, "It follows that *jouissance* alone causes the abject to exist as such. One does not know it, one does not desire it, one joys in it. Violently and painfully. A passion."[34]

This is the same pleasure that we derive from the perverse, from sadomasochistic acts, or from the wild orgiastic immersion of the carnivalesque—pleasure combined with pain, with revulsion, and with terror. It is also the strange pleasure and longing that we find in particular subjects of horror—a type at once recognizable in the fiction of both Poe and Lovecraft: the *deject*. The deject, according to Kristeva, is one who has developed a peculiar type of pathology—one defined by the lack of "place," a stray who is constantly in search of an ever-receding location. That is to say, the deject is one who has *become* the abject—a thing rejected and expelled from humanity, lost and wandering in search of that wholeness of which it can never again be a part: "For it is out of such straying on excluded ground that he draws his jouissance. The abject from which he does not cease separating is for him, in short, a *land of oblivion* that is constantly remembered."[35]

Compare this description to any of a number of Poe's or Lovecraft's narrators who are constantly in search of, or wandering through, nameless lands, strange seascapes, "Cyclopean" architectures, or books of forgotten lore. These are placeless places that defy any sense of real space or time — and yet, they are experienced as real and concrete scenes of encounter, violence, and physical horror. They are also places secretly longed-for and sought-out by these narrators with perverse determination (I am thinking particularly of Poe's Arthur Gordon Pym or Lovecraft's narrators in "Call of Cthulhu" or *At the Mountains of Madness*, among others). The same might be said of Mr. Harvey, the serial killer in *The Lovely Bones*, who constructs an elaborate underground bunker for his own violent excesses (and perhaps of Suzy Salmon who cannot resist the allure of the cornfield); or, in a different way, of Eleanor Vance, whose journey to the Hill House is at once a literal escape from her previous reality, and "a straying onto excluded ground" where she will indulge her longing for self-torment. All are dejects, and all are drawn to the very places and things that threaten their own destruction.

So is this, then, the only value of the abject — to point the way towards self-annihilation through an embrace of our own rejected otherness, or, on the other hand, to serve as a warning never to stray too far from our "placid islands of ignorance"? Those are, of course, the two options offered by Lovecraft, at least in his fiction, where anxious narrators repeatedly warn us not to follow in their footsteps, never to open the forbidden books, or else be prepared for madness and oblivion. But Kristeva hints at another possibility, and it is one which recognizes the place of the abject, and of horror more generally, in our lives — and particularly in our art and literature. She notes the centrality of the abject in religious ritual, especially rituals of defilement and cleansing. The rejection or expulsion of the taboo, the exile of the other, and the condemnation of transgression (sin) are, of course, inherent to most religious traditions — they are, in fact, the central catharses of religious ritual.

They are also, she argues, the central catharsis of art — but not in the same way. Poetic catharsis is not a "purifying" act, meant to rid us of the abject and deny its power over us, but rather a "harmonizing" ritual that attempts to summon the abject and open the subject to its *jouissance*, without abandoning us to its destructive excesses. It is an act of "immersion" in the abject that "arranges, defers, differentiates and organizes, harmonizes pathos, bile, warmth, and enthusiasm."[36] In this sense, artistic horror bears a close, and not incidental, resemblance to the Dionysian rituals of the ancient Greeks, or the modern celebrations of Carnivale and Mardi Gras — performances of *jouissance* that can evoke the abject, even revel in it, but also mingle it with the more temperate waters of imagination and symbolic meaning. Horror in these guises, while still real and powerful, is not, of necessity, self-destructive. So it is in great works of art, poetry, music, and dance — they have the power to "harmonize" even those forces which, in our everyday lives, seem dissonant and irreconcilable.

This is not to say that art can fully tame or integrate the abject — that remains forever outside the grasp of human imagination. But it can make the abject approachable and, perhaps, useful, without being annihilating. Anyone who has ever thrilled at the terrors, shocks, and even the gory excesses of their favorite horror movies can appreciate how pleasure, and a certain degree of pain, can be strangely comingled — not so far as to make us wish for that reality outside of the theater or the pages of the book, but far enough to satisfy our irrational longing for the *jouissance* of the forbidden. This observation of the ritualistic value of horror also brings us back to the question of pedagogy, and how we might approach the teaching of horror in a setting that, in many ways, mimics that of the ritual stage. A classroom, like a church or a therapeutic setting, offers a relatively safe and bounded space in which to explore the otherwise unexplorable — to speak about the unspoken, and the barely imagined levels of consciousness that art can evoke. The goal, as Kristeva suggests, is "harmonization" through "immersion."

Really Teaching Horror

What Poe, Lovecraft, Kristeva and other purveyors of what I'm calling "the horror of the real" suggest to us is that horror begins at home, in the mundane, everyday experiences of life. It often occurs while we are engaging in our most basic animal functions: eating, sleeping, defecating, having sex, wiping our noses. Kristeva famously opens her meditation on the abject with a story/memory of a certain food-loathing ("the most elementary and most archaic form of abjection") that serves as a catalyst for horror:

> When the eyes see or the lips touch that skin on the surface of milk — harmless, thin as a sheet of cigarette paper, pitiful as a nail pairing — I experience a gagging sensation and, still farther down, spasms in the stomach, the belly; and all the organs shrivel up the body, provoke tears and bile, increase heartbeat, cause forehead and hands to perspire. Along with the sight-clouding dizziness, *nausea* makes me balk at that milk cream, separates me from the mother and father who proffer it.[37]

Because of this primal revulsion, the body rejects the milk, and as a result is separated from it as well as from the human imagos associated with it. And because the infant still doesn't distinguish "self" and "other," this rejection is experienced as a rejection of a part of "me"—the beginning of an abjection that at once includes and excludes the nascent self; the beginning, also, of that sense of "outsideness" that infuses all later experiences of horror.

When I share this example with students, many are puzzled by the word "skin" in Kristeva's description of the milk. Most have never tasted fresh milk, or even milk with heavy cream, so the notion of "skin" on milk is, as intended, repulsive, but unfamiliar. This observation inevitably leads to a discussion of what they, the students, find repulsive or horrifying about certain foods, liquids, textures, tastes, etc. The idea that horror can be so basic is strangely appealing—it makes horror personal—and the enthusiasm with which many leap into detailed descriptions and dissections of nausea-inducing sensations can be, well, nauseating. But the exercise makes Kristeva's point beautifully: we all know horror intimately, and while repulsed by it, we also revel in the sharing of it.

A similar exercise can be conducted concerning less visceral, more amorphous sensations, such as aversions to certain sounds, mannerisms, places, or even colors and words. What makes us uncomfortable, anxious, or fearful of these things, and why? Can we explain or embody those fears in some concrete example, like the skin on the milk, or are we forced to use vague, elusive descriptions, re-enactments, or even recreations of the experience in order to fully understand it? I've encouraged students to try each of these methods—within the bounds of personal comfort and safety—and to share them, if possible, in the classroom. The results, including written journals, drawings, recordings, and performances, often provide us with our first "texts" for our analysis of horror; texts which require the eye of the analyst as well as of the literary critic. One such exercise, done together, involves a reading from Herman Melville's *Moby Dick*—the chapter entitled, "The Whiteness of the Whale." After reading the chapter, I ask the students to do a simple pencil drawing, on dark construction paper, of an object or animal that provokes a sense of terror in them. A host of spiders, snakes, dogs, and the occasional odd duck or rabbit emerges. I then ask them to reflect on what about that animal provokes such feelings of terror or nervousness—personal experience, imagined dangers, stories or legends, films they've seen, or perhaps just its appearance, shape, or color. Finally, I ask them to color their drawings *white*, like Ahab's whale, and to reflect once again on the possible effects of such a simple alteration in the creature's appearance. Does it evoke a greater sense of terror or strangeness? Does it appear absurd and comical? Does it sap the horrific power of the initial image by "white-washing" its salient features? Whatever the answers, the exercise lends a deeper level of personal awareness to our reading of Melville's whale, and more importantly, of the subtle, nameless causes behind both Ahab and Ishmael's obsession with the animal. If anyone in the room can be horrified by the sight of a white snake, or, to echo another famous literary text, "a dimpled spider fat and white," then perhaps the horror of the white whale becomes a little more real as well.

To extend such personal encounters with physical horror into the realm of art and literature, though, also requires an understanding of the boundaries that separate the two. While Kristeva's abject can be echoed in simple feelings of revulsion or nausea, what lies beyond those sensations remains obscure. Can art reflect "the real" more concretely and directly, or, is it, as Lacan suggests, beyond the scope of imagination? In a recent seminar on "American Gothic," I posed the question another way: "Can the gothic be real? Or can the real be gothic?" My question was aimed at drawing out the distinction between lived experience and the representation of that experience in a form often defined by its conventionality, traditions, and recurrent patterns of meaning. Could we, for example, view the Maysles brothers' 1975 documentary, *Grey Gardens*, as a "gothic" text, or does its foundation in autobiography and documented history remove it from the realm of genre fiction and its inherited conventions?[38] Here, the distinction was really between what we might consider the mundane, everyday "reality" of two women's lives and the artfully filmed, directed, and edited "story" of those lives as captured by the artists. But it also raises the question of whether even the most seemingly "objective" technology or method — in this case the camera and the documentary style — can pierce the boundary between our highly symbolic cultural forms and imagined meanings, and something that could be considered "real."

Similarly, I read to the class an account of a World War II survivor of the bombing of Nagasaki, in which the narrator details his childhood memories of the event in language that might evoke the most fantastic descriptions found in an Edgar Allan Poe or H. P. Lovecraft tale:

> What a sight! The biggest thing I ever saw, the biggest that ever was, was sticking way up into the sky from the other side of the mountain. It was like a cloud but it was like a pillar of fire too. It looked hard and soft and alive and dead all at the same time, and beautiful and ugly, too, all at once. The light it sent out was all the colors of the rainbow. It almost blinded me with the glare. It kept getting taller and taller all the time, and wider and wider, twisting and rolling around just like smoke from a chimney. It was growing from the top; I mean the top was getting pushed up from the inside. Then the top began to spread out, so that it looked like an umbrella opening up...After a few minutes I saw something coming up the road that looked like a parade of roast chickens. Some of them kept asking for "Water! Water!" I wasn't burning up any more. I shivered. I ran back to the cottage. I would rather blind myself than ever have to see such a sight again![39]

Here, the vivid, fantastical imagery, the contradictory descriptions of the mushroom cloud, and the mixture of the sublime and the surreal (or absurd) in the contrasting vision of the burned victims causes both a physiological reaction in the speaker and that fleeing from the reality of the events that is the hallmark of gothic fiction. The contrived language of the gothic seems to be the only one capable of describing what was, to its victims, a very real horror. But given the historicity of the event, and its consequences for those who lived through it, would it be reductive, even offensive, to call this account "gothic" in nature?

The question proved more daunting than it first seemed, as the class offered example after example of similar accounts drawn from their own lives. Being in Louisiana, many had vivid memories of Hurricane Katrina and other experiences of real suffering and terror, some of which certainly bore a resemblance to events that we'd been reading about and seeing on film. However, when pressed to decide if these experiences were, indeed, "gothic" in nature, many of the students had trouble reconciling their own understandings of their experience with the highly artificial narratives and metaphoric complexities of the fiction.

The results changed, however, when I re-stated the question this way: "Is 'horror' real, or can the real be 'horrific'?" At this, I received a resounding "Yes!" Citing not only their own experience, but the definitions offered by our authors and theorists, the students argued that "horror," rather than "gothic," is the term that most clearly draws the experience of the real and its various literary and cinematic representations together. Horror, they seemed to feel, is not a genre, but a function, a category of experience, like love or faith or the sublime — it carries with it, not a set of conventions and forms, but a set of sensations and effects. Thus it could more adequately convey the *reality* of the lived experience.

This, of course, only solves the problem of terminology, not the problem of representation. If we call a book or a film a "horror" text, rather than a "gothic" text, does that bring us any closer to understanding what that text is doing or revealing to us? Here, the medium of film seems to have certain advantages over literary texts. While applying the term "gothic" to real-life experiences seems clumsy and artificial, students generally have no problem identifying it as a form of literary representation — its conventions are well-established, its language and effects are easily identified, and even its psychological depths are readily analyzable through the tools of psychoanalysis and literary theory. Using "horror" rather than the "gothic" seems to open up the range of texts available for study, and introduces elements not always associated with traditional gothic conventions — realism, objective narration, scientific analysis, literal horrors that defy psychological or supernatural speculation. But still, the language of horror fiction is limited, as all language is, by its inevitably closed system of signification, by the weight of its history and intertextuality, and by its frequent failure to adequately convey "horror" in a way that is experiential, rather than referential.

The same might be said of film, of course — a medium rich in its own history and referentiality, as well as with its own set of conventions, techniques of artifice, and "authorial" manipulation. But there does seem to be something more visceral about the experience of horror on film that students find especially enticing, or especially repulsive. Film confronts the senses in a way that literary texts can only gesture towards or reproduce in the imagination; it attacks our eyes, our ears, sometimes even our sense of touch, as our skin crawls and the hair rises on the back of our neck as the ominous music rises in the background. When the monster springs on its victims, we leap from our seats, scream, cry, laugh, and experience that unique feeling of *jouissance* that thrills and terrifies us into a passionate frenzy. At least it can do these things, if we are sensitive and attentive enough to become immersed in the experience of the film.

I use films extensively in courses on gothic and horror fiction precisely because they seem to bring us a bit closer to the lived experience of horror in a way that can be experienced, contained, and analyzed in a group setting. I ask my students to be attentive, not only to the familiar elements of plot, character, language, allusion, and cinematic technique, but also to the individual *effects* of the film: their own emotions, physical sensations, thought processes, and even their moral reactions to what they are witnessing. These elements of the cinematic experience are usually the first things that we discuss in the immediate aftermath of our viewing, when they're fresh and powerful, saving the meta-analysis for later. I also ask them to write down such impressions either during or immediately after the first viewing of the film, and save those notes for comparison after a few days of discussion or writing on the larger themes and ideas. Did their physical and emotional reactions to the film influence their formal analysis? What did they find most "horrifying" and why; was it related to their own experiences of "the uncanny," "the perverse," or "the abject"? Did those sensations conflict with what they thought they wanted to say about the film's ideas, formal qualities, or cultural significance? Were there certain reactions that couldn't be adequately theorized or put into language, and why do they think this is so?

This way of analyzing film is certainly not technical or critical in the formal sense — but it is analytical, and in some cases, therapeutic, as students are encouraged to explore their own subjective responses both before and after they try for objective reasoning. The results, I think, can be enlightening. Students come to recognize the difficulty of reconciling the various levels of horror into a single cohesive "interpretation." They start to distinguish between craft or method (intention) and individual effects. They begin to draw out the important distinctions and boundaries between how horror is experienced and how it is represented. Most importantly, perhaps, they are given room to "immerse" and "harmonize" themselves with any aspects of the abject that their own experiences of horror might evoke.

The last part, of course, is one that must be approached with caution. To evoke and confront the abject can be, for many students, unsettling and potentially traumatic. I have had students burst into tears at the sight of violence or gore on film, leave the room when the sensations become over-powering, or refuse to discuss certain details of their own responses that touched on something too personal to share in a group setting. I warn students of these risks before the course begins, and when we prepare to watch or read texts that have the potential for such complications. Fortunately, students who take such courses or watch such films are generally a self-selecting group of horror-buffs, or at least adventurers, for whom the pleasant nervousness of horror is more salient than its terrors. Still, some are not prepared for the degree of personal emotion or unsettling thought that can accompany this more introspective approach to reading.

I have several strategies for channeling and containing these kinds of reactions: the first, which I've already mentioned, is the group "debriefing" that occurs immediately after a film or particularly intense reading. These are not class "discussions" in the usual sense, in which we'd do a more formal analysis of texts and ideas, but rather an opportunity to express and record something more spontaneous and personal. Finding that others shared their reactions, or had similar ones, can often be cathartic in itself—it reveals the collective, ritualistic nature of horror. Secondly, their own notes and journals allow for a more private response and working through of individual feelings, memories, or ideas evoked by the texts or films. These are a required part of the class—but when the assignments are due, I make sure to allow them to withhold or edit any entries that they prefer not to share in their raw form. This gives them the freedom to respond spontaneously and without censure, but also to protect whatever aspects of their experience that they feel are too private. Finally, I give every student the opportunity to meet and discuss their reactions with me outside of the classroom, not just for scholarly guidance, but to share or explain what they prefer to withhold from their formal discussions and assignments. These are not "therapy" sessions, but individualized conversations about our subject and their thoughts about its significance to their own writing or thinking about the texts. If I or they feel that actual therapy is required, I stand ready with referrals to the appropriate counseling services. But in my experience, this has never been necessary—given multiple outlets for conversation and expression, plus their own innate curiosity, and perhaps their own experience of the *jouissance* of their immersion in horror, most students thrive on the encounter.

NOTES

1. Edgar Allan Poe, *Poe: Poetry and Tales* (New York: the Library of America, 1984), 317.
2. Shirley Jackson, *The Haunting of Hill House* (New York: Penguin, 2006), 1.
3. Alice Sebold, *The Lovely Bones* (Boston, New York, London: Little, Brown, and Company, 2002), 186.
4. I should note the similarities of this argument to Noël Carroll's elaboration of what he calls "art-horror." See Noël Carroll, *The Philosophy of Horror, or, Paradoxes of the Heart* (New York and London: Routledge, 1990). While I agree with his essential definition and description of art-horror as an aesthetic genre — namely one that focuses on instilling in the audience a particular type of affect, characterized by fear and revulsion — I do not maintain his distinction between "art-horror" and what he terms "natural horror," or the horror experienced in real life, outside of the text or artistic construct. For Carroll, art-horror is a "cross-art, cross-media genre whose existence is already recognized in ordinary language" (12). But, as I will argue below, I believe that the "horror of the real," as I am defining it, breaks down our psychic distinctions between real and imagined experience and affects us in much the same ways as if our beliefs and thoughts (i.e. the knowledge that what we are reading is a fiction) mirrored our feelings and emotions (i.e. that what we are experiencing is, in fact, *real*). What's more, I am suggesting, along with Lacan and Kristeva, that the essence of horror resides outside the boundaries of what is "already recognized in ordinary language"; indeed, our experience of horror, whether in texts or in everyday life, arises from a pre-linguistic level of psychic development that resists generic definitions like Carroll's.
5. See Jacques Lacan, *The Four Fundamental Concepts of Psycho-Analysis* (New York, London: W. W. Norton, 1981); and Julia Kristeva, *Powers of Horror: An Essay on Abjection* (New York: Columbia University Press, 1982).
6. Alice Sebold, *Lovely Bones*, 186.
7. Jacques Lacan distinguishes what he calls "the Real" — an element of the sub-conscious connected to physical sensations, bodily functions, and basic animal instincts — from those later cognitive functions, the Imaginary and the Symbolic, which, respectively, allow us to form the conception of a coherent self and link that self to the social world of symbols and language. I will discuss the relationship of "the Real" to the Imaginary and the Symbolic further in the section on "The Horror of the Real," below.
8. H. P. Lovecraft, *The Annotated H.P. Lovecraft*, ed. by S.T. Joshi (New York: Dell, 1997), 341.
9. Ibid., 340.
10. For the most direct representation of this existential awareness, see Lovecraft's tale, "The Outsider" in H. P. Lovecraft, *Tales of H. P. Lovecraft*, ed. by Joyce Carol Oates (Hopewell, NJ: Ecco, 1997).
11. H.P. Lovecraft, *The Annotated Supernatural Horror in Literature*, ed. by S.T. Joshi. (New York: Hippocampus, 2000), 22.
12. Ibid., 23.
13. Here it may be useful to utilize Noël Carroll's explanation of "emotions" as states that involve both "physical perturbations" (i.e. the sensation of fear or revulsion toward an object of horror) and "evaluative thoughts" (i.e. the belief that the object/monster is a danger to us). See Carroll, 26. Here, the "evaluative thought" that coincides with the experience of horror is Lovecraft's "sense of outsideness." Thus, thoughts and feelings coincide to create the full affect of "horror."
14. Lovecraft, *Annotated Supernatural*, 37.
15. Ibid., 42.
16. Ibid., 43.
17. Ibid., 45.
18. Ibid., 44.
19. Poe, 485.
20. Lovecraft, *Annotated Supernatural*, 46.
21. Lovecraft, *Annotated Lovecraft*, 340.
22. Ibid., 340.
23. Lovecraft, *Tales*, 52.

24. Ibid., 52
25. Ibid., 52
26. Kristeva, 1.
27. I am, of course, not the first to apply Kristeva's theories to the analysis of horror fiction and film. See, especially, Barbara Creed's "Horror and the Monstrous-Feminine: An Imaginary Abjection," in *Feminist Film Theory: A Reader*, edited by Sue Thornham (New York: New York University Press, 1999). Others who have looked specifically at American fiction and film include Michael Davis, "'What's the Story Mother?': Abjection and Anti-Feminism in Alien and Aliens" Gothic Studies, 2000 August; 2 (2): 245–56.; and Kate Sullivan, "Meeting Monsters, Loving Men: Abjection and Community in Peter Straub's Ghost Story and Stephen King's 'The Breathing Method,'" *Paradoxa: Studies in World Literary Genres (Paradoxa)* 2002; 17: 176–99. And for applications of Kristevan analysis to the classroom setting, see Anne Williams, "The Horrors of Misogyny: Feminist Psychoanalysis in the Gothic Classroom," in *Approaches to Teaching Gothic Fiction: The British and American Traditions*, ed. by Diane Long Hoeveler and Tamar Heller (New York: Modern Language Association of America, 2003), 73–82.
28. Sigmund Freud, "The Uncanny," in *On Creativity and the Unconscious: Papers on the Psychology of Art Literature, Love, Religion* (New York: Haper & Row, 1958).
29. Kristeva, 5.
30. Lacan, 58.
31. Kristeva, 2.
32. Ibid., 4
33. Ibid., 11.
34. Ibid., 9
35. Ibid., 8.
36. Ibid., 28.
37. Ibid., 2.
38. *Grey Gardens*, DVD, directed by Albert Maysles, David Maysles, Elle Hovde, and Muffie Myer (Portrait Films, 1975).
39. Takashi Nagai, *We of Nagasaki: The Story of Survivors in an Atomic Wasteland,* translated by Ichiro Shirato and Herbert B.L. Silverman (New York: Duell, Sloan and Pearce, 1951).

The Pedagogical Value of Mary Shelley's *Frankenstein* in Teaching Adaptation Studies

BEN KOOYMAN

As Thomas Leitch observes in a 2008 survey of adaptation studies, the field has overcome various challenges and prejudices to achieve scholarly legitimacy. Leitch praises the recent "pioneering work" of scholars like Deborah Cartmell, Imelda Whelehan, and Robert Stam for elevating adaptation studies out of "the backwaters of the academy."[1] Where previously the scholarly study of adaptations adhered to a "fundamentally conservative, based-on-the-literary-text model" of analysis,[2] thanks to the efforts of the aforementioned authors and others, it is now moving on from those problems and preoccupations "inherited from literary studies—fidelity, hierarchy, canonicity"[3] and engaging with wider methodologies. However, Leitch notes that "the field is still haunted by the notion that adaptations ought to be faithful to their ostensible sourcetexts,"[4] and as I know from personal experience, attachment to this notion, despite the best efforts of a new generation of scholars to shake it off, still haunts the classroom environment.

From 2009 to 2010 I taught adaptation studies at a South Australian university. While it would be sweeping to suggest that my experiences teaching this topic are emblematic of all teaching experiences in this area, I wager that a number of the obstacles and challenges I encountered would be shared by other teachers in this field. Of particular note, as suggested above, was the disjunction between the scholarly investment in adaptation studies as an evolving discipline and the students' sense of adaptation studies as a practice amounting to little more than evaluations of textual fidelity or infidelity. Julie Sanders argues that "it is usually at the very point of infidelity that the most creative acts of adaptation and appropriation take place."[5] However, in the classroom environment, students continued to cling to fidelity as a measure of successful or unsuccessful adaptation. Furthermore, class discussions often degenerated into the trading back and forth of value judgments, reducing the analysis of adaptations to subjective film criticism rather than fostering genuine engagement with how texts are transformed from one medium to another. This is perhaps symptomatic of studying film texts in an English literature context — the course was part of the English (rather than film) major — where baggage pertaining to what qualifies as high art (i.e. literature) and low art (i.e. film), despite the best efforts of more progressive teachers, continues to haunt the field.

The intentions of this chapter are twofold. Firstly, drawing from my own experiences teaching adaptation studies, I illustrate some of the challenges faced by teachers of adaptation studies in the tertiary sector. Secondly, I argue that Mary Shelley's *Frankenstein* and two of its most notable film adaptations, James Whale's *Frankenstein* (1931) and Kenneth Branagh's *Mary Shelley's Frankenstein* (1994), can be useful tools for teaching adaptation studies and overcoming the disjunctions between scholarly and student practices. Once again drawing from personal classroom experience, I contend that close analysis of a key passage from Shelley's text and equivalent scenes from its film variations illustrates several important points: firstly, adaptations must be evaluated as self-contained texts rather than secondary iterations or offshoots of their primary sources; secondly, there is no objective criteria for measuring the success or failure of a film adaptation, and no such thing as 'authentic' or 'inauthentic' adaptations; and finally, adaptations produced in different eras will be shaped by different historical contexts, production determinants, ideological systems, and narrative conventions.

In 2009 and 2010, I taught in a course titled "Adaptations: From Text to Film" at Flinders University, South Australia.[6] This course revolved around the comparison, contrast, and close analysis of literary texts and their film adaptations. The range of texts covered was diverse, from classic novels and heritage films to contemporary works and their adaptations. While teaching this topic, I observed various disjunctions between recent scholarly attitudes towards adaptation studies and student attitudes, as reflected in the tutorial environment and in written work.

First and foremost, there was a tendency in class discussion to digress from close analysis and interpretation of the adaptation process towards subjective film criticism and the exchange of value judgments. Imelda Whelehan calls evaluating film adaptations "an inexact science dogged by value judgments about the relative artistic worth of literature and film,"[7] and students take enormous pleasure in this inexact science. In tutorial discussions, Keira Knightley's work in Joe Wright's *Pride and Prejudice* (2005) and *Atonement* (2007) was reviled, and it surfaced that Heath Ledger talked funny in Ang Lee's *Brokeback Mountain* (2005), Gregory Peck talked funny in Robert Mulligan's *To Kill a Mockingbird* (1962), and the black and white photography of William Wyler's *Wuthering Heights* (1939) and *To Kill a Mockingbird*, not to put too fine a point on it, sucked. The fact that such relatively superficial attributes impeded scholarly engagement with the films suggests an inherent divide in the attitude of the average English student (save those also studying film) between literature as an object to be read for study and film as an object to be viewed for recreation, and an inability to reconcile those impulses. Students privileged and held the literary text in higher regard than the film precisely because it was literature, while the film was often dismissed as inferior simply because it was film.

The assumption that film is inherently inferior to literature is problematic and pervasive, not just in the classroom but in the collective consciousness. Robert Stam believes that much adaptation scholarship has perpetuated "the axiomatic superiority of literature to film."[8] These "deeply rooted and often unconscious assumptions about the relations between the two arts" are partly linked to the "valorization of historical anteriority and seniority: the assumption, that is, that older arts are necessarily better arts."[9] Deborah Cartmell and Imelda Whelehan similarly note that scholarship has "historically privileged the literary over the cinematic,"[10] and observe that, in turn, the supposed superiority of literary texts to their film adaptations has become an "entrenched belief prevalent in the popular press."[11] Courses devoted to studying adaptation are at constant risk, however unintentionally, of reinforcing this increasingly anachronistic but still pervasive high art-low art divide.

Most adaptation scholars working today have abandoned such high-low divides and ceased to look at film adaptations as works of secondary importance. Cartmell and Whelehan strive in their work to ensure films are "not derided as sycophantic, derivative, and therefore inferior to their literary counterparts."[12] Linda Hutcheon argues that "the act of adaptation always involves both (re-) interpretation and then (re-) creation" and is best seen as "a form of intertextuality."[13] Stam likewise advocates for "adopting an intertextual as opposed to a judgmental approach rooted in assumptions about a putative superiority of literature."[14] In other words, students must consider adaptations autonomous, intertextual texts in their own right, and not automatically deride them as inferior.

Another problem encountered in the classroom was that students brought firm ideas of what constituted authenticity and inauthenticity to each week's screenings, and it soon became clear that students equated a film's textual fidelity with authenticity and success, and textual infidelity with inauthenticity and failure. This was especially evident when comparing different adaptations of Jane Austen's *Pride and Prejudice* and Emily Brontë's *Wuthering Heights*. Where Simon Langton's six episode BBC miniseries *Pride and Prejudice* (1995) was praised as the superior version of Austen's novel because of its near-exhaustive treatment of the story, Wright's two-hour film version was dismissed as unsuccessful because it supposedly skimmed the narrative. Similarly, where Wyler's melodramatic *Wuthering Heights* was panned by students for only adapting the first half of Brontë's novel, Peter Kosminsky's more comprehensive *Emily Brontë's Wuthering Heights* (1992) was praised.

This sort of approach to evaluating the success or failure of an adaptation is highly reductive: it diminishes both films and their literary sources to mere repositories of story, characters, and scenes, and the success of an adaptation ultimately depends upon its comprehensive inclusion of all those attributes from the original source. Whelehan notes:

> For many people the comparison of a novel and its film version results in an almost unconscious prioritizing of the fictional original over the resulting film, and so the main purpose of comparison becomes the measurement of the success of the film in its capacity to realize what are the core meanings and values of the originary text.[15]

While this sort of fidelity criticism was once the "critical orthodoxy" of this field,[16] most adaptation scholars have abandoned this reductive approach. As Stam observes:

> The shift from a single-track verbal medium such as the novel to a multi-track medium like film, which can play not only with words (written and spoken) but also with music, sound effects, and moving photographic images, explains the unlikelihood, and I would suggest even the undesirability, of literal fidelity.[17]

Elsewhere, Stam notes that film adaptations have been "especially castigated and held to an absurdly rigorous standard of fidelity" compared to adaptations in other art forms,[18] and argues that "it's important to move beyond the moralistic and judgmental ideal of fidelity."[19] Brian McFarlane concurs with Stam, describing fidelity as "a wholly inappropriate and unhelpful criterion" given that "every reading of a literary text is a highly individual act of cognition and interpretation."[20] That is to say, when readers demand fidelity from a film adaptation of a text, they are demanding fidelity to their own interpretation of that text rather than, say, Jane Austen's or Emily Brontë's. Consequently, fidelity and infidelity become unreliable markers of successful adaptation because they are highly subjective.

Another problem prevalent in the classroom was that students often did not take into account the various determinants that inform a film's production. McFarlane argues that "We need to have in mind… the parameters of cinematic production at the time of the film's production, the proclivities of the film's director and writer, the auras that attach to the film's stars."[21] Moreover, as Sanders notes, "adaptations and appropriations are impacted upon by movements in, and readings produced by, the theoretical and intellectual arena as much as by their so-called sources."[22] A comparison of students' treatment of Wyler's and Kosminsky's films of *Wuthering Heights* crystallizes some of these issues. Wyler's film was criticized for adapting only half the book, for turning the story into a romantic melodrama rather than familial tragedy, and for its sanitized treatment of the novel's dark subject matter. Meanwhile, Kosminsky's film was praised for tackling the subject matter ignored in Wyler's film, for telling the whole story, and for being dark and gritty like its source. Thus the latter film achieved the label of authenticity, while the former was dismissed as inauthentic.

However, students did not take into account the context for many of the so-called flaws in Wyler's film. Hollywood studio filmmaking in the 1930s was calibrated towards commerce, not art, so it was necessary to streamline Brontë's complex narrative. Furthermore, it was necessary to mould the story into a recognizable film genre and the romantic melodrama was the most logical fit, especially in an era when women rather than teenage boys were the dominant target audience for mainstream studio films.[23] The sanitized treatment of the subject matter was also a product of context: the film was made under the Motion Picture Production Code (or Hays Code) which dictated what could and could not be shown on film. Thus the domestic and child abuse that figure largely in the novel were ignored — much of this content appears in the jettisoned second half of the novel — and the severity of Heathcliff's personality was toned down to make him a more acceptable leading man: his villainy becomes a product of nurture (poor treatment as a child) rather than nature.

Just as students did not contextualize the supposed flaws of Wyler's film, they likewise did not see that the so-called positives of Kosminsky's film were also a product of context. Kosminsky's film was a boutique art film, not a costly mainstream studio film, and it was produced in the permissive 1990s without the severe restrictions of the Hays Code hanging over the production. As such, it had greater liberty to translate the more taboo content of Brontë's novel to film. And while it certainly tackles the second half of Brontë's book, it does so in an abridged manner, rushing through this section: while Wyler's film tells only half the story, I would argue that it tells half the story much more coherently than Kosminsky tells the full story. Ultimately, Kosminsky's film of *Wuthering Heights* is no more comprehensive an adaptation of Brontë's novel than Joe Wright's maligned *Pride and Prejudice* is an adaptation of Jane Austen's novel, but where one appears faithful compared to a 1930s Hollywood melodrama that tells only half the story, the other seems scandalously unfaithful compared to a six-hour BBC miniseries. As for the film's darkness and grittiness, this was an aesthetic choice typical of many adaptations of the time, where darkness and grittiness became a marker of authenticity.[24] Ultimately, there is no objective criteria for labeling Kosminsky's film a superior adaptation of *Wuthering Heights*, and the supposed qualities which, according to students, elevated it above its precursor — greater fidelity, grittier direction, more risqué subject matter — are primarily products of context.

Having illustrated a range of pedagogical issues facing novel-to-film adaptation studies, the second section of this chapter, also drawing from personal classroom experience, discusses how close analysis of Mary Shelley's *Frankenstein* and two of its adaptations can help address some of these pedagogical challenges and reinforce current scholarly directions in the field of adaptation studies.

Mary Shelley's *Frankenstein*, first published in 1818, has been a staple of popular literature for nearly 200 years, but its status as canonical text is relatively recent, largely due to feminist and cultural concerns. Fred Botting writes that its newfound literary status:

> testifies to the changes that have already occurred in literary and critical theory and practice, marking a shift of focus in which literary and popular fiction is studied in relation to a network of other writings from political, historical and cultural spheres. Subject, in recent decades, to increasing and serious academic appraisals from various critical perspectives, *Frankenstein*'s place in courses, if not within the once established and now contested literary tradition, seems assured.[25]

While Botting identifies Shelley's novel as "a byword for horror,"[26] *Frankenstein*, alongside Bram Stoker's *Dracula*, Robert Louis Stevenson's *Strange Case of Dr. Jekyll and Mr. Hyde*, and the works of Edgar Allan Poe, is generally subsumed in academia under the banner of "Gothic" literature, a label which validates its inclusion in the canon by distancing it from "horror fiction" per se. Ironically, as Botting notes, "*Frankenstein*, though one of the texts now synonymous with Gothic, deploys standard Gothic conventions sparingly to bring the genre thoroughly and critically within the orbit of Romanticism."[27]

Hutcheon comments that when we watch adaptations of a canonical text, "we may not actually have direct experience of it [the original], but may rely on a generally circulated cultural memory."[28] Few canonical novels have had as vivid a cultural memory or as diverse a cinematic afterlife as *Frankenstein*. However, like adaptations of Stoker's *Dracula*, most films of *Frankenstein* take liberty with their source material. It is the iconography of *Frankenstein* that attracts filmmakers, rather than the specific narrative beats of Shelley's text, and that iconography has circulated far and wide throughout popular culture. In addition to what we might call straight (relatively speaking) adaptations of *Frankenstein*, from the Universal Monster series (1931–1944) to the Hammer Horror series (1957–1974) to Kenneth Branagh's film, we have comic riffs on the story — *Abbott and Costello meet Frankenstein* (1948), *Young Frankenstein*

(1974), and the TV series *The Munsters* (1964–1966)—and ensemble monster mashes—*The Monster Squad* (1987) and *Van Helsing* (2004)—and variations on the classic *Frankenstein* theme of humankind usurping God and creating sentient beings—*Metropolis* (1927), *Re-Animator* (1985), and *Splice* (2010).[29] Stephen King speculates that *Frankenstein* "has probably been the subject of more films than any other literary work in history, including the Bible," and through this dissemination it has entered into the "myth pool... of fictive literature in which all of us, even the non-readers and those who do not go to the films, have communally bathed."[30]

When I surveyed students about their familiarity with Shelley's text, I discovered that only a few had read the novel and/or watched a film of *Frankenstein* from start to finish. However, all students had been exposed to the story in one form or another, whether in cartoons, while flicking channels, via secondhand intertextual citations, or through any number of the footprints left across popular culture by Shelley's creations. Thus while few students were intimately familiar with *Frankenstein*, most were acquainted to varying degrees with its broader mythos and iconography. I imagine this would be a common pattern across different universities and student groups, and this is one of the greatest advantages of using horror texts like *Frankenstein*, *Dracula* or *Dr. Jekyll and Mr. Hyde* in adaptation studies: students are usually acquainted with the wider mythos, and to some degree curious about how their own accumulated understanding of the mythos corresponds to or differs from its source. Another advantage is that, as a horror text, *Frankenstein* connotes thrills and fun at the same time that it connotes "serious" canonical literature.

The remainder of this chapter examines how a key passage from Mary Shelley's novel has been adapted to film by two different directors, James Whale and Kenneth Branagh. In doing so, I hope to demonstrate how this canonical horror text and its film spin-offs provide a means of addressing some of the issues discussed in the previous section, including misplaced investment in textual fidelity as a measure of success and authenticity in adaptation, indifference towards important contextual matters, and misguided high art/low art hierarchies that elevate novels while denigrating films. I myself have employed the below passage from Shelley's novel and its interpretations by Whale and Branagh in the classroom to address these issues, and the exercise and resulting class discussion have been productive each time.

Below is the selected excerpt from Shelley's novel, taken from the beginning of Chapter Five:

> It was on a dreary night of November that I beheld the accomplishment of my toils. With an anxiety that almost amounted to agony, I collected the instruments of life around me, that I might infuse a spark of being into the lifeless thing that lay at my feet. It was already one in the morning; the rain pattered dismally against

the panes, and my candle was nearly burnt out, when, by the glimmer of the half-extinguished light, I saw the dull yellow eye of the creature open; it breathed hard, and a convulsive motion agitated its limbs.

How can I describe my emotions at this catastrophe, or how delineate the wretch whom with such infinite pains and care I had endeavored to form? His limbs were in proportion, and I had selected his features as beautiful. Beautiful! Great God! His yellow skin scarcely covered the work of muscles and arteries beneath; his hair was of a lustrous black, and flowing; his teeth of pearly whiteness; but these luxuriances only formed a more horrid contrast with his watery eyes, that seemed almost of the same color as the dun-white sockets in which they were set, his shrivelled complexion and straight black lips.

The different accidents of life are not so changeable as the feelings of human nature. I had worked hard for nearly two years, for the sole purpose of infusing life into an inanimate body. For this I had deprived myself of rest and health. I had desired it with an ardor that far exceeded moderation; but now that I had finished, the beauty of the dream vanished, and breathless horror and disgust filled my heart. Unable to endure the aspect of the being I had created, I rushed out of the room and continued a long time traversing my bedchamber, unable to compose my mind to sleep.[31]

Shelley's depiction of the creation of the Monster differs from how most films have interpreted it. Where Shelley obscures the process of creation, filmmakers tend to elaborate on it in creative and bombastic ways. On reading *Frankenstein*, students conditioned by popular culture would likely expect a similarly energetic and detailed scene, complete with all the thunderclaps, lightning flashes and hunchbacked manservants popularized in films of *Frankenstein*. But Shelley's interests lie elsewhere.

The strengths of Shelley's passage are the gloomy, mysterious atmosphere it generates and the insights it provides into Frankenstein's diseased, unraveling mind. The drama of the passage resides in its power of suggestion: it leaves the creation of the Monster entirely to the reader's imagination. However, as many critics contend — often reductively — the strengths of the film medium are action rather than suggestion, forward narrative momentum rather than reflection, and exteriority rather than interiority. Critic Pauline Kael argued that "Movies are good at action; they're not good at reflective thought or conceptual thinking. They're good for immediate stimulus."[32] Many adaptation scholars would disagree with this, among them Linda Hutcheon, who rejects the cliché that "literary fiction, with its visualizing, conceptualizing, and intellectualized apprehension, 'does' interiority best; the performing arts, with their physical immersion, are most suited to representing exteriority."[33] However, in the case of *Frankenstein*, most filmmakers appear to have adopted Kael's rationale. James Whale's adaptation of *Frankenstein* uses the creation of the Monster as the basis for an extravagant and imaginative set piece, and most filmmakers since have followed suit, but have rarely equaled Whale.

Universal Studios' 1931 production of *Frankenstein* was the first sound adaptation of Shelley's novel, and remains the most important and famous film of *Frankenstein* to date. As indicated earlier, only a handful of my students were closely acquainted with Shelley's novel or any of its adaptations, but all were familiar with the popular image of the Monster established by Whale's film: the "physically overbearing monster with the shovel forehead and the sunken, stupidly crafty eyes," to quote Stephen King.[34] Michael Mallory, in his book commemorating the Universal Monster canon, argues that "While some of these characters pre-existed in mythology or literature, the iconic forms, images and identities that we immediately recognize in them today all emanated from... Universal Studios."[35] Jack Pierce's iconic make-up and Boris Karloff's performance as the Monster, and subsequent approximations of that performance by Lon Chaney, Jr., Bela Lugosi, and Glenn Strange, have made Universal's vision of Frankenstein's Monster definitive in what King calls the "cultural echo chamber."[36] However, Whale's film is not an especially faithful adaptation of the novel, as its depiction of the Monster's creation attests.[37]

Mallory observes that "The creation scene — all ablaze with sights and sounds of all manner of strange, sparkling equipment... set the prototype for all subsequent laboratory sequences."[38] The scene opens with a radical departure from the novel: in Shelley's text Victor Frankenstein is alone when he brings the creature to life, but here the scientist — renamed Henry Frankenstein — is aided in his work by his hunchbacked assistant Fritz, and observed by fiancée Elizabeth, friend Victor, and former teacher Waldman. The group dynamic significantly changes the nature of Shelley's passage, which depicted Frankenstein at the tail end of prolonged isolation. Given Whale's emphasis on spectacle in this scene, it is fitting that he incorporates an element of spectatorship: Whale's background was in the theatre, and Paul M. Jensen argues that he found in Shelley's passage "something that taps into his own sense of demonstration, of presentation, of theatricality."[39] Linda Costanzo Cahir observes that "the most successful films based on literary works translate the words into images by both interpreting and exploiting the source text. The literary text is strip-mined for the riches the filmmakers can use to promote their own vision."[40] Whale's auteurist identification and exploitation of the theatricality inherent in Shelley's passage is an excellent example of this.

Whale stated that he accepted the assignment of making *Frankenstein* because he "thought it would be amusing to try and make what everybody knows is a physical impossibility seem believable. Also it offered fine pictorial chances."[41] The creation scene reflects these two impulses. Whale creates visually arresting and dynamic cinema, with cinematography influenced by Expressionist filmmaking, impressive panning shots following the monster's body as it is raised to the skylight on a grill and lowered again, shots of electrical currents crackling around scientific equipment, and dramatic contrasts of nature (thunder and lightning) and Old Worlds (Gothic architecture) with New Worlds (eye-catching scientific apparatus). As well as providing cinematic spectacle, by explicitly illustrating the process of the Monster's creation and lavishing detail on the devices used, Whale makes the physical implausibility of bringing the Monster to life believable. The director contended that "if the audience did not believe the thing had been really made they would not be bothered with what it was supposed to do afterward."[42] Consequently, by the time the scene ends with Henry shouting "It's Alive!" repeatedly, the audience has most likely suspended disbelief in the physical impossibility of the concept, thanks to Whale's detailed (if fantastical) illustration of the scientific process.

Overall, Whale's depiction of the scene entails radical departures from the novel: private and obscured occurrences become public spectacle, implied actions become explicit, the interiority of Frankenstein's first person narration becomes external performance, and the repulsion that ends Shelley's passage becomes celebration. Where Shelley's scientist immediately recoils in disgust from the Monster, in Whale's film the scientist is at first ecstatic, and his subsequent, gradual realization of the error of his ways is consistent with conventional film characterization: without the interiority afforded by the novel's first-person narration, a sudden change in Frankenstein's attitude towards the Monster would be slightly implausible.

Despite the many alterations made from text to screen, it would be misguided and naive to accuse Whale of infidelity to Shelley. Quite simply, Shelley's passage, adapted faithfully, would not have made successful cinema in the context of 1930s Hollywood film production, and audiences largely unfamiliar with the novel (though undoubtedly familiar with the story) would likely have found a deliberately obscured creation scene dramatically unsatisfying. As a result, the adaptation process necessitated many of the creative decisions illustrated above to make the scene work in this radically different medium. Furthermore, despite some significant departures from the source material, the creation scene still fulfils its narrative function in the overall architecture of the story, pays lip service to many of the Gothic staples present in Shelley's work, and articulates the idea of Frankenstein as usurper of God in Frankenstein's final lines in the scene: "Now I know what it feels like to be God."[43]

On reading the selected passage from Shelley's novel in the classroom, many students were taken aback by its difference from their accumulated cultural knowledge of *Frankenstein*, a body of knowledge founded largely upon Whale's film and its iconography. However, on watching Whale's depiction of the creation scene, students faulted the film for its lack of fidelity to Shelley's writing, indicating the almost-reflex privileging of literature over film discussed earlier. But on closer analysis of the sequence, and after I contextualized it in light of Whale's biography and 1930s Hollywood production practices, the rationale for Whale's tinkering with the text became clearer and students became more comfortable with the scene as a cinematic elaboration on— rather than direct translation of—Shelley's passage, one largely determined by historical context and auteurist vision.

While Whale's sequel *Bride of Frankenstein* (1935) playfully incorporates Mary Shelley into its narrative—its opening scene features Shelley, husband Percy Shelley, and fellow poet Lord Byron at Byron's estate in Switzerland in 1816, where the idea for the novel originated—Kenneth Branagh's film of *Frankenstein*, made 60 years later, is a far more serious attempt to court association with *Frankenstein*'s original author. *Mary Shelley's Frankenstein* (1994), while a mainstream Hollywood production, strives for what Andrew Higson characterizes as the "discourse of authenticity" common to British heritage cinema.[44] The whiff of heritage cinema that the film carries can be partly attributed to Branagh's pedigree as his generation's foremost adapter of Shakespeare, and the casting of various heritage stars like Helena Bonham Carter and Ian Holm. However, it is also due to the film's foregrounding of its original author, and what Higson calls the "reverence for source material" which permeates heritage cinema.[45]

The film opens with the following voiceover narration, taken from the novel's Introduction and "spoken" by Mary Shelley:

> I busied myself to think of a story which would speak to the mysterious fears of our nature and awaken thrilling horror. One to make the reader dread to look around, to curdle the blood, and quicken the beatings of the heart.[46]

The title card *Mary Shelley's Frankenstein* accompanies these lines, reinforcing the film's status as an "authentic" rendition of Shelley's novel. Eckart Voigts-Virchow argues that Branagh cites Shelley in the film's title to "invoke the (untenable) primacy of literature as a cultural norm."[47] Meanwhile, both Deborah Cartmell and Will Brooker locate the title's citation of Shelley as part of a broader commercial trend at the time of production, a trend encompassing other works like the aforementioned *Emily Brontë's Wuthering Heights*, *William Shakespeare's Romeo + Juliet* (1996), Branagh's own *William Shakespeare's Hamlet* (1996) and, most significantly, *Bram Stoker's Dracula* (1992). For Cartmell:

> Although their names serve to distinguish the films from previous adaptations, they are also signifiers of a return to authenticity.... The presence of the author privileges "authority" and sanctions the adaptation as "authoritative," faithful to the author because of their very presence within it.[48]

Brooker, meanwhile, sees this movement as a "trend for claiming a return to the "authentic" ur-text in literary adaptations."[49]

Just as Whale's film of *Frankenstein* followed on from the success of Tod Browning's *Dracula* (1931), Branagh's film capitalized on the success of the aforementioned *Bram Stoker's Dracula*. That film's director, Francis Ford Coppola, served as a producer on Branagh's film, strengthening ties between the two productions. *Mary Shelley's Frankenstein* imitates Coppola's film in generating its "discourse of authenticity" through courting association with the work's original author in its title and deploying actors who serve as signifiers of heritage cinema in its cast, as mentioned above. It also follows Coppola's lead in attempting to cover more narrative territory from the novel than any prior adaptation. In his Introduction to the book chronicling the film's production, Branagh states that "our intent was always to arrive at an interpretation that's more faithful than earlier versions to the spirit of the book."[50] He dismisses the Universal Monster adaptations of *Frankenstein* as "very entertaining but rather melodramatic black-and-white features that were rather camp, even when they first came out," insisting that "many elements of the story have still to be put on film" and that his "idea was to use as much of Mary Shelley as had not been seen on film before."[51] Elsewhere, he says that "I hope Mary Shelley would at least approve" of his production, further courting association with and approval from *Frankenstein*'s creator.[52]

However, both Coppola's and Branagh's films take more liberties with their source texts than their surface veneer of faithfulness suggests. Margaret Montalbano argues that in Coppola's film, Stoker's novel is "refracted through twentieth century concerns with, among other things, gender roles and sexuality."[53] Furthermore, Coppola incorporates into the narrative a Hollywood-style doomed romance between Mina Harker and the titular predator. Meanwhile, Branagh's film significantly revises the fate of Frankenstein's wife Elizabeth, among various other textual alterations and additions. R. Barton Palmer argues that "valorizing 'faithfulness' seems a desperate gesture at recuperating an outmoded concept of textual production whose foundational concept is the irreproducible original."[54] Ultimately, this gesture is incongruous and at odds with the realities of film production, as both *Bram Stoker's Dracula* and *Mary Shelley's Frankenstein* demonstrate.

The relationship between Whale's and Branagh's films of *Frankenstein* is comparable to that between Wyler's and Kosminsky's adaptations of *Wuthering Heights* mentioned earlier. Where one film tells only part of the story (though in fairness Whale's sequel *Bride of Frankenstein* does continue the story), the other provides greater narrative coverage and invites association as a superior, authentic adaptation, aided in part by the citation of the author in the title and the incorporation of the author's voice and/or person into the narrative (Emily Brontë, played by musician Sinéad O'Connor, appears at the beginning and end of Kosminsky's film). However, like *Emily Brontë's Wuthering Heights*, just because *Mary Shelley's Frankenstein* covers more ground does not mean it is automatically superior to Whale's film or other films based on the story. If an adaptation's value depends solely on its status as a repository of story, scenes, and characters from the original narrative, then *Mary Shelley's Frankenstein* may well be a better adaptation. But fidelity is not the sole measure of a film adaptation's success or authenticity. I do not wish to imply that Branagh's film is "bad" for courting a veneer of authenticity it does not necessarily warrant, as this would only perpetuate the sort of "gratuitous value judgments"[55] about adaptations that scholars wish to abandon. Rather, I simply wish to reiterate that Branagh's claims must not be taken at face value, and that we must evaluate his film on the basis of what it does rather than what it says it does or what we ourselves want it to do.

Close scrutiny of the film's creation scene — more precisely, the first of its two creation scenes — helps to clarify this point, and analysis of where Branagh's version of the scene overlaps with and digresses from Whale's reinforces certain important tenets of the adaptation process. Branagh praises Shelley's "very unspecific evocation of the creation process" as "a stroke of brilliance... because it has allowed artists in other mediums to interpret that part of the story in many imaginative and exciting ways."[56] Branagh follows in the footsteps of Whale in embellishing the scene, realizing as Whale did that a deliberately obscured rendering of Shelley's original passage would lack cinematic possibility. This reinforces the fact that Branagh's film can never *really* be *Mary Shelley's Frankenstein*.

The scene opens with Frankenstein racing into his laboratory after an encounter with Elizabeth, shedding his robe, and diving into action. The first part of this sequence unfolds at a hectic pace, with Frankenstein darting around the room single-handedly overseeing every stage of the creation process. Much as Whale's version of the scene served as a set piece showcasing his directorial skills, so too does Branagh turn the scene into a set piece, showcasing not only his skills as a director but his respectably sculpted body as well. The camera pans, tracks, sweeps up and down, and is constantly on the move throughout: Branagh notes "the operatic fervor of the creation process ... with the camera swinging and swooping across the lab."[57] This energetic camerawork is a stock characteristic of Branagh's directorial style, best exemplified prior to *Mary Shelley's Frankenstein* in his films *Dead Again* (1991) and *Much Ado About Nothing* (1993). Like Whale's film, Branagh's film is also informed by its immediate precursors — not just Coppola's film of *Dracula*, but other horror films and thrillers of the time as well as Branagh's own Shakespeare adaptations — and consequently borrows their established codes and conventions. Consistent with popular action movies and thrillers of the period, the editing is fast-paced and the score, composed by Branagh's regular musical collaborator Patrick Doyle, is bombastic. This is a notable contrast to the soundtrack accompanying Whale's version of the scene, which contains only sound effects and no incidental music. Once the creation process draws to a close and the sequence slows down, Branagh incorporates the types of jump scares common in the modern horror film—sudden scares following long stretches of suspenseful silence—first when the Monster's hand suddenly brushes against the glass of its sarcophagus tank, and again when the Monster dramatically rises from the tank.

As indicated earlier, Whale's production of *Frankenstein*, and that film's version of this scene, casts a long shadow over popular culture, and Branagh's big-budget studio spectacle inevitably pays tribute to Whale's famous film. Branagh is a highly intertextual director, and belongs to what Peter Brooker describes as "a more intensively palimpsestic, ironic, and self-reflexive film culture" than his predecessors.[58] Samuel Crowl argues that "Popular film culture lies deep at the soul of Branagh's creative sensibility"[59]:

> Branagh is a product of the postmodern movement dominated by a sense of belatedness; a sense that originality is exhausted and that only parody and pastiche and intertextual echo remain. Rather than finding such a condition enervating, Branagh's work seizes on its possibilities. Branagh is, in Ihab Hassan's term, a reconstructionist; an artist who creates out of the bits and shards of the postmodern moment.[60]

There are various homages and allusions to Whale's creation scene throughout Branagh's version of the scene. The hanging grill on which the Monster's body lies, which Frankenstein elevates, sends across the room, and then lowers into the sarcophagus tank, is an obvious example, as are the electrical currents that crackle around Frankenstein's scientific apparatus. One of the first signs of life from the Monster is its hand brushing violently against the glass of the tank, much as the first sign of life in Whale's film is the Monster's hand twitching. Frankenstein's response to this sign of life—"It's Alive! It's Alive!"—similarly pays homage to Whale's film. Robert Stam argues that "the diverse prior adaptations [of a text] taken together can form a larger, cumulative hypotext available to the filmmaker who comes relatively 'late' in the series."[61] In the case of *Frankenstein*, Branagh is a latecomer to Shelley's text, with a wealth of hypotextual material at his disposal, and it is important to recognize the presence of these prior textual traces in Branagh's film, as well as traces of other notable films and styles. As Brian McFarlane notes, when it comes to analyzing adaptations, "we need to realize and allow for the fact that the anterior novel or play or poem is only one element of the film's intertextuality."[62]

Like Whale, Branagh emphasizes the notion of Frankenstein playing God in the creation scene, but takes this one step further by incorporating "explicit sexual imagery"[63] into the sequence, reinforcing the notion that the

Monster's creation is akin to an act of procreation. The sarcophagus tank in which the Monster lies symbolizes the womb, the large sack of electric eels — nicknamed the "bollock" by the filmmakers[64] — stands in for the scrotum filled with sperm, and the tube which connects this "bollock" to the womb and shoots electric eels into it symbolizes the penis ejaculating. Frankenstein invests his Monster with life through creating and commanding this man-made sexual apparatus, and through this Branagh articulates the alternative procreation theme inherent in Shelley's text. The overtones of procreation and childbirth also further articulate the idea that Frankenstein's rejection of the Monster is a rejection of his own child. After the Monster lunges from the tank, tipping it over and emptying its contents onto the floor, Frankenstein and the creature squirm in the slimy liquid as the scientist tries to help the newborn creature stand and walk, with little success. Frankenstein is repulsed by the Monster's inability to function and, thinking the creature dead after it becomes entangled in chains and hung from above, vows to destroy his work. As mentioned earlier, Frankenstein's sudden repulsion towards and rejection of his creature in Shelley's novel would appear extreme and unfeasible on film without the crutch of Shelley's neurotic narration. Branagh's depiction of Frankenstein's struggle to help the creature stand and walk to some degree legitimizes this repulsion and rejection. However, even as Branagh legitimizes Frankenstein's response, he also condemns it. As the director noted, he imagined "a child being born to parents who then walk out of the delivery room and leave this bloodstained, fluid-covered thing to just crawl around on its own."[65]

Branagh's adaptation of this key passage from Shelley's novel elaborates on the themes of procreation and the blasphemous usurpation of God present in the novel. However, contrary to the "discourse of authenticity" which the film perpetuates, changes have been made in the adaptation process, as illustrated above, to make this passage work in a very different medium — a medium which, as indicated earlier, thrives on action rather than suggestion, forward narrative momentum rather than reflection, and exteriority rather than interiority — and to make it consistent with the dominant codes and conventions of the time of production. The film also inevitably refers to its most famous precursor adaptation of Shelley's text, James Whale's film, and other notable works. This seemingly more "faithful" and "authentic" adaptation of Shelley's novel ultimately takes as many liberties with its source material as Whale's earlier adaptation. Consequently, to think of *Mary Shelley's Frankenstein* as Mary Shelley's *Frankenstein* would be misguided. However, it would be even more misguided to condemn or dismiss the film for not being Mary Shelley's *Frankenstein*.

While Branagh's film is the more recent of the two productions discussed here, it became evident in classroom discussion that fewer students were acquainted with the iconography of Branagh's film than Whale's, which is indicative of the precursor production's greater cultural longevity as well as the corporate stamina of the Universal Monsters brand. Nonetheless, most students recognized Branagh, either associating him with Shakespeare or his work as an actor in films like *Harry Potter and the Chamber of Secrets* (2002), and the actor-director's Shakespearean pedigree, as well as his film's evocation of Mary Shelley in its title, generated expectations of fidelity to Shelley's passage, which the screened sequence sometimes did and sometimes did not satisfy. Being a recent production, students found it easier to recognize modern film and horror film tropes, like the aforementioned jump scares. More interestingly, having viewed the equivalent scene from Whale's precursor film just minutes earlier, students were able to identify those moments where Branagh's film explicitly riffed on or significantly departed from Whale's scene. This identification helped drive the point home that film adaptations of literary works derive as much from broader film culture and historical determinants as they do their original literary sources.

In conclusion, I do not wish to suggest that Mary Shelley's *Frankenstein* and its film adaptations provide the only, or indeed the very best, means of addressing the disjunctions between scholarly and student practices and attitudes towards adaptation studies. However, the work's prominent status in the collective "myth pool"[66] and "cultural echo chamber,"[67] its wealth of adaptations and appropriations from different eras and contexts, and its dual status as both canonical and popular literature make it a suitable candidate, and my own experiences using the selected passage from *Frankenstein* and the selected depictions of this passage in the classroom to discuss these pedagogical issues have been productive and educational for students.[68]

As this chapter has demonstrated, this text and its adaptations are extremely useful for addressing three key challenges that haunt the adaptation studies classroom. Firstly, *Frankenstein* and its adaptations testify that there is no objective criteria for measuring the success or failure, or authenticity or inauthenticity, of a film adaptation, and that the most consistently used measures, fidelity and infidelity, are inherently unreliable. In both films discussed here, the different demands of the film medium necessitated significant creative alterations. Secondly, *Frankenstein* and its adaptations reinforce the point that different films of a single text produced in different eras will yield significantly different results. Both Whale's and Branagh's films were triggered and informed by the commercial success of a preceding adaptation of Stoker's *Dracula*, yet very different production modes, historical contexts, commercial imperatives, and narrative conventions resulted in very different adaptations of Shelley's work. Finally, *Frankenstein* and its films assert that adaptations must be regarded as autonomous texts as well as adaptations, on the grounds of what they achieve rather than what they do not achieve, and should not be relegated to secondary or derivative status simply because they are adaptations. To diminish these films for their reinventions of the novel is to diminish their own formidable cinematic achievements and their own broader contributions to the larger *Frankenstein* mythology.

NOTES

1. Thomas Leitch, "Adaptation Studies at a Crossroads," *Adaptation* 1.1 (2008): 63. See also Deborah Cartmell and Imelda Whelehan, eds., *Adaptations: From Text to Screen, Screen to Text* (London: Routledge, 1999); Deborah Cartmell and Imelda Whelehan, eds., *The Cambridge Companion to Literature on Screen* (Cambridge: Cambridge University Press, 2007); and Robert Stam, *Literature through Film: Realism, Magic, and the Art of Adaptation* (Malden: Blackwell, 2005).
2. Leitch, 65.
3. Leitch, 76.
4. Leitch, 64.
5. Sanders, *Adaptation and Appropriation* (London: Routledge, 2006), 20.
6. This is an undergraduate course in the university's Department of English, Creative Writing, and Australian Studies, and is coordinated by Dr. Giselle Bastin.
7. Imelda Whelehan, "Adaptations: The Contemporary Dilemmas," in *Adaptations: From Text to Screen, Screen to Text*, eds. Deborah Cartmell and Imelda Whelehan (London: Routledge, 1999), 9.
8. Robert Stam, "Introduction: The Theory and Practice of Adaptation," in *Literature and Film: A Guide to the Theory and Practice of Film Adaptation*, eds. Robert Stam and Alessandra Raengo (Malden: Blackwell, 2005), 4.
9. Stam, "Introduction: The Theory and Practice of Adaptation," 4.
10. Deborah Cartmell and Imelda Whelehan, "Introduction: Literature on Screen: a synoptic view," in *The Cambridge Companion to Literature on Screen*, eds. Deborah Cartmell and Imelda Whelehan (Cambridge: Cambridge University Press, 2007), 2.
11. Cartmell and Whelehan, "Introduction: Literature on Screen: A Synoptic View," 3.
12. Cartmell and Whelehan, "Introduction: Literature on Screen: A Synoptic View," 2.
13. Linda Hutcheon, *A Theory of Adaptation* (New York: Routledge, 2006), 8.
14. Stam, "Introduction: The Theory and Practice of Adaptation," 46.
15. Whelehan, 3.
16. Hutcheon, 7.
17. Stam, *Literature Through Film*, 4.
18. "Introduction: The Theory and Practice of Adaptation," 15.
19. Stam, "Introduction: The Theory and Practice of Adaptation," 14.
20. Brian MacFarlane, "Reading film and literature," in *The Cambridge Companion to Literature on Screen*, eds. Deborah Cartmell and Imelda Whelehan (Cambridge: Cambridge University Press, 2007), 15.
21. MacFarlane, 26.
22. Sanders, 13.
23. Maltby, *Hollywood Cinema*, 2d ed. (Malden: Blackwell, 2003), 20.
24. For example, Kenneth Branagh's *Henry V* (1989) was praised for its authenticity to Shakespeare's play, but was no more authentic to its source than Laurence Olivier's glossier 1944 film. Rather, its gritty anti-war inclinations were more authentic to contemporary cultural sensibilities, just as Olivier's film—a patriotic, jingoistic wartime drama released during World War Two—was more authentic to its own era.
25. Botting, "Introduction," in *Frankenstein*, ed. Fred Botting (New York: St. Martin's, 1995), 1.
26. Fred Botting, *Gothic* (London: Routledge, 1996), 105.
27. Botting, *Gothic*, 101. Like *Frankenstein*, the rise of Gothic literature's stock in the academy has been relatively recent and informed by broader movements in the academy: as Botting

writes, "By challenging the hierarchies of literary value and widening the horizons of critical study to include other forms of writing and address different cultural and historical issues, recent critical practices have moved Gothic texts from previously marginalised sites designated as popular fiction or literary eccentricity" (*Gothic*, 17). Ironically, while the Gothic label licenses the canonisation of literature from the maligned horror genre, Botting aligns the 20th century horror film with "the non-literary, cultural tradition that conventionally remains the true locus of Gothic" (*Gothic*, 14).

28. Hutcheon, 122.
29. There are also films which dramatize and recreate the conception of Shelley's novel, like *Gothic* (1986) and *Frankenstein Unbound* (1990), and a film that deals with Whale's production of *Frankenstein*: *Gods and Monsters* (1998).
30. Stephen King, *Danse Macabre* (New York: Everest House, 1981), 62.
31. Mary Shelley, *Frankenstein* (London: Puffin, 1994), 69–70.
32. Hutcheon, 57.
33. Hutcheon, 56.
34. King, 62.
35. Mallory, *Universal Studios Monsters: A Legacy of Horror* (New York: Universe, 2009), 11.
36. King, 65.
37. It is also, it is worth noting, a work borne of many creators, not just Shelley and Whale, or Karloff and Pierce. The title card in the film's opening credits traces its genealogy of authors and marks the text as a product derived from multiple sources: "Based upon the composition by John L. Balderston; From the novel by Mrs. Percy B. Shelley; Adapted from the play by Peggy Webling; Screen Play by Garrett Fort [and] Francis Edwards Paragoh." In addition, another director, Robert Florey, worked on the project before Whale, and the influence of German Expressionist cinema on the film largely derives from Florey. Furthermore, the success of Tod Browning's *Dracula* (1931) not only kick-started the project, but informed its casting — actors Dwight Frye and Edward Van Sloan appear in both films, and *Dracula*'s star Bela Lugosi nearly played the Monster — and aesthetic design, ensuring the continuity and consistency of a corporate brand — the Universal Monster movie — that soared throughout the 1930s and 1940s and continues to this day in films like *Van Helsing* (2004) and *The Wolf Man* (2010). Ultimately, numerous cooks contributed to the broth and informed the look, feel and reception of the film.
38. Mallory, 69.
39. *The Frankenstein Files: How Hollywood Made a Monster*, prod. David J. Skal, dir. David J. Skal, 45 min., Universal, 1999, DVD.
40. Linda Costanzo Cahir, *Literature into Film: Theory and Practical Approaches* (Jefferson, NC: McFarland, 2006), 97.
41. Rudy Behlmer, audio commentary, *Frankenstein*, prod. Carl Laemmle, Jr., dir. James Whale, 1 hr. 10 min., Universal, 1999, DVD.
42. Behlmer, DVD.
43. *Frankenstein*, prod. Carl Laemmle, Jr., dir. James Whale, 1 hr. 10 min., Universal, 1931, DVD.
44. Andrew Higson, *English Heritage, English Cinema: Costume Drama since 1980* (Oxford: Oxford University Press, 2002), 42. Branagh's film's cultivation of a heritage veneer is likely due, I suspect, to its director's desire to distinguish his work from pulpier, more maligned adaptations: while Shelley's novel is an established classic, its film incarnations, as products of the horror genre, have not been invested with the same prestigious veneer as, say, adaptations of Dickens or Austen. However, while Branagh's film surpasses earlier adaptations as a heritage film, it appears markedly less successful as both a film and a horror film per se, as critical responses attest. Where Whale's film is 100 per cent fresh on rottentomatoes.com (a website compiling and archiving film reviews), Branagh's film earns a not-so-fresh 44. Also ranking higher are *Bride of Frankenstein* (100), *Young Frankenstein* (94), and even Andy Warhol's *Flesh for Frankenstein* (91). Also fresher are the similarly calibrated *Bram Stoker's Dracula* (80) and *Interview with the Vampire* (60), as well as earlier and subsequent Branagh films, including *Henry V* (100), *Much Ado about Nothing* (90), *Hamlet* (94) and *Thor* (78). On imdb.com, meanwhile, Branagh's film's average user rating is 6.3 compared to Whale's film's average of 8.0. While there are undoubtedly flaws in both these approaches to ranking a film's critical reception, they nonetheless provide useful yardsticks of a film's reputation and longevity.

45. Higson, 42.
46. *Mary Shelley's Frankenstein*, prod. Francis Ford Coppola, James V. Hart and John Veitch, dir. Kenneth Branagh, 2 hr. 3 min., TriStar, 1994, DVD.
47. Eckart Voigts-Virchow, "Heritage and Literature on Screen: *Heimat* and Heritage," in *The Cambridge Companion to Literature on Screen*, eds. Deborah Cartmell and Imelda Whelehan (Cambridge: Cambridge University Press, 2007), 123.
48. Deborah Cartmell, "Introduction," in *Adaptations: From Text to Screen, Screen to Text*, eds. Deborah Cartmell and Imelda Whelehan (London: Routledge, 1999), 26.
49. Will Brooker, "Batman: One Life, Many Faces," in *Adaptations: From Text to Screen, Screen to Text*, eds. Deborah Cartmell and Imelda Whelehan (London: Routledge, 1999), 186. This frequent privileging of the author in film marketing in the early–to mid–1990s is fascinating in this post–"Death of the Author" landscape, though as Sean Burke notes, much of Roland Barthes' own post–"Death of the Author" work remained author-centered, albeit with the author's authority displaced. As Burke argues, Barthes' subsequent work was concerned with "returning the author to the house without shaking its foundations, quietly, inconspicuously, an author who can leave by the front door only if he enters from the back." In this respect, the figure of the author was never entirely eradicated. See Sean Burke, *The Death and Return of the Author: Criticism and Subjectivity in Barthes, Foucault, and Derrida*, 2d ed. (Edinburgh: Edinburgh University Press, 1998), 33. It is also worth noting that 1968, the year Barthes' essay was published in France, also saw the publication of Andrew Sarris, *American Cinema: Directors and Direction 1929–1968* (New York: Dutton, 1968), one of the most extensive English language applications of French auteur theory. The death of the author thus coincided with the rise of the auteur and increasing cultural investment in filmmaking as a form of authorship. The citation of Shelley, Shakespeare, Bronte and Stoker bespeaks not only the ongoing relevance of the author, but an attempt to further legitimize film authorship by emphasizing its lineage with literature.
50. Diana Landau, ed., *Mary Shelley's Frankenstein: The Classic Tale of Terror Reborn on Film* (London: Pan, 1994), 9.
51. Landau, 9.
52. Landau, 29.
53. Montalbano, "From Bram Stoker's *Dracula* to *Bram Stoker's Dracula*," in *A Companion to Literature and Film*, eds. Robert Stam and Alessandra Raengo (Malden: Blackwell, 2004), 387.
54. R. Barton Palmer, "The Sociological Turn of Adaptation Studies: The Example of Film Noir," in *A Companion to Literature and Film*, eds. Robert Stam and Alessandra Raengo (Malden: Blackwell, 2004), 264.
55. Leitch, 64.
56. Landau, 9.
57. Landau, 19.
58. Peter Brooker, "Postmodern adaptation: pastiche, intertextuality and re-functioning," in *The Cambridge Companion to Literature on Screen*, eds. Deborah Cartmell and Imelda Whelehan (Cambridge: Cambridge University Press, 2007), 110.
59. Samuel Crowl, "Flamboyant realist: Kenneth Branagh," in *The Cambridge Companion to Shakespeare on Film*, ed. Russell Jackson (Cambridge: Cambridge University Press, 2000), 222.
60. Crowl, 223.
61. Stam, *Literature through Film*, 5.
62. MacFarlane, 26–27.
63. Landau, 20.
64. Landau, 166.
65. Landau, 20.
66. King, 62.
67. King, 65.
68. Whether there was a quantitatively measurable correlation between the staging of this exercise in the classroom and any positive increase in overall assignment grades or topic evaluations I cannot say, and such a study is outside the scope of this project, though an investigation would certainly be worthwhile.

About the Contributors

Aalya **Ahmad** teaches at Carleton University in Ottawa, Ontario. Her doctoral dissertation was a comparative literary study of horror fiction. She teaches and publishes about monstrosity, horror, feminist activism, zombies and politics.

John Edgar **Browning** is a Ph.D. student and Arthur A. Schomburg Fellow in the American Studies Department at the State University of New York at Buffalo. He is the author or coauthor of eight books, including *Draculas, Vampires, and Other Undead Forms: Essays on Gender, Race, and Culture* (2009), *Dracula in Visual Media* (2010), and *The Vampire, His Kith and Kin* (2011), as well as numerous articles and chapters on the subjects of horror and monstrosity.

Lance **Eaton** is a visiting lecturer at Emerson College, University of Massachusetts, and North Shore Community College. His areas of research include comics, gender and sexuality, horror, film, and popular culture. He regularly teaches a course on monsters and another on popular culture and media. He has published articles and encyclopedia entries on vampires, zombies, and horror comics.

Brian **Johnson** is an associate professor of English at Carleton University in Ottawa, Ontario, where he teaches theory, horror, and Canadian literature. Recent and forthcoming publications include essays on intersections between environmentalism and eroticism in Alan Moore's *Swamp Thing*, indigeneity and northern Gothic in the detective fiction of Michael Slade, and the role of the Jewish superhero in Mordecai Richler's novels of apprenticeship.

Ben **Kooyman** is a language and learning advisor at the University of South Australia who earned his Ph.D. in English in 2010. His doctoral thesis examined film adaptations of Shakespeare's plays and the strategies through which filmmakers fashioned their identities through cultivating association with Shakespeare. He has published essays on Stuart Gordon and John Landis, Eli Roth and Diablo Cody, and is currently working on a monograph on horror directors.

About the Contributors

K. A. **Laity** is an associate professor at the College of Saint Rose and a Fulbright Fellow at the Moore Institute at the National University of Ireland Galway. She is the award-winning author of *Pelzmantel* (2010) and *Unikirja* (2009), a collection of short stories and a play based on the *Kalevala, Kanteletar,* and other Finnish legends, for which she won the 2005 Eureka Short Story Fellowship as well as a 2006 Finlandia Foundation grant.

John Edward **Martin** is an assistant professor of English at Louisiana Tech University. He specializes in early American literature, Romanticism, Gothic fiction, poetry, and religion and literature. His Ph.D. dissertation was on "Confession and the Gothic Poetic in Edgar Allan Poe and Emily Dickinson" (Northwestern University, 2006). He has recently presented papers at the International Poe Conference and the American Literature Association Conference.

Lisa Marie **Miller** received her Ph.D. from New York University and teaches in the English Department of Pace University. She has published articles on film, education, literature and popular culture and, since 1996, has served as chair of the Horror Area she created for the Mid-Atlantic Popular Culture Association. She has presented numerous conference papers on the subjects of horror and the paranormal.

Sean **Moreland** earned his Ph.D. at the University of Ottawa, where he teaches courses on American literature, Gothic and horror fiction, and literature and psychology. His poetry and short fiction have appeared in several Canadian periodicals. He has recently contributed essays to the collections *Generation Zombie* (McFarland) and *Terror of the Soul: Essays on Canadian Horror Film* (University of Toronto Press.)

Summer **Pervez** holds a B.A. and an M.A. from the University of Western Ontario and a Ph.D. from the University of Ottawa. She teaches in the English department at Kwantlen Polytechnic University. Her research area is postcolonial/world literature and film, with an emphasis on South Asia. Specific interests include cinema studies, diaspora studies and the globalization of terrorism.

Miles **Tittle** is completing a dissertation on William Morris and medieval paratextuality at the University of Ottawa. He holds degrees from Dalhousie University, the University of Victoria, and NSCAD University. He teaches horror and other genre fiction courses at the University of Ottawa and Carleton University, and his research interests include book culture in Victorian and modern literature.

Jeffrey Andrew **Weinstock** is a professor of English at Central Michigan University and associate editor for *The Journal of the Fantastic in the Arts*. He is the author of *Scare Tactics: Supernatural Fiction by American Women, The Rocky Horror Picture Show,* and *Charles Brockden Brown* and is the editor of *the Ashgate Encyclopedia of Literary and Cinematic Monsters*.

J. A. **White**, an associate professor of English at Morgan State University in Baltimore, Maryland, is the author of *Hero-Ego in Search of Self: A Jungian Reading of* Beowulf (Peter Lang, 2004). His "The Monkees: A Happily but Safely Diverse Portrait for a New America" and "Construction of a Post-Racial Identity in Popular Film Media: Revolution and Resistance" recently appeared in *Popular Culture Review*.

Index

abjection 7, 64, 82, 84, 109–113, 233–238, 244n27; *see also* Kristeva, Julia
academic approaches to horror topics 2, 6–7, 13, 49, 60, 76, 99–100, 158–161, 163–4, 178, 181, 250; *see also* classroom (pedagogical experiences and practices)
adaptations 8, 14, 25, 67, 139, 141–153, 154n10, 245–263; *see also* remakes
affect 7–13, 15n3, 16n22, 25, 66, 80, 86, 95–96, 100–101, 104, 108–109, 111, 116, 121, 159, 201, 243n4, 243n13
Ahmad, Aalya 12
Aickman, Robert 1
Alien trilogy 68, 96, 202, 244n27
Althusser, Louis 41, 47–50, 53
American literature (horror in) 268
American Psycho 11, 179–199
Anima, animus 201, 206, 207, 211, 214–18, 220, 222n9; *see also* Jung, Carl Gustav
archetype 66, 82, 139, 153, 201–202, 204, 207–208, 211–212, 221, 222n9, 222n10
Argento, Dario 11, 124–136
art-horror 10, 13, 16n22, 122n28, 201, 203, 205, 210, 243n4; *see also* Carroll, Noël
audiences 5, 8–9, 11–12, 14, 34, 58, 61, 64–66, 68–69, 71, 76–81, 83, 87, 89–90, 92n11, 93n19, 124, 126–136, 138, 140–146, 151, 153, 187, 205–206, 208, 211–212, 214, 216–219, 226, 243n4, 249, 254
Audition 68, 70–71

Barker, Clive 67, 212
Barker, Martin 9, 15n3; *Ill Effects* (with Julian Petley) 12
Belanger, Jeff (*The Ghost Files*) 163, 166–167, 171–173 179
Benshoff, Harry 6
Beowulf 204, 206, 222n18
Berenstein, Rhona J. 58, 60, 69
Bhoot (*Spirit*) 75, 78, 79–83, 85–90, 93n26, 94n41; *see also* Bollywood
bhutagraha 79, 88
Bhutavidya 78, 92n14

Bierce, Ambrose 231
The Bird with the Crystal Plumage 125, 128; *see also* Argento, Dario
Bloch, Robert 12
the body 36, 59, 61, 64, 67–68, 72, 81, 86, 89–91, 123n28, 126, 139, 144, 182, 234–235, 237
Bollywood 3, 15, 75–92n11, 94n43
Bourdieu, Pierre 12, 16n41
Branagh, Kenneth (*Mary Shelley's Frankenstein*) 246, 250, 251, 255–260, 261n24, 262n44
Bride of Frankenstein 255–256, 262n44
Brophy, Philip 8
Browning, John Edgar 12
Butler, Judith 64, 127

camp 20, 23–25, 256
Campbell, Bruce 19, 21, 27, 34
Campbell, Joseph 203, 206, 222n5, 222n13
Candyman 207, 211–218, 221, 223n33
Capitalism 76, 115–116
Carroll, Noël 6, 10, 13, 16n22, 39n42, 61, 96, 99, 101, 113, 121, 122n28, 201, 210, 222n2, 222n3, 243n4, 243n13
Carter, Angela 67, 123n28
Caruth, Cathy 13
censorship 16n35, 38n6, 163, 182–184
Cherry, Brigid 58, 61, 69, 126–127
Chesterton, G. K. 12
Chowdhury, Purna 90–91
Cixous, Hélène 107
class (socio-economic) 1, 3, 6, 12, 36, 45, 50, 52, 68, 63, 68, 70, 89–90, 96, 110, 114–116, 118, 121, 143, 185, 209, 213, 225
classroom (pedagogical experiences and practices) 2, 5–9, 11–14, 20, 22–28, 30, 32, 35–38, 38n10, 41–54, 55n18, 56–57, 62–63, 67, 69–73, 75–77, 91, 92n3, 95–101, 103–105, 107–109, 111, 113–115, 117–121, 122n19, 124–130, 133, 135, 138–143, 145–146, 149–150, 153, 156–187, 188–191,

194, 195–196, 198n11, 198n12, 198n15, 198n20, 201–204, 219–221, 226–227, 237–242, 245–251, 253–254, 259–60, 263n68
Clemens, Valdine 13
Clover, Carol 6, 9, 51, 62–65, 68–70, 75–76, 80, 81–87, 89–91, 92n3, 93n20, 93n26, 94n38, 94n42, 125–127, 206, 210; *see also* Final Girl
Cohen, Jeffrey Jerome 53, 138
Colavito, Jason 98–99, 121
Cold War 145, 152
Coleridge, Samuel Taylor 200
comedy 24, 88, 193–194, 197n8, 200
cosmic horror (cosmic fear) 16n22, 26, 227–229, 231, 235
Crane, Jonathan Lake 13
Craven, Wes 25–26, 38n10, 62, 86
Creed, Barbara 7, 61, 64, 67, 79–80, 82, 85, 88, 93n19, 94n39, 96, 222n25, 244n27; *see also* abjection; monstrous-feminine
cultural studies 5, 14, 16n35, 43, 49, 77, 140
cyborg 20, 36–37, 39n42, 53; *see also* Haraway, Donna

Daniels, Les 7
Dante, Alighieri: *De Monarchia* 182, 186; *The Divine Comedy* 179–197, 198n13, 198n16, 198n24, 199n27, 199n35; *Inferno* 180, 182, 185, 187, 189–190, 192, 194–195, 198n16, 199n27
The Dark Half 12
Darwaza Band Rakho (*Keep the Door Closed*) 78; *see also* Bollywood
Darwin 231
death 32, 61–62, 65, 69–70, 72, 81–83, 87–88, 114, 125, 141, 143, 156–161, 166–168, 170–173, 175, 177, 186–188, 196, 198n24, 204–205, 211, 213–214, 216, 218, 230; of the author 263n49
defamiliarization 102, 112–113, 116
Derrida, Jacques 24, 26, 29, 30
Do Gaz Zameen Ke Neeche (*Two Yards Under the Ground*) 77; *see also* Bollywood
Dracula 41, 43, 45, 52, 54n3, 96, 250–251; in film 45, 51, 202, 205, 221, 250, 255–258, 260, 262n37

Eaton, Lance 14
Edmundson, Mark 28
Educators (instructors, teachers) 15, 20, 33, 25, 41–43, 46, 52–53, 140, 142–143, 145–146, 156–157, 177, 227; *see also* class (pedagogical experiences and classroom practices)

Edwards, Amelia B. "The Phantom Coach" 100–103, 106
Edwards, Paul: *Immortality* 156
Ellis, Bret Easton 179–189, 192, 196, 199n27
English literature 5, 246
Evil Dead trilogy 19–38, 39n15
excess 10, 12, 19, 24, 99–100, 109–110, 120–121, 186, 235–237
exorcism 75, 80, 83, 87, 94n37, 105–106; *see also* possession
The Exorcism of Emily Rose 85, 88, 93n20
The Exorcist 71, 79–80, 83, 85, 87–88, 93n18, 93n35

fandom 7, 8, 11–14, 16n35, 16n41, 24, 56–62, 66, 69, 101, 126–127, 136
the fantastic 95–96, 102–106, 108, 110–111, 115, 117–119, 122n24, 122n28, 225, 228, 230; *see also* Todorov, Tzevtan; the marvelous; the fantastic-marvelous
fear 9–10, 16n22, 40, 42, 44–45, 50, 53, 58–59, 62, 65, 71–72, 101, 109, 112, 118, 121, 126–127, 131–133, 138–139, 144, 147, 158, 164, 166, 177–178, 182–183, 187–188, 193, 200–204, 208, 213, 219, 222n3, 227–228, 230–232, 238, 243n4, 243n13; *see also* affect; art-horror; cosmic horror
feminism 12, 44, 46, 56–64, 66–72, 81, 93n26, 107–110, 112–113, 117, 119–120, 122n17, 123n28, 149, 159, 212, 250
fidelity criticism 14, 248
Final Girl 56, 62–65, 68–69, 73, 127, 206, 210, 221; *see also* Clover, Carol
Fish, Stanley 8–9
Foucault, Michel 27, 30–31
Frankenstein 14, 67, 138, 140, 145, 246, 250–252, 254, 259, 261n27; films 27, 146, 202, 221, 246, 250–263, 262n29, 262n37, 262n44
Freedman, Carl 98–99
Freeland, Cynthia 6, 60, 64, 69
Freud 1–2, 81, 85, 96, 104, 107–108, 124–126, 128, 206, 222n25, 228, 231–233, 235; *see also* the uncanny
Friday the 13th 205, 208, 219, 221
Funny Games 12

Gangoli, Geetanjali 89, 92
Gelder, Ken 6, 66
gender 1, 3, 6–7, 9, 28, 36–37, 44–45, 48, 50–51, 53, 56–72, 75–76, 80, 85, 89–90, 92, 93n20, 96, 98, 108–112, 118–120, 123n28, 125–129, 133, 136, 140, 157–158, 163, 169, 188, 206–207, 213–214, 256
genre 1, 5, 7, 10, 11, 14, 21, 24–29, 34, 38,

41, 45, 51, 58–63, 66, 68, 77, 79, 88, 95–96, 98–99, 101–105, 108–110, 120–121, 122n24, 122n28, 126–127, 140, 160, 182, 183, 200, 221, 226, 231, 239–240, 243n4, 249–250, 262n27, 262n44; subgenre 15, 65, 92n3, 93n26, 95
ghosts 1–2, 10, 26, 66, 81, 95, 101–102, 103–107, 110–111, 115–116, 118, 120, 123n28, 130, 156–166, 168–178, 205, 218, 231
Gilbert, Sandra, and Susan Gubar: *The Madwoman in the Attic* 117
Giles, Dennis 9
Gilman, Charlotte Perkins: "The Yellow Wallpaper" 67, 231
Ginger Snaps 61, 67, 69–72
goblin 161, 166
Goblin (band) 130
gore 24, 61, 68, 141, 242
Gothic 5–6, 40, 42, 46, 50–52, 54n3, 55n36, 56, 67, 89, 96, 98, 111, 157, 164, 182, 212, 224–229, 231, 239–241, 250, 254, 261n27
Grand Guignol 24
Grant, Barry Keith (ed.): *The Dread of Difference* 6
Grey Gardens 239
Grodal, Torben 200

Halberstam, Judith: *Skin Shows* 12, 40–41, 54n3, 57, 64, 212
Halloween 71, 160
Halloween (film) 62, 202, 207, 219
Hammer Studios 89, 250
Hantke, Steffen 12, 66
Haraway, Donna 12, 20, 36; *see also* cyborg
Hawthorne, Nathaniel 1, 231
Hellboy 14
Heller, Tamar 6, 244n27
heritage cinema 255–256
the hero/heroine 33–34, 60–61, 89–90, 129, 139, 145, 148, 150, 152, 155n29, 200–209, 214, 218, 220–221, 222n13, 229
Hester-Williams, Kim D. 212
Hickey, Dave 2
Hills, Matt: *The Pleasures of Horror* 6–8, 10–11, 13, 60, 62, 69; *see also* fandom
The Hills Have Eyes 25–26, 70
Hirshberg, Glen 3
Hitchcock, Alfred 62, 140
Hoeveler, Diane Long 6, 244n27
Hoffmann, E. T. A. 107
Hollywood 14, 17n52, 20–22, 29, 33, 70, 77–78, 91, 249, 254–256
Hurricane Katrina 13, 240
Hutcheon, Linda 14, 24–25, 27, 31–32, 39n39, 247, 250, 252

Iaccino, James 202, 222n10, 222n11
The Incredible Hulk 14, 139–140, 145–149, 151–152, 155n29
international horror 14, 66, 76–77, 79, 80, 90–91, 145
intersectionality 44, 70
intertextuality 8, 14, 15n9, 20, 25–28, 62, 69, 139, 140, 247, 251, 258

Jacobs, W. W.: "The Monkey's Paw" 97, 100, 110, 113, 118
James, Henry 1, 108, 122n28, 123n45, 231
James, M. R. 97, 100–102, 105, 106–107, 110, 112, 115, 118, 231
Jameson, Frederic 20, 39n30
Jancovich, Mark 6, 11, 16n35, 16n41
Jaws 25–26
Jenkins, Henry 8
Johnson, Brian 8
Johnson-Bailey, Juanita 46–49, 55n18
jump scares 258, 260
Jung, Carl Gustav 2, 11, 200–208, 211, 219–221, 222n9, 222n10, 222n11

Kael, Pauline 252
Kastenbaum, Robert 156–158, 166, 168, 172
Kaun? (Who?) 78; *see also* Bollywood
King, Stephen 7, 10, 12–13, 65, 67, 204, 251, 253
Kipling, Rudyard 110, 118
Kooyman, Ben 14
Kristeva, Julia 7, 15n9, 64, 82, 96, 107, 110–113, 226–228, 233–239, 243n4, 244n7; *see also* abjection

Lacan, Jacques 22, 35, 107, 122n19, 226–228, 233–235, 239, 243n4
Laity, K. A. 11
The League of Extraordinary Gentlemen 149–150
Leatherface 43, 51, 72, 204, 207; *see also The Texas Chainsaw Massacre*
LeFanu, J. S. 110
Les Misérables 192
Levine, George 120
Levine, Lawrence 68
Lewis, Matthew: *The Monk* 12, 187
Looney Tunes 141, 145
Lord Dunsany 231
Lovecraft, Howard Phillips 7, 10, 12, 16n22, 96, 101, 232–233, 235–237, 239, 243n10, 243n13
The Lovely Bones 224–225, 236
Lunar Park 188; *see also* Ellis, Bret Easton
Lyotard, Jean-François 9, 20, 37

Machen, Arthur 231
Mailer, Norman 185
Mallory, Michael 253
Martin, John Edward 13
Marvel Comics 139, 145
the marvelous 102, 106, 117, 122–123*n*28; the fantastic-marvelous 95, 102–105, 108, 111, 115, 117–119, 122*n*24, 122*n*28; *see also* the fantastic; Todorov, Tzevtan
Marxism 41, 51, 98, 108–110, 113–114, 116, 120
Mary Reilly 142
masculinity 71, 76, 83, 123*n*28, 127, 136, 147, 149, 188, 201
Mayne, Judith 9, 91
McDonagh, Maitland 127, 128, 136
McHale, Brian 24, 27, 29–30, 32, 39*n*24
Mears, Derek 208
Mehta, Rini Bhattacharya 77
Melville, Herman 1, 238; *Moby Dick* 238
metafiction 19, 20, 21, 25, 32, 33, 103, 188; metanarratives 20, 29, 37, 65, 99
metaphor 5, 24, 31, 36, 64, 89, 91, 102, 104, 184, 204–205, 213, 219, 240
Metz, Christian 11
Miller, Lisa Marie 11
Les Misérables 192
Modleski, Tania 61, 68
the monster 12, 14, 27–28, 37, 39*n*42, 40–46, 52–54, 56, 58–60, 64, 67, 70, 82, 92*n*11, 110–112, 116, 118, 120, 122*n*28, 126, 128, 138–141, 143, 146–148, 151, 153, 200–201, 203–210, 212, 219–221, 225, 230, 241, 251, 243*n*13, 250–254, 256, 258–260
monster pedagogy (MPT) 44–46, 52–4
the monstrous-feminine 67, 82, 85–86, 222*n*25; *see also* Creed, Barbara
Moore, Alan 150–151, 153
Moreland, Sean 15
Motion Picture Production Code (Hays Code) 249
Mulvey, Laura 11, 57–59, 62, 80, 91–92, 124–126, 133
myth 40, 67, 78–79, 201–203, 213–214, 222*n*13, 223*n*33, 228, 232, 251, 253, 260–261

Navarro, Yvonne 14
Ndalianis, Angela 24–25, 28, 34, 38*n*10
Necronomicon 25–27, 30–31, 33
Nesbit, Edith: "Man-Size in Marble" 100, 110, 113, 117–119
Neumann, Erich 202, 222*n*5; *see also* Jung, Carl Gustav
New Age 157, 161–163
A Nightmare on Elm Street 17*n*52, 58, 62

1920 (film) 75, 79–90; *see also* Bollywood
normativity 7, 50, 72
Nosferatu 205, 219

Oates, Joyce Carol 66–67
the occult 15, 63, 65, 75, 78–84, 90–91, 94*n*38, 115, 205; *see also* Clover, Carol
Opera 125, 134; *see also* Argento, Dario
the other 31, 89, 110, 112, 116, 121, 236

the paranormal 11, 23, 29, 85, 87, 92, 93, 156–177
Paranormal Activity 85, 87, 92*n*2, 93*n*20
penny dreadfuls 12
Pervez, Summer 15
Pinedo, Isabel Cristina 6, 57, 60–61, 68–70, 90, 94*n*49, 127, 212
Poe, Edgar Allan 1, 62, 122*n*28, 224–226, 228–231, 233–237, 239, 250
Poltergeist 26, 174
pornography 10, 58, 60–61
possession 3, 15, 65, 75–76, 78–92, 93*n*19, 93*n*25, 93*n*27, 94*n*38, 94*n*41, 94*n*42, 94*n*44
postmodernism 8, 19–27, 29–32, 34–38, 39*n*30, 60, 67, 68, 188, 258
poststructuralism 98, 107
Pound, Ezra 187, 198–199*n*24
Powell, Anna 6, 7, 9
Pride and Prejudice 246–247, 249
Propp, Vladimir 95, 102
Psycho 140
psychoanalysis 1, 6, 11, 59, 62–65, 70, 75, 83–85, 96, 98, 104, 107–111, 113–114, 118, 122*n*19, 201, 204, 226, 228, 232–234, 240

Raat (*Night*) 79; *see also* Bollywood
Raaz 2 75, 79–90, 94*n*41; *see also* Bollywood
Radcliffe, Anne 10, 67
Raimi, Sam 19–20, 23, 25–26, 35, 38*n*10; *see also Evil Dead* trilogy
Ramsay brothers (F. U., Tulsi, Shyam) 77–78, 90
Randi, John 173
the real 224–230, 232–234, 237, 239–240, 243*n*4, 243*n*7
remakes 14, 17*n*52, 67–68, 70
retroactive continuity (retcon) 26, 33
Rice, Anne 45, 66–67
Romanticism 224, 227–233, 249–250, 268

safe space 42
Sagan, Carl 161–162, 164, 172, 177
Schneider, Stephen Jay 6, 8, 66
Schwartz, Gary E. 160–161

science 37, 40, 63, 83, 86–87, 102, 147, 156–157, 161, 166, 171–174, 177, 205, 228, 232
science fiction 26, 29, 31, 39n24, 63, 98–99, 212
scopophilia 11, 57, 63, 124–125, 127–128, 131, 133–134, 136
Sedgwick, Eve Kosofsky 41, 53, 110
serial killers 181, 183, 186, 219; Joseph Edward Duncan III 198n20
sexuality 2, 43, 45, 48, 50, 57, 64, 72, 90, 93n25, 94n39, 96, 98, 111, 126, 158, 187, 188, 213, 256
the shadow 201, 202, 204–205, 207–213, 218–221, 233; *see also* Jung, Carl Gustav
Shelley, Mary 14, 67, 140, 246, 250–260; *see also Frankenstein*
The Shining 26, 28
The Silence of the Lambs 64
Silverman, Kaja 38n2, 125
Smith, Frederick M. 80, 88, 91–92, 92n14, 93n25, 94n37
Sontag, Susan 23–24
spectatorship 19, 21–22, 23, 33–36, 58–59, 91, 95, 126, 217, 253
Stabile, Carol 43–45
Stam, Robert 245, 247–248, 258
Stevenson, Robert Louis 150; adaptations 140–153, 154n10, 154n20; character of Jekyll/Hyde 14, 139–153, 154n10, 154n13; *The Strange Case of Dr. Jekyll and Mr. Hyde* 139–140, 146
students *see* classroom
Sullivan, Jack 10
the supernatural 1, 3, 15, 28–32, 82–84, 86, 103–106, 110–111, 114–119, 157, 160, 162, 172, 189, 224, 226–228, 230, 232, 240
Suspiria 125, 130; *see also* Argento, Dario
Suvin, Darko 98

The Texas Chainsaw Massacre 14, 51, 69–70, 73, 207
Thakur, Gautam Basu 76
Theory (general) 2–3, 5, 7, 8–9, 10, 34, 41–42, 49–50, 62, 95–101, 108–113, 120–121, 122n17, 122n19, 228, 240, 250
threshold 104, 130, 189, 203
Tittle, Miles 11
Todorov, Tzevtan 95, 96, 102–105, 107–110, 113, 115, 122n24; *see also* the fantastic
Tombs, Pete 66, 77, 79, 92n11, 93n18
torture porn 16n26, 67
transgression 20, 99–100, 102, 108–109, 113, 116, 186–188, 235–236
Tudor, Andrew 11
The Turn of the Screw 108–109, 114, 116
Twitchell, James 6–7

the uncanny 85, 96, 104, 107–110, 112, 116, 119, 162, 170, 233, 241

vampires 1, 54, 66, 160, 162, 171, 175
Vampyr 26
Varma, Ram Gopal 75, 78, 79, 94n43
Videodrome 12

Weinstock, Jeffrey Andrew 8
Whale, James 27, 146, 246, 251–260, 262n37, 262n44
Whelehan, Imelda 245–248
White, J. A. 11
Witchboard 80, 83, 87
Wood, Robin 6, 14, 41, 43, 45, 56
Wuthering Heights 247–250, 255–256

Zombie, Rob 14
zombies 5, 15, 67, 70–72, 79, 138, 210

www.ingramcontent.com/pod-product-compliance
Lightning Source LLC
Chambersburg PA
CBHW030338240426
43661CB00052B/1670